This work also appears under the title of

MASTERPIECES OF WORLD LITERATURE IN DIGEST FORM

PREFACE

THE array of literature represented in this fifteen-volume set is drawn from the vast reservoir of literary achievements which has been accumulating since the legendary beginnings of Western civilizations. All the great literature is not here; perhaps all that is here is not great. But these works are representative of the places and the times from which they sprang and they have helped to tint the fabric which makes up the composite imprint of our culture. Romance and adventure, laughter and illusion, dreams and desperate hopes, fear and angry resentment — these things have prodded men's minds as they walked toward our century. Their insight is our heritage.

Along with this heritage, our generation has fallen heir to a Busy Age. Never in history has there been so much competition for the attention of the average individual. But although ours is a Busy Age, unparalleled technological advancements have made it an age in which the chances for enlightenment and cultural development, at all levels, have never before been approached even remotely. Out of this increased "exposure" must surely come a more intellectually alert society. From such a society we may reasonably expect an acceleration of our cultural development. It is in the light of all these circumstances that a work such as MASTERPLOTS can have a place and a purpose.

The fifteen-volume Combined Edition of MASTERPLOTS comprises a collection of digests and essay-reviews covering 1,510 titles from world literature. This work is not an anthology or a collection of "reprints." The two million words of material it contains were newly written expressly for this set. Two styles are employed: the synopsis and the essay-review. 1,287 of the entries are handled as synopses, 223 as essay-reviews. Most of the essays are devoted to poetry, philosophy, and other types of literature that have no plots to summarize.

Designed primarily for reference, the format of MASTERPLOTS is styled and standardized to afford maximum information in the quickest time. Each of the digests is preceded by carefully checked, concisely stated reference data which furnish at a glance the type of work, authorship, type of plot, time of plot, locale, and first publication date. Following this will be found a list of principal characters and their relationships, often a highly useful feature. Next is the *Critique,* a short, incisive critical analysis of the original book. Finally there is the plot-summary, given as a well-rounded story and devoid of quotations from the original work. Editorial comments having been confined to the *Critique,* the reader is afforded an uninterrupted opportunity to study the action, characterizations, and development of the theme as the plot-story progresses. For clarity, a character is usually referred to by one designated name throughout the digest. Stories are arranged alphabetically by title. They average twelve to fifteen hundred words in length, though some exceed twenty-five hundred words.

In contrast to the plot-summaries, the 223 essay-reviews sometimes include quotations from the original works to illustrate salient points. This is especially true of those critical articles dealing with poetry. It will be noted that some novels and plays are handled as essay-reviews instead of plot-summaries. Sometimes such a procedure was followed so that a general discussion of the author's other work could be included in the article dealing with a specific title. In a few cases the essay-review method was employed in compliance with the wishes expressed by authors or copyright owners who preferred to be represented in essay-reviews rather than plot-summaries.

A total of 753 authors are presented in the fifteen-volume Combined Edition of MASTERPLOTS. The range is from Homer and Hesiod to the present day and such wide author representation assures the reference value of MASTERPLOTS. In keeping with the interest ratio, however, later writers predominate. More than one-third of the authors included were active in the twentieth century. Forty-one are winners of the Nobel Prize in Literature. A complete Author Index appears at the end of Volume Fifteen.

Of primary importance from the beginning was the selection of titles intended for inclusion in MASTERPLOTS. Interests and requirements vary, but almost any worth-while literary work will influence in some measure the writings that follow it and for this reason a number of titles of historical significance were chosen regardless of whether they still enjoy a

PREFACE

wide audience today. In almost every case living authors were consulted about their own books which were under consideration. Because the relative merit of contemporary writing is likely to be a subject of some controversy, the assistance of authors themselves concerning their own works was valuable.

Consultations with specialists here and abroad have resulted in the inclusion of titles which are important but which are often overlooked when standard book lists are compiled. For example, a number of excellent but little-known Spanish and Latin American works are represented, some of which have been translated into English only recently. We have also drawn, to a small degree, on the vast reservoir of Oriental literature, an area of world culture long neglected by Western readers. However, we are now in an age of world-wide cultural intercourse, a force that — happily — transcends temporary political considerations, and as the wisdom, the humanity, the delights of Oriental literature come to the attention of the mass Western audience, interest in this field is sure to widen.

Actual preparation of this work required an enormous amount of active assistance from a carefully selected staff that included scores of English Faculty associates chosen from dozens of universities and colleges throughout the United States. I wish to express my appreciation for the able and cheerful assistance received from these staff members, some of whom have been active in the project continuously since its inception.

Throughout the preparation of this work the cooperation of authors, publishers, agents, and literary trustees has been solicited and I wish to acknowledge the assistance received from these sources. Copyright notices and credit lines appear as footnotes accompanying the appropriate titles.

This Preface would be incomplete without special reference to Story Editor Dayton Kohler's masterful survey of world literature entitled "Books and Reading," which appears on pages xxxi-lxi in the front part of this volume. Professor Kohler's brief, lucid treatment of his subject is superior to any we have seen. It is "must" reading for all those who are interested in a concise, erudite guide to the major currents of world literature from Homer to the most recent Nobel Prize winner.

PREFACE

Some will find in the pages of MASTERPLOTS a pleasant renewal of an old acquaintance, a chance meeting with an almost forgotten literary friend. Others may wish to pursue further an interest encountered here for the first time. In either case, this work will have served its purpose.

FRANK N. MAGILL

COMPLETE LIST OF CONTENTS

ix

COMPLETE LIST OF CONTENTS

COMPLETE LIST OF CONTENTS

COMPLETE LIST OF CONTENTS

COMPLETE LIST OF CONTENTS

COMPLETE LIST OF CONTENTS

COMPLETE LIST OF CONTENTS

xxi

Pilgrim's Progress, The — *Bunyan*
Pillars of Society, The — *Ibsen*
Pilot, The — *Cooper*
Pioneers, The — *Cooper*
Pirates of Penzance, The — *Gilbert*
Pit, The — *Norris*
Plague, The — *Camus*
Plaideurs, Les — *Racine*
Plain Dealer, The — *Wycherley*
Platero and I — *Jiménez*
Playboy of the Western World, The —
   Synge
Plough and the Stars, The — *O'Casey*
Plumed Serpent, The — *D. H. Lawrence*
Plutus — *Aristophanes*
Poem of the Cid — *Unknown*
Poems, Chiefly in the Scottish Dialect —
   Burns
Poetical Works of Edward Taylor, The —
   Taylor
Poetics, The — *Aristotle*
Poetry of Auden, The — *Auden*
Poetry of Bashô, The — *Bashô*
Poetry of Blake, The — *Blake*
Poetry of Bryant, The — *Bryant*
Poetry of Carducci, The — *Carducci*
Poetry of Christina Rossetti, The —
   C. Rossetti
Poetry of Dante Gabriel Rossetti, The —
   D. G. Rossetti
Poetry of Donne, The — *Donne*
Poetry of Drayton, The — *Drayton*
Poetry of Emily Dickinson, The —
   Dickinson
Poetry of Freneau, The — *Freneau*
Poetry of Frost, The — *Frost*
Poetry of Gray, The — *Gray*
Poetry of Hopkins, The — *Hopkins*
Poetry of Horace, The — *Horace*
Poetry of Lanier, The — *Lanier*
Poetry of Lewis, The — *C. D. Lewis*
Poetry of Lindsay, The — *Lindsay*
Poetry of Lovelace, The — *Lovelace*
Poetry of Mallarmé, The — *Mallarmé*

Poetry of Marvell, The — *Marvell*
Poetry of Ronsard, The — *Ronsard*
Poetry of Spender, The — *Spender*
Poetry of Stefan George, The — *George*
Poetry of Theocritus, The — *Theocritus*
Poetry of Yeats, The — *Yeats*
Point Counter Point — *A. Huxley*
Polyeucte — *Corneille*
Poor People — *Dostoevski*
Poor White — *S. Anderson*
Porgy — *Heyward*
Portrait of a Lady, The — *H. James*
Portrait of the Artist as a Young
   Man, A — *Joyce*
Possessed, The — *Dostoevski*
Pot of Gold, The — *Plautus*
Power — *Feuchtwanger*
Power and the Glory, The — *G. Greene*
Power of Darkness, The — *Tolstoy*
Pragmatism — *W. James*
Prairie, The — *Cooper*
Praise of Folly, The — *Erasmus*
Precious Bane — *Webb*
Prejudices: Six Series — *Mencken*
Prelude, The — *Wordsworth*
Pride and Prejudice — *Austen*
Prince, The — *Machiavelli*
Prince and the Pauper, The — *Twain*
Prince of Homburg, The — *Kleist*
Princess of Clèves, The — *Lafayette*
Prisoner of Zenda, The — *Hope*
Private Life of the Master Race, The —
   Brecht
Private Lives — *Coward*
Private Papers of Henry Reycroft, The —
   Gissing
Professor, The — *C. Brontë*
Professor's House, The — *Cather*
Prometheus Bound — *Aeschylus*
Prometheus Unbound — *P. B. Shelley*
Promised Land, The — *Pontoppidan*
Proserpine and Ceres — *Folk tradition*
Purple Dust — *O'Casey*
Purple Land, The — *Hudson*

COMPLETE LIST OF CONTENTS

COMPLETE LIST OF CONTENTS

COMPLETE LIST OF CONTENTS

BOOKS AND READING

A SURVEY OF WORLD LITERATURE

by
DAYTON KOHLER
Story Editor of
MASTERPLOTS

I
AN INTRODUCTION TO READING

"Each of us, then, makes his own illusion of the world—illusion poetic, sentimental, joyous, melancholy, foul, or dismal—according to his nature. And the writer has no mission other than to reproduce faithfully this illusion, with all the processes of art he has learned."

GUY DE MAUPASSANT

There are many roads into the world of books, but the way of fiction is probably the most common. The reason is plain. The novel and the short story come closer to the experience of the modern reader than any other form of contemporary writing. They are to us what epic poetry was to the Greeks and Romans, what stage drama was to the Elizabethans. Then, too, the appeal of the story, whether told as poem, play, history, biography, or novel, is primitive and strong.

Mankind's delight in stories has never been limited to any period or place. It is as timeless and universal as the art of the storyteller, which stretches in an unbroken line back to the unrecorded oral beginnings of literary history. Men and women of earlier times were moved by the same impulse that makes us, before we turn the page, anticipate the next chapter of a good novel. The craftsmanship of structure, realistic character portrayal, evocation of atmosphere and setting, and the writers' strategy with symbol and language can add much to our appreciation of the art of fiction, but always it is the story, a time sequence of events relating fiction to life, which first captures our interest and then compels a sense of recognition and belief.

But the appeal of fiction may go deeper. We all live, perhaps more intensely than we realize, in our imaginings and emotions. Aware of our own difficulties in the uncertain business of living, we are all the more interested in other men and their problems, and stories provide a sort of life extension course by which we try to vary or lengthen our own lives.

We begin a story with the hope that it will be faithful, in Hawthorne's words, "not merely to the possible, but to the probable and ordinary in man's experience." When the writer adds perspective and meaning to that experience and gives it beauty of form, his story becomes a record of human interest and permanent value. And what is true of the story is true of all other types of literature as well. Lyric poetry, the essay, philosophy, each in its own way, touch our imagination and emotions and satisfy our sense of belief.

The aim of all literature is truth. There are, however, two kinds of truth. One we call factual. It is the material of the daily newspaper, a scientific treatise, history, biography. Many able novelists, from Daniel Defoe to John Dos Passos, have reshaped this body of observed and proved fact into the form of fiction. The other is inner or imaginative truth. It, too, is grounded in the physical world, but its vision is inward and downward, not outward. Less concerned with the appearances of things than it is with deeper realities of human personality and conduct, this is the kind of truth we find in literature that we call creative. It is more than the thing which seems true merely because it conforms to our knowledge of the world. We do not need to believe in men six inches tall, for example, in order to understand Swift's criticism of human society in *Gulliver's Travels*. In the same way, modern disbelief in ghosts and witches takes away nothing from our appreciation of *Hamlet* and *Macbeth*. Whether realistic or romantic, imaginative truth penetrates deeply into the experience of the individual or the race. The result is a fuller interpretation of life as we know it.

Books which continue to gratify our sense of truth over a long period of time we call classics. The name is unfortunate, suggesting classroom lectures and dusty library shelves, but we have no other. Age, however, does not make a classic, for time quickly sends to the rubbish pile the outdated books of every literature. A book is a classic because it tells us something so undeniably true that it becomes part of our experience as we read, because it presents a character who seems to embody in one person a significant phase of human personality or fate. Ulysses is immortal as the far-seeking wanderer. Chaucer's Wife of Bath has the earthy vitality of life itself. Hamlet is for all time the tragic hero broken under a load of duty too heavy for the spirit to sustain. Don Quixote will ride forever as the romantic idealist tilting against windmills. Jean Valjean is society's outcast who shows man's inhumanity to man. Huck Finn's adventures reveal a boy's world, the restless energy of a young nation, the goodness and shoddiness of human nature. Books can do no more than vary timeless themes of birth and striving, endurance and death, but they can make life more real, more understandable. Although the conditions of men change, man does not, and so the classic is capable of renewing its meaning for each generation.

We read for a variety of reasons: for relief from boredom, for information, for culture, for pleasure. All of these aims are in some measure justified by the pressures and necessities of the world we live in today. But, as W. Somerset Maugham has pointed out, no reading is of lasting value unless it gives us pleasure. Many people, unfortunately, think of pleasurable reading in terms of "light" fiction, escapist books which offer only temporary release from daily routine or commonplace surroundings. The enjoyment we get from good reading is a quality more positive than simple diversion, for which there is nowadays no need of books at all. Reading for information serves a practical but limited purpose. All on one factual level, it adds to our store of information without enriching personality.

Much so-called cultural reading is no more than genteel snobbery. Culture is for use; its ends are goodness and truth. There are no absolute values in literature, and the only real meaning a book can have is the meaning it holds for its reader. We should read our books as we eat a good dinner, with appreciation and zest, not take them in prescribed doses, like a tonic. Reading for pleasure is an exercise which enables us to live with our whole bodies as well as our minds.

In one of his essays Robert Louis Stevenson describes his experience when he read Dumas' *Vicomte de Bragelonne* for the first time: "I carried the thread of that epic into my slumbers, I woke with it unbroken, I rejoiced to plunge into the book at breakfast, it was with a pang that I must lay it down and turn to my own labors; for no part of the world has ever seemed to me so charming as these pages, and not even my friends are quite so real, perhaps quite so dear, as D'Artagnan."

This is what we mean by the true magic of reading. Not all of us are so temperamentally constituted that we can read with the same thoroughgoing gusto, but every reader comes, at one time or another, upon some book which in substance or style seems written for his particular delight. No one can say what this book will be. For one it may be the essays of Montaigne, who has been called the first modern man, for another the passionate search for truth and beauty in the poetry of John Keats, for still another one of the great novels—*Pickwick Papers, Father Goriot, Moby Dick, War and Peace, Wuthering Heights*. No matter what the starting point, the world of books will never again be a dreary, uncharted wasteland. A few lines of type, a chance reference, and we are off with Tom Jones on the highroad to London, riding with D'Artagnan to save the honor of a queen, at our ease with Hazlitt over a supper of bread, cheese, and ale in an old English inn, or embarking with Ishmael on the bedlam voyage of the *Pequod*.

Books can never be a substitute for life.

They can, as we have already seen, add much to our knowledge of the world and the people in it. For instance, we may be certain that a neighbor's wife is carrying on a secret love affair with the golf professional at the country club, but we can never understand her motives and feelings as clearly as we know those of Emma Bovary. Or a poem like Edwin Arlington Robinson's "Miniver Cheevy" may give us better insight into the true nature of an impractical, tippling, day-dreaming friend. In real life our knowledge of people is usually limited to what they say and do; we can only guess at the vital inner life which lies, like the submerged portion of an iceberg, below the surface. The novelist and the poet, however, go beneath externals of speech and action to show life at its source, in the hidden world of thought and feeling.

Reading makes us citizens of the world at large. Sam Weller, Soames Forsyte, Becky Sharp, Emma Bovary, Raskolnikov, Mrs. Proudie, and a thousand other figures from the world's literature belong to all ages and all countries. Like Chaucer's Canterbury Pilgrims and the boarders in Balzac's Pension Vauquer, they are a part of all humanity. To know them is to cross national and racial boundaries and to shed our complacency and provincialism at the same time.

Great books not only record and interpret life for us but also console our griefs, expose our vices, redeem our weaknesses. When we read wisely, we are always in the process of becoming. No one could read Thoreau's *Walden* and remain insensible to his own natural environment. Poetry shows us that in our daily lives we think in imagery and talk in figurative language. Books teach us how to live more completely within ourselves. Proust's *Remembrance of Things Past* contains a revealing episode. There the narrator, a grown man, dips a small cake into a cup of tea. The taste of this morsel brings back childhood memories of a tea-moistened cake his aunt had given him years before at Combray, and with this recollection all the impressions of that time return. "In that moment all the flowers in our garden and in M. Swann's park, and the water lilies on the Vivonne, and the good people of the village and their little dwellings and the church and all Combray and its surroundings, came into being, both town and gardens, from my cup of tea."

We are all like Proust's narrator, but we may need the example of a discerning writer before we can realize our own resources of memory and imagination.

The trivial writer offers entertainment and asks little except our time in return. The serious writer, on the other hand, may make greater demands on his readers. Although some poems and novels must be read with disciplined, attentive minds, the qualities which make for hard or easy reading are no test of literary value. The final test for any book is what we get out of it, according to our tastes and capacities. One of the greatest pleasures in reading is the discovery of the unexpected or purposeful in a work we once took for granted. Sometimes a book leads us into strange bypaths. Browning's *The Ring and the Book,* for example, is on one level a murder melodrama laid in seventeenth-century Italy. So complex is his poem, however, so rich and varied its background, that if we were to follow all the threads of interest in his story we would find ourselves reading many volumes on painting, literature, science, religion, history, psychology, law, architecture, and costume. To master such a work gives us a feeling of power as well as pleasure.

Since there are no absolute values in literature, it follows that all reading must be selective. But the *what* of reading is often as perplexing as the *why* and *how.* No one can read everything. It has been estimated that one would have to read more than twenty volumes a day to keep up with books published each year. Even Dr. Bookworm could not exhaust the shelves of a fair-sized library in a normal lifetime. For most readers some kind of guide is necessary; without a sense of direction we flounder among books past or present and are likely to fall back on whatever is currently popular.

We should learn at the outset to distrust the book whose chief recommendation is its popularity. Public favor is too fickle to mark any book for survival, as the forgotten, unread titles on the best seller lists of the last fifty years will show. If we cannot rely on our own judgment, mistrust the enthusiasms of our friends, and rebel against the dictates of our teachers, there are other aids for our guidance. Reviews in newspapers and magazines will keep us informed on new books as they appear. There are also scholarly lists of many kinds—Ten Books to Take to a Desert Island, the Twenty Best Novels, One Hundred Great Books, all compiled as if some virtue existed in round numbers. We need only consult these lists, however, to discover how widely literary experts disagree, and their differences of critical opinion may throw us back upon our own resources.

Probably the best course for the reader who has some half-defined idea of what he wants to read, or thinks he should read, would be to examine a comprehensive book of literary synopses. If the condensed versions are presented objectively along with some background information on the book and its writer, they become an excellent basis for appraisal and selection. From such a book pick out a group of titles which in substance and treatment seem to suit your taste or mood. Then sample. Since tastes differ, there is little point in reading a book which does not promise an adequate return for your effort.

Perhaps a preference for humor and the oddities of human character has led you to the novels of Charles Dickens, but on closer inspection you find his sentimentality and melodramatic plots distasteful. Try Thackeray, whose satire may be a proper corrective, or Jane Austen. If you tire of the novel of manners, read *Wuthering Heights,* a story of human passion as wild and bleak as its Yorkshire moorland setting. From Tennyson's lyricism turn to the philosophical poems of Wordsworth or the psychological portraits of Browning. If you prefer something more modern, you may find what you are looking for in Hemingway, who in *The Sun Also Rises* and *A Farewell to Arms* expresses the violence and despair of his generation. Somewhere along the line you will find those books which make reading a true pleasure, and your literary perspectives will have widened considerably in the meantime. An adventure story like *Treasure Island* may lead you to Melville or Conrad. Conrad may take you to the French novelists whom he acknowledged as his masters or to Henry James, his contemporary, who in turn may carry us back to Hawthorne, another writer concerned with man's moral problems. Stephen Vincent Benet's fine narrative poem of the Civil War, *John Brown's Body,* may send us to Sandburg's biography of Lincoln or Freeman's life of Lee. Eugene O'Neill's *Mourning Becomes Electra* may stir our curiosity about the plays of Aeschylus. Literary paths cross and recross and we are free to choose our reading wherever they may lead.

The brief survey of reading that follows is selective as well. There has been no attempt to make a complete outline of world literature and much has necessarily been omitted. This survey is intended only to relate certain literary works to their periods and to indicate whenever possible why they have stirred the imaginations and emotions of their readers.

II
A SURVEY OF READING

GREECE AND ROME

Life in ancient Greece must have been intensely absorbing and rewarding, for on that small, rocky peninsula at the edge of a continent the Greeks made for themselves a place of many beginnings. Surrounded by barbarian tribes, they came into history with the assets of every civilized people: inquiring, imaginative minds and a beautiful and precise language. Knowing nothing of the past, they created an enduring body of folk tradition. Ignorant of geography, they sailed their ships into the unknown Mediterranean. They loved games and relished learning. Their gods they made in their own image—expedient, quarrelsome, witty, wise. Their small city states were models of government upon which our own is based.

The time, the place, and the people were right for a great civilization. During the Age of Pericles, for example, more men of genius lived in Athens than the world has seen since in any other place at one time. There the Greeks brought to perfection a literature and a style of architecture which have left deep imprints on the arts for more than two thousand years. They discovered principles and invented systems, and so laid the foundations of philosophy, natural science, mathematics, medicine. It has been truly said that the Western world goes back to Greece for everything but its religious faith.

The Greeks were a practical, realistic people, never mystics. In their need to understand the world they lived in they created myths to account for origins of things and to explain why life must be as it is. Stories like those of Pandora's box, Cupid and Psyche, Orpheus and Eurydice, Icarus, goat-footed Pan, the rape of Proserpine, are never childish; they are filled with beauty and wisdom. Also in the oral tradition were later tales of legendary heroes and tribal history, such as the labors of Hercules, the expedition of the seven against Thebes, the quest of the Argonauts, Theseus and the killing of the Minotaur. Out of this background of myth and heroic legend came the two great Homeric epics, the *Iliad* and the *Odyssey*.

Whether Homer was one man or ten is a secret lost in the shadowy past. What is more important, the two stories told in his name survive, as fresh and vivid as they were thousands of years ago. To citizens of Greek towns that had known assault and siege the *Iliad* was a great poem of battles. Beginning in the tenth year of the war with Troy, it tells of Achilles' terrible wrath and the death of Hector. It is a tale of violence and doom, compassion and grief, the earthly and the divine, for Homer is one of the few writers capable of making the gods seem at home in the human world, at the same time lifting men almost to the stature of gods.

The *Iliad* is the tragic epic of man's ambition for conquest and glory. The *Odyssey* is romantic comedy dealing with his desire for peace and home. Crafty Ulysses is a hero who emerges triumphant over every disastrous circumstance during his ten years of wandering after the fall of Troy, and his reward at the end is the comfort of his own hearth and the love of Penelope, his faithful spouse.

The Greeks prized their other poets—Hesiod, Sappho, Pindar, Theocritus, and all the singers of the *Greek Anthology*—but Homer was their master writer. To them his poems were more than heroic epics richly told. They were a storehouse of literature, history, religious tradition, social custom, moral instruction. Because he touched on whatever is universal in human thought and deed, Homer remains a poet for all moods and all ages.

Aeschylus, first of the Greek writers of tragedy, called his plays "morsels from the banquet of Homer," but this statement we must credit in part to the patriotic feelings of an Athenian who wished to be remembered only as one who had fought at Marathon. His work is filled with pride of country, poetic grandeur, tragic insight. Of his seven surviving plays the most interesting are the three relating to the descendants of Atreus. *Agamemnon, The Libation-Bearers,* and *The Furies* tell on one level a story of faithlessness, murder, revenge, and expiation. On another level this trilogy is a tremendous fable of a moral order overthrown and then reëstablished. Equally powerful is *Prometheus Bound,* the story of the titan who stole fire from the gods and gave it to mankind.

These plays have a bold and austere quality we do not find in the work of his successor and rival, Sophocles. A superior craftsman, especially in *Oedipus the King, Electra,* and *Antigone,* Sophocles is more restrained in his treatment of the problem of evil and divine retribution. He is the humanist among Greek playwrights. Even mocking Aristophanes paid him high tribute when he showed Sophocles in the underworld, as gentle among the shades as he had been in life.

Euripides, third of the tragic dramatists, lived in a later age. Faith in the gods was waning in his day, and skepticism and speculative philosophy had begun to weaken traditional morality. Lacking the religious fervor of Aeschylus and the moral serenity of Sophocles, he came closer to realistic studies of personality. *Alcestis* and *The Trojan Women* are stories of devoted, suffering womanhood. In *Medea* and *The Bacchae* he made fatal flaws of character the secret of man's tragic destiny.

Behind all of these plays is deep concern with the fate that pursues mankind, a subject of perennial interest to writers of all periods. Thomas Hardy, William Butler Yeats, Eugene O'Neill, and Robinson Jeffers are among modern writers who have found in Greek drama the themes and symbols of their own novels, poetry, and plays.

The lighter side of Greek nature found expression in comedy. Aristophanes is a master of irreverence and satire. Demagogues and political quackery are nothing new under the sun, and it is not necessary to know Athenian politics in order to enjoy his plays. Whether he is ridiculing politics in *The Knights* and *Lysistrata,* philosophy in *The Clouds,* or artistic rivalry in *The Frogs,* there is a serious purpose beneath his hilarity and bite. He is pleading for a return to the private and public morality of the earlier democracy.

Among the glories of Greece were the great minds it produced, thinkers and philosophers like Socrates, Plato, and Aristotle. Our knowledge of Socrates we get chiefly from the writings of Plato, his pupil and friend. What we owe most to Socrates is his method of teaching, the dialogue of questions and answers going deeply into the heart of a problem. Plato gave form to abstract thought. His conception of the ideal state, as outlined in *The Republic,* may seem outdated in our day of conflicting ideologies, but his views on love, friendship, and ethics are among the world's permanent possessions. A good beginning for the interested reader would be *The Apology* and *Phaedo,* dialogues dealing with the trial and death of Socrates.

Aristotle has been called "the master of those who know." No abstract speculator, he broke with Plato's idealism and translated thought into action. Churchmen and scholars of the Middle Ages called him "The Philosopher" and found in his writings not only the wisdom of a way of life but also the principles of Christian conduct. From him the modern world has inherited theology, logic, biology, rhetoric, politics, literary criticism, and even the terms that philosophers use today.

The Greeks, vitally interested in every form of human activity, found their first historian in Herodotus. His history of the wars between Greeks and Persians is more than a chronicle of events, for he was a student of mankind who poured into his books a flood of informative detail, anecdote, and hearsay, bringing life and drama to his pages. He is the great storyteller among historians, and his picture of the Greek state against a wider background of world culture gives us history in its proper perspective. Thucydides was a more sober, and at times sounder, writer. His *History of the Peloponnesian War* is largely an eyewitness account of the struggles between Athens and Sparta. Xenophon wrote also as a participant in the events he describes. He was a general in the famous army of ten thousand Greeks during their retreat from Persia, as told in his *Anabasis.*

If Herodotus is the father of history, then Plutarch stands in the same relationship to biography. Living in a world dominated by the Roman Empire, he was able to make comparisons between great men of both civilizations. His method in *Lives of the Noble Grecians and Romans* was to place two figures side by side— Alexander and Caesar, Alcibiades and Coriolanus, Demosthenes and Cicero— and then subject them to the tests of Greek philosophy. Modern scholars may deplore his carelessness with dates and scientific detail, but our knowledge of many of his subjects remains almost as he presented them. Plutarch, in fact, answered his later critics when he wrote: "Nay, a slight thing, like a phrase or a jest, often makes a greater revelation of character than battles where thousands fall." The *Lives* is still one of the great source books in history and literature. Shakespeare is only one of many writers who have borrowed from the first and one of the best of biographers.

Although Greek literature was to supply Latin writers with their best models, no two peoples were ever less alike than the Greeks and the Romans. The Greek genius was for the arts of beauty and daily living, that of the Romans for conquest, law, and engineering. One aspect of the Latin character is clearly revealed in Caesar's *Gallic War,* once the property of every schoolboy. The book is more than an account of military campaigns and the administration of conquered tribes; it is a classic example of forceful, incisive prose. In Caesar, as in many Roman writers, the style reflects the energy and practicality of the race.

The history of Greece began with Homer, but Rome had known more than five hundred years of history before her first writers appeared. Then, at the end of the third century B.C., Plautus and Terence wrote comedies adapted chiefly from Menander, a Greek comic poet, just as Seneca, several hundred years later, imitated the tragic drama of Athens. Certainly Romans had no literature they could call their own until the period of Vergil, Ovid, Horace, Cicero, and Lucretius, in the first century B.C.

Vergil wished for his country a literature as great as that of Greece. Toward this end he wrote the *Aeneid,* its theme borrowed in part from the Homeric epics. His story of the wanderings of Aeneas and the founding of Rome shows deep reverence for the past. But Vergil was a gentle poet who also loved country life and rustic virtues, as he described them in his *Eclogues* and the *Georgics,* and his epic lacks the stirring clash of arms and vivid pageantry we find in the *Iliad.* Perhaps the autumnal serenity of his verse made him all the more loved by the Romans. He was one of the few pagan writers esteemed by scholars and churchmen of the Middle Ages.

Horace is another beloved classic poet. Urbane, temperate, humorous, he expresses the spirit of Roman society in its Golden Age. At the other extreme from his gentle philosophy are Martial's caustic wit and Juvenal's savage pessimism and satire. Among Latin poets, however, Lucretius fills a place of his own. *On the Nature of Things* is a long philosophical poem unlike anything else in classic literature. In it he examines natural phenomena, religion, science, philosophy, and in the process he anticipates several scientific discoveries of the past hundred years. A man centuries ahead of his time, he has gained in our own day the recognition he deserves.

Cicero survives as the most famous of Latin prose writers. Lawyer, politician, and a master of eloquence, he shaped a lasting prose style which even in translation is powerful in clarity and rhythm. Fifty-seven of his speeches have been preserved, along with fragments of many others. His treatises on friendship and old age and his collection of letters have influenced many later writers, among them Montaigne, Sir Francis Bacon, Jonathan Swift.

The leading historians of the Roman Empire were Livy and Tacitus. Livy wrote the history of Rome from its founding to the fall of Carthage. Much of his material he drew from Polybius, a Greek historian who had lived through the period of the Punic Wars. The effectiveness of Tacitus as the historian of his own age lies in his powers of analysis, his excellent character sketches, and his lucid, ironic style. Suetonius presents a different and more scandalous picture of Roman history and life in his *Lives of the Twelve Caesars.* His account is one of imperial baseness and intrigue.

What Suetonius did with historical characters, Petronius, friend of the Emperor Nero, did in prose fiction. His *Satyricon* is a sly, unvarnished tale of magnificence and vice, a shameless comedy of manners laying bare a decadent society that had lost all sense of shame. Several generations later Lucius Apuleius wrote *The Golden Ass,* a satirical story of witchcraft and picaresque adventure. *Daphnis and Chloë* belongs to the same period, a romantic idyl of pastoral life and young love attributed to Longus, a Greek writer of the Hellenistic revival.

Under happier circumstances these tales might have speeded the development of the novel, but by the second century Roman culture had grown stagnant and the empire was crumbling from within. Only two other literary works stand out in the closing centuries of Roman rule and the long twilight of Greek culture. One of these is the *Meditations* of Marcus Aurelius, an emperor influenced by the Stoic philosopher, Epictetus. Written in Greek, the *Meditations* reveals the inner thoughts of a wise and humane ruler who believed that virtue is its own reward and that the ways of the gods, inscrutable to man, are just. The other is *On the Consolation of Philosophy,* by Boethius, who has been called the last Roman writer. This work, which bridges the gap between pagan philosophy and Christian belief, was a favorite book among scholars and writers of the Middle Ages.

Through the writings of St. Jerome, St. Augustine, St. Ambrose, and others, Latin survived as the language of the medieval Church. But in the centuries which followed the fall of Rome the great Greek and Latin classics were to have little influence on literature or thought. Their revival came only with the beginning of the Italian Renaissance in the fifteenth century.

It would be impossible to pass from the classic world without some consideration of the Bible as a literary work. For the Bible is an anthology of fine literature—myth, history, biography, poetry, short stories, letters, prophecy—as well as a tremendous religious document. In *Joseph and His Brothers,* Thomas Mann has shown that the Joseph story is the outline of a novel perfect in construction. Milton went directly to the Bible for his subject in *Paradise Lost.* Certainly no other book has had a more profound or far-reaching influence on human conduct and belief. Here again we are partly indebted to Greece and Rome. At Alexandria, in the second century B.C., Jewish scholars began the Greek translation of the Old Testament known as the Septuagint. The New Testament was written entirely in Hellenistic Greek. When St. Jerome prepared the Latin translation of the Bible— the Vulgate—he worked with Greek texts as well as Hebrew and Aramaic manuscripts. Wycliff's translation was made from the Vulgate. The Authorized, or King James, Version was prepared from Hebrew and Greek texts. Published in 1611, it has in large measure determined English prose style. So the Bible as most of us know it today is a religious and literary heritage transmitted through the great cultures of the past.

THE MIDDLE AGES

The Middle Ages is the name historians gave to the period between the pillage of Rome by the Visigoths in 410 and the fall of Constantinople in 1453. These dates are convenient but hardly accurate, for we know that the return to barbarism began with the recall of the Roman legions and that the Renaissance had its roots planted deeply in the feudal system which replaced the authority of Rome.

The Middle Ages were the Dark Ages. The period was one of wars, famine, pestilence, and gross superstition. Aside from the monasteries, there was no place where a writer could work, and there were few men who would have been capable of reading his manuscript. But the age was not as benighted as was once supposed. In the Arab universities at Damascus, Cairo, and Cordova the Greek philosophers and scientists were studied as carefully as the Koran. It is said that the tutor of St. Thomas Aquinas was a Moor, and in the second half of the Middle Ages many French and English scholars studied in the Moorish schools. In England and Ireland, less ravaged by turmoil after the collapse of Rome, there were famous scholars like the Venerable Bede or the Irish monks Charlemagne summoned to his court when he planned to revive the schools. The Benedictine monks collected classic manuscripts and preserved them in their libraries. Medieval scholasticism, dry and schematic as it was, did more than keep learning alive. The schools produced both a Friar Bacon and a François Villon.

The period was also one of great faith which gave meaning and dignity to men's lives. During the Middle Ages man's hope of forgiveness and salvation inspired the building of magnificent cathedrals and sent knightly Europe on crusades to reclaim Jerusalem from the Saracens. It was only natural that this same faith should find expression in literature. St. Augustine was both a father of the Church and a profound thinker. In his *Confessions* he wrote an intimate and revealing autobiography. *The City of God,* written to refute the charge that the sack of Rome was punishment by the gods because of the spread of Christianity, is a religious treatise over which theologians have been disputing ever since. In it he wrote: "The greatest city in the world has fallen in ruin, but the City of God abideth for ever." His argument established the tradition of spiritual and temporal power for the medieval Church. Although St. Augustine lived in the fifth century, he is as much a citizen of the Middle Ages as St. Francis of Assisi, St. Bonaventure, and St. Thomas Aquinas.

Meanwhile, out of the pine forests and frost-rimed harbors of the North, a new type of literature was emerging, tales of Germanic tribal heroes that come down to us in the Anglo-Saxon poem *Beowulf* and the German *Nibelungenlied,* stories of heroic adventure, enchantments and strange monsters, bloody family feuds. From the same sources at a later date came the Scandinavian eddas and sagas, long chronicles in verse or prose of legendary Viking days and the early history of Iceland and Norway.

As the ideals of the chivalric code began to change the old, rough feudal life, metrical romances dealing with King Arthur and other chivalric heroes followed the primitive, vigorous Germanic stories of the earlier period. In France troubadours sang graceful poems in praise of their loves and created the knightly cult of woman-worship. Most famous of the French romances were *The Song of Roland* and *Aucassin and Nicolette.*

By the thirteenth century medieval society was almost as formalized in its literature as it was in its social structure. For the knight and his lady there were the courtly romances sung by minstrels and troubadours; for the churchman, stories of saints and martyrs and collections of moral tales like those in the *Gesta Romanorum;* for the artisan and peasant, folk ballads and beast fables in which they satirized the clergy and nobility; for scholars, chronicles like those of Froissart and Commines.

The figure of Dante towers high above all other writers of the fourteenth century. *The Divine Comedy*—in Dante's day it was simply the *Commedia,* a story with a happy ending—is his master work, a long poem revealing the whole mind and spirit of the Middle Ages. In it the poet records the splendor and faith of the medieval Church, the idealism of chivalry, the scope of philosophy and science in his day. The framework of the story is simple. Dante, lost in the darkness of a deep wood, is rescued by Vergil, who guides the younger poet through Hell, Purgatory, and Heaven. The poem may be read for story, for poetic imagery, for allegorical interpretation. No other literary work has the scope and depth of Dante's narrative poem, and no other writer has ever expressed so vividly man's need for wisdom and spiritual guidance.

Geoffrey Chaucer is the great figure in English literature of the Middle Ages. *The Canterbury Tales* is a work of realism and humor that has not staled with time. *Troilus and Criseyde,* although written in verse, is our earliest example of the psychological novel. When Chaucer assembled his thirty-two pilgrims at the Tabard Inn at Southwark and set them on their way with gaiety and gusto, he was representing almost the whole of medieval society. But his people are never types. They are as strongly individualized as the stories they tell. And what stories! Chaucer is worth knowing. If the Middle English in which he wrote confuses you, read him in one of the excellent modern versions now available. There is no better introduction to English literature than the characters and tales of the Canterbury pilgrims.

Some of his stories Chaucer borrowed from Boccaccio, his Italian contemporary. Boccaccio lived and wrote in the Middle Ages, but his work points unmistakably toward the Renaissance. Author of various books, including a biography of Dante, he is best known for *The Decameron,* a collection of one hundred court and tavern tales retold in his graceful, lively prose. The stories range from the bawdy and the grotesque to the poetic and the pathetic. They are told, supposedly, by young men and women who have retired to a country villa to escape a plague. In *The Decameron,* however, the writer directs our interest to the stories and not, as Chaucer does, to their tellers. The collection demonstrated for Boccaccio's time the possibilities of fiction in prose. He is one of the forerunners of the modern novel.

Sir Thomas Malory performed the same service in English literature when he collected all the stories of King Arthur and his knights of the Round Table and retold them in *Le Morte d'Arthur.* Malory's tales, written in quaint, simple prose, still mean for most readers the romantic side of medieval life. The book is historically important, as it was one of the first printed by Caxton on his press at Westminster.

One last figure, and the most picturesque of all, stands between the old medieval world and the new. He is François Villon, scholar, poet, tosspot, gallows bait, associate of thieves and drabs. In his poetry he paints a realistic picture of the Paris underworld of violence and sin. His work also reveals his touching devotion to his aged mother and his adoration of the Virgin. Medieval and modern, he is the spiritual ancestor of Baudelaire. It has been said with justification for the claim that Villon, Rabelais, and Montaigne shaped French literature between them.

THE RENAISSANCE

The Renaissance was a period of rebirth, in art, science, and literature.

Again the change had come more slowly than men realized at the time. Artists of the Renaissance knew the earlier paintings of Cimabue and Giotto. Writers had before them the examples of Dante, Boccaccio, Chaucer, and Petrarch's sonnets. Medieval alchemists had never changed lead into gold, but they had made other discoveries adding to man's knowledge of his world. Coster in Holland and Gutenberg in Germany had invented the printing press and ended forever the slow process of copying books by hand. Marco Polo had traveled to Cathay and returned to Venice to stir men's imaginations with accounts of strange lands beyond the boundaries of Europe. And everywhere men were growing restless under the feudal domination of Church and state.

Perhaps the deciding impulse came when Constantinople fell to the Turks in 1453. Greek scholars, taking with them to Italy a knowledge of classic literature that Western Europe had almost forgotten, gave medieval man a new sense of continuity with the past. Suddenly, it seemed, a new age was dawning. It was Shakespeare's "brave new world," in which anything was possible.

Columbus, Vasco da Gama, the Cabots, Magellan, Sir Francis Drake, and all the great navigators and freebooting captains of the age widened men's physical horizon and claimed new lands beyond the seas for their sovereigns. Meanwhile men were exploring new frontiers of the mind as well as unknown continents. Galileo invented the telescope and Copernicus changed man's conception of the world when he viewed the earth as only one small dot in a universe of stars and planets. Painters learned from Greek sculpture the singleness of body and spirit. Da Vinci, Michelangelo, Raphael, and Titian were pioneers and masters in the greatest period of painting the world has ever known. Men began also to assert the right to worship as they pleased. Martin Luther and the Reformation are as much a part of the Renaissance as Michelangelo's *Last Judgment* or Shakespeare's plays.

It is against this larger background that the literature of the period must be viewed, for to the Renaissance man scholarship, art, science, statecraft, poetry, and philosophy were one unit of human thought and activity, not divided into separate departments as we know them today. Da Vinci was, among other things, a painter, musician, inventor, architect, mathematician, chemist, and botanist. Michelangelo wrote beautiful sonnets. Spenser, Sidney, and Raleigh were poets as well as soldiers. Benvenuto Cellini, sculptor and goldsmith, painted indelibly his own swaggering portrait in his *Autobiography*, in which he showed the age more vividly alive than Vasari revealed it in *Lives of the Painters*.

Italy, having inherited the relics of Greek and Roman civilizations, was the first country to feel the stirrings of the new age. At Florence, Lorenzo de Medici, patron of poets and artists, gathered about him a notable group of writers. There Machiavelli, Florentine diplomat, studied the career of the Medici and as the result of his observations wrote *The Prince*, a realistic treatise on statecraft. Ludovico Ariosto, at Ferrara, wrote *Orlando Furioso*, based on the French *Song of Roland*. In the same court Torquato Tasso completed his heroic poem, *Jerusalem Delivered*, a story of the Crusades.

In 1494 there was born at Chinon, France, a writer whose name is inseparably connected with the Renaissance spirit. François Rabelais, scholar and physician, poured his deep wisdom and racy humor into his two tales, *Gargantua* and *Pantagruel*. These books are a blend of seriousness and ribald laughter, and their humor still rings true after four centuries. A lusty rebel against medieval asceticism and scholastic dogma, Rabelais wrote in such fashion that the phrase "Rabelaisian wit" has passed into common usage.

A very different writer, but typical in his own fashion, is Michel de Montaigne, who tried to express in his essays what he felt as a man. "I am my book," he declared, and his writing covers a wide segment of human experience, all recorded with critical skepticism and complete intellectual honesty. His gifts to French literature are the frankness and irony of the Gallic spirit.

In England the Renaissance reached its peak during the reign of Queen Elizabeth. The sixteenth century was an age of great names and titles—Sir Thomas More's *Utopia*, Sidney's *Astrophel and Stella*, Spenser's *The Shepherd's Calendar* and *The Faerie Queene*, Bacon's essays, the plays of Christopher Marlowe, master of the resounding line—but Shakespeare stands far above his contemporaries. Like Homer and Dante, he is the poet of his own place and of all the world as well. It would require a book to analyze the many aspects of his genius. We read him for the entertaining stories he tells. Most of them, we know, were borrowed from other sources, from playwrights of his own day, from Holinshed's *Chronicles*, from Plutarch's *Lives*, but we can still admire the creative skill of a writer able to take a slight or threadbare story and shape it into a work of art. We read him for his matchless poetry, the sheer beauty of language we find even in his poorer plays. We read him for characters who seem as various as life itself—braggart Falstaff, noble Othello, perplexed Hamlet, ambitious Macbeth, tragic Lear, Malvolio, Prospero, Brutus, Dogberry, Pistol, Romeo, Shylock, Rosalind. The list is almost endless. We read him because he brings history dramatically before us, for the sweeping range of his thought, for the lyrics scattered through his plays. He stands at the center of Elizabethan England, but, as Ben Jonson wrote of him, "He was not of an age, but for all time."

While Shakespeare was at work on his tragedies, Miguel de Cervantes, an old Spanish soldier imprisoned for debt, began to write the first part of *Don Quixote*, published in 1605. This novel is more than the great book of the Spanish Renaissance—it is universal. The old Don is noble in his illusions, dignified in disaster. Beside him in his quest for adventure rides his lazy, shrewd, devoted squire. They are among the immortal characters of fiction. Perhaps Cervantes began his book, as some critics assert, with the intention of laughing antiquated chivalry out of Spain. Whatever his purpose, he produced a work which is both realistic and romantic and our one great example of the comic novel. The two parts of *Don Quixote* and the plays of Lope de Vega and Calderón mark the Golden Age of Spanish literature.

THE SEVENTEENTH CENTURY

When Shakespeare died in 1616, his laurels passed to Ben Jonson, whom the next generation ranked as the better playwright. One of Jonson's contributions to the theater was his revival of classical tragedy. More pleasing to modern taste, however, are his great comedies of humors —*Every Man in His Humour, The Silent Woman, Volpone, The Alchemist*—satires on the men and foolish foibles of his day. In Jonson's time the English stage seemed as brilliant as ever, but we know now that its light was little more than the afterglow of the bright Elizabethan day. The romances and tragi-comedies of Beaumont and Fletcher and the poetic violence of Webster are good, but the thinning vitality runs out in the sentimental melancholy of Ford and Shirley's artificiality. The closing of the theaters by law in 1642 ended officially the great decades of Elizabethan drama.

The translators of the Bible and Sir Francis Bacon wrote the most notable prose of the period. Bacon, like Montaigne, made all knowledge his province and natural experience his guide in the study of mankind. His essays he called "certain brief notes, set down curiously rather than significantly" on a wide range of topics. Many of his pithy sentences have passed into proverbial usage: "To choose time is to save time." "Silence is the virtue of fools." "Hope is a good breakfast, but it is a bad supper." A voluminous writer, he made his most important contributions to scientific thought in his *Advancement of Learning* and *Novum Organum,* in which he set forth his theory of inductive reasoning.

In the seventeenth century, an age of religious controversy and wars all over Europe, England was to reap the bitter fruits of the Reformation. Expansion of trade during the Renaissance had created a new, prosperous middle class. Industrious, thrifty, tenacious of rights, dissenting in religious views, this class owed nothing to the tradition of the medieval Church and little to the spirit of Renaissance humanism. In England the rebellion that began in 1642 was social, political, and religious warfare—middle class against the nobility, Parliamentarian against Royalist, Puritan against Established Church.

Today we see that the confusion and strife of the period were signs of painful readjustment to forces and drifts set in motion by Renaissance individualism. But to men of that time it seemed, as John Donne wrote, as if the world were "all in peeces, all cohearance gone, All just supply, and all relation." Few writers of the period escaped being swept along by the cross-currents of the time. Among prose writers, Milton's *Areopagitica,* Hobbes' *Leviathan,* Taylor's *Holy Living and Holy Dying,* Dryden's *Absalom and Achitophel,* Fuller's *Holy and Profane States,* and Locke's *Of Civil Government* reflect the religious and political sentiments of the age. Herrick, Lovelace, Suckling, and Waller were Royalist poets.

In John Milton, Puritanism found its great spokesman. Time has drained away much of the Puritan dogma from *Paradise Lost;* what remains in this greatest of English epics is spiritual exhaltation that dramatizes the conscience of a man and the conscience of his century. Writing to "justify the ways of God to man," Milton's majestic poem is a testament to faith and the same austere but sublime certainties in man's struggle between good and evil that we find in the work of Aeschylus and Sophocles. Pagan and Puritan were moved alike by the spectacle of divine redress redeeming mankind.

John Bunyan stands out as the great amateur among English storytellers. Setting out to write a simple parable of human life and Christian conduct, he produced a fervent allegory whose worldwide appeal is indicated by its translation into more than one hundred languages and dialects. This tinker and unlicensed preacher who learned the art of writing from his Bible is a master of eloquent prose. *Pilgrim's Progress* is a pious tale, an adventure story, a realistic novel. Many readers will be entertained also by the naïveté and disarming simplicity of Bunyan's autobiography, *Grace Abounding to the Chief of Sinners.*

With the Restoration of Charles II in 1660 the English stage had a brief but brilliant revival. Restoration comedy is witty and artificial, often shocking in its lack of moral taste. Written to please dissolute courtiers of a profligate court, it has had little popularity or influence beyond its own period. William Wycherley's *The Country Wife* and *A Plain Dealer* and William Congreve's *The Way of the World* are far superior to other plays of the time.

A Restoration work certain to find many readers in the long future is Samuel Pepys' *Diary.* Pepys is one of the truth tellers of our literature, and the diary he kept from 1660 to 1669 gives us our most intimate picture of men, manners, and morals in the days of the Merry Monarch.

The seventeenth century was rich in scientific writing. Descartes published *An Essay on Method;* Kepler formulated his mathematical laws of astronomy, and Newton in his *Principia* outlined his findings in physics, including the law of gravitation.

While English drama was declining, the French theater was entering its classic age. French drama was an outgrowth of the luxury and magnificence of the court during the long reign of Louis XIV, whose "L'état, c'est moi" created monarchial absolutism and prepared the way for the French Revolution. Pierre Corneille and Jean Racine wrote notable plays which have had a continued popularity in France, where the neo-classical elements of their dramas seem to satisfy Gallic passion for precision and form. A playwright more universal in his appeal is Molière, whose *Tartuffe,* and *The Misanthrope* are comedies of rich fun and good-natured satire. He has been called the Cervantes among playwrights.

When we look back on the seventeenth century, we are most likely to be attracted to its minor works: Donne's metaphysical poems, Herrick's lovely lyrics, La Fontaine's *Fables,* Madame de Sévigné's *Letters,* La Rochefoucauld's ironic *Reflections,* and Walton's *Compleat Angler,* the best book ever written on the "Contemplative Man's Recreation." These writers often seem closer to the true spirit of the age than the major figures who voiced its confusion and fury.

THE EIGHTEENTH CENTURY

The eighteenth century was an age of great prose. This is not to say that its poetry was inferior—only that its poets were few. Early in the period Alexander Pope polished the heroic couplet to epigrammatic perfection and in *The Rape of the Lock* and his *Essay on Man* made poetry a vehicle for social criticism and philosophic speculation. In the closing decades of the century Robert Burns brought poetry back to the simplicity of common things when he wrote of the sorrows, joys, and loves of the Scottish peasant.

But prose is the language of thought, and the eighteenth century has been aptly called the Age of Reason. It was a time when many men believed a perfect social order possible by systematizing all knowledge, thought, and activity. If science could be explained rationally, they argued,

the same laws could be extended to society, government, religion, and the arts. Deism became the characteristic religious tendency, its essence the attempt to rationalize faith by reason and evidence. Constitutionalism became the ideal principle of government and *laissez faire* the dominant theory in trade and industry. To understand the underlying temper of the time, read its philosophers and scientists—Montesquieu's *The Spirit of the Laws,* Voltaire's treatises and his devastating satire in *Candide,* Rousseau's *The Social Contract,* Adam Smith's *An Inquiry into the Nature and Causes of the Wealth of Nations*—and you will see why the typical figures of the century are Franklin, Jefferson, Thomas Paine, Edmund Burke, Samuel Johnson. The age was trying to give order and meaning to what the Renaissance had promised and the seventeenth century had preserved.

The literature of the age reflects that common-sense point of view which sets a premium on truth. "The value of any biography depends on its being true," declared Dr. Samuel Johnson, and Boswell's biography of the great lexicographer is for all time a model of the factual and the real. Johnson's essays and his novel, *Rasselas,* are little read today, his dictionary is no more than a literary landmark; but the man himself, burly, slovenly, opinionated, yet great in spirit and revealingly human, lives in Boswell's work. The same deep and informed passion for truth makes Edward Gibbon's *The Decline and Fall of the Roman Empire* one of the greatest histories of all time.

Their purpose "to expose the false arts of life, to pull off the disguises of cunning, vanity, and affectation," Richard Steele and Joseph Addison reclaimed the essay from philosophy and science, gave it characters and the interests of the everyday world, made it familiar and entertaining as a picture of life. Good-humored, they stand at the opposite pole from Jonathan Swift, for whom the way to truth was the method of satire. *Gulliver's*

Travels is a classic of fantastic adventure and a savage indictment of civilized society, a story to entertain children and a moral lesson for older readers. It can be two different books in one because Swift masked his unpleasant truths about man, his pettiness, grossness, stupidity, and appalling animalism, within a framework of travel adventure in strange lands.

The development of the English novel, in fact, grew out of the truth-telling impulse of its creators. For most of us, probably, the first novel compelling our sense of belief is one we read in childhood—*Robinson Crusoe.* Daniel Defoe was a citizen of the country called by the derisive French a nation of shopkeepers, and his middle-class practicality and interest in factual detail are apparent in all of his books. *Moll Flanders* and *The Journal of the Plague Year* have one quality in common: both are fiction. His use of real names and places, his autobiographical method, even his stripped clarity of style, are devices to convince us of the truth of his narratives.

What Defoe did for the seamier side of human character, Samuel Richardson did for its virtues. His intention being "to promote the cause of religion and virtue," he told in *Pamela* and *Clarissa Harlowe* stories of high-minded and good young women. But he was less successful in portraying a noble young man in *Sir Charles Grandison.* His novels are awkward in their letter form and heavy with analysis of character, but they are models for sentimental fiction from his day to the vogue of the latest serial queen.

Henry Fielding, lawyer and playwright, believed that Richardson's moral views were conventional and shallow. In protest, he began a burlesque of *Pamela* in his own *Joseph Andrews,* but he forgot his fun-making purpose when Parson Adams walked into the pages of his novel. Fielding's masterpiece is *Tom Jones,* the realistic story of a hearty, vigorous young man of eighteenth-century England. This work is one of the world's great novels, filled as it is with the writer's robust humor and deep, mellow philosophy of life. Fielding's novels have the realism and shrewd insights we find in Hogarth's paintings.

A writer similar in material but without Fielding's warm sympathies is Tobias Smollett. His humor is crude and boisterous, his view of life critical and coarse. For all that, *Roderick Random, Peregrine Pickle,* and *Humphry Clinker* present a clear picture of the social life of the time.

Lawrence Sterne is a unique figure in the history of the novel. In one sense *Tristram Shandy* is not a novel at all but an elaborate cock-and-bull story in which Sterne allows his foibles and whimsical nature to lead him into all kinds of digressions on any topic that comes into his head. His biographical novel becomes a picaresque of the mind, wayward, witty, with flashes of sly sentiment and deep feeling. But his characters live. Uncle Toby, Corporal Trim, Mr. Shandy, and Parson Yorick are as real as Parson Adams and Tom Jones. *A Sentimental Journey* is in the same vein, a narrative unlike any other travel book ever written, entertaining because it reflects Sterne's own delight in the oddities of human character and experience.

Like the previous age, the eighteenth century has its literary residues, lesser works that still provide entertainment. Goldsmith's *She Stoops to Conquer* and Sheridan's *The Rivals* and *The School for Scandal* are delightful comedies. René Le Sage's *Gil Blas* is one of the earliest and best of picaresque novels; it is difficult to explain why it is not more widely known today. Then there are the comedies of Beaumarchais on which popular operas have been based—*The Barber of Seville* and *The Marriage of Figaro.* Fanny Burney's *Evelina* is dated now, but Goldsmith's *The Vicar of Wakefield* still holds its cheerful sentiment for many readers. Mention must also be made of John Gay's *The Beggar's Opera,* forerunner of the buoyant merriment of Gilbert and Sullivan.

A literary colossus, Johann Wolfgang von Goethe stands astride the neo-classicism of the eighteenth-century and nineteenth-century romanticism. Emerging from the Storm and Stress period of German literature, he became our last example of the universal mind. His influence began in 1774, when *The Sorrows of Young Werther* infected a whole generation with pleasurable melancholy. He wrote plays as popular as those of Schiller, his friend and contemporary, and lyrics as lovely as those of Heine. His *Wilhelm Meister's Apprenticeship* is one of the great novels. But the true measure of his genius is *Faust*, the story of man's thirst for all knowledge and all power, reckless of consequences, regardless of moral and religious law. Perhaps the widespread interest which in 1949 attended his two hundredth anniversary will reclaim Goethe from awe-stricken neglect. He is the only modern writer to challenge the statures of Shakespeare, Dante, and Homer.

In general, the literary history of the nineteenth century is the story of romanticism in retreat and the triumph of the commonplace. The literature of the age we view in clearer perspective, for its great names were those we studied in high school and college, its titles the books we found on library shelves when we were children. Closer to these writers in time, we have a better understanding of their problems and achievements.

The age, which began with the Napoleonic Wars as an aftermath of the French Revolution, saw the peace muddled by the Congress of Vienna, knew disillusionment, and lived through financial panics, has more than surface resemblances to our own cycle of World Wars, the Russian Revolution, the Treaty of Versailles, dictators, depression, and spiritual bankruptcy. Today we know that the writers of the Romantic Age were not always romantic and that the great Victorians were not as full of sweetness and light as they seemed to their readers.

But for a time, at least, English romanticism spoke in its poets: Wordsworth, who found intimations of immortality in the beauty of nature and the heart of man; Coleridge, poet of imagination and dream; visionary Shelley; Byron, eternity's pilgrim and society's critic; Keats, who found life's joys and sorrows in the world of the senses.

It spoke also in the essays of Charles Lamb and Thomas De Quincey, and in that strange offshoot, the Gothic romance. Horace Walpole in *The Castle of Otranto* and Mrs. Radcliffe in *The Mysteries of Udolpho* created a literary fashion, a spine-tingling fiction of ghosts, sleepwalkers, ruined castles, dismal crypts, birds of ill omen, plots of abduction and murder. This literature was to cross the Atlantic and reach its final flowering in Edgar Allan Poe's poems and his *Tales of the Grotesque and Arabesque.*

In a Hampshire village a quiet spinster turned her back on terror and stormy passion and in *Pride and Prejudice* brought the novel of manners to a point of perfection it has not achieved since. Perhaps *Emma,* or *Persuasion,* is a better novel in construction and detail, but her story of the five Bennett sisters will always hold first place among Jane Austen's readers. For her the materials of fiction were not the clash of events in that uncertain time. She took her subjects from provincial society, the only life she knew. A country dance or a strawberry tea was to her an occasion filled with dramatic possibilities, but she created great effects with her small cast and single scene. Her shrewd observations of life, ironic wit, and agreeable good sense make her a writer whose popularity is not likely to fade.

At the same time Sir Walter Scott was creating the historical novel, perhaps the most lasting contribution of English romanticism to world literature. Scott's style seems awkward to us now and his fiction weighted with excessive detail, but he has never been surpassed in sheer storytelling ability or the variety of characters we find in his books. Pick any six titles from his long list of novels—*Guy Mannering, The Heart of Midlothian, Old Mortality, Ivanhoe, Kenilworth, Quentin Durward*. Each is an invitation to renew old pleasures in Scott's stirring pictures of the past.

Tennyson and Browning began their careers as romantics; they ended them as chief poetic spokesmen of the Victorian Age. Tennyson summed up its indecisions, hopes, and fears when he published *In Memoriam* in 1850. Browning's master work did not appear until 1868. *The Ring and the Book* is a long narrative poem pointing toward the modern psychological novel. Poetry interpreted the age; the essay criticized it in the work of Matthew Arnold, John Ruskin, Thomas Carlyle.

The parade of books which were to affect the contemporary world began in mid-century. John Stuart Mill published his *Principles of Political Economy* in 1848, the year in which Marx and Engels issued their *Communist Manifesto*. Charles Darwin's *Origin of Species* appeared in 1859, *The Descent of Man* in 1871. Marx spoke out again with the first volume of *Das Kapital* in 1867. In the next year Huxley's *The Physical Basis of Life* disturbed many readers. The next decade brought Henry George's *Progress and Poverty*. The 1880's saw the publication of Nietzsche's *Thus Spake Zarathustra* and *Beyond Good and Evil*. By 1890 only the writings of William James, Sigmund Freud, Henri Bergson, and Albert Einstein were needed to complete seasonal changes in the intellectual climate of our time.

The lasting effects of these world movers were still hidden in the future, however, when Charles Dickens published *Pickwick Papers* in 1836. This early work contains all the qualities we continue to associate with his name: the vivid characterizations, droll humor, pathos, a mastery of scene and situation. Today we know that his books sin against almost every canon of the novel, but we still read him because he carries us forward with a creative vitality that seldom loosens his hold upon our sense of belief. Again we can pick our titles at random—*David Copperfield,* the immortal *Pickwick, A Tale of Two Cities, Great Expectations*. In them Dickens remains the most popular of nineteenth-century writers.

Thackeray's *Vanity Fair* we read for the character of Becky Sharp in a novel which has unfortunately overshadowed the greater art of his historical masterpiece, *Henry Esmond*. Of George Eliot we are no longer quite so sure. *Adam Bede, Silas Marner, Middlemarch* and *Romola* are impressive monuments to her fame, but we miss in her moral seriousness and critical point of view the saving grace of humor which redeems Dickens' melodrama and sentimentality. Yet *Middlemarch* remains, as Virginia Woolf has pointed out, one of the few novels ever written for adult minds.

A writer more to the modern taste is Anthony Trollope, restored to popularity after several decades of neglect. Trollope is another of the great truth tellers. With reckless haste that paid little heed to niceties of style he turned out scene after scene of English provincial life, and as a result the social and cultural picture of his age stands before us today as meaningful and whole as it was when the ink dried on his page. Because he hurried to get everything in, his Barchester *is* nineteenth-century England. In novels like *The Warden* and *Barchester Towers* we recognize it for what it was, a very real and self-contained world.

Trollope presents his Slopes and Proudies with keen awareness of their social and moral values but without mocking irony. For that we go to George Meredith's *The Ordeal of Richard Feverel* and *The Egoist*. Meredith asks much of his readers, who must realize that his poised humor and subtle, figurative style are a comic mask over a view of life that was essentially tragic.

From art as discipline we turn to the world of the Brontës, where everything is natural and free. The heroine of Charlotte Brontë's *Jane Eyre* owes nothing to the conventions of Victorian society as she tells her own story with frankness and passion that brought new insights into English fiction. *Wuthering Heights*, by Emily Brontë, is a work of pure genius. Charlotte called her sister's novel a "wild" book, and it is that. Heathcliff and Catherine Earnshaw are human beings in speech and form, but their natures are as wild and stormy as nature itself. The brooding spirit of the Yorkshire moors sweeps into Emily Brontë's prose, filling it with harsh poetry. The result is a book that stands high among the world's great novels.

On the continent, meanwhile, novelists had carried realism to a point where no English writer of the time dared venture. The realists had not won their place without a struggle. Victor Hugo's *Les Miserables* and *The Hunchback of Notre Dame* keep alive the romantic spirit of his work. Few characters in fiction are as well known as D'Artagnan, Athos, Porthos and Aramis, the gallant heroes Alexandre Dumas immortalized in *The Three Musketeers, Twenty Years After,* and *The Vicomte de Bragelone.* Stendhal, author of *The Charterhouse of Parma* and *The Red and the Black,* is another writer marked for survival. Realism came into its own, however, when Gustave Flaubert wrote *Madame Bovary* and *A Sentimental Education.* Honoré de Balzac, most fertile of French novelists, wrote more than ninety novels and tales in his tremendous Human Comedy. Here, again, we pick our titles at random—*Father Goriot, Cousin Bette, Eugénie Grandet.* Guy de Maupassant, master of the short story, is the connecting link between Flaubert's realism and the naturalism of Émile Zola, who in *Nana, The Downfall,* and *The Land* carried realism to its farthest edge in his attempt to make fiction an exact transcription of life.

Nikolai Gogol, author of *Dead Souls,* is one of the fathers of the Russian novel, which reached its peak in the work of Ivan Turgenev, Fyodor Dostoevski, and Count Leo Tolstoy. Turgenev is the great critic of his society in *Smoke* and *Fathers and Sons,* a master of form and a writer of deep humanitarian spirit. Dostoevski's province is the black night of the human soul in the world of the outcast and the oppressed. In *Crime and Punishment, The Idiot,* and *The Brothers Karamazov* he plumbs the depths of man's shame and guilt. Tolstoy brought his passion for reform into much of his fiction. *War and Peace* stands far above his other novels, just as it towers over all fiction of the past or present. A story of the Napoleonic Wars, its vast enclosures of time and space seem to hold the whole of human experience within its pages. Anton Chekhov is the fourth of the great nineteenth-century Russians. Best known for his short stories, he wrote in *The Cherry Orchard* and *The Seagull* plays which convey the same terse, impressionistic pictures of Russian life.

Neither Robert Louis Stevenson's revival of romance in *Treasure Island* and *Kidnapped* nor Rudyard Kipling's brilliantly vigorous short stories—good as these writers are—measure up to European literature at the end of the nineteenth century. The only English writer to stand beside his continental contemporaries is Thomas Hardy. In novels like *The Return of the Native, The Mayor of Casterbridge,* and *Tess of the d'Urbervilles* he explored tragic relationships between character and environment. The individual, good or bad, against the vast, imponderable forces of the universe is Hardy's vision of life, and this spectacle he treats with detached awareness of the parts played by tragic circumstance and the irony of fate in the lives of men. In his work we feel that an Aeschylus or Sophocles has been reborn in a modern writer.

The nineteenth century in Europe closed with a revival of dramatic literature. Henrik Ibsen brought realism and social problems into the theater in *The Doll's House* and *Ghosts,* plays which prepared the way for George Bernard

Shaw and John Galsworthy. Bitterness and pessimism also marked the plays of August Strindberg. Maxim Gorky dramatized sheer human misery in *The Lower Depths*. The novel, the short story, and the drama were now realistic. Europe had entered the twentieth century.

More important to American readers, however, is the fact that the nineteenth century saw the development of our national literature. The early beginnings had been tentative and far apart. Benjamin Franklin's *Autobiography*, written without thought of publication, has become one of our permanent possessions, but it is an exception. The writings of Thomas Paine and Philip Freneau belong only to the period of the Revolution; the Connecticut wits are as dated as Michael Wigglesworth's *The Day of Doom*; the novels of Charles Brockden Brown are no more than titles in literary histories. But if William Cullen Bryant had written nothing but "Thanatopsis" and "To a Waterfowl" he would still be remembered, for he was our first true poet, finding food for moral reflection in the woods and fields of the American landscape. Washington Irving wrote the folklore of a new continent in "Rip Van Winkle" and "The Legend of Sleepy Hollow." Lover of legend and tradition, a writer perfect in the short flight, he bridged the gap between the old world and the new in *The Sketch Book* and *Bracebridge Hall*.

James Fenimore Cooper brought into American fiction a knowledge of rivers and woods and the wild, free life of the frontier. He wrote our best novel of the Revolutionary War in *The Spy* and our first true sea novel in *The Pilot*, but his fame is even more secure in the Leatherstocking Tales—*The Deerslayer, The Last of the Mohicans, The Pathfinder, The Pioneers,* and *The Prairie*. The figure of the lone hunter in the American wilderness possessed Cooper's imagination, and in his novels, carelessly written as they are, he gives us our heroic picture of pioneer life. There was a time when Cooper was read chiefly for his thrilling stories of escape and pursuit. Nowadays we know that his values run deeper. There is almost a prophetic quality in his writing; long before the actual frontier disappeared he dramatized the fate of the Indian and the frontiersman in that short interval between wilderness life and an expanding industrial society. Beneath their blood-and-thunder plots the Leatherstocking Tales reflect Cooper's interest in the westward movement and the social tensions it created.

The American renaissance came suddenly in New England. For a good picture of that spacious time read Van Wyck Brooks' *The Flowering of New England*, a book neither biography, chronicle, nor analysis, but a mixture of all three. The opening chapters on Ticknor and Everett, scholars of genius who gave the age its taste for learning, and the closing chapters on Holmes and Lowell—the lesser men of the period—enclose the book in a frame of reference. Everywhere else is the passionate stir of a new day. The background is of two parts: first the clear New England landscape of hills and meadows, quiet villages, orchards, and dark sea, a region marked by the trades and traits of its people; then the indoor world of the library, where men studied the philosophies of Greece and the Orient and poets discovered in lays of the troubadours and roaring sagas the literature of a romantic past. Against this background the great writers come to life, and as they move— Longfellow, Prescott, Emerson, Hawthorne, Thoreau, Whittier, Holmes, Lowell, and many others—through an age that begins in Gilbert Stuart's Boston and ends in Concord with the death of Thoreau, Brooks distills into flowing, luminous prose the essence of their work.

Something in the keen, bracing atmosphere of Concord seemed for a time to lift men above themselves. There Ralph Waldo Emerson, social rebel and ethical thinker, wrote his poems and essays to set forth his doctrine of self-knowledge and self-reliance. He preached no formal philosophy, only a transcendental belief in the possible in man, but he brought the democratic ideal into our intellectual and moral life. There Henry David Thoreau went into the woods in quiet protest against growing materialism in the society about him, and the record of his experience he wrote in *Walden* has become twentieth-century man's text in essential living. Nathaniel Hawthorne was never far from Concord in spirit. Working in solitude, he explored his regional and ancestral past. Out of his brooding concern for the Puritan spirit and the problem of evil came *The Scarlet Letter* and *The House of the Seven Gables* as well as the allegorical short stories, all works of quiet but sure art.

At Cambridge, meanwhile, Longfellow and Lowell lived in a mellower, more scholarly atmosphere. *Evangeline* and *The Courtship of Miles Standish* have the same academic echoes we hear in *The Vision of Sir Launfal* and *The Biglow Papers*. Oliver Wendell Holmes was a Boston wit. At Amesbury, not far off, Whittier preserved in *Snow-Bound* and other poems a nostalgic picture of rural New England already passing.

There were other great figures in America's Golden Day. In the South, Edgar Allan Poe had expressed in musical verse the mysteries of love and death, and he had brought the short story to its finished form in his tales of imagination and the supernatural. West of Boston, Herman Melville, having written *Typee* and *Omoo* among other books of seafaring adventure, was ready to publish *Moby Dick*. His own generation read *Moby Dick* for information and romance. Today we read it as a fable of man's self-destroying pursuit of natural evil in the world, the white whale a symbol of all the forces creating rage and hatred in man's long history. The novel is a reflection of America's unquiet mind, its magnificent hopes, despair, and defiance.

Walt Whitman published the first edition of *Leaves of Grass* in 1855. The decade was already one of stress when he spoke out bravely in the face of the gathering storm. Many of his poems are weakened by bombast and fustian, but at his best his work is filled with eloquence and beauty. It is a saddening commentary on our way of life to say that Whitman is our only great poet of democratic beliefs and institutions, a writer who spoke for himself, his country, and his time. Only Carl Sandburg in *The People, Yes* has echoed Whitman's vision of the greatness and simple dignity possible in the life of Western Man.

Mark Twain was in many ways Whitman's common, democratic man. He was born at the end of an era, and in his best books—*Huckleberry Finn, Tom Sawyer, Life on the Mississippi*—he looked back to a place and a way of life the Civil War had ended forever. The Mark Twain who looked toward the future was the tired, disgusted pessimist of *The Man That Corrupted Hadleyburg* and *The Mysterious Stranger*. His Hannibal is a place of idyl and myth, the enchanted world of boyhood in a young nation, between the forest and the river. All the life of America moved up and down the Mississippi in those years; Huck Finn and Nigger Jim are only a part of its restless humanity. Although the river offered tranquillity and freedom, its currents sometimes flowed into violence or into backwaters where a clear-eyed boy could see whatever was shoddy or soiled in human character. Twain was a curiously uneven writer. Much of his clowning as a public entertainer has already worn thin, but the virility and hearty laughter and sane pessimism are in the durable American grain, the drawling voice of the frontier in protest against mediocrity and conformity.

William Dean Howells, Twain's contemporary and friend, had the even temperament Twain lacked, but he was not sufficiently a rebel to break with the genteel tradition of most American writing after the Civil War. Admirer of Balzac and Zola, he created in his own novels only a domestic realism which has been

1

called "the romance of the commonplace." *The Rise of Silas Lapham* is his most representative book.

On this side of the Atlantic the new realism first made itself heard in the novels of Stephen Crane and Frank Norris. Crane's *Maggie: A Girl of the Streets* was the shocking book of the mauve decade, a novel Howells thought "too honest" for readers of the 90's. Crane's great book is *The Red Badge of Courage,* a vividly realistic story of war from the point of view of a soldier in the ranks. Norris, a more somber writer, wrote *McTeague* and in *The Octopus* and *The Pit* completed two novels of a planned trilogy on American economic life, before his death at thirty-two.

Henry James, who wrote at the end of the nineteenth century and the beginning of the twentieth, belongs to British literature as well as American. An expatriate almost all of his life, he wrote on English and European society from the viewpoint of a sensitive American. His themes are the artist in a materialistic society and the American who is always a pilgrim to old world tradition and sometimes its victim. James' craftsmanship is so scrupulous and exquisite in detail that he has become one of the great influences on the technique of the novel, so that his fame, at least as a writer's writer, seems assured. *The Portrait of a Lady* is the best novel of his early period. *The Wings of the Dove, The Ambassadors,* and *The Golden Bowl,* written shortly after the turn of the century, are more complex in structure but more revealing as art. His novelette, *The Turn of the Screw,* is one of the great psychological horror stories in the language.

A few more names and we finish with the nineteenth century. These include Emily Dickinson, who wrote distilled lyrics on love, death, immortality, in the hidden privacy of her Amherst garden; Sidney Lanier, belated romantic; Bret Harte, whose tales of the gold rush created the vogue of the local color story; and Sarah Orne Jewett, who in *The Country of the Pointed Firs* re-created a picture of New England life after its great days had passed.

THE TWENTIETH CENTURY

When twentieth-century science invented the atomic bomb, it made fate more planetary than personal; otherwise our cares and concerns seem very much as they were a generation ago. Our attitudes toward our problems change more quickly —that is all. We have had the boob-baiting satire of the generation represented by H. L. Mencken in the essay and by Sinclair Lewis in the novel, the private anguish of Hemingway and others of the lost generation, and the proletarian dialectics of John Dos Passos and James T. Farrell in the depression 30's. Nowadays we are told that ours is the Age of Anxiety, but the telling has a familiar sound. Most of it was said, and more emphatically, by the major prophets of the Victorian Age. So while we wait to learn the mid-century *Zeitgeist,* the voices to whom we listen are mostly those from the recent past.

Looking back to the beginning of the century, for example, we know that Henry Adams and Theodore Dreiser speak to us more truly than Booth Tarkington and Winston Churchill, the popular writers of the period. *The Education of Henry Adams* is more than one man's examination of himself in relation to his background and his age. Adams viewed with detached appraisal a modern society which "ran in every conceivable and inconceivable direction," but without ethical purpose or significance. His importance is historical if nothing else, for he was the first serious writer to consider philosophically the relationship between modern man and the mechanical symbols of his civilization.

When Stuart Sherman complained that Dreiser "has chosen only to illustrate the unrestricted flow of temperament," he was pointing unknowingly to the trait which makes Dreiser a modern. There is a primitive, monolithic quality in his writing, "something grey and bleak and hurtful, that has been in the world perhaps forever," as Sherwood Anderson once wrote. Into his long, unwieldy novels and cumbersome short stories he poured all the accumulated facts resulting from his patient brooding over the activities and psychology of the animal man. In his world the divine fury of Aeschylus becomes the inward compulsions of nature and the external drives of a competitive society. *Sister Carrie, Jennie Gerhardt, The Financier,* and *The Titan* brought the American novel close to Balzac's achievement in his Human Comedy. *An American Tragedy* is documentary analysis of social morality. If *The Bulwark* and *The Stoic,* published after Dreiser's death, are less powerful than his earlier fiction, they gain serenity as the last words of a writer who dedicated his art to a search for truth concerning human behavior. There are no tricks in his novels; his artlessness is the secret of his simple and often terrifying sincerity.

Edith Wharton maintained for the novel its last hold upon a traditional society. Born into a Jamesian world of wealth and culture, she arrived on the scene too late to sustain its values and so became the historian of its disintegration as the old aristocracy of dignity and breeding was giving way to a new plutocracy of easy money and vulgar display. Having known what the traditional society once stood for, she let her characters stand or fall by its old-fashioned but recognizable standards. Her titles (*The House of Mirth, The Age of Innocence*) reveal the ironic temper of her art. Critic of the society she knew best, she made few excursions beyond her own fashionable world. One of these is *Ethan Frome,* a starkly realistic, almost timeless tragedy of New England life.

These three writers stand out among the literary cross-currents of the time. Local color, carrying over from the nineteenth century a minor art based on landscape, created effects as diverse as Owen Wister's sagebrush stereotype ("When you call me that, smile.") and brisk tales in which O. Henry re-

created New York as Baghdad-on-the-Subway. Regionalism took on firmer outlines in Ellen Glasgow's novels. "What the South needs," she declared, "is blood and irony." *Barren Ground, The Romantic Comedians,* and *The Sheltered Life* are among the social chronicles and novels of manners that grew out of her determination to write about the South not sentimentally, as a stricken province, but as a part of the larger world. But writers were not satisfied to get America stated; they also wanted to remake it. When Upton Sinclair exposed the evils of the meatpacking industry in *The Jungle,* he assumed leadership of a group of writers who stood for political, social, and economic reforms. James Branch Cabell took the way of evasion and mockery. His romances of mythical Poictesme are escapes into ironic fantasy and nose-thumbing gestures toward Comstockery and Mrs. Grundy.

Suddenly America was reading its new poets: the psychological portraiture of Edwin Arlington Robinson's character studies; the pastoral meditations and narratives of Robert Frost, Yankee farmer and poet-sage; Carl Sandburg's American scene of prairie wheat fields, Chicago, steel mills, and the laboring life; Vachel Lindsay's chants of salvation in ragtime. These writers were already well established when T. S. Eliot published *The Waste Land* in 1922. Most influential poem of its period, *The Waste Land* presents in historical and literary image a contrast between the heroic past and an ignoble present.

Revolt from the village had already begun. In *Winesburg, Ohio,* Sherwood Anderson viewed with poetic perception the quiet bravery and longings of repressed, inarticulate lives. Edgar Lee Masters wrote as a poet in *Spoon River Anthology,* but his brief chronicles of drabness and disillusionment belong to the tradition of prose rather than to poetry.

The country roads of village fiction led inevitably to *Main Street.* Sinclair Lewis gave us an America of small-town smugness, stupidity, and sham, of billboards, realtors' conventions, adding machines, corner drug stores, filling stations, telephone operators, the movies, suburbia, high-pressure salesmanship, pepped-up religion, boosters' clubs, commercialized medicine. Critics might protest that the strident tones and confusion of his novels showed no depths of wisdom and repose, but we read *Main Street* and *Babbitt* as soon as they appeared. Lewis' people were two-dimensional caricatures, paper-thin, but they were close enough to the real to let us see ourselves and our neighbors. Although we realize now that Lewis loved best what he satirized most, he did succeed in doing perfectly what Mark Twain had attempted in *The Gilded Age*. His novels show America talking loud and acting big to conceal the poverty of spirit beneath its gadget-minded civilization.

One true artist of the period stood apart from literary cliques and fashions. Willa Cather was the last of a generation of writers who lived through the passing of the frontier, who saw the land of the homesteader transformed into a countryside of tidy farms and cramped, ugly towns; and she found in pioneer virtues her own values as an artist. Her first important novels—*O Pioneers!, The Song of the Lark, My Antonia*—enclosed vast areas of prairie, hills, and sky in a world rich and sustaining with homely realism. *A Lost Lady* belongs to a later period. Its theme, like that of *The Professor's House,* is decay, the spectacle of a way of life that was once great and spacious giving place to a new way that is paltry and crude. Having written the elegy of the frontier, Miss Cather found in more traditional societies realities of the spirit which have been almost overwhelmed in the complexities and confusion of the present. *Death Comes for the Archbishop,* a story of the Southwest, is an American masterpiece reclaiming a significant segment of our national past.

But Willa Cather's concern for lasting values offered little comfort, in the period between the wars, to young writers facing realities of disaster from want and destruction by war. By that time the Jamesian pilgrim had become the drifter, a rootless generation looking for emotional release in Paris night life or in the hot violence of Spain. To the young expatriates who drift between Left Bank cafés and Spanish fiestas in Ernest Hemingway's *The Sun Also Rises,* life has become the physical sensations of drink, sport, lovemaking, and the bullfight. The tragic love story and the disastrous retreat from Caporetto in *A Farewell to Arms* told us how the old values had been lost. The sense of retrieval which Hemingway expressed in an inferior novel, *To Have and Have Not,* found complete affirmation in *For Whom the Bell Tolls,* a novel of the Spanish civil war. Master of a stripped prose style that conveys the immediate realities of experience, Hemingway is important as the spokesman and technical innovator of his generation. His short stories, ranging from familiar anthology pieces like "The Killers" to the less familiar but more impressive "The Snows of Kilimanjaro," are probably the best being written today.

The 1930's gave us John Dos Passos, James T. Farrell, Thomas Wolfe, John Steinbeck, and William Faulkner. Dos Passos' best-known work is *U.S.A.*, a trilogy made up of *The 42nd Parallel, 1919,* and *The Big Money.* This novel attempts to show, through the experiences of a dozen or so representative characters, the vast and complicated structure of American life between 1900 and 1930 and to trace the slow cleavage of its social and economic system, which by the depression years had created a nation divided between the possessors and the dispossessed. The note of social protest is loud in everything Dos Passos has written between *Manhattan Transfer,* a kaleidoscopic picture of New York life, and his recent novels of the New Deal era. To create the effect of contemporary life in *U.S.A.*, he hit upon three time-fixing devices: Newsreel, The Camera Eye, and a series of impressionistic biographies. Farrell is a realist more in the tradition of Zola. His Studs Lonigan trilogy and the series of novels dealing with Danny O'Neill are purely objective studies of life on Chicago's mean streets.

Thomas Wolfe's four novels— *Look Homeward, Angel* and *Of Time and the River, The Web and the Rock* and *You Can't Go Home Again*—present in the experiences of two different heroes a thinly disguised autobiography of Wolfe himself. Whether the hero's name is Eugene Gant or George Webber, he is the same undisciplined personality, a reflecting screen for his author's exuberance and confusion and despair. Wolfe's virtues as a writer are as great as his faults: on one side an unsurpassed realism of sense impressions, an expert command of language, the dream of lost time, the marvelous reporting, the vivid character sketches; on the other his failure to achieve form, the impassioned rhetoric and hymns to death and time that stand outside the framework of the novels, the overpowering egoism. His books make life seem the thing he said it was, a common haze of loneliness and groping shot through with private fantasy and furious outbreak against a materialistic society.

Wolfe's novels, diffuse in form, are in spirit all of one piece. Steinbeck is a more uneven writer. He has veered from primitive mysticism to the issues of class conflict, from sentimental exploitation of Whitman's dear love of comrades to quaintly humorous idealization of the simple life. His one really fine performance is *The Grapes of Wrath*, a bitter saga of migration and hardship in the experiences of a dispossessed dustbowl family lured to California during the depression and there betrayed by economic exploitation.

William Faulkner is another writer who has followed his own course. His subject is the destruction of the old order in the South and the further corruption of the descendants of that order by a ruthless and competitive industrial society; and his novels, experimental in form, poetic in style, are haunted alike by the beginnings of Southern culture and the threat of its extinction. Most of his fiction has for background imaginary Yoknapatawpha County in Mississippi. The Yoknapatawpha novels— *The Sound and the Fury, As I Lay Dying, Light in August, Absalom, Absalom!*, and *Intruder in the Dust* are among the best— elaborate a tremendous myth of Southern life and history. *The Sound and the Fury* tells of social and moral decay in a family of gone-to-seed aristocrats. *Light in August* and *Intruder in the Dust* reflect racial problems. *Absalom, Absalom!*, key novel of the series, brings together all of Faulkner's themes: the old order in the South, chattel slavery and the evils it engendered, the poor white, miscegenation, fratricide, community shame and guilt, social decay.

F. Scott Fitzgerald is a writer whose posthumous reputation has added greatly to his stature. During the 1920's he created three fashions in fiction: the younger generation novel, the college novel, and the gangster novel. *This Side of Paradise* has the wit and brilliance of a rebellious talent. *The Great Gatsby*, mature in theme and construction, is the story of one man's education in the emotional erosion and waste the boom period imposed upon the human spirit. *Tender Is the Night* is another picture of the lost generation, grown older and sadder but little wiser, and still lost.

In spite of recent vulgarization, regional and historical novels make up an interesting and varied body of work: the blend of realism and folk poetry in *The Time of Man* and *The Great Meadow*, by Elizabeth Madox Roberts of Kentucky; Glenway Wescott's stories of rural life in Wisconsin in *The Apple of the Eye* and *The Grandmothers*; Walter D. Edmonds' re-creation of Erie Canal days in *Rome Haul*; Elsie Singmaster's stories of the Pennsylvania German country; novels of the West by H. L. Davis, Vardis Fisher, Walter Van Tilburg Clark, and A. B. Guthrie; Conrad Richter's remarkable trilogy of pioneer life in *The Trees, The*

Fields, and *The Town;* Carl Sandburg's panorama of American history in *Remembrance Rock.* A list of books out of the ordinary in theme or treatment would include E. E. Cummings' *The Enormous Room,* a story of life in a French military prison; Pearl Buck's *The Good Earth;* Elinor Wylie's *The Venetian Glass Nephew;* Katherine Anne Porter's *Pale Horse, Pale Rider* and her short stories in *Flowering Judas;* Thornton Wilder's *The Bridge of San Luis Rey,* and Erskine Caldwell's tall-story exaggeration in *Tobacco Road.*

The vitality and techniques of the American novel have greatly influenced contemporary world literature. In England, on the other hand, the century has seen a decline in the tradition of the novel. Signs of change are most apparent in the work of H. G. Wells, who made the novel a literary packsack in which to peddle his views on science, education, religion, history, politics, and war. He began his career as a writer of pseudo-scientific romances like *The Time Machine* and *The War of the Worlds,* both still readable, and he ended it with didactic studies excellent for social and political analysis but of little value as fiction. *Tono-Bungay,* a satire on modern business practices, and *Mr. Britling Sees It Through,* a study of a rational, liberal-minded Englishman in wartime, will probably be read after his Utopian novels have been forgotten.

Polish-born Joseph Conrad was unequaled in his generation for technical and aesthetic effects which are only now being properly evaluated. He has been called a novelist of the sea, a romanticist, a realist, a writer of atmosphere, and a philosopher in fiction. His own experiences as a sailor provided many of the plots and exotic settings of his novels, but he is more than a writer of sea stories in the Marryat tradition, for his novels take shape around the moral issues of courage, love, fidelity, honor. Man he saw in conflict with powers of evil—savagery in *Almayer's Folly,* cowardice in *Lord Jim,* greed in *Nostromo,* lawlessness in *Victory,* madness in *Heart of Darkness.* To him, as he showed in *The Nigger of the Narcissus,* the sea was the testing ground of human character and action. He stated his literary creed in his preface to the same novel, when he wrote: "My task which I am trying to achieve is, by the power of the written word, to make you hear, to make you feel—it is, before all, to make you see."

John Galsworthy's deep humanitarian sympathies and impartial realism set the pattern for his novels and plays. What he did, quite simply, was ask the English upper middle class to re-examine its social structure and morality. In his novels the forces of conflict are always social, between the conservative group to whom property means goods acquired and possessed, a symbol of class responsibility and position, and the rebellious artist or lover of beauty. The three novels of *The Forsyte Saga—The Man of Property, In Chancery* and *To Let*—present a family whose collective life is dominated by things. This trilogy is both family chronicle and a social history of English life between the Victorian Age and the period immediately following World War I, in which Galsworthy analyzes with patient, scrupulous detail not only the acquisitive instincts of his ruling class but also its clannishness, stubborn pride, inverted sentimentalism, and indifference to the arts. *A Modern Comedy,* made up of *The White Monkey, The Silver Spoon,* and *Swan Song,* continues the story of the Forsytes in order to show postwar forces at work among the younger generation. Soames Forsyte, the man of property, is the central character giving unity to the whole work, a frank materialist whose life is nevertheless touched with greatness because he stands for order and recognized values in a world drifting toward no values whatever. He became so real to Galsworthy's readers that when *Swan Song* was published a London newspaper appeared with the heading, "Death of Soames Forsyte."

Although Arnold Bennett wrote a number of novels about the manufacturing district he called the Five Towns, *The Old Wives' Tale* is his greatest achievement in fiction. Time is the real theme of this novel, which relates the life stories of two sisters, Constance and Sophia Baines. Everything contributes to a sense of time passing. It condemns Constance to meek endurance of provincial routine and tedium. It carries Sophia to Paris and a precarious existence there, as well as to the accumulation of a modest fortune. In the end she goes back to the town of her birth, where the sisters end their days together as time rounds out its circle. *The Old Wives' Tale* is a cleanly built, powerfully realistic novel giving the impression of life itself. The Clayhanger tetrology and *Riceyman Steps* are other fine novels by Bennett, each as detailed and painstakingly realistic as a painting of the Dutch school.

The contemporary British novel reflects a variety of aims and means if not a great tradition. D. H. Lawrence wrote as a social prophet who wished to bring back to everyday existence a closer relationship between man and nature, an understanding of life less of the intellect than of the five senses. *Sons and Lovers,* a study of human personality thwarted by possessive mother love, is a powerful psychological novel written in vigorous, poetic prose. *The Rainbow* and *Women in Love* uncover subconscious tensions in sexual relationships to show that many moderns are lost in the confusion of their own emotions. W. Somerset Maugham is an unsparing realist and expert craftsman whose best novel, *Of Human Bondage,* is the partly autobiographical story of a young man who learns through disillusionment and hardship the limitations of his nature and talent. *The Moon and Sixpence* provides an exotic South Seas background for a grimly realistic study of self-centered genius in a novel based on the life of Paul Gauguin. *Cakes and Ale* is a wickedly satirical portrait of literary genius in shirt sleeves. Hugh Walpole was a more tradi-

tional writer. *Fortitude* is a modern version of *David Copperfield. The Herries Chronicle,* his most ambitious work, carries an English family through more than two hundred years of social and political history. Virginia Woolf experimented daringly with technique in her attempt to convey the true nature of reality. In prose as delicate and impressionistic as that of Katherine Mansfield in her short stories, Mrs. Woolf went even beyond Joyce in her use of symbols to make objects in the outer world correspond to inward states of thought and feeling. In *Mrs. Dalloway* and *To the Lighthouse* she was most successful in piercing the "luminous halo" of experience to show the fleeting, fragmentary interior life of her people. *Orlando* is fantasy on themes of English history and literature. *The Waves,* most intricate of her novels, attempts to record impressions of memory and sensation simultaneously in the lives of six different characters. Like Wells, Aldous Huxley has used the novel as a vehicle of ideas. Unlike Wells, however, he has no faith in science as a cure for mankind's ills. In *Brave New World* he satirizes with the savagery of a modern Swift all concepts of a scientific Utopia. *Crome Yellow* and *Point Counter Point* show modern man divided between the sensualism of his animal impulses and the frustration of his intellectual processes. The wisdom and insight of E. M. Forster are illustrated in *A Passage to India,* a study of racial tensions. *Memoirs of a Midget,* by Walter de la Mare, combines poetic fantasy and realistic social criticism.

One of the most remarkable and influential novels of modern times is James Joyce's *Ulysses,* a novel that records the events of a single day in the lives of a small group of Dubliners. In telling his story, Joyce has given his stream-of-consciousness technique a kind of order by superimposing his characters and the events of their day upon a structure of Homeric myth. Thus *Ulysses,* beneath its confusion of incident and subjective probings, parallels the story of the *Odyssey,* so that Leopold Bloom, frustrated advertising salesman, is recognizable as Ulysses, his earthy wife Molly as Penelope, and Stephen Dedalus, a young writer, as Telemachus. Joyce's bewildering system of cross-references, parodies, and parallels makes a first reading of this novel a bewildering experience for the uninitiated, for his purpose is not only to reproduce the sights, sounds, and smells of his scene but also to reveal the memories, desires, and emotions of his people. Standing, as it does, between his more objective and beautifully written autobiographical novel, *A Portrait of the Artist as a Young Man*, and the later, nightmare dreamworld of *Finnegan's Wake*, *Ulysses* considerably enlarged the technical resources and scope of the novel. There are only a few contemporary novelists who have not borrowed either directly or indirectly from Joyce's symbolism and technique.

Evelyn Waugh and Graham Greene are the outstanding figures among younger novelists. Waugh at his best has powers of comic invention and satire reminiscent of a younger and less didactic Shaw. Under his hilarious improvisations in *Decline and Fall* and *Vile Bodies*, however, a serious writer is at work, whose theme is the shoddiness of fashionable Mayfair and the vicious frivolity of overcivilized society. *A Handful of Dust* shows class and country on the brim of a moral abyss. From these not-so-funny comedies of morals Waugh has turned in *Brideshead Revisited* and later novels to themes just as devastating but leavened by an undercurrent of religious significance. Graham Greene, who has written entertaining melodramas in *Stamboul Train*, *The Ministry of Fear*, and *It's a Battlefield*, and more realistic novels in *Brighton Rock*, *The Power and the Glory*, and *The Heart of the Matter*, carries an almost militant Christianity into the themes and style of his books. He writes always with an acute sense of surrounding evil and man's eternal conflict with a malignant universe.

In the drama George Bernard Shaw looms above all other playwrights of his own and later generations, just as Eugene O'Neill occupies the foremost place in the American theater. Shaw's wit and moral fury in such plays as *Candida, Man and Superman, Back to Methuselah, Heartbreak House,* and *Saint Joan* have lifted doctrine to the level of art and stripped away sentimentality and bourgeois morality from the English stage. Ireland's William Butler Yeats is still the giant among English poets of the last half century. The Sitwells—Edith, Osbert, and Sacheverell —represent aesthetic trends of the present time, and W. H. Auden and Stephen Spender speak for a more intellectual and critical school of poets trying to express in their verse the anxiety and turmoil of our industrial civilization.

Except for a few writers whose work holds immediate, topical interest, as in the case of the French Resistance group or the current Existentialists, the continental writers with whom we are most familiar are those whose established reputations make them available in excellent translations. The number of good books out of Europe seems all the more remarkable when we consider the wars, putsches, and purges which have ravaged the continent for more than two generations.

From France we have had the sophisticated satires of the writer who signed his country's name to his novels. Although Anatole France began his career in the 1880's, he did not publish *Penguin Island, The Gods Are Athirst,* and *The Revolt of the Angels* until the early decades of the present century. Roger Martin du Gard gave us an important domestic chronicle in *The Thibaults*. André Gide, eminent stylist and neo-classicist, is the author of *The Counterfeiters. Man's Fate* and *Man's Hope,* by André Malraux, reflect modern ideological issues. François Mauriac, author of *Thérèse,* is a deeply religious writer. Jules Romains presents a panoramic view of modern history in the series of novels called *Men of Good Will*. Albert Camus has brought new techniques into French fiction. Antoine de Saint-Exupéry has given us our only classic examples of the literature of flight in *Night Flight* and *Wind, Sand and Stars*. There is also American-born Julian Green, whose somber work, particularly in *The Closed Garden* and *The Dark Journey*, is Gallic in theme and treatment as well as language.

The most important writer in modern French literature, however, is Marcel Proust. His *Remembrance of Things Past* traces with subjective realism and profound psychological analysis the decay of French bourgeois society. In form *Remembrance of Things Past* is a novel without plot or crisis, unfolding with every lavish detail that Proust could invoke. From the dream-trance reverie which introduces Proust's themes and characters to that long last sentence with its slow echoes of the word *time,* the novel is art distilled out of the processes of memory and time itself, the structure being dictated entirely by the movement of memory and the illusion of the way time passes, or seems to pass, recurs, or seems to recur. The story begins against the idyllic setting of Combray, when the narrator was a child. It ends with a scene in which Proust collects his corrupt and aging people for the last time at a reception in the Faubourg Saint-Germain, and shows us a death's-head in every chair. It is an indecent spectacle of the end of an age, the will to death of an effete society, as revealed by an introspective storyteller whose observations and perceptions we follow from childhood to disillusioned middle age.

Close to Proust in stature stands Thomas Mann, German author who has now become an American citizen, a writer whom many regard as the greatest man of letters in the world today. Mann's international reputation rests chiefly upon his four great novels. *Buddenbrooks*, published in 1901, preceded *The Forsyte Saga* as a novel carrying the story of a single family through several generations. In this book the author traces the decline and dissolution of a wealthy mercantile family of Lübeck, where he himself had been born into the society he describes.

The Magic Mountain is a symbolic and philosophical novel that attempts to take in the whole range of contemporary thought. To a sanatorium high in the Alps come diseased people from many countries. They are the citizens of a sick world, and their stories reflect the ills of an age and a continent. *Joseph and His Brothers* is an ambitious retelling of the Bible story in the light of anthropology, modern psychology, and historical perspectives. *Doctor Faustus* is another novel of modern Europe, in which a German musician symbolically sells his soul to the devil in return for two decades of creative genius. It is an allegory of moral and political crisis told with smoky medieval overtones of doom and damnation.

Franz Kafka is another writer who has imposed his vision of illusion and reality upon the twentieth-century consciousness. *The Castle* is a strange fable of spiritual quest, an inverted *Pilgrim's Progress* through the modern world in which science has established everything except the guideposts leading to human salvation. *The Trial* reads more like a modern *Book of Job,* for in it divine justice is as inscrutable and difficult to fathom as divine grace.

Norwegian literature has given us two novelists of wide range and power. Knut Hamsun is best known for *Growth of the Soil,* the story of a peasant farmer around whose land a small community grows, its growth paralleling the development of civilization itself. In *Kristin Lavransdatter* and *The Master of Hestviken,* Sigrid Undset created against the background of the past a fictional world of solid reality, so that these historical novels make the remote medieval age as real as the present. Her men and women live in a violent and picturesque time, yet they are true to the everyday experiences of life which have been common to men in all ages. When Sigrid Undset brought realism and modern psychology into the historical novel, she made the first important contribution to this form since the days of Scott. Another outstanding woman novelist was

Selma Lagerlöf of Sweden. Her most popular book, *The Story of Gösta Berling,* appeared at the end of the nineteenth century, but she did important work, in *Jerusalem* and *The Ring of the Lowenskölds,* during the present period. Her contemporary, Verner von Heidenstam, was a poet and novelist of strongly romantic and nationalistic temperament. Another Swedish writer who has achieved a world reputation in recent years is Pär Lagerkvist, a poet, dramatist, and novelist concerned with the problem of faith in a world of cosmic malevolence and human guilt. Special mention should also be made of Johan Bojer and Olav Duun, Norwegian novelists whose work had deep roots in peasant life; Johannes V. Jensen, author of *The Long Journey,* and Isak Dinesen, a writer in the Gothic tradition, of Denmark, and Halldór Laxness and Gunnar Gunnarsson, Icelandic novelists. The promising career of Kaj Munk, Danish playwright, was cut short when he was killed by the Nazis in 1944.

Under the Soviet regime the tremendous scope and vitality of Russian literature in the nineteenth century has been curbed by the masters in the Kremlin. Maxim Gorky continues to hold his place of importance among Russian writers whose careers began before the Red Revolution. Of the novelists who have received official approval, the best known outside Russia are Boris Pilnyak, Konstantin Fedin, Leonid Leonov, Ilya Ehrenburg, and Mikhail Sholokhov, and of these Sholokhov is the only writer who approaches the stature of the generation of Turgenev, Dostoevski, and Tolstoy. His epic work is *The Silent Don,* which, ironically enough, deals with counter-revolutionary activities of stubbornly independent Cossacks in the period between 1912 and 1922. A rather special work is Vladimir Dudintsev's *Not by Bread Alone.* Published during the brief period of seeming liberalism in 1957, this novel aroused considerable excitement both inside Russia and abroad when it appeared. An even greater furor arose over Boris Pasternak's *Doctor Zhivago* in 1958.

The only long work of fiction by one of the leading Russian poets of the century, this novel in the great moral tradition of Russian literature presents a vivid picture of a disordered revolutionary age which, through loneliness, violence, cruelty, and fear, involves a whole society in the common ruin. The impact of this novel outside Russia has led to the translation of Pasternak's poems and also to interest in two other poets of the early revolutionary period, Sergey Esenin and Vladimir Mayakovsky.

In Italy the collapse of Fascist dictatorship was marked by a tremendous resurgence of literary activity. During the period of political domination of the arts only Riccardo Bacchelli achieved a critical stature matching that of the older generation of writers represented by Giovanni Verga, Luigi Pirandello, and Grazia Deledda. Although *Fontamara* had established the international reputation of Ignazio Silone, that bitter indictment of man's inhumanity to man had been written in exile; at home, Alberto Moravia had been the object of official censorship. But after the war a new generation of writers in the realistic tradition made their influence felt in such works as Moravia's *The Woman of Rome, Two Adolescents, Conjugal Love,* and *The Conformist;* Elsa Morante's *House of Liars;* Vasco Pratolini's *A Tale of Poor Lovers* and *A Hero of Our Time;* Giuseppe Berto's *The Sky Is Red* and *The Brigand;* Elio Vittorini's *In Sicily* and *The Twilight of the Elephant;* and Carlo Levi's *Christ Stopped at Eboli.* These writers in no sense comprised a school or another Italian Renaissance, but in these books and later ones they continue to attract the attention of readers abroad. Meanwhile the older classics have not been neglected. Alessandro Manzoni's *The Betrothed* has appeared in a new translation for English-speaking readers, and *Le Confessioni di un ottuagenario;* Ippolito Nievo's long chronicle of the struggle for Italian independence, is now available under a new title, *The Castle of Fratta.* The same theme of national freedom serves as the framework of *The Leopard,* by Giuseppe di Lampedusa. This story of the rise of Garibaldi and the unification of Italy was hailed as a masterpiece when it appeared in 1959. In the same year Salvatore Quasimodo, a controversial figure among modern Italian poets, was awarded the Nobel Prize for literature.

Greece is another nation now in the process of an active literary revival. The leading figures of the movement were Kostis Palamis and Constantine Kavafis in poetry and Nikos Kazantzakis in prose. Three of Kazantzakis' novels — *Zorba the Greek, The Greek Passion,* and *Freedom or Death,* as well as his epic retelling of the *Odyssey* — have been widely translated. Other novelists who have found an English-speaking audience are Stratis Myrivalis and Elias Venezis.

In Spain, on the other hand, the deaths of Jacinto Benavente y Martínez, José Ortega y Gasset, Pío Baroja y Nessi, and Juan Ramón Jiménez have left no figures of comparable stature in the fields of drama, philosophy, fiction, and poetry. Among the younger novelists Camilo José Cela, author of *The Hive,* and José María Gironella, who has written a trilogy of the Spanish Civil War, are the most outstanding.

The situation is quite different in Latin America, where in the past three decades Spanish American literature, having shed much of the revolutionary concerns of Mariano Azuela and Martín Luis Guzmán, the Parnassianism of Rubén Dario, and the provincialism of such writers as José Hernández, Rómulo Gallegos, Ricardo Palma, and Hugo Wast, has come of age. Two important influences on this new literature were Gabriela Mistral, Chilean poet and Nobel Prize winner, and Alfonso Reyes, Mexican poet, critic, essayist, and short story writer, who by their examples and their work helped to realign Hispano-American letters with the cultural tradition of the past and the rich, meaningful resources of the present beyond the limits of the national experience. Writers of the new generation have added the techniques

of Joyce, Hemingway, Faulkner, and Eliot to their own native materials and models. The result is writing that is experimental, fresh, and indigenous without being provincial: in Argentina the novels and tales of Eduardo Mallea and Jorge Luis Borges; in Chile the poetry of Pablo Neruda; in Ecuador the novels and plays of Jorge Icaza; in Peru the novels of Ciro Alegría; in Mexico the verse of Octavio Paz and Alí Chumacero, the short stories of Francisco Rojas González, and Juan José Arreola, and the novels of Agustín Yáñez, Carlos Fuentes, Juan Rulfo, and Jorge López Paez. The late Xavier Villarrutia still remains an important figure in the Mexican theater, as does Florenzio Sánchez in Argentina and Uruguay. Eunice Odio, born in Costa Rica, is a poet of individual temperament and great talent. Although contemporary Brazilian literature has not produced a writer of the stature of Joaquim Maria Machado de Assís, Manuel Bandeira and Carlos Drummond de Andrade in poetry, Nelson Rodrigues in drama, and Jorge Amado and José Lins do Rego in the novel have made important contributions to the national literary tradition.

In Japan, since the end of World War II, a new literary tradition seems to be taking shape, a grafting of Western techniques and influences upon the older forms of Japanese literature. In present-day Japan the *Kabuki* theater and the classical *Noh* dramas still flourish; the change is most apparent in poetry and fiction. Both forms reveal a fusion of native and Western traditions. Of the novelists now known outside Japan, Junichiro Tanizaki is possibly the least affected by Occidental influences. His *Some Prefer Nettles* is regarded as a modern classic, and *The Makioka Sisters* is a beautifully presented study of the old merchant culture destroyed by the war. One of the most popular of contemporary writers is Yukio Mishima, whose *Confessions of a Mask, The Sound of Waves,* and *The Temple of the Golden Pavilion,* as well as a collection of his plays, are now available in translation. His range includes both the pastoral and the deeply psychological. Like Osamu Dazai and Jiro Osaragi, he also reflects in some of his novels the cultural tensions of a nation trapped by history between the power of the past and the processes of change. Another traditionalist is Yasunari Kawabata, author of *Snow Country*. *Fires on the Plain*, by Shohei Ooka, is a tragically compelling novel dealing with Japanese resistance in the Philippines during World War II. In *The Heiké Story*, Eiji Yoshikawa turned away from the confusion of the present to give an account of twelfth century history in his chronicle of the warring Genji and Heiké clans. The novel suggests Lady Murasaki Shikibu's *The Tale of Genji* in theme and treatment, but in Yoshikawa's work the events of the medieval past are viewed through the modern sensibility.

China, wracked by internal strife, war with Japan, and ideological domination throughout the present century, has produced no writing of any real significance; however, a number of the celebrated Chinese classics have recently been translated. These include Shih Nai-an's *Shui Hu Chuan (All Men Are Brothers)*, Tsao Hsueh-chin's *Hung Lou Meng (Dream of the Red Chamber)*, and the *Chin P'ing Mei*, now attributed to Hsü Wei.

In India another active literary movement, partly nationalistic, partly regional, partly social, is now in progress, and the time has passed when the native literature spoke to Western readers chiefly through the poems of Rabindranath Tagore and Mohammed Iqbal. Although E. M. Forster's *A Passage to India* remains the dominant image of Anglo-Indian life, writers in all fifteen major languages of Indian and in English are now attempting to create their own image of that vast and varied land. In some ways the situation is like that which existed in Ireland at the turn of the century, for many of the new Indian writers, particularly in the field of the novel, are engaged in creating a national literature in English. Of the novelists,

R. K. Narayan has almost achieved classic dimensions. His fictional world is Malgudi, an imaginary town in South India, and within this setting, as in *The Guide, Swami and Friends, The Financial Expert*, and *The Man-Eater of Malgudi*, he shows himself a master of themes and moods that range from the tragic to the farcical. A writer of completely somber effect is Kamala Markandaya, whose *Nectar in a Sieve* presents dramatically the poverty, ignorance, and squalor of millions of Indian peasants. Another novel, *Some Inner Fury*, deals with the more familiar theme of Anglo-Indian relationships. The background picture of India's struggle for power, especially the influence of Gandhi on ideals of leadership, makes Anand Lall's *The House at Adampur* an impressive first novel. Politics is again the theme of Nayantara Sahgal's *A Time to Be Happy*. R. Prawer Jhabvala, although not a native Indian, is able through marriage and association to present with intimate knowledge the witty yet sympathetic pictures of Indian social life shown in *Amrita* and *The Nature of Passion*.

When we read or discuss these writers of our time, we are on more familiar but less certain ground. Contemporary judgments are likely to be more contemporary than final, however, and it is impossible to tell which books of the past sixty years speak only for a generation and which are the classics of the future.

To tell completely the story of the world's literature would require a book of many pages. This survey, as was stated at the beginning, is no more than tentative, an attempt to indicate the pleasurable reading of various literary ages. There have been many omissions, as the reader undoubtedly discovered for himself. But since every reader must eventually revise any reading list according to his own findings, this brief survey is not aimed at completeness or finality. Its usefulness is therefore limited to its stated purpose—an introduction to reading.

MASTERPLOTS
FIFTEEN-VOLUME
COMBINED EDITION

Volume One
Abbe-Barb

THE ABBÉ CONSTANTIN

Type of work: Novel
Author: Ludovic Halévy (1834-1908)
Type of plot: Sentimental romance
Time of plot: 1881
Locale: France
First published: 1882

Principal characters:
ABBÉ CONSTANTIN, a French priest
JEAN REYNAUD, his godson
MRS. SCOTT, an American
MISS PERCIVAL, her sister

Critique:

This tale has long been a favorite book for use in French classes. The story is full of pleasant places and pleasant people. There is little if any conflict; the one character who might possibly be considered the villain is too polite to offer much resistance to the plans of the hero and heroine. The novel was crowned by the French Academy.

The Story:

The kindly old curé, Abbé Constantin, stopped before the chateau of Longueval to look at posters which proclaimed that the chateau and its surroundings were to be sold at auction either in four pieces, or as a unit. The abbé, like the rest of the neighborhood, smiled at the idea that anyone might be able to buy the entire estate; more than two million francs was too large a sum for anyone to have. As he walked along by the old estate, he thought of all the delightful days he had spent with the old marchioness and her family. He dreaded the thought of a new owner who might not ask him to dinner twice a week, who might not contribute generously to the poor, who might not attend all the services of his little church. The abbé was too old to desire a change.

He walked on to the little house where Madame de Lavardens lived with her son Paul. Paul had not turned out well. His mother gave him a generous allowance to spend every year. After spending his money within three months in Paris, he stayed the rest of the year with his mother in the country. At the de Lavardens home, the abbé learned that Madame de Lavardens was hoping that her agent had secured at least one part of the estate for her. She was awaiting news of the auction, and she invited the abbé to wait with her and her son to hear what had happened.

When the agent arrived, he informed them that Mrs. Scott, a wealthy American, had bought the whole estate. The abbé's heart sank. An American! She would be a Protestant—no doubt a heretic. His hopes for his little church grew weak. No longer would the hothouses of the estate keep his altar full of flowers; no longer would the poor be relieved by the charity of the chateau. With a

1

gloomy heart he went home to supper.

Jean Reynaud, the abbé's godson, was his guest at supper that night. Jean's father had been an officer in the same regiment in which the abbé had been chaplain, and the two had been the best of friends. When Jean's father had been killed, the abbé had taken care of Jean as if he were his own son. The boy had insisted on following his father in a military career. Jean's kindness was well-known in the area. He gave a yearly income to the destitute families of two men who had been killed on the same day as his father, and he was always doing charitable deeds for the abbé's poor.

On his arrival Jean set about cutting garden greens for the salad. He was startled when he looked up and saw two beautifully but simply dressed young women who asked to see the abbé. They introduced themselves as Mrs. Scott and Miss Percival, her sister. In a flurry of excitement the old abbé came out to meet his unexpected guests, and to his great pleasure they announced that they were Catholics of French-Canadian blood. When each of the women gave the abbé a thousand francs to give to the poor, the happy man almost burst into tears. The inhabitants of the chateau were still to be a blessing for the town.

Jean, overcome by the beauty of the two women, could not decide who was the more handsome. Miss Percival was the younger and more vivacious, but the serene charm of Mrs. Scott was equally attractive. The women told the abbé the story of their lives; of their poverty as children, of the lawsuit which their dying father had made them promise never to give up, and of the final success of the suit and the millions that became theirs because of it. Mrs. Scott said that she and her husband intended to spend much time in France at their new home. When the ladies left, the abbé and Jean were profuse in their praise.

This meeting was the first of many. The ladies had grown tired of social gaiety during their stay in Paris, and Miss Percival had become disgusted with the great number of men, thirty-four in all, who had proposed marriage to her, for she knew that it was her money, not herself, they were after. The women hoped to spend a quiet few weeks in the chateau, with the abbé and Jean as their only visitors. During the visits Jean fell in love with Miss Percival. He was upset when Paul de Lavardens insisted on being introduced.

Miss Percival knew at once that Paul's proposal would be number thirty-five. He was polite and made conversation easily, but he did not have the qualities she had come to admire in Jean. The more she saw of Jean the more she liked him, and it was not long before she realized that she was in love with the young officer.

At the first ball held at the chateau, Jean's manner showed Miss Percival that he loved her. But he said nothing, for he believed that army life would not be a happy one for her. As he had neither social graces nor the wealth which could be substituted for them, he did not dare to dance with her at the ball for fear he would blurt out his love. When she approached him to ask for a dance, he left abruptly.

Jean's regiment went away for twenty days. When he returned, he realized that he loved Miss Percival more than ever. Finally he decided that his only course was to be transferred to a regiment stationed in another area. On the night he was to leave he sent his excuses to the chateau and went to explain his actions to the abbé, who listened to his story with deep interest. Suddenly there was a knock on the door and Miss Percival walked in. She apologized for her intrusion, but said that she had come to confess to the abbé. She asked Jean not to leave, but to stay and hear her.

She announced that she loved Jean and felt sure that he loved her. Jean had to admit that it was true. She said she knew he had not dared to ask her to marry him because of her wealth. Consequently she was forced to ask him to marry her. The abbé commending her action, they became engaged.

When the marriage ceremony for the happy couple was performed in the little church, a fine new organ played the music for the service. It was Miss Percival's marriage gift to the church. The abbé was happy; the sale of the old chateau had brought more good to the town than it had known before.

ABE LINCOLN IN ILLINOIS

Type of work: Drama
Author: Robert E. Sherwood (1896-1955)
Type of plot: Historical chronicle
Time of plot: 1831-1861
Locale: New Salem and Springfield, Illinois
First presented: 1938

Principal characters:
MENTOR GRAHAM, a schoolmaster
ABE LINCOLN
ANN RUTLEDGE, Abe's early love
JUDGE BOWLING GREEN, Justice of the Peace
NINIAN EDWARDS, a politician
JOSHUA SPEED, a merchant
WILLIAM HERNDON, Abe's law clerk
MARY TODD, Abe's wife
STEPHEN A. DOUGLAS, Abe's political opponent
SETH GALE, Abe's friend
JIMMIE GALE, Seth's young son

Critique:

Robert Sherwood saw in the struggles of Abe Lincoln a symbol of democracy in action. The playwright was able to stick fairly close to the facts of Lincoln's life in working out his allegory of the growth of the democratic spirit, but in several scenes he was forced to invent fictitious characters or incidents to make his point. Whether the play be viewed as history or allegory, it remains as authentically American as its leading character.

The Story:

In the summer of 1831, when Abe Lincoln was twenty-two years old, he arrived in New Salem, Illinois, at that time a frontier village of fifteen log cabins. Shortly afterward the lanky young man opened a general store in partnership with a friend named Berry. Their stock included whiskey. Berry continued to tap the keg until he drank up all their liquid assets, and the store went bankrupt. Abe voluntarily assumed all the obligations for the partnership and went into debt for about fifteen hundred dollars.

At that time Abe boarded with Mentor Graham, the neighborhood schoolmaster, who began the task of teaching the young backwoodsman the rudiments of grammar. He awakened in Abe an interest in great oratory as well as a love for' poetry. Graham sensed his pupil's extreme melancholy and preoccupation with death as well as his marked disinclination to do anything which required much effort. He advised Abe to go into politics, declaring wryly that there were only two professions open to a man who had failed at everything else—schoolteaching and politics.

Abe's opportunity came a year later while he held the job of local postmaster. A young politician, Ninian Edwards, a vigorous opponent of President Jackson, appeared at the Rutledge tavern in New Salem. He was looking for a possible candidate for the State Assembly. Edwards so much admired Abe's deft handling of several quarrelsome Jackson supporters that he offered Abe the candidacy.

In making his offer he was supported by Abe's two loyal and influential friends in Salem, Joshua Speed, a merchant, and Judge Bowling Green, the justice of the peace. But Abe, who had been considering going farther west, refused. Then several circumstances arose to change his mind. Seth Gale, the friend with whom

Abe had planned to make the trip, received news that his father was sick and he had to return to his native state of Maryland at once. And Ann Rutledge, daughter of the local tavernkeeper, with whom Abe had been secretly in love, received a letter from New York State to the effect that a young man named McNeil, with whom Ann had been in love, would not be able to return to New Salem. When Abe declared his devotion, Ann, disillusioned with her former lover, encouraged him. As a consequence, Abe sent word by his friend Judge Bowling Green that he would be a candidate for the State Assembly.

Fate brought about another, more disastrous, turn in Abe's fortunes. Ann Rutledge fell suddenly ill of a fever, and nothing that the doctor or Abe did could save her. After Ann's death, Abe became completely obsessed by a feeling of melancholia from which none of his friends could rouse him. He opened a Springfield law office with his friend, Judge Stuart, but he refused to take much interest in politics, in spite of the urgings of his clerk, William Herndon, who was a firebrand Abolitionist. Although Abe disliked slavery, he failed to see that the Abolitionists were helping their cause by threatening to split the country.

Knowing that something must be done to pull Abe out of his lethargy, his old political mentor, Ninian Edwards, introduced him to his ambitious sister-in-law, Mary Todd. Mary saw immediately that Lincoln was a man she could inspire to great things. Her aristocratic sister, Elizabeth, could not understand what Mary saw in this raw-boned frontiersman, but Mary saw in him the satisfaction of her own frustrated yearnings. They became engaged.

But Abe had not forgotten Ann Rutledge. On the day of his wedding to Mary Todd, he pleaded with his friend, Joshua Speed, to deliver to Mary a letter he had written to tell her that he did not love her. Speed insisted that Abe go to Mary himself and explain that he

was afraid of her, of the demands she would make upon him. After he had humiliated Mary Todd with his explanation, Abe drifted back to the prairie frontier once more.

One day he encountered his old friend, Seth Gale, with whom he had once planned to go west. Seth had set out from Maryland with his wife and child, and was headed for Oregon. But his child, Jimmie, was ill, and Seth felt that if his son died neither he nor his wife would have the courage to continue the journey. In a flash of insight, Abe saw in his friend's predicament a symbol of the plight of the country as a whole. The Dred Scott Decision had made it possible to extend slavery in the West, a circumstance that would be fatal to those who, like Seth Gale, were trying to build a new country there. That vision crystallized Abe's purpose in life; and when he offered up a prayer to the Almighty for the life of little Jimmie, he was thinking of the country as a whole. Filled with a new purpose, he pocketed his pride and went back to Mary Todd. Still believing in him, she accepted Abe without a moment's hesitation.

From that day on his career followed one straight line, culminating in his nomination for the presidency. There were his debates with Stephen A. Douglas, who was to be his opponent in the election that followed. Within his own party there were political considerations which Lincoln handled with dignity and tact. But most important of all, there was his own life with Mary Todd. In the years since their marriage she had borne him four sons, one of whom had died, and through those years she had grown more tense and irritable, until the home life of the Lincolns became almost intolerable. Abe patiently endured her tirades in their own home, but when Mary began criticizing him in public, he resisted. On the night of his election she had one of her tantrums, and Abe was forced to send her home on the very eve of her triumph.

5

With his election to the highest office in the land, Lincoln's troubles increased. The old melancholia returned, the old preoccupation with death. On an eventful day in 1861, standing on the rear platform of the train which was to take him from Springfield to Washington, he tried to express to his old neighbors and friends his ideals for the future of America. As the presidential train pulled out he could hear his well-wishers singing the last strains of "John Brown's Body"—"His soul goes marching on!"

ABRAHAM AND ISAAC

Type of work: Drama
Author: Unknown
Type of plot: Biblical story
Time of plot: Biblical antiquity
Locale: Beersheba
First presented: Fifteenth century

Principal characters:
ABRAHAM
ISAAC, his son
DEUS, God
ANGELUS, the Angel
THE DOCTOR, a commentator

Critique:

One of the fifteenth-century mystery plays performed by guild members in various towns in England, *Abraham and Isaac* tells the biblical story of Abraham's willingness to sacrifice his son. The Brome version is distinguished from others by its greater length and its fuller development of the characters of Abraham and Isaac. The mystery plays, although often simple in both plot and design, helped to provide the background and tradition from which Elizabethan drama later emerged. The play is in verse, sometimes written in five-line stanzas rhyming *abaab* and sometimes in eight-line stanzas with alternate rhymes, these stanzas often ending in a shortened line. At other times the poetry conforms to no clear rhyming or stanzaic pattern. It is difficult to determine whether the play was originally written in a more careful poetic pattern, now lost through successive copyings and oral repetition, or whether it was originally written in a form close to the present version.

The Story:

Abraham, offering a prayer of Thanksgiving to God, counted his blessings— his land, his peaceful life, his children— and told of his delight in his favorite child, Isaac. He stood, while praying, in a field near his home in Beersheba. After the prayer he called to Isaac to return to their home.

God, in Heaven, summoned an Angel and told him that He intended to test Abraham's steadfastness by asking him to sacrifice Isaac, and he ordered the Angel to announce his wish to Abraham. Meanwhile, Abraham prayed again, asking God what gift or offering might please Him most. The Angel then appeared and told Abraham that God had commanded the sacrifice of Isaac as an indication of Abraham's love for the Lord.

Abraham immediately experienced great inward conflict. He kept repeating that Isaac was the most loved of all his children, that he would rather sacrifice anything else of his, including his own life, than to offer up Isaac. At the same time he was aware that God's will must be obeyed and that the sacrifice, no matter how painful, must be made. Abraham then called Isaac, who had been praying, and told him that they must perform a sacrifice for the Lord. Isaac declared his willingness to help. Abraham felt his heart breaking as they walked toward Mount Vision to make the sacrifice.

On their arrival at the mount, Isaac asked why Abraham seemed so concerned. The boy began to quake at the sight of the sharp sword in his father's hand because, aware of his father's acute misery, he guessed that he was to be the offering in the sacrifice to the Lord. Abraham then tried to explain to Isaac that they must follow God's commandment, having no other choice. But Isaac prayed to his father, asking him to spare his life and wishing his mother were there to intercede for him. Isaac also wondered what crimes he had committed that his life should be demanded by God. Abraham, in his misery, explained that God's will must simply be obeyed. At last Isaac understood and yielded to God's will. He asked, however, that Abraham not tell his mother he had been killed. Instead, she was to believe that he had gone into another land.

Resigning himself to death, Isaac asked for his father's blessing. Abraham gave his blessing, lamented further, and proceeded to bind Isaac's hands. Abraham then repeated his hope that he could be sacrificed in Isaac's place, but the brave Isaac reminded him that God must be obeyed and asked that the killing be done quickly. Abraham covered Isaac's face with a cloth and made ready to lift his sword.

But just as he was about to strike Isaac, the Angel appeared and took the sword from his upraised hand. The Angel said that Abraham had proved his willingness to obey God's command, an act which fully displayed Abraham's mind and heart. Therefore, the Angel continued, Abraham would not be compelled to sacrifice his son, but might substitute a young ram, tied nearby, for the offering. Abraham was overjoyed and after the Angel's departure gave thanks to God for Isaac's deliverance. Isaac, too, welcomed his reprieve, but only did so after Abraham had assured him that God would regard the ram as a worthy substitute.

Isaac, at his father's bidding, ran to bring the ram. Returning with it, Isaac expressed his happiness that the beast, rather than he, was to be sacrificed. When Abraham offered up the ram, Isaac still showed a great fear of Abraham's sword and did not wish to look at it.

After the sacrifice, God again spoke to Abraham, acknowledging his goodness and promising that his family would multiply. Abraham then returned with Isaac to their home, recounting on the way his pleasure that his favorite child had been spared. Isaac was also grateful, but realistically he mentioned his fear and stated that he never wanted to see the hill again. Both thanked God and both showed great relief to be returning home together. Abraham praised the gentleness and understanding of his young son.

(At that point the Doctor appeared on the scene to make the moral of this happening explicit. The Doctor brought out the fact that the story showed how one should follow God's commandments without quarreling. The Doctor asked how many would be willing to smite their children if God so commanded. He thought that several might do so, though their women would wail and protest. But, the Doctor continued, God would mend everything for those truly willing to follow his commandments, for those who served God faithfully would be certain to benefit from their loyalty.)

ABRAHAM LINCOLN

Type of work: Biography
Author: Carl Sandburg (1878-   )
Time: 1809-1865
Locale: Kentucky, Illinois, Washington, D. C., and areas of the Civil War campaigns
First published: The Prairie Years, 1926; The War Years, 1939

Carl Sandburg's *Abraham Lincoln* is a monumental work on a monumental theme, the life, works, and times of a symbolic American of history and legend. There is nothing of its kind, ancient or modern, with which it may adequately be compared. Among Civil War biographies its closest counterpart is Douglas Southall Freeman's *R. E. Lee* (q.v.), but even on this common ground point of view and the use of salient detail create vastly different effects of organization and presentation. In the Freeman biography Lee holds the center of the stage at all times, and the background panorama of people and events, even the battles and campaigns of the war, are shown only as they throw light on Lee's personality and labors. Sandburg, on the other hand, sets Lincoln against a tremendous movement of history as he tells simultaneously, on different levels, the story of a man, a war, an age, and a people. In the end the qualities which set this work apart seem appropriate and significant. Lincoln, that ungainly, complex, humorous, melancholy, and sadly serene man, was also one of the great solitaries.

When *The War Years* appeared in 1939, more than one reviewer commented on the happy conjunction of the perfect writer and the perfect subject. In Sandburg's case there is more truth in this critical generalization than in most, for he brought to his tremendous task a greater familiarity with the regional and folk aspects of Lincoln's life than anyone had possessed since Lincoln's own day. In the late nineteenth century there was still no wide gap between Sandburg's boyhood in Galesburg, Illinois, and Lincoln's growing years in the Sangamon River country. Familiar with New Salem, Vandalia, Springfield, and other landmarks of Lincoln's early life, the Swedish immigrant's son had known the men and women of Lincoln's day and had listened to their stories. Poet, fabulist, folklorist, and singer of the American dream, Sandburg felt in time that the Lincoln story had become a part of himself, not in the sense of blind hero worship but as evidence of the believable reality and fulfilled promise of American life.

More than thirty years of preparation, research, and writing went into the two divisions of *Abraham Lincoln*. At first Sandburg had in mind a story of Lincoln as the prairie lawyer and politician, but as his investigations continued he realized that his book was outgrowing its projected length and purpose. His increasing desire to tell all the facts of Lincoln's life as they existed in books already published, documentary records, or in the memories of men and women finally led him to divide his material into two parts, the first the story of the country boy and lawyer-politician, the second an account of Lincoln in the White House.

The Prairie Years was published in 1926. In these two volumes Sandburg deals with the more legendary aspects of the Lincoln story: boyhood days and backwoods life; a young man's journeys down the Mississippi; a masculine schooling, mostly self-taught, in grammar, mathematics, surveying, debate, and law; the years of clerking in grocery stores and working at odd jobs; military service in the Black Hawk War; his relations with Ann Rutledge, Mary Owens, Mary Todd; his law practice, and his early political career. This material is presented with a wealth of anecdote—stories about Lincoln and by him—so that it resembles at times an anthology of Lincoln lore. This period of Lincoln's life lends itself at times to fabulous or lyric treatment of which Sandburg the poet takes full advantage. There are passages that read like poetry, sentences and paragraphs that celebrate the beauty of nature and the mystery and wonder of life. Yet these occasional flights of poetic fancy are held firmly within bounds by realistic portrayal and strict regard for fact. In these volumes Sandburg's Lincoln emerges as a man of the people but no hero in the ordinary sense. Circumstances had shaped him into a man of vision and resource, but he was also a troubled, threatened, doubted man when he left Springfield in 1861 on the eve of his inauguration as President of the United States.

The War Years was published in four volumes thirteen years later. In the meantime Sandburg had traveled widely to gather material from every available source, read extensively in histories, biographies, newspapers, pamphlets, diaries, letters, and handbills, looked at pictures and cartoons, collected memorabilia of every sort, and written steadily while he studied, pondered, and re-created—in effect, relived—Lincoln's life during the Civil War period. The result, in the opinion of historians and critics, is a biography not likely soon to be surpassed of a man linked inseparably to his country's history and the folk imagination of all time.

Sandburg makes no attempt to gloss over the dark years of 1861-1862. Lincoln, who had incurred ridicule by arriving in Washington in a military cape and a Scotch plaid cap—in disguise, his enemies jeered—found himself hated in the South, handicapped by his Cabinet and the Congress, and faced with the crisis of Fort Sumter. Having taken over the leadership which William Henry Seward, Secretary of State, had tried at first to withhold from the chief executive, Lincoln then proceeded to display a temporizing attitude which history finds hard to explain. His declaration at the end of 1862—"Fellow-citizens, we cannot escape history."—is open to various interpretations. But Lincoln was to ride out of the storm of public disfavor. The Emancipation Proclamation, the turn of the tide at Gettysburg, the appointment of Ulysses S. Grant to the high command, and the Gettysburg Address mark what Sandburg calls the "Storm Center" of the war years. Although the mid-term elections of 1863 were against Lincoln and his own party was prepared to abandon him for the sake of political expediency, he won the campaign of 1864 in the face of the bitterest opposition of his enemies and the apathy of his party. From this time on Sandburg shows the tide in full flood—the aggressive final phase of the war, Sherman's march to the sea, the passing of the Thirteenth Amendment, the surrender at Appomattox, and the night at Ford's Theater on April 14, 1865. The end of the story is starkly, movingly, eloquently told with a poet's power of words and the historian's respect for truth.

In handling the massive reportage of *Abraham Lincoln,* Sandburg never pretends to be more than a storyteller, a recorder. Ever since the publication of *The Prairie Years* critics had tried to find a term to describe his method as a biographer, since his work could not be judged by any of the accepted schools from Herodotus to Lytton Strachey. *The War Years*, with all its vast accumulation of fact piled on fact, detail on detail, gave them the answer. Sandburg's method is the way of the old chronicles and sagas in telling the stories of folk and tribal heroes. This biography is a work which expands within the consciousness of the reader because of its continuous addition and multiplication of concrete and evocative details—battle summaries, character sketches, anecdotes, letters, quotations of every kind—all presented without analysis or interpretation so that in the end they shape themselves to their own pattern and carry their own weight of meaning.

Nothing is too vast or too commonly known to be glossed over without patient attention to every living detail; nothing is too trivial to be included. Never has there been such a summoning of witnesses to testify to a man and his age.

Foreign diplomats, members of the Cabinet and the Congress, military men of the North and the South, Tolstoy, Ibsen, Hawthorne, Mrs. Mary Chesnut, that shrewd, ardent Secessionist, and hundreds of obscure men and women appear briefly, make their gesture or have their say, and then disappear. His enemies make their insults and accusations; his detractors voice their ridicule; his friends speak in his praise. All leave behind them something that adds to our understanding of Lincoln, something more important than the opinions of politicians or the decisive outcomes of battles and accounts of military campaigns in creating the illusion of life itself.

These details, great and small, are the background setting against which Lincoln looms with increasing stature as his story unfolds. Against this backdrop of history he appears as a man all too human in his weaknesses and failures, just as he appears greater than other men in the strength, wisdom, and sad serenity of his last months. "Unfathomable" is the adjective Sandburg most frequently applies to him. Many writers have tried to analyze Lincoln. It remained for Sandburg simply to show the man, letting him speak and act for himself. This also was the method of the anonymous writers of the ancient sagas.

The War Years, more somber in tone, offers less opportunity than *The Prairie Years* for bardic song. Occasionally, however, the poet breaks in on the biographer and historian. One such passage occurs after the account of the Gettysburg Address when Lincoln, a wet towel over his tired eyes, was on his way back to Washington, and a moonlit hush had fallen over the battlefield and the new-made graves. Then in Whitmanesque measures Sandburg speaks his requiem for the buried dead in the silent cemetery as he looks out over the land and into the homes where the son, the husband, or the father is missing from his familiar place and the clocks of time and destiny tick on. Again, at the beginning the chapter titled "The Calendar Said Good Friday," he employs another passage to set the mood for coming tragedy. Nowhere, however, is he more moving than in the solemn intensity of the three simple sentences that bring the Lincoln story to its irrevocable close.

Sandburg's *Abraham Lincoln* is the biography of an American whose true story lends itself to the spirit of legend, a pageant of history, a poet's dream, a national myth. It is a story that is vast, implicative, at times contradictory. It is the stubborn, time-defying stuff of life itself, a story in which Sandburg finds in Lincoln's life the meaning of all America. But it is a poet's biography only in the sense that every true poet is a biographer providing insights to human experience. Unfortunately, not all biographers are poets. Carl Sandburg, to our enrichment, is the rare writer who is both. If America has an epic, it is this story of a national hero re-created from the testimony of the men and women of Lincoln's time.

ABSALOM, ABSALOM!

Type of work: Novel
Author: William Faulkner (1897-1962)
Type of plot: Psychological realism
Time of plot: Nineteenth century
Locale: Mississippi
First published: 1936

Principal characters:
THOMAS SUTPEN, owner of Sutpen's Hundred
ELLEN COLDFIELD SUTPEN, his wife
HENRY, and
JUDITH, their children
ROSA COLDFIELD, Ellen's younger sister
GOODHUE COLDFIELD, Ellen's and Rosa's father
CHARLES BON, Thomas Sutpen's son by his first marriage
QUENTIN COMPSON, Rosa Coldfield's young friend
SHREVE McCANNON, Quentin's roommate at Harvard

Critique:

This novel is the most involved of William Faulkner's works, for the narrative is revealed by recollections years after the events described have taken place. Experience is related at its fullest expression; its initial import is recollected and its significance years thereafter is faithfully recorded. The conventional method of story-telling has been discarded. Through his special method Faulkner is able to re-create human action and human emotion in its own setting. Sensory impressions gained at the moment, family traditions as powerful stimuli, the tragic impulses—these focus truly in the reader's mind so that a tremendous picture of the nineteenth-century South, vivid down to the most minute detail, grows slowly in the reader's imagination. *Absalom, Absalom!* is a novel of tremendous and tragic import.

The Story:

In the summer of 1910, when Quentin Compson was preparing to go to Harvard, old Rosa Coldfield insisted upon telling him the whole infamous story of Thomas Sutpen, whom she called a demon. According to Miss Rosa, he had brought terror and tragedy to all who had dealings with him.

In 1833 Thomas Sutpen had come to Jefferson, Mississippi, with a fine horse and two pistols and no known past. He had lived mysteriously for a while among people at the hotel, and after a short time he disappeared. Town gossip was that he had bought one hundred square miles of uncleared land from the Chickasaws and was planning to turn it into a plantation.

When he returned with a wagon load of wild-looking Negroes, a French architect, and a few tools and wagons, he was as uncommunicative as ever. At once he set about clearing land and building a mansion. For two years he labored and during all that time he hardly ever saw or visited his acquaintances in Jefferson. People wondered about the source of his money. Some claimed that he had stolen it somewhere in his mysterious comings and goings. Then for three years his house remained unfinished, without windowpanes or furnishings, while Thomas Sutpen busied himself with his crops. Occasionally he invited Jefferson men to his plantation to hunt, entertaining them with liquor, cards, and savage combats between his giant slaves—combats in which he himself sometimes joined for the sport.

At last he disappeared once more, and when he returned he had furniture and furnishings elaborate and fine enough to make his great house a splendid showplace. Because of his mysterious actions, sentiment in the village turned against him. But this hostility subsided somewhat when Sutpen married Ellen Coldfield, daughter of the highly respected Goodhue Coldfield.

Miss Rosa and Quentin's father shared some of Sutpen's revelations. Because Quentin was away in college many of the things he knew about Sutpen's Hundred had come to him in letters from home. Other details he had learned during talks with his father.

He learned of Ellen Sutpen's life as mistress of the strange mansion in the wilderness. He learned how she discovered her husband fighting savagely with one of his slaves. Young Henry Sutpen fainted, but Judith, the daughter, watched from the haymow with interest and delight. Ellen thereafter refused to reveal her true feelings and ignored the village gossip about Sutpen's Hundred.

The children grew up. Young Henry, so unlike his father, attended the university at Oxford, Mississippi, and there he met Charles Bon, a rich planter's grandson. Unknown to Henry, Charles was his half-brother, Sutpen's son by his first marriage. Unknown to all of Jefferson, Sutpen had got his money as the dowry of his earlier marriage to Charles Bon's West Indian mother, a wife he discarded when he learned she was partly of Negro blood.

Charles Bon became engaged to Judith Sutpen but the engagement was suddenly broken off for a probation period of four years. In the meantime the Civil War began. Charles and Henry served together. Thomas Sutpen became a colonel.

Goodhue Coldfield took a disdainful stand against the war. He barricaded himself in his attic and his daughter, Rosa, was forced to put his food in a basket let down by a long rope. His store was looted by Confederate soldiers. One night, alone in his attic, he died.

Judith, in the meanwhile, had waited patiently for her lover. She carried his letter, written at the end of the four-year period, to Quentin's grandmother. About a week later Wash Jones, the handyman on the Sutpen plantation, came to Miss Rosa's door with the crude announcement that Charles Bon was dead, killed at the gate of the plantation by his half-brother and former friend. Henry fled. Judith buried her lover in the Sutpen family plot on the plantation. Rosa, whose mother had died when she was born, went to Sutpen's Hundred to live with her niece. Ellen was already dead. It was Rosa's conviction that she could help Judith.

Colonel Thomas Sutpen returned. His slaves had been taken away, and he was burdened with new taxes on his overrun land and ruined buildings. He planned to marry Rosa Coldfield, more than ever desiring an heir now that Judith had vowed spinsterhood and Henry had become a fugitive. His son, Charles Bon, whom he might, in desperation, have permitted to marry his daughter, was dead.

Rosa, insulted when she understood the true nature of his proposal, returned to her father's ruined house in the village. She was to spend the rest of her miserable life pondering the fearful intensity of Thomas Sutpen, whose nature, in her outraged belief, seemed to partake of the devil himself.

Quentin, during his last vacation, had learned more of the Sutpen tragedy. He now revealed much of the story to Shreve McCannon, his roommate, who listened with all of a Northerner's misunderstanding and indifference.

Quentin and his father had visited the Sutpen graveyard, where they saw a little path and a hole leading into Ellen Sutpen's grave. Generations of opossums lived there. Over her tomb and that of her husband stood a marble monument from Italy. Sutpen himself had died in 1869. In 1867 he had taken young Milly Jones, Wash Jones' grand-

13

daughter When she bore a child, a girl, Wash Jones had killed Thomas Sutpen.

Judith and Charles Bon's son, his child by an octoroon woman who had brought her child to Sutpen's Hundred when he was eleven years old, died in 1884 of smallpox. Before he died the boy had married a Negro woman and they had had an idiot son, Jim Bond. Rosa Coldfield had placed headstones on their graves and on Judith's she had caused to be inscribed a fearful message.

In that summer of 1910 Rosa Coldfield confided to Quentin that she felt there was still someone living at Sutpen's Hundred. Together the two had gone out there at night, and had discovered Clytie, the aged daughter of Thomas Sutpen and a Negro slave. More important, they discovered Henry Sutpen himself hiding in the ruined old house. He had returned, he told them, four years before; he had come back to die. The idiot, Charles Bon, watched Rosa and Quentin as they departed. Rosa returned to her home and Quentin went back to college.

Quentin's father wrote to tell him the tragic ending of the Sutpen story. Months later, Rosa sent an ambulance out to the ruined plantation house, for she had finally determined to bring her nephew Henry into the village to live with her, so that he could get decent care. Clytie, seeing the ambulance, was afraid that Henry was to be arrested for the murder of Charles Bon many years before. In desperation she set fire to the old house, burning herself and Henry Sutpen to death. Only the idiot, Charles Bon, the last surviving descendant of Thomas Sutpen, escaped. No one knew where he went, for he was never seen again. Miss Rosa took to her bed and there died soon afterward, in the winter of 1910.

Quentin told the story to his roommate because it seemed to him, somehow, to be the story of the whole South, a tale of deep passions, tragedy, ruin, and decay.

14

ABSALOM AND ACHITOPHEL

Type of work: Poem
Author: John Dryden (1631-1700)
Time: Late seventeenth century
Locale: London
First published: 1681

Principal characters:
    DAVID, King of Israel
    ABSALOM, his illegitimate son
    ACHITOPHEL, chief of the rebels

Dryden claimed that *Absalom and Achitophel* was carefully planned to promote political reform. To gain this end, Dryden used satire, the true aim of which he defined as "the amendment of vices by correction." The particular vices he wanted corrected were those of the Whigs of his day, who were seeking to secure the succession of the Duke of Monmouth, illegitimate son of Charles II, to his father's throne. Second, realizing that direct satire might defeat its purpose by incurring resentment, Dryden chose to attack the Whigs by casting them as characters in the Biblical story of Absalom's revolt against David. Third, to dull the edge of the satire even more and thus increase its effectiveness proportionately, he cast it in verse, "for there's a sweetness in good verse, which tickles even while it hurts."

The poem is loosely organized, but several main divisions can be noted. The first of these, an account of the political situation in Israel (England), opens with a joking reference to David's (Charles II's) virility, which though wasted on a barren queen, produced a host of illegitimate progeny, of which by far the fairest and noblest was Absalom (Duke of Monmouth). David's kingly virtues were equally strong but unappreciated by a great number of Jews (Whigs), who because of a perverse native temperament wanted to rebel. Although David had provided no cause for rebellion, as the wiser Jews (Tories) pointed out, a cause was found in the alleged Jebusite (Catholic) plot to convert the nation to the Egyptian (French) religion. The plot miscarried, but it did create factions whose leaders were jealous of David and opposed his reign.

The second section consists of a portrait of Achitophel, the chief of these leaders (the Earl of Shaftesbury, leader of the Whigs), and an account of his efforts to persuade Absalom to seize the throne. Dryden characterized Achitophel as a brilliant wit touched by the madness of ambition. Unwilling to be remembered only for his distinguished career as a judge, he "Resolv'd to ruin or to rule the State," using the king's alleged sympathy for the Jebusites as an excuse for rebellion. Achitophel first used flattery to win over Absalom, proclaiming that the nation was clamoring for him—a "second Moses." At first Absalom resisted, pointing out that David was a wise and just king, and that David's brother (the Duke of York) was the legal heir. These half-hearted objections Achitophel met with sophistry. David's mildness, he claimed, had deteriorated into weakness; the public good demanded Absalom's strength; the rightful heir was planning to murder Absalom; David himself secretly wanted Absalom to be king and would support his claim as heir to the throne. To these specious arguments Absalom succumbed, whereupon Achitophel proceeded to organize all the Jewish malcontents into a single seditious party.

The third section of the poem lists the motives of these misguided patriots, opportunists, republicans, and religious fanatics. In a series of satiric character studies Dryden ridiculed their chieftains. In the character of Zimri, which Dryden considered "worth the whole poem," he poked fun at the fickleness and "extremity" of Buckingham, Shaftesbury's lieutenant in the Whig Party. Shimei repre-

15

sented the Sheriff of London, who had betrayed the king's interests, and Corah, the notorious Titus Oates, who had fabricated many of the details of the Catholic plot.

The next section of the poem describes Absalom's nation-wide tour, planned by Achitophel to gauge the extent of the people's support for their plan to exclude the legal heir from the throne and to establish Absalom's right to the succession by law. Traveling up and down the land, Absalom craftily represented himself as the people's friend, opposed to Egyptian domination, the Jebusite plot, and a senile king, but powerless to act because of his loyalty to the crown and the lawful succession. The Jews, always easy to delude, proclaimed Absalom a new messiah.

A long tirade follows in which Dryden attacked the Jews' naïve support of Absalom and their willingness to overthrow legally instituted authority. Though not a believer in absolute monarchy, Dryden was a conservative who upheld the supremacy of established law over the voice of the people. He feared that the government would quickly deteriorate into anarchy if the people were given the power to make and break kings at will by changing the order of the succession. Dryden, like all the conservatives of his time, feared the judgment of the people, and, therefore, any movement toward democracy.

In the next section Dryden sketched portraits of David's supporters—the Tory leaders. Here, of course, there was no satiric intent. Barzillai (the Duke of Ormond) was lavishly praised as the noblest adherent to David's cause and one of Israel's true heroes. Two members of the clergy, namely Zadoc (the Archbishop of Canterbury) and the Sagan of Jerusalem (the Bishop of London), were commended for their services to the crown. Other loyalists, praised for their services in Sanhedrin (Parliament), include Adriel (the Earl of Mulgrave), Jotham (the Marquis of Halifax), Hushai (Laurence Hyde), and Amiel (Edward Seymour). These loyal chieftains who defied the powerful rebel faction ultimately convinced David that concessions to the people would but feed their leaders' ambition, and that Absalom was being used as a tool by the treacherous Achitophel.

The last section of the poem consists of a long speech in which David finally reasserted the royal prerogative. Realizing that his enemies had been scoffing at his moderation and clemency as a sign of weakness and fear, he resolved to show his strength. David, regretting that Absalom would be compelled to suffer, expressed his willingness to forgive at the sign of repentance, but he refused to condone disloyalty. The Sanhedrin's attempt to change the line of succession he denounced, scorning their deceitful claim that they were trying to protect him from a scheming brother. Finally, he stated his reluctance to resort to force but declared his readiness to use it to defend the supremacy of established law over both Sanhedrin and king. In the last lines of the poem, heaven clapped its thunder in approval of David's words and the new era which they heralded.

Absalom and Achitophel failed, of course, to reform the Whigs; their attempts to put the Duke of Monmouth rather than the Duke of York on the throne were defeated only some fifteen years after the publication of the poem, which is remembered for its literary, not historical, significance.

16

THE ABSENTEE

Type of work: Novel
Author: Maria Edgeworth (1767-1849)
Type of plot: Social criticism
Time of plot: Early nineteenth century
Locale: England and Ireland
First published: 1812

Principal characters:
> LORD CLONBRONY, an absentee landlord
> LADY CLONBRONY, his affected, ambitious wife
> LORD COLAMBRE, their son
> GRACE NUGENT, a cousin
> MISS BROADHURST, an heiress
> ARTHUR BERRYL, Lord Colambre's friend
> COUNT O'HALLORAN, an Irish gentleman
> SIR TERENCE O'FAY, an impecunious nobleman
> LADY DASHFORT, a designing noblewoman
> LADY ISABEL, her daughter
> MR. MORDICAI, one of Lord Clonbrony's creditors
> MR. BURKE, an honest estate agent
> NICHOLAS GARRAGHTY, a dishonest estate agent

Critique:

The Absentee, published in the second series of Miss Edgeworth's "Tales of Fashionable Life," is a novel of protest against the system of landlordism under which the owners of Irish estates disported themselves in fashionable London society while their tenants lived in misery and squalor, at the mercy of agents who were often unscrupulous and concerned only with their own interests. The Irish scenes of this novel are as fresh and vivid as those in the earlier Castle Rackrent, and the picture of London society, a world of thriftless absentees, wealthy snobs, fortune hunters, and match-making mothers, is excellent in critical and satirical detail. In this work the writer displayed a talent for caricature as well as deep regional feeling. Her vulgar Lady Clonbrony, Nicholas Garraghty, the dishonest agent, and Sir Terence O'Fay, an impecunious sponger, suggest later figures in the work of Surtees and Dickens.

The Story:

Lord Clonbrony was an absentee landlord. The owner of large but encumbered Irish estates, he lived in England because Lady Clonbrony, an extravagant, ambitious woman, would have nothing to do with Ireland or the Irish. People of wealth and position laughed at her and the silly determination with which she aped English manners and speech. Lord Clonbrony they ignored. A respected peer in Dublin and a good landlord when he had lived on his own estates, he was a nobody in his wife's fashionable world, and so he associated with questionable and dissipated companions like Sir Terence O'Fay. Little was known about Lord Colambre, the Clonbrony heir, except that he was a student at Cambridge and a young man of considerable expectations from a distant relative. A cousin, Grace Nugent, was well thought of because of her beauty and good manners.

Lady Clonbrony was anxious to have her son marry Miss Broadhurst, a young woman of much sense and large fortune. Although Lady Clonbrony and Mrs. Broadhurst did their best to promote the match, the young people, while friendly, were not drawn to each other, Lord Colambre because he was too much attracted by Grace's amiability and charm, Miss Broadhurst because she respected his feelings for his cousin.

In execution of a commission for Arthur Berryl, a Cambridge friend, Lord

17

Colambre went to the establishment of Mr. Mordicai, a coachmaker and money-lender. There he overheard some talk which revealed that his father's financial affairs were not in good order. Questioned, Lord Clonbrony admitted that his situation was grave but that he relied on Sir Terence, often his intermediary with his creditors, to prevent legal action against him. The father reflected with some bitterness that there would be no need for such expediency if landowners would live on their own estates and kill their own mutton.

Lord Colambre saw for himself the results of reckless borrowing when Sir John Berryl, the father of his friend, was taken suddenly ill. Mordicai, demanding immediate payment of a large debt, attempted to have the sick man arrested and thrown into prison. Only Lord Colambre's presence and firm words of rebuff kept the money-lender from carrying out his intention. Mordicai left with threats that Lord Colambre would someday regret his insults. Sir John Berryl died that night, leaving his family almost penniless.

Deeply concerned for his own family's welfare, Lord Colambre decided to visit Ireland and see for himself the state of his father's affairs. Lady Clonbrony used every possible argument to dissuade her son, and Sir Terence suggested that the young man could best help his father by marrying a woman as wealthy as Miss Broadhurst. When Lord Colambre left suddenly for Ireland, his mother, refusing to give up her matrimonial plans for her son, allowed her friends to believe that he had gone to attend to private business in connection with his marriage settlement. Since many people expected him to marry Miss Broadhurst, that story satisfied the Clonbrony creditors for the time being.

Arriving in Dublin, Lord Colambre met Sir James Brooke, a British official well informed on Irish affairs, and the two men became good friends. The young nobleman, pleased with everything he heard and saw, was unable to understand his mother's detestation of the Irish. He tried to meet Nicholas Garraghty, his father's agent, but the man was away on business. Instead, he was entertained by the agent's sister, a silly, affected woman named Mrs. Raffarty.

He also met Lady Dashfort, who saw in him a possible husband for her widowed daughter, Lady Isabel. Although he heard no good reports of Lady Dashfort or her daughter, he became a frequent visitor in their home. At last, interested in securing an alliance for her daughter, Lady Dashfort proposed that he accompany her to Killpatrickstown, where she was going to visit Lord and Lady Killpatrick. It was her intention to show him Irish life at its worst, so that he would have no desire to live on the Clonbrony estates after his marriage to Lady Isabel. Aware of his affection for Grace, Lady Dashfort arranged matters so that Lady Killpatrick asked her to exhibit her genealogical table, which had been prepared as evidence in a lawsuit. She did so with seeming reluctance, on the grounds that she was ashamed of her remote connection with the scandalous St. Omars. She then revealed that Grace's mother had been a St. Omar.

Lord Colambre wrote to his mother to ask the truth. She replied that the girl's mother had been a St. Omar but that she had taken the name Reynolds after an affair with a gentleman of that name. When the Reynolds family refused to acknowledge her child, she had married a Mr. Nugent, who had generously given the daughter his own name. The young man realized that this disclosure put a bar between Grace and himself.

Through the Killpatricks, Lord Colambre met Count O'Halloran, regarded by his neighbors as an oddity because of his learning, his fondness for animals, and his liking for the Irish. When the count returned the visit, Lady Dashfort took issue with him because he criticized the improper conduct of an English officer with whom both were acquainted. Lady

18

Dashfort's lack of good manners and moral sense, and the further revelation of Lady Isabel as a malicious flirt, showed the two women to Lord Colambre in their true light. He decided to leave the Dashforts and continue his tour alone.

Count O'Halloran prevailed upon him, however, to accompany that gentleman to Oranmore. There Lord Colambre found a family of taste and breeding, interested in affairs of the day and the welfare of their tenants. Stimulated by the example of Lord and Lady Oranmore, he planned to go immediately to his father's estate, but incognito, so that he could observe more accurately the conditions of the tenantry and the conduct of the estate agents.

He found the village of Colambre neat and prosperous, well looked after by Mr. Burke, the agent. After a dinner with the Burkes, the agent showed him over the estate with evident pride in all he had accomplished. He regretted, however, that the absentee owner took no interest in the land or the tenants, aside from the revenues derived from them. Burke's fears that Lord Clonbrony was displeased with his management were confirmed by the arrival of a letter in which his lordship dismissed the agent and directed him to turn over his accounts to Nicholas Garraghty.

Lord Colambre went next to Clonbrony. From a driver he learned that the tenants hated and feared Nicholas Garraghty, the factor, and Dennis Garraghty, his brother and assistant. The carriage breaking down, Lord Colambre spent the night with Mrs. O'Neill, a widow whose niece had been named after Grace Nugent. The next day the young nobleman was present when Dennis Garraghty refused to renew a lease promised to Mrs. O'Neill's son Brian. The arrival of Mrs. Raffarty and her identification of Lord Colambre caused Garraghty quickly to change his mind. Disgusted by the man's methods of doing business and by the unkempt, poverty-stricken appearance of the village, Lord Colambre wrote to his father and asked him to have no further dealings with the Garraghtys.

During the voyage back to England Lord Colambre's ship was delayed by a storm, so that the Garraghtys arrived in London ahead of him. He returned, however, in time to confront the agent and his brother with a report on their transactions. Hearing his son's story, Lord Clonbrony would have dismissed them on the spot if he had possessed the cash necessary to settle their entangled accounts. Lord Colambre then asked his father and Sir Terence for a full accounting of the distressed nobleman's obligations. In return, he proposed to settle the debt with the inheritance he would receive when he came of age, a date only a few days off, if his father would end all business relations with the Garraghtys and go to Ireland to live. Lord Clonbrony welcomed the proposal, but his wife, when she heard of it, treated the idea with scorn. She was already displeased with her son because he had not pressed his suit upon Miss Broadhurst and the heiress was to marry his friend, Sir Arthur Berryl. When Lord Colambre expressed pleasure over his friend's good fortune, Lady Clonbrony retired in disgust.

Under persuasion by every member of her family, Lady Clonbrony at last ungraciously agreed to return to Ireland. Meanwhile Lord Colambre, busy with his father's accounts, discovered that many of the London bills had been deliberately overcharged and that Nicholas Garraghty was in reality his lordship's debtor, not his creditor, as the agent had claimed. With some ready money sent by Lady Berryl, the former Miss Broadhurst, through her husband, Lord Colambre was able to settle his father's most pressing debts and Sir Terence was able to reclaim Mordicai's bond at a discount. Garraghty having been dismissed in disgrace, Mr. Burke was appointed agent of the Colambre and Clonbrony estates.

On the day he came of age Lord Colambre's first duty was to execute a bond for five thousand pounds in Grace's name, that amount of her own inheritance having been lent to her guardian years before. The young man's secret regret was that he could not offer his heart with his cousin's restored property.

Count O'Halloran, arriving in London, called on Lord Colambre. When the young nobleman confided his true feelings for Grace and told his friend something of her story, the count recalled a Captain Reynolds whom he had known in Austria. Dying, the officer had told of his secret marriage with a Miss St. Omar and had entrusted to the count a packet of private papers, among them a marriage certificate. The count had given the papers to the English ambassador and they had passed in turn into the keeping of Sir James Brooke, the executor of the ambassador's estate. Acting on this information, Lord Colambre went to Sir James and obtained the papers, which had never been carefully examined. When he presented them to the dead officer's father, old Mr. Reynolds accepted with delight the proof of his granddaughter's legitimacy and declared his intention to make her his heiress. Because Grace had never known of the shadow cast on her birth, Lady Berryl was delegated to tell her the whole story, a task which that friendly young woman performed with great delicacy and tact.

Acquainted with the true state of affairs, Lady Clonbrony offered no objections to her son's marriage with Grace. Lord Clonbrony and his wife returned to Ireland and there, in due time, Grace became Viscountess Colambre, much to the satisfaction of Lady Clonbrony, who saw so happily fulfilled her hopes that her son would marry an heiress.

THE ACHARNIANS

Type of work: Drama
Author: Aristophanes (c. 448-c. 385 B.C.)
Type of plot: Social satire
Time of plot: The time of the Peloponnesian War, 431-404 B.C.
Locale: Athens
First presented: 425 B.C.

Principal characters:
> DICAEOPOLIS, a peace-loving citizen
> AMPHITHEUS, his friend
> EURIPIDES, the playwright
> LAMACHUS, a general
> AMBASSADORS TO THE ALLIES OF ATHENS
> THE ACHARNIANS, a chorus of charcoal burners

Critique:

The Acharnians is the earliest known comedy of Aristophanes and, deservedly, his first prize-winner. Thematically, it is the most inclusive of his plays; in it we find his powerful wit and satire against militarism and war, his contempt for petty politicians and informers, his delight in earthy sex play, and his spirited spoofing of Euripides—qualities which make it the most personal of Aristophanes' works. When Dicaeopolis speaks directly to the audience in the parabasis, he does so with the voice of Aristophanes eloquently asserting his intellectual honesty and independence and declaring that he will always fight for the cause of peace and justice in his comedies.

The Story:

Dicaeopolis, waiting for the assembly to convene, sat musing, making figures in the dust, pulling out his loose hairs, and longing for peace. He was fully prepared to harass and abuse the speakers if they talked of anything but peace with Sparta. Immediately after the citizens had gathered, his friend Amphitheus began to complain of hunger because of the wartime diet. He was saved from arrest only by the intervention of Dicaeopolis.

The assembly then listened to a series of fantastic claims made by the pompous ambassadors to Athens' allies, each speech punctuated by a scoffing aside from Di-

caeopolis, who knew full well that the entire alliance was wasting away from the effects of the Peloponnesian War. The high point of absurdity was reached when the last of the ambassadors ushered in a few scraggly, miserably dressed troops, introducing them as a Thracian host sent to assist in the war. Dicaeopolis, knowing of the assembly's willingness to adjourn upon the slightest provocation, then brought about the end of the session by claiming to have felt a drop of rain.

Finding himself unable to bring about the end of the war, Dicaeopolis determined to effect a personal, separate peace. Amphitheus, his own ambassador, returned from the enemy with three bottles of wine—the first five years old, the second ten years old, and the third thirty years old. The first two tasted vile, but the last was rich with a bouquet of nectar and ambrosia. Drinking it down, Dicaeopolis personally accepted and ratified a thirty-year peace. The Acharnians, whose vineyards had been ravaged by the enemy, having got wind of this traitorous act, arrived in pursuit of Amphitheus just as Dicaeopolis was leaving his house to offer up a ritual prayer to Bacchus in thanks for the peace that allowed him to resume once more a normal existence with his wife. Upon hearing his prayer, the Acharnians began to stone him as he tried in vain to persuade them that peace was good. Threatened with further violence, Dicaeopolis seized a covered basket of coals and announced that it was an Acharnian child, a hostage, which he would disembowel if he were not permitted to plead his cause. When the Acharnians agreed, he asked further to be allowed to dress properly for the occasion.

Dicaeopolis then went to the house of Euripides to borrow the costume of Telephus, the most unfortunate and pathetic of all the heroes of Euripides' tragedies. The great playwright, in the midst of composing a new tragedy, was hardly in the mood to be disturbed, but Dicaeopolis could not resist the opportunity to tease him about his wretched heroes and about the fact that his mother had sold vegetables. Finally the irate Euripides gave him the miserable costume and turned him out.

The eloquent plea for peace that Dicaeopolis delivered to the Acharnians was so moving that the chorus was divided on the issue. At that moment Lamachus, a general dressed in full armor, arrived on the scene. He declared that nothing could dissuade him from eternal war on the Spartans and their allies. Dicaeopolis countered with a proclamation that his markets were henceforth open to all the enemies of Athens, but not to Lamachus.

Shortly thereafter a starving Megarian appeared in Dicaeopolis' market place with his two daughters, who had agreed with their father that it would be better to be sold than to die of hunger. After disguising them as pigs by fitting them with hoofs and snouts, the Megarian stuffed them into a sack and offered them to Dicaeopolis as the finest sows he could

possibly offer to Aphrodite. Dicaeopolis, aware of the deception, nevertheless accepted them in exchange for a supply of garlic and salt. The next trader was a fat, thriving Boeotian with a tremendous supply of game birds, animals, and fish. All he asked in exchange was some item of Athenian produce not available in Boeotia. Careful bargaining revealed, however, that the only such item was an informer—a vessel useful for holding all foul things, a mortar for grinding out lawsuits, a light for looking into other people's accounts. At last the bargain was made, and the next meddling informer to enter the market place and threaten Dicaeopolis with exposure to the authorities was seized, bound, and carefully packed in hay for the Boeotian to carry home.

Suddenly General Lamachus was ordered to take his battalions to guard the borders against invasion during the forthcoming Feast of the Cups. At the same time the priest of Bacchus ordered Dicaeopolis to prepare for joyous participation in the feast. The chorus wished them both joy as Lamachus donned his heavy armor and Dicaeopolis dressed in festival clothes, as Lamachus unhooked his spear and Dicaeopolis unhooked a sausage. After the feast Lamachus was carried in, hurt in a fall in a ditch before encountering the enemy; and Dicaeopolis entered, hilariously drunk and supported by two voluptuous courtesans. The blessings of peace were emphasized by the fact that, in the end, Lamachus the militarist was carried off to the surgeon while Dicaeopolis was conducted before the judges to be awarded the wineskin of victory.

ADAM BEDE

Type of work: Novel
Author: George Eliot (Mary Ann Evans, 1819-1880)
Type of plot: Domestic romance
Time of plot: 1799
Locale: England
First published: 1859

Principal characters:
ADAM BEDE, a carpenter
SETH BEDE, his brother
MARTIN POYSER, proprietor of Hall Farm
MRS. POYSER, his wife
DINAH MORRIS, her niece, a Methodist preacher
HETTY SORREL, another niece
CAPTAIN ARTHUR DONNITHORNE, the young squire

Critique:

This novel of English pastoral life probably shows George Eliot's quality as a novelist better than any other of her works, with the possible exception of *Middlemarch*. When George Eliot was writing of the peasants, the artisans, the yeomen, the clergy, and the squires of Warwickshire, she was writing out of memories of her own childhood, and her characters come to life as people she had known. Moreover, she superimposes upon them an awareness of fate, not majestic as in Hardy, but growing out of her convictions that there is a cause and effect relationship in human behavior as there is in the rest of nature.

The Story:

In the village of Hayslope at the close of the eighteenth century, there lived a young carpenter named Adam Bede. Tall and muscular, Adam was respected by everyone as a good workman and an honest and upright man. Even the young squire, Captain Arthur Donnithorne, knew Adam and liked him, and Adam in turn regarded the squire as his best friend.

Adam was, in fact, so good a workman that his employer, Mr. Jonathan Burge, the builder, would have welcomed him as his son-in-law and partner. But Adam had no eyes for Mary Burge; his only thoughts were of distractingly pretty Hetty Sorrell, niece of Mrs. Poyser, whose husband, Martin, ran the Hall Farm. Hetty, however, cared nothing for Adam. She was interested only in Captain Donnithorne, whom she had met one day in her aunt's dairy.

No one in Hayslope thought Hetty would make Adam a good wife, least of all Adam's mother, Lisbeth, who would have disapproved of any girl who threatened to take her favorite son from her. Her feelings of dependence upon Adam were intensified after her husband, Matthias Bede, drowned in Willow Brook while on his way home from the village inn.

In the meantime, Adam's brother Seth had fallen in love with the young Methodist preacher, Dinah Morris. Dinah was another niece of Mrs. Poyser, as unlike her cousin Hetty as Adam was unlike Seth. Hetty resembled nothing so much as a soft, helpless kitten, but Dinah was firm and serious in all things. One evening while she and Seth were walking home together from the village green, he had proposed marriage. Dinah sadly declined, saying she had dedicated her life to preaching the gospel.

When funeral services for Matthias Bede were held in Hayslope Church on the following Sunday, the thoughts of the congregation were on many things other than the solemn occasion they were attending. Adam's thoughts of Hetty blended with memories of his father.

23

Hetty's thoughts were all of Captain Donnithorne, who had promised to make his appearance. She was disappointed, however, for Donnithorne had already departed with his regiment. When he returned on leave, the young squire celebrated his twenty-first birthday with a great feast to which nearly all of Hayslope was invited. Adam was singled out as a special guest to sit at Donnithorne's table. Adam's mother was both proud and jealous lest her son be getting more and more out of her reach.

One August night, exactly three weeks after the Donnithorne party, Adam was returning home from his work on the Donnithorne estate when he saw two figures in close embrace. They were Donnithorne and Hetty Sorrel. When Adam's dog barked, Hetty hurried away. Donnithorne, embarrassed, tried to explain that he had met the girl by chance and had stolen a kiss. Adam called his friend a scoundrel and a coward. They came to blows, and Donnithorne was knocked senseless. Adam, frightened that he might have killed the young squire in his rage, revived him and helped him to a nearby summerhouse. There he demanded that Donnithorne write a letter to Hetty telling her that he would not see her again.

The next day Donnithorne sent the letter to Hetty in Adam's care, thus placing the responsibility for its possible effect upon Adam himself. Adam gave her the letter while they were walking the following Sunday. When, in the privacy of her bedchamber, she read the letter, Hetty was in despair. Her dreams shattered, she thought only of finding some way out of her misery. Then in November Adam was offered a partnership in Mr. Burge's business, and he proposed to Hetty. Mr. and Mrs. Poyser were delighted to find that their niece was to marry the man they so much admired.

But the wedding had to be delayed until two new rooms could be added to the Bede house. In February, Hetty told her aunt she was going to visit Dinah Morris at Snowfield. Actually, however, she was determined to find Donnithorne. When she arrived at Windsor, where he was supposed to be stationed, she found that his regiment had been transferred to Ireland. Now in complete despair Hetty roamed about until in a strange village, and in the house of a widow named Sarah Stone, her child by Donnithorne was born. Frightened, Hetty wandered on, leaving her baby to die in a wood. Later, tortured by her conscience, she returned to find the child gone.

When his grandfather died, Donnithorne returned to Hayslope to discover that Hetty was in prison, charged with the murder of her child. He did everything in his power to free her, and Dinah Morris came to her prison cell and prayed with her to open up her heart and tell the truth. Finally poor Hetty broke down and confessed everything that had happened since she left Hayslope. She had not intended to kill her baby; in fact, she had not actually killed the child. She had considered taking her own life. Two days later, Donnithorne, filled with shame and remorse, brought a reprieve. Hetty's sentence was committed to deportation. A few years later she died on her way home. Donnithorne went to Spain.

Dinah Morris stayed with the Poysers often now, and gradually she and Adam were drawn to each other. But Dinah's heart was still set on her preaching. She left Hall Farm and went back to Snowfield. Adam Bede found his only satisfaction toiling at his workbench. Then one day his mother spoke again of Dinah and her gentle ways. Adam could wait no longer. He went to find her.

ADDRESSES

Type of work: Formal speeches
Author: Abraham Lincoln (1809-1865)
First delivered: 1838-1865

Abraham Lincoln, sixteenth President of the United States and author of the Gettysburg Address, has come to be recognized as a creative speaker with an individual and appealing style. He had a perceptive sense of humor and an awareness of human dignity and of the tragedy which occurs with the loss of it. His arguments were logically respectable and responsive to the problems of his times. Although he always retained a directness of statement and feeling which reflected the conditions of his boyhood in Kentucky and Indiana, he was by no means a merely homespun speaker or writer; his poetic phrasing and imagery, Biblical allusions, and rhetorical devices all testify to the fact that he was a well-educated and intelligent man who could speak to any kind of audience in a manner and with the diction appropriate to the occasion.

But Lincoln was not perfect. If it is relevant to state the fact of his imperfection, the reason is that Lincoln's compassion and understanding and his contribution to the creation of American democracy as we know it have so impressed his fellow citizens that sometimes romantic legends lead us to believe that he never spoke without winning assent and admiration from those whom he addressed. But since he was human and to err is human, and since he was sometimes called upon to speak when there was no great problem to resolve or attack, he was on occasion ineffective in what he said.

Once the legend of Lincoln's perfection is dispelled, the fact of his greatness as a man, a President, and a speaker emerges. The Gettysburg Address of 1863 was no isolated phenomenon; the ideas, the sentiments, the clear eloquence had all been heard before, but never with such economy and depth.

"The Perpetuation of Our Political Institutions," one of the earliest of Lincoln's speeches, was an address given to the Young Men's Lyceum of Springfield, Illinois, on January 27, 1838. Lincoln began by recalling the political and social legacy bequeathed the American people of the nineteenth century by their fathers, and he asked how the task of maintaining the liberties transmitted to them might best be performed. He argued that the danger of loss came not from abroad but only from Americans themselves: "If destruction be our lot, we must ourselves be its author and finisher." Lincoln then referred to several violent instances of mob action and argued that such disregard for law could result in the loss of the legacy of freedom. Although the passion of revolution had helped Americans achieve their liberty, it was necessary to let reason and a reverence for law prevail.

In this early speech there is ample evidence of Lincoln's power, a power partly literary and partly spiritual. The young speaker reflected his sense of his role, as a citizen, to transmit the American heritage. Like his contemporaries, he placed his faith in reason, law, the orderly processes of government, and a sense of human dignity; but he added to this conventional faith his own clear conviction and commitment, applying the principles of democracy to the immediate danger he found about him. His philosophy of government was conservative; he did not speak for abolition—but what he conserved were the principles needed in critical times. His character, not the particular strain of his politics, was already the most persuasive element in his addresses; the demands of the Presidency in a time of civil war were to realize the nobility of that character.

At the close of the Republican State Convention at Springfield, Illinois, on

June 16, 1858, Lincoln delivered an acceptance of the senatorial nomination. This speech marked the beginning of the campaign that was to involve him in the series of debates with Stephen A. Douglas. After referring to the increase in slavery agitation, Lincoln declared:

> In my opinion, it will not cease, until a crisis shall have been reached, and passed—
> "A house divided against itself cannot stand."
> I believe this government cannot endure, permanently half slave and half free.
> I do not expect the Union to be dissolved—I do not expect the house to fall—but I do expect it will cease to be divided.
> It will become all one thing, or all the other.

Lincoln went on to discuss the Nebraska Bill, which allowed the people of any state or territory to determine whether slavery was to be allowed in their state or territory, the Dred Scott Decision, and the opinions of Senator Douglas. Lincoln maintained that Douglas cared nothing about halting the advance of slavery, and he implied that Douglas' policy tended to divide the Union.

In the first Lincoln-Douglas debate at Ottawa, Illinois, on August 21, 1858, Douglas referred to Lincoln's acceptance speech and quoted Lincoln's remarks concerning the "house divided against itself." He argued that the founders of the nation had believed it possible for the union to exist with both free and slave states, and he suggested that Lincoln could hardly disagree with such men as Washington, Jefferson, Franklin, and Hamilton. He endorsed the Dred Scott Decision, declaring that if Lincoln's opinions prevailed "black settlements" would "cover your prairies." "I am in favor of confining citizenship to white men, men of European birth and descent," Douglas asserted, "instead of conferring it upon Negroes, Indians, and other inferior races."

Lincoln replied by correcting a number of misrepresentations made by Senator Douglas, and in order to counter the charge that he was an abolitionist he quoted from a speech he had made at Peoria, Illinois, in 1854. Although he stated that he had no intention of introducing political and social equality between the white and the black races, he added that "notwithstanding all this, there is no reason in the world why the Negro is not entitled to all the natural rights enumerated in the Declaration of Independence—the right to life, liberty, and the pursuit of happiness." Even when, for the sake of politics, Lincoln agreed with Douglas that the black man was not his equal, he qualified his admission: "I agree with Judge Douglas that he [the Negro] is not my equal in many respects—certainly not in color, perhaps not in moral or intellectual endowment." Then, although the "perhaps" made a world of difference, Lincoln closed that particular subject: "But in the right to eat the bread, without the leave of anybody else, which his own hand earns, he is my equal, and the equal of Judge Douglas, and the equal of every living man."

Even now, more than a hundred years after the debates, the speeches by Douglas and Lincoln bring the living man before the imagination. Douglas is the clever, urbane debater; but Lincoln is at least as clever, and he has the words to reach all minds and to express sentiments which make up the American ideal. In debate, Lincoln was as relentless as his opponent in the attempt to win his points, but he was never vicious, even when he was not as candid as a man could be. His homely sense of humor remained an invaluable instrument in his bag of rhetorical devices. Immediately after considering Douglas' charge that he was an abolitionist, Lincoln passed on to the question of whether he had ever been a grocery-keeper. He said, "I don't know that it would be a great sin if I had been; but he is mistaken. Lincoln never kept a grocery anywhere in the world. It is true that Lincoln did work the latter part of one winter in a little still-house up at the head of a hollow."

At Springfield, Illinois, in his last speech of the campaign of 1858, Lincoln repeated that he admitted the right of the South to reclaim its fugitives and that he denied the right of Congress to interfere with the states. He declared that he had found the campaign painful, particularly because former friends accused him of wishing to destroy the union. Then he concluded that some had charged him with ambition, but that he would gladly withdraw if he could be assured of "unyielding hostility" to the spread of slavery. The candor and intensity of this brief speech make it one of Lincoln's most moving addresses.

Lincoln's courage became most evident with his address at Cooper Union in New York on February 27, 1860. He took issue with Douglas' claim that the authors of the Constitution understood the "question" as well as the men of his own day. He agreed with Douglas that the fathers of the Constitution understood the issue, but he disagreed with Douglas' assertion that they sided with Douglas' view that the Constitution forbids federal control of slavery. Lincoln argued strongly against any interpretation of the Constitution which would have permitted the extension of slavery to the Free States and the territories. He referred to the secessionist threat to destroy the union if a Republican president were elected, and he urged that the Republicans do their part to maintain peace. He concluded, "Let us have faith that right makes might, and in that faith, let us, to the end, dare to do our duty as we understand it."

Later in the year, in May, Lincoln was nominated for the office of President by the Republican Party; although he had been defeated in his senatorial campaign against Douglas, his speeches had brought him into national prominence. In February, 1861, after having been elected to the Presidency in November of the preceding year, Lincoln said farewell to the people of Springfield, Illinois, with a few poignant sentences in which he asked for the assistance of "that Divine Being" who had attended Washington. The Civil War began in April.

Lincoln's inaugural addresses, his message to Congress on July 4, 1861, and his annual messages to Congress presented the facts of the national crisis with clarity and compassion. The Gettysburg Address of November 19, 1863, brought all of Lincoln's sincere idealism into focus and related it to the grief of a nation. His addresses will continue to remain a cherished part of the American heritage and a significant segment of the world's literature.

THE ADMIRABLE CRICHTON

Type of work: Drama
Author: James M. Barrie (1860-1937)
Type of plot: Humorous satire
Time of plot: Early twentieth century
Locale: Loam House, Mayfair; a desert island
First presented: 1903

Principal characters:
THE EARL OF LOAM
LADY MARY,
LADY CATHERINE, and
LADY AGATHA, his daughters
THE HON. ERNEST WOOLLEY, his nephew
WILLIAM CRICHTON, his butler

Critique:

One of the best of Barrie's comedies, *The Admirable Crichton* contains a more definite theme than Barrie generally put into his plays. His satirical portrait of an English aristocrat with liberal ideas is the most skillful that has been done on the subject. Lord Loam, like many liberals, is a kind of social Jekyll and Hyde, accepting the doctrine of the rights of man in theory, but holding tightly to his vested interests in practice.

The Story:

Once every month, the philanthropic Earl of Loam gave expression to his views on human equality by forcing his servants to have tea with him and his family in the great hall of Loam House in Mayfair. It was a disagreeable experience for everyone concerned, especially for his butler, Crichton, who did not share his master's liberal views. Lord Loam alone enjoyed the occasion, for he was the only one who remained completely himself. He ordered his daughters and his nephew about and treated them exactly as he treated his servants on the remaining days of the month.

Lady Mary, his oldest daughter, was a spirited young woman who resented her father's high-handed methods with his family. Her indignation reached a climax one day when Lord Loam announced that his three daughters were to have but one maid among them on a yachting trip on which the family was about to embark. Lady Mary was furious, but she assumed that her maid, Fisher, would go along. When Fisher learned that she was expected to look after the two younger sisters in addition to Lady Mary, she promptly resigned, and the two maids attending Catherine and Agatha followed suit. Lord Loam was left without any servants for his projected cruise, for his valet also resigned. Although it hurt his pride deeply, Crichton finally agreed, out of loyalty to his master, to act as his valet on the trip. Moreover, he persuaded Tweeny, the housemaid upon whom he had cast a favorable eye, to go along as maid to Lord Loam's daughters.

The cruise ended unhappily when the yacht was pounded to pieces during a violent storm in the Pacific, and the party was cast away on a tropical island. All reached shore except Lord Loam. The other survivors had watched him throw away his life in a frantic but vain attempt to get into the lifeboat first.

On the island all tried to preserve as much as possible the class distinction which had prevailed in England. But the attempt was unsuccessful. Crichton alone knew exactly what he was doing, and it was upon him that the others had to depend. So Crichton, the servant, became on the island the natural leader, and he ruled his former superiors with a gentle but a firm hand. For example, he found the epigrams of the Hon. Ernest, which had seemed so brilliant in England, a bit trying; as a consequence, Crichton adopted the policy of submitting Ernest to a severe ducking whenever he came forth with an epigram. The aristocrats worried over the rising authority of their former butler and the decline in their own prestige. When Lord Loam finally appeared, after washing ashore with some wreckage, they urged him to take a stand of authority. Lord Loam's only recourse was to remove his little party to another section of the island apart from Crichton. But hunger, which the aristocrats by their own efforts could not assuage, brought them meekly back. Crichton became the acknowledged leader of them all.

Crichton took full advantage of his newly acquired authority. Having none of the earl's ideas about equality, he found no necessity for pretending that on the island his former betters were his equals in any sense. Each was kept in his place and required to do his own work according to the needs of the camp.

Under Crichton's rule the aristocrats were happy for perhaps the first time in their lives. The hard physical labor made something approaching a man out of Ernest, and the task of helping to prepare Crichton's food and waiting on him at the table turned Lord Loam's snobbish daughters into attractive and useful women. Lord Loam, dressed in animal skins, was merely a harmless and rather genial old man with no particular talents, whom everyone called Daddy. But the greatest change occurred in Lady Mary. She alone realized that in any environment Crichton was superior to them all, and that only the conventions of so-called civilized society had obscured that fact. Consequently she fell in love with the butler and did everything in her power to make herself his favorite. Crichton, attracted to the beautiful Lady Mary, considered making her his consort on the island. He indulged in the fancy that in some past existence he had been a king and she a Christian slave. But when a ship appeared on the horizon, Crichton realized that his dreams were romantic nonsense. On their return to England he again would be a butler, and she would be Lady Mary.

It was as Crichton had expected. After the rescue Lord Loam and his family returned to their old habits of thought and behavior. Crichton was again the butler. The Hon. Ernest wrote a book about their experiences on the island and made himself the hero of their exploits. Crichton was barely mentioned. Lady Mary reluctantly renewed her engagement to the rather asinine Lord Brocklehurst, whose mother was greatly worried over what had happened on the island and not sure that a daughter of Lord Loam was a fit wife for her son.

But Lady Mary still recognized Crichton's superiority, and told him so frankly. Crichton was shocked. Her views might have been acceptable on the island, he said, but not in England. When she expressed the radical view that something might be wrong with England, Crichton told her that not even from her would he listen to a word of criticism against England or English ways.

ADOLPHE

Type of work: Novel
Author: Benjamin Constant (1767-1830)
Type of plot: Psychological romance
Time of plot: Late eighteenth and early nineteenth centuries
Locale: Germany and Poland
First published: 1815

Principal characters:
ADOLPHE, the narrator
ELLÉNORE, his mistress

Critique:

From one point of view it may be said that the modern psychological novel sprang full-blown from the brain of Benjamin Constant; from other points of view, however, *Adolphe* is too much of a sport in nineteenth-century literature to shed much light on the historical development of the novel. The work might be described as a little seventeenth-century tragedy written in lucid eighteenth-century prose about a nineteenth-century situation by a twentieth-century analytical consciousness. The brevity and the apparently effortless progression of the story result in a deceptive simplicity. Ostensibly about an unhappy love affair—from the first fixation of an abundant and unattached vitality, through the luminous point of love, to the final disillusionment, or dissolution—*Adolphe* represents a remorseless survey of a familiar modern interior waste land whose most marked characteristic is gradual emotional atrophy.

The Story:

Having creditably completed his studies at Göttingen in spite of a somewhat dissipated life, Adolphe was expected, after a preliminary period of travel, to take his place in the governmental department of which his father was the head. The hopes entertained by his father, the minister of a German Electorate, inclined him to leniency regarding his son's indiscretions, but because of an inherent timidity shared by father and son—a timidity combined, on the part of the father, with a defensive outward coldness—no real sympathy was possible between the two.

The constraint generated by this relationship had a considerable effect on Adolphe's character, as did a period he spent as the protégé of a woman much older than he whose strong and unconventional opinions made on him an indelible impression. This period, spent in long, passionately analytical conversations, culminated with the woman's death.

On leaving the university, Adolphe went to the small German principality of D——. At first he was welcomed at court, but eventually he attracted to himself the malicious judgments of those who resented the mannered frivolity, alternating with scathing frankness, which stemmed from his profound indifference to the available society. The woman who had formed his mind had bequeathed to him an ardent dislike of mediocrity and all its expressions, and he found it difficult to reconcile himself with the artificiality of society and the necessity for arbitrary convention. Moreover, his only interest at that time was indulgence in passionate feelings which lead to contempt for the ordinary world.

One thing which did impress him was the spectacle of a friend's joy at making a conquest of one of the less mediocre women of the court. His friend's reaction not only developed in Adolphe the regrets connected with piqued vanity, but also other, more confused emotions related to newly discovered aspects of his desire to be loved. He could discover in himself no marked tastes, but on making the acquaintance of Count P——, Adolphe soon determined to attempt establishing a liaison with the woman who had shared the count's life for ten years and whose two illegitimate children had been acknowledged by their father. Ellénore was a spirited woman who came from a good Polish family ruined in her childhood by political troubles. Her history was one of untiring devotion to the count and constant conflict between her respectable sentiments and her position in society—a position which had gradually become sanctioned, however, through the influence of her lover.

Adolphe did not think of himself as being in love, but as fulfilling obligations to his self-esteem; yet he found his thoughts increasingly occupied with Ellénore's person as well as his project and, unable to make a verbal declaration, he finally wrote to her. His inner agitation and the conviction he sought to express rebounded, however, and his imagination became wholly entangled when Ellénore refused to receive him. Becoming perfectly convinced of his love, he finally succeeded in overcoming her resistance to his suit. When the count was called away on urgent business, Adolphe and Ellénore basked for a few weeks in the charm of love and mutual gratitude. But Adolphe began almost immediately to be annoyed at the new constraint imposed on his life by this attachment, rewarding though he found it. The idea that it could not last calmed his fears, and he wrote to his father upon Ellénore's importunings, asking permission to postpone his return for six months. When his father gave the desired consent, Adolphe was immediately confronted again by all the drawbacks involved in his remaining at D——. He was irritated at the prospect of prolonging the deceptions required by his affair; of continuing the profitless life he led under Ellénore's exacting domination; above all, of making her suffer by compromising her position, for the count had become suspicious on his return.

Adolphe's resentment led to a quarrel with Ellénore in which were made the first irreparable statements that once spoken, cannot be recalled. The quarrel and the forced intimacy which followed

it only increased Ellénore's anxiety and ardor, and she decided to break with Count P—— when he ordered her not to see Adolphe. Adolphe could not summon the courage to reject her sacrifice, even though it caused him great anguish and destroyed in a moment the social respect which Ellénore had acquired through years of effort. His sense of duty increasing as his love weakened, he was willing to fight a duel at the slightest disparaging remark about her; yet he himself wronged her in inconsequential social conversation. When the time came for him to leave, he promised to return, fearing her violent grief. Moreover, he discovered that the arrival of the break he had longed for filled him with keen regret, almost with terror. He wrote regular letters to her, each begun with the intention of indicating his coldness, but always ended with words calculated to restore her confidence in his passion. Meanwhile, he relished his independence.

Having understood from Adolphe's letters that it would be difficult for him to leave his father, Ellénore decided to join him. He wrote advising her to postpone her coming, with the consequence that her indignation was aroused and her arrival hastened. Adolphe had resolved to meet her with a show of joy, concealing his real feelings, but she sensed the deception immediately and reproached him, putting his weakness in such a miserable light that he became enraged. Finally, the two turned on each other in a violent scene.

On returning to his father's house, Adolphe learned that his father had been informed of Ellénore's arrival and had taken steps to force her to leave the town. His father's concern with Adolphe's future was undoubtedly genuine, but it unfortunately took the form of adherence to the standard values of a corrupt society and could only have the effect of strengthening the bond between the lovers. Adolphe made hurried arrangements and carried Ellénore off precipitately, smothering her with passion. Always astute, she detected contradictions in his actions and told him that he was moved by pity rather than by love—thereby revealing something which he would have preferred not to know and giving him a new preoccupation to conceal.

When the two reached the frontier, Adolphe wrote to his father with some bitterness, holding him responsible for the course he had been forced to take. His father's reply was notable for its generosity; he repeated everything Adolphe had said and ended by saying that although Adolphe was wasting his life, he would be allowed complete freedom. In the absence of the necessity to defend Ellénore, Adolphe's impatience with the tie became even more pronounced.

The two settled for a time in Bohemia where Adolphe, having accepted the responsibility for Ellénore's fate, made every effort to restrain himself from causing her suffering. He assumed an artificial gaiety and with the passing of time once again came intermittently to feel some of his feigned sentiment. When alone, however, his old unrest gripped him and he made vague plans to flee from his attachment.

At this point Adolphe learned of a fresh sacrifice which Ellénore had made, the refusal of an offer from Count P—— to settle her again in suitable circumstances. Adolphe, grasping at this opportunity, told her that he no longer loved her, but at the sight of her violent grief he pretended that his attitude was all a ruse. Another possibility of escape oc-

curred after Ellénore's father had been reinstated in his property in Poland: she was notified that he had died and that she had been made the sole heir. Because the will was being contested, Ellénore persuaded Adolphe to accompany her to Poland. Meanwhile, their relationship continued to deteriorate.

Letters came from Adolphe's father asserting that since Adolphe could no longer be considered Ellénore's protector there was no longer any excuse for the life he was leading. The father had recommended Adolphe, the letters said, to Baron T—— (a friend of the father's and the minister from their country to Poland) and wished Adolphe to call on him. When the young man did so, Baron T—— assumed the father's role and attempted to separate Adolphe and Ellénore. Adolphe spent a night wandering in the country, engaged in confused meditations in which he told himself that his mind was recovering from a long degradation.

Ellénore made another futile effort to penetrate the closed sanctuary of his mind, but a new alignment of forces emerged as Adolphe succumbed more and more to the influence of Baron T——. He continued to procrastinate in putting a definite end to the relationship, but he wrote incriminating letters which the baron forwarded to Ellénore. At last she became fatally ill. Adolphe was finally freed by her death, which produced in him a feeling of great desolation.

THE AENEID

Type of work: Poem
Author: Publius Vergilius Maro (70-19 B.C.)
Type of plot: Heroic epic
Time of plot: The period immediately following the Trojan War
Locale: The Mediterranean region
First transcribed: Augustan manuscript

Principal characters:

AENEAS, Trojan hero destined to found the Roman race
DIDO, Queen of Carthage, in love with Aeneas
ANNA, her sister
ASCANIUS, son of Aeneas
ANCHISES, father of Aeneas
VENUS, goddess of love and beauty, mother of Aeneas
JUNO, queen of the gods and enemy of the Trojans
CUMAEAN SIBYL, prophetess who leads Aeneas to Hades
LATINUS, king of the Latins, whom Aeneas defeats in battle
LAVINIA, his daughter
TURNUS, Latin hero ambitious for the Latin throne and hand of Lavinia
EVANDER, Arcadian king, ally of Aeneas
PALLAS, his son

Critique:

This poem is the distinguished Latin epic which celebrates the glory of Rome in great poetry. It records the traditional story of the establishment of the Roman race and thus traces the lineage of the Romans back to Aeneas and Troy. It has already stood the test of time and will go down in history as one of the world's great epics.

The Story:

Aeneas, driven by storm to the shores of Libya, was welcomed gladly by the people of Carthage. Because Carthage was the favorite city of Juno, divine enemy of Aeneas, Venus had Cupid take the form of Ascanius, son of Aeneas, so that the young god of love might warm the heart of proud Dido and Aeneas come to no harm in her land. At the close of a welcoming feast Aeneas was prevailed upon to recount his adventures.

He described the fall of his native Troy at the hands of the Greeks after a ten-year siege, telling how the armed Greeks had entered the city in the belly of a great wooden horse and how the Trojans had fled from their burning city, among them Aeneas with his father Anchises and young Ascanius. Not long afterward, Anchises had advised setting sail for distant lands. Blown by varying winds, the Trojans had at length reached Buthrotum, where had been foretold a long and arduous journey before Aeneas would reach Italy. Having set sail once more, they had reached Sicily. There Anchises, who had been his son's sage counselor, had died and had been buried. Forced to leave Sicily, Aeneas had been blown by stormy winds to the coast of Libya. Here he ended his tale, and Dido, influenced by Cupid disguised as Ascanius, felt pity and admiration for the Trojan hero.

The next day Dido continued her entertainment for Aeneas. During a royal hunt a great storm drove Dido and Aeneas to the same cave for refuge. There they succumbed to the passion of love. Aeneas spent the winter in Carthage and enjoyed the devotion of the queen. But in the spring he felt the need to continue his destined course. When he set sail, the sorrowing Dido killed herself. The light of her funeral pyre was seen far out at sea.

Again on the shores of Sicily, Aeneas bade his men refresh themselves with food, drink, and games. First of all there was a boat race in which Cloanthus was the victor. The second event was a foot race, won by Euryalus. Entellus engaged Dares in a boxing match, which Aeneas stopped before the obviously superior Entellus achieved a knock-out. The final contest was with bow and arrow. Eurytion and Acestes made spectacular showings and to each was awarded a handsome prize. Following the contests, Ascanius and the other young boys rode out to engage in war games. Meanwhile, the women were grieving the lost guidance of Anchises, and at the instigation of Juno set fire to the ships. Aeneas, sustained by the gods, bade his people repair the damage. Once more the Trojans set sail.

Finally, they reached the shores of Italy, at Cumae, famous for its sibyl. The sibyl granted Aeneas the privilege of visiting his father in the underworld. After due sacrifice, the two of them began their descent into Hades. At length they reached the river Styx and persuaded the boatman Charon to row them across. Aeneas saw the spirits of many people he had known in life, including the ill-fated Dido. Then they came to the beginning of a forked road. One path led to the regions of the damned; the other led to the land of the blessed. Following this latter road, they came at last to Anchises, who showed Aeneas in marvelous fashion all the future history of Rome, and commanded him to found his kingdom at the place where he would eat his tables. On his return to the upper regions Aeneas revisited his men and proceeded to his own abode.

Again the Trojans set sail up the coast of Italy, to the ancient state of Latium, ruled over by Latinus. On the shore they prepared a meal, laying bread under their meat. As they were eating, Ascanius jokingly observed that in eating their bread they were eating their tables. This remark told Aeneas that here was the place Anchises had foretold. Next day the Trojans came to the city of King Latinus on the Tiber. Latinus had been warned by an oracle not to give his daughter Lavinia in marriage to any native man, but to wait for an alien, who would come to establish a great people. He welcomed Aeneas as that man of destiny.

A Latin hero, Turnus, became jealous of the favor Latinus showed Aeneas, and stirred up revolt among the people. Juno, hating Aeneas, aided Turnus. One day Ascanius killed a stag, not knowing that it was the tame favorite of a native family. There grew from the incident such a feud that Latinus shut himself up in his house and ceased to control his subjects. Meanwhile Aeneas made preparations for battle with the Latins under Turnus.

In a dream he was advised to seek the help of Evander, whose kingdom on the Seven Hills would become the site of mighty Rome. Evander agreed to join forces with Aeneas against the armies of Turnus and to enlist troops from nearby territories as well. Now Venus presented Aeneas with a fabulous shield made by Vulcan, for she feared for the safety of her son.

When Turnus learned that Aeneas was with Evander, he and his troops besieged the Trojan camp. One night Nisus and Euryalus, two Trojan youths, entered the camp of the sleeping Latins and slaughtered a great many of them before they were discovered and put to death. The enraged Latins advanced on the Trojans with fire and sword and forced them into open battle. When the Trojans seemed about to beat back their attackers, Turnus entered the fray and put them to flight. But the thought of Aeneas inspired the Trojans to such bravery that they drove Turnus into the river.

Aeneas, warned in a dream of this battle, returned and landed with his allies on the shore near the battlefield, where he encountered Turnus and his armies. Evander's troops were being routed when Pallas, Evander's beloved son, began to urge them on and himself rushed into the fight, killing many of the enemy before he was slain in combat with

Turnus. Aeneas sought to take the life of Turnus, who escaped through the intervention of Juno.

Aeneas decreed that the body of Pallas should be sent back to his father with appropriate pomp during a twelve-day truce. The gods had watched the conflict from afar; now Juno relented at Jupiter's command, but insisted that the Trojans must take the Latin speech and garb before their city could rule the world.

Turnus led his band of followers against Aeneas in spite of a treaty made by Latinus. An arrow from an unknown source wounded Aeneas, but his wound was miraculously healed. The Trojan hero reëntered the battle, was again wounded, but was able to engage Turnus in personal combat and strike him down. Aeneas killed his enemy in the name of Pallas and sacrificed his body to the shade of his dead ally. No longer opposed by Turnus, Aeneas was now free to marry Lavinia and establish his long-promised new nation. This was Rome, the mistress of the ancient world.

AESOP'S FABLES

Type of work: Didactic fiction
Author: Aesop (fl. sixth century B.C.?)
First published in English: 1484

A mid-nineteenth-century French lawyer, M. L. Hervieux, wanting his daughters to know something of Roman literature, decided to translate some of the animal stories which had been put into Latin verse by Phaedrus, a Macedonian servant freed by Emperor Augustus. The trouble was to find a definitive edition of the work. Years later, after visiting most of the important libraries of Europe, M. Hervieux published *Les fabulistes latins* in two volumes and fifteen hundred pages, attributing only sixty-seven fables to this Greek who translated into Latin verse the Greek prose of Demetrius Phalereus of the third century B.C. In the third century of the Christian era, Valerius Babrius, Latin tutor to the son of Emperor Alexander Severus, had also put into Greek verse the fables in Latin prose by Nicostratus, a hanger-on at the court of Marcus Aurelius. Three quarters of the fables set down by Nicostratus were attributed to Aesop.

Some scholars believe that Aesop was as much a fable as his fables. Of course, there is a *Life of Aesop,* written by a certain Planudes Maximus, a thirteenth-century Byzantine monk who prefaced his collection of fables in Latin prose with what he claimed was a true biography of their author. According to the Byzantine monk, Aesop was a slave born in, Samos and killed in Delphi in the sixth century B.C. One statue shows him as deformed and animal-like as the characters of his tales.

History does provide a few details. There is reference to a "noble statue" of him that once existed in Athens, the work of Lysippus, but that may have been as much a creation of the imagination as the sturdy, brown-clad figure in Velázquez' painting. Herodotus, writing less than a century after Aesop was supposed to have flourished, in describing the lovely courtesan Rhodopis, who lived about 550 B.C., mentioned (II,134) the fact that the girl was a slave of Iadmon of Samos, and added: "Aesop, the maker of fables, was a fellow slave." Also, Herodotus recorded the payment of an indemnity paid by the Delphians to the grandson of Iadmon for the murder of Aesop, supposedly because some fable symbolizing the misdeeds of one citizen had angered the others.

Aristotle, in his *Rhetoric,* II, xx, is the authority for Aesop's use of a fable in oratory, as he defended a demagogue accused of embezzling. The slave told of a fox who was infested by fleas but refused to let a hedgehog remove them: "These have already taken their fill of me and do not continue to suck my blood. If you remove them, others less satiated will come to extract what blood I have left." The story was a hint to the Samians to let his client continue in office, since he had already made his fortune.

Also tagged with Aesop's name is the story of the frogs who asked for a king and were sent a stork who gobbled them up, a fable intended to dissuade the citizens of Athens from deposing Pisistratus. But when researchers seek in Greek manuscripts other fables that can definitely be attributed to Aesop, they find hardly a dozen, of which that of the nightingale is the oldest. True, seven collections were ascribed to Aesop, but without proof, and usually their content goes still farther back into antiquity, to early Indian tellers of tales or even to Egyptian poets of the fourteenth century B.C.

One explanation of the infrequent references to the Greek beast-fables is that they were so well known that nobody bothered to mention them. The interesting thing is that Aesop has been called "Father of the Animal Fable," even though the form had existed centuries before his assumed time.

Seventy years ago, Joseph Jacobs, an English investigator engaged in cataloguing fables attributed to Aesop, gave as good an answer as any. Before the time of Aesop, these stories, regarded as jokes, were told for amusement. Aesop, by his use of them, as Aristotle acknowledged, raised them in dignity to the ranks of serious oratorical material, worthy of use when a life was at stake and, if deductions about the cause of his death be correct, taken seriously enough to cause the death of their author.

Ninety-seven of the fables attributed to Aesop composed the first book printed in English with initial letters, printed by William Caxton at Westminster in 1484. Only one perfect copy remains, in the possession of the Queen of England. Others, damaged, are found in the Bodleian Library and the British Museum. The rest were probably as popular as Aesop's fables today and were read to pieces. The tales were equally popular in other lands. In 1496, the Infante Henrique made a Spanish translation that inspired Tomás Iriarte (1750-1791) and his contemporary Samaniego to versify fables memorized by every Spanish school child. Marie de France, at the beginning of the thirteenth century, put more than a hundred of them into French, antedating what has probably been the most elegant form in which they have ever appeared, the twelve books of *Fables* written in verse by Jean de La Fontaine (1668-1694).

"Esope, man of Greece," explained William Caxton in 1484, "subtyll and ingenyous, techeth in his fables how men ought to kepe and rewle them well. And to thende that he shold shewe the lyf and customes of al maner of men, he induceth the byrdes, the trees, and the bestes spekynge to thende that the men may know wherfore the fables were found . . . the whiche yf thou rede them, they shalle aguyse and sharpe thy wytte and shal gyve to thee Cause of Joye." Then follow the fables, in their crude Gothic type and quaint spelling, each illustrated by a grotesque woodcut.

First comes the fable of the cock and the precious stone, in which the bird, discovering a diamond in the filth, saw no possible use for it. The fable writer ends with the implication that those who see no wisdom in "this fayre and playsaint book," are as stupid as the cock. The second tells of the wolf who accused the lamb of enough crimes for an excuse to eat him. The fifth deals with the greedy dog crossing the stream with meat in his mouth and trying to snap up also the piece he saw reflected in the water.

Part II begins with the famous fable of the frogs who asked Jupiter for a king and ends with the story of the frog who tried to swell up to equal the size of the ox. Book III contains the fable of the nightingale to whose nest the "spere-hawk" came with the demand that the songster entertain him; otherwise, he would eat one of the little birds. But a hunter came by and caught the marauder. This story follows a set form. It begins: "He that oppresseth the Innocent shalle have an evyle end, whereof Esope reherceth to us such a fable." At the end the story restates the moral: "And therefore he that doth harm and letteth the Innocent is worthy to dye of evylle dethe, as Cayn dyd which slewe his broder Abel."

This is the formula of all the fables in this ancient volume, the forerunner of so many editions that have appeared throughout the centuries with or without their morals stated, to delight readers who know nothing about Aesop himself and care even less.

AGAINST THE GRAIN

Type of work: Novel
Author: Joris Karl Huysmans (Charles Marie Georges Huysmans, 1848-1907)
Type of plot: Exotic romance
Time of plot: Nineteenth century
Locale: Paris
First published: 1884

Principal character:
JEAN DES ESSEINTES, an aesthete

Critique:

Huysmans, profoundly influenced by Baudelaire and Mallarmé, is perhaps the outstanding prose writer of the decadent school. His writing has the characteristics of the movement: detailed, sensuous description and precise, erudite vocabulary. *Against the Grain (À Rebours)* is a novel in which almost nothing happens; what one learns of the action is through retrospect. Most of the book is concerned with the hero's library, his taste in interior decoration, his illusions, and the complete decadence which stems directly from his conception of Catholicism.

The Story:

The Des Esseintes were an old family. In the Chateau de Lourps the portraits of the ancestors were those of rugged troopers and stern cavalry men. But the family had followed a familiar pattern; through two hundred years of intermarriage and soft indulgence the men had become increasingly effeminate. Now the only remaining Des Esseintes was Jean, a man of thirty. By a kind of atavism, Jean resembled in looks his first grandsire. The resemblance was in looks only.

Jean had had an unhappy childhood. His father, living in Paris most of the time, visited Jean briefly at school once in a while when he wished to give moral counsel. Occasionally he went to see his wife at the chateau. Jean was always present at those hushed interviews in which his mother took little interest. Jean's mother had a strange dread of light. Passing her days in her shaded boudoir, she avoided contact with the world.

At the Jesuit school Jean became a precocious student of Latin and acquired a fair knowledge of theology. At the same time he was a stubborn, withdrawn child who refused all discipline. The patient fathers let him follow his own bent, for there was little else they could do. Both his parents died while he was young; at his majority he came into complete control of his inheritance.

In his contacts with the world Jean went through two phases. At first he lived a wild, dissolute life. For a time he was content with ordinary mistresses. His first love was Miss Urania, an American acrobat. Because she was strong and healthy Jean yearned for her as an anemic young girl might long for a Hercules. But Miss Urania was quite feminine, even prudish in her embraces. Their liaison prematurely hastened his impotence.

Another mistress was a brunette ventriloquist. One day he purchased a tiny black sphinx and a chimera of polychrome clay. Bringing them into the bedchamber, he prevailed on her to imitate Flaubert's famous dialogue between the Sphinx and the Chimera. His mistress, however, was sulky at having to perform offstage.

After that phase Jean began to be disgusted with people. He saw that men brought up in parochial schools, as he was, were timid and boring. Men who had been educated in the public schools were more courageous but even more boring. In a frantic effort to find companionship, he wildly sought out the most carnal pastimes and the most perverted pleasures.

Jean had never been strong, and from childhood he had been afflicted with scrofula. Now his nerves grew weaker. The back of his neck always pained him; his hand trembled when he lifted a light object. In a burst of despairing eccentricity he gave a farewell dinner to his lost virility. The meal was served on a black table to the sound of funeral marches. The waitresses were nude Negresses. The plates were edged in black; the menu included dark bread, meat with licorice sauce, and wine served in dark glasses.

At thirty Jean decided to withdraw from the world. Having concluded that artistry was much superior to nature, he vowed that in his retreat he would be completely artificial. He found a suitable house in a remote suburb of Paris and made elaborate preparations for his retirement.

The upper floor was given over to his two elderly servants, who had to wear felt coverings on their shoes at all times. The downstairs he reserved for himself. The walls were paneled in leather like book binding, and the only color for ceilings and trim was deep orange. In his dining-room he simulated a ship's cabin and installed aquariums in front of the windows. The study was lined with precious books. With great art he contrived a luxurious bedroom which looked monastically simple.

Among his paintings Jean treasured two works of Moreau which depicted Salomé and the head of John the Baptist. He pondered long over the meaning of the scenes. History being silent on the personality of Salomé, Jean decided that Moreau had recreated her perfectly. To him she was the incarnation of woman.

His library was his chief concern. Among the Latin writers he had no love for the classicists: Vergil, for example, he found incredibly dull. But he took great delight in Petronius, who had brought to life Roman decadence under Nero. He loved ardently a few of the French sensualists, Verlaine and Baudelaire among them. He had also a small collection of obscure Catholic writers whose refinement and disdain for the world suited his own temperament.

For months his life was regular and satisfying. He breakfasted at five and dined at eleven. About dawn he had his supper and went to bed. Because of his weak stomach he was most abstemious in his diet.

After a time his old ailments came back to plague him. He could eat or drink very little and his nerves pained him. After weeks of torture he fainted. When his servants found him, they called a neighborhood doctor who could do little for him. At last Jean seemed to recover, and he scolded the servants for having been so concerned. With sudden energy he made plans to take a trip to England.

His luggage having been packed, he took a cab into Paris. To while away the hours before train time, he visited a wine cellar frequented by English tourists and had dinner at an English restaurant. Realizing afresh that the pleasure of travel lies only in the anticipation, he had himself driven home that same evening and thus avoided the banality of actually going somewhere.

At one stage of his life Jean had loved artificial flowers. Now he came to see that it would be more satisfying to have real flowers that looked artificial. He promptly amassed a collection of misshapen, coarse plants that satisfied his aesthetic needs.

But Jean's energy soon dissipated. His hands trembled, his neck pained him, and his stomach refused food. For weeks he dreamed away his days in a half-stupor. Thinking of his past, he was shocked to realize that his wish to withdraw from the world was a vestige of his education under the Jesuits. Finally he became prey to hallucinations. He smelled unaccountable odors, and strange women kept him company.

One day he was horrified to look into his mirror. His wasted face seemed that of a stranger. He sent for a doctor from Paris. After the physician had given him injections of peptone, Jean returned to something like normal. Gradually the doctor began injecting cod liver oil and other nourishing food into his veins. For a while Jean was entranced with the notion of getting all his sustenance through injections. One more activity would thus be unnecessary.

Then the doctor sent his little artificial world crashing; he ordered Jean to leave his retreat and go live a normal social life in Paris. Otherwise his patient would be in danger of death or at least of a protracted illness with tuberculosis. Jean, more afraid of his illness than he was of the stupid world, gave the necessary orders and glumly watched the movers begin their work.

THE AGE OF INNOCENCE

Type of work: Novel
Author: Edith Wharton (1862-1937)
Type of plot: Social criticism
Time of plot: Late nineteenth century
Locale: New York City
First published: 1920

Principal characters:
NEWLAND ARCHER, a young attorney
MAY WELLAND, his fiancée
COUNTESS ELLEN OLENSKA, her cousin

Critique:

This novel is an incisive but oblique attack on the intricate and tyrannous tribal customs of a highly stratified New York society with which the author herself was familiar. Her psychological probing of the meaning and motivation behind the apparent façade of her characters' social behavior shows her to be a true disciple of Henry James. The method is indeed that of James, but Edith Wharton's style is clearer and less involved. Here is a well-made novel, the work of a craftsman for whom form and method are perfectly welded, and the action results inevitably from the natures of the characters themselves.

The Story:

Newland Archer, a handsome and eligible young attorney engaged to lovely May Welland, learned that the engagement would be announced at a party to welcome his fiancée's cousin, Countess Ellen Olenska. This reception for Ellen constituted a heroic sacrifice on the part of the many Welland connections, for her marriage to a ne'er-do-well Polish count had not improved her position so far as rigorous and straight-laced New York society was concerned. The fact that she contemplated a divorce action also made her suspect, and, to cap it all, her rather bohemian way of living did not conform to what her family expected of a woman who had made an unsuccessful marriage.

Newland Archer's engagement to May was announced. At the same party

Archer was greatly attracted to Ellen. Before long, with the excuse that he was making the cousin of his betrothed feel at home, he began to send her flowers and call on her. To him she seemed a woman who offered sensitivity, beauty, the promise of a life quite different from that he could expect after his marriage to May.

He found himself defending Ellen when the rest of society was attacking her contemplated divorce action. He did not, however, consider breaking his engagement to May, but constantly sought reasons for justifying what was to the rest of his group an excellent union. With Ellen often in his thoughts, May Welland's cool beauty and correct but unexciting personality began to suffer in Archer's estimation.

Although the clan defended her against all outsiders, Ellen was often treated as a pariah. Her family kept check on her, trying to prevent her from indulging in too many bohemianisms, such as her strange desire to rent a house in a socially unacceptable part of town. The women of the clan also recognized her as a dangerous rival, and ruthless Julius Beaufort, whose secret dissipations were known by all, including his wife, paid her marked attention. Archer found himself hating Julius Beaufort very much.

Convincing himself that he was seeing too much of Ellen, Archer went to St. Augustine to visit May, who was vacationing there with her mother and her hypochondriac father. In spite of her cool and conventional welcome and her gentle rebuffs to his wooing, her beauty reawakened in him a kind of affection, and he pleaded with her to advance the date of their wedding. May and her parents refused because their elaborate preparations could not be completed in time.

Archer returned to New York. There, with the aid of the family matriarch, Mrs. Manson Mingott, he achieved his purpose, and the wedding date was advanced. This news came to him in a telegram sent by May to Ellen, which Ellen read to him just as he was attempting to advance the intimacy of their relationship. Archer left Ellen's house and found a similar telegram from May to himself. Telling his sister Janey that the wedding would take place within a month, he suddenly realized that he was now protected against Ellen and himself.

The ornate wedding, the conventional European honeymoon which followed, and May's assumption of the role of the proper wife, soon disillusioned Archer. He realized that he was trapped, that the mores of his society, helped by his own lack of courage, had prepared him, like a smooth ritual, for a rigid and codified life. There was enough intelligence and insight in Archer, however, to make him resent the trap.

On his return to New York, he continued to see Ellen. The uselessness of his work as junior attorney in an ancient law firm, the stale regimen of his social life, and the passive sweetness of May did not satisfy that part of Archer which set him apart from the rest of his clan.

He proposed to Ellen that they go away together, but Ellen, wise and kind, showed him that such an escape would not be a pleasant one, and she indicated that they could love each other only as long as he did not press for a consummation. Archer agreed. He further capitulated when, urged by her family, he advised Ellen, as her attorney and as a relative, not to get a divorce from Count Olenski. She agreed, and

Archer again blamed his own cowardice for his action.

The family faced another crisis when Julius Beaufort's firm, built upon a framework of shady financial transactions, failed, ruining him and his duped customers. The blow caused elderly Mrs. Mingott to have a stroke, and the family rallied around her. She summoned Ellen, a favorite of hers, to her side, and Ellen, who had been living in Washington, D. C., returned to the Mingott house to stay. Archer, who had not met Ellen since he advised her against a divorce, began seeing her again, and certain remarks by Archer's male acquaintances along with a strained and martyrlike attitude which May had adopted, indicated to him that his intimacy with Ellen was known among his family and friends. The affair came to an end, however, when Ellen left for Paris, after learning that May was to have a baby. It was obvious to all that May had triumphed, and Archer was treated by his family as a prodigal returned. The rebel was conquered. Archer made his peace with society.

Years passed. Archer dabbled in liberal politics, interested himself in civic reforms. His children, Mary and Dallas, were properly reared. May died when Archer was in his fifties. He lamented her passing with genuine grief. He watched society changing, and saw the old conservative order give way, accepting and rationalizing innovations of a younger, more liberal generation.

One day his son Dallas, about to be married, phoned him and proposed a European tour, their last trip together. In Paris, Dallas revealed to his father that he knew all about Ellen Olenska and had arranged a visit to her apartment. But when they arrived, Archer sent his son ahead, to pay his respects, while he remained on a park bench outside. A romantic to the end, incapable of acting in any situation which made demands on his emotional resources, he sat and watched the lights in Ellen's apartment until a servant appeared on the balcony

42

and closed the shutters. Then he walked slowly back to his hotel. The past was the past; the present was secure.

AGNES GREY

Type of work: Novel
Author: Anne Brontë (1820-1849)
Type of plot: Sentimental romance
Time of plot: Mid-nineteenth century
Locale: England
First published: 1847

Principal characters:
AGNES GREY, a young governess
EDWARD WESTON, a curate, later Agnes' husband
MARY GREY, Agnes' sister
RICHARD GREY, Agnes' father
MRS. GREY, Agnes' mother
MRS. MURRAY, owner of Horton Lodge, Agnes' second employer
ROSALIE MURRAY, her older daughter
MATILDA MURRAY, her younger daughter
MR. HATFIELD, Rector at Horton, Rosalie's suitor
SIR THOMAS ASHBY, later Rosalie's husband
HARRY MELTHAM, and
MR. GREEN, Rosalie's other suitors
NANCY BROWN, an old widow at Horton
MRS. BLOOMFIELD, owner of Wellwood, Agnes' first employer
TOM BLOOMFIELD, her oldest child
MARY ANN BLOOMFIELD, her older daughter
FANNY BLOOMFIELD, her younger daughter
UNCLE ROBSON, Mrs. Bloomfield's brother

Critique:

This novel, written in the first person, is the account of the tribulations of a poor governess trying to achieve respectability and independence in nineteenth-century England. Agnes Grey, a governess because of economic necessity, finds the people among whom she works either bleak or frivolous representatives of the upper classes. They are neither understanding nor helpful, and Agnes, saddled with impossibly arrogant charges, is not a great success as a governess. Fortified by a loving though poor family and by an irreproachable character, she eventually marries the sterling and attractive clergyman. Agnes is the sentimental heroine, and the plot is not to be distinguished from that of the conventional sentimental romance. The good and the true ultimately triumph; the evil and the frivolous are ultimately unhappy. In spite of Agnes' pious sentiments, however, the novel is marked by sharp observations of contemporary life and a gentle and penetrating sarcasm in some of Agnes' comments on her employers. Anne Brontë never became an important novelist, but this novel suggests her ability lay more in the direction of Jane Austen than in that of her sister Emily.

The Story:

Mrs. Grey, a squire's daughter, had offended her family by marrying for love a poor parson in the north of England. She bore him six children, but only two, Mary and Agnes, survived. Nevertheless, the Greys were happy with their humble, educated, pious life in their small house and garden.

Mr. Grey, never wholly at his ease because his wife had been forced to give up carriages and fine clothes in order to marry him, attempted to improve their fortunes by speculating and investing his patrimony in a merchant's sea voyage. But the vessel was wrecked, everything was lost, and the Greys were soon left penniless. In addition, Mr. Grey's health, never robust, began to fail more perceptibly under the strain of his guilt for bringing his family close to ruin. Mary and Agnes, reared in the sheltered atmosphere of a clergyman's household, had spent their time reading, studying, and working in the garden. When the family situation became desperate, however, Mary began to try to sell her drawings to help with the household expenses, and Agnes, the younger daughter, decided to become a governess.

Overcoming the qualms her family felt at the idea of her leaving home, Agnes found a situation and, on a bleak and windy autumn day, arrived at Wellwood, the home of the Bloomfield family. She was received rather coldly by Mrs. Bloomfield and told that her charges, especially Tom, a seven-year-old boy, were noble and splendid children. She soon found that the reverse was true. Tom was an arrogant and disobedient little monster whose particular delight was to pull the legs and wings off young sparrows. Mary Ann, his six-year-old sister, was given to tantrums of temper and refusal to do her lessons. The children were frightened of their father, a peevish and stern disciplinarian, and the father, in turn, blamed Agnes when the children, as frequently happened, got out of control.

Agnes found it impossible to teach the children anything because all her efforts to discipline them were undermined by Mrs. Bloomfield, who felt that her angels must always be right. Even four-year-old Fanny lied consistently and was fond of spitting in people's faces. For a time, Agnes was heartened by Mr. Bloomfield's mother's visit, but the pious old lady turned out to be a hypocrite who sympathized with Agnes verbally and then turned on her behind her back.

Matters became a great deal worse with the visit of Uncle Robson, Mrs. Bloomfield's brother, who encouraged young Tom to torture small animals. One day, after he had collected a whole brood of young birds for Tom to torture, Agnes crushed them with a large stone, choosing to kill them quickly rather than to see them suffer a slow, cruel death. The

family felt she had deprived Tom of his normal, spirited pleasure. Shortly after this incident she was told that her services would no longer be required; the Bloomfields felt that she had not disciplined the children properly or taught them very much.

Agnes spent a few months with her family at home before taking up her next post. She found the Murrays, the owners of Horton Lodge, more sophisticated, wealthier, and less bleak and cruel than the owners of Wellwood; but they were still hardly the happy, pious, warm family that Agnes had hoped to encounter. Her older charge, Rosalie, was sixteen, very pretty, interested only in flirting and in eventually making the most suitable marriage possible; her younger charge, Matilda, fourteen, was interested only in horses and stables. Although they treated her with politeness, neither girl had any respect for the learning and piety that Agnes had to offer. If Agnes' work was less unpleasant than it had been at Wellwood, it was equally futile.

After living at Horton Lodge for nearly a year, Agnes returned home for a month for her sister's wedding. During this time, the Murrays had given Rosalie a coming-out ball, after which she began to exercise her charms on the young men at Horton. Agnes was shocked, when she returned, to find Rosalie flirting with all the men and summarizing the marital possibilities of each with such a hardened and materialistic eye. In the meantime a new curate had come to Horton. Edward Weston was a sober and sincere churchman, neither climbing nor pompous like the rector, Mr. Hatfield. Edward Weston and Agnes, attracted to each other, found many opportunities to meet in their sympathetic visits to Nancy Brown, an old widow who was almost blind. At first Rosalie found Weston both dogmatic and dull, but Agnes found him representative of the true piety and goodness which she believed were the qualities of a clergyman. Rosalie, continuing to play the coquette, conquered first the unctuous rector, Mr. Hatfield, and then after Mr. Hatfield had proposed and been quickly rejected, turned her charms on Mr. Weston. Although Agnes was fiercely jealous of Rosalie's flirtation, she never really acknowledged her own growing love. Finally, Rosalie accepted Sir Thomas Ashby; his home, Ashby Park, and his fortune were the largest in the vicinity of Horton.

Shortly after Rosalie's marriage, before Agnes had the opportunity to see much of Edward Weston, she was called home by the death of her father. She and her mother decided to start a school for young ladies in the fashionable watering place of A———. Although Agnes returned to Horton Lodge for another month, she did not see Weston before she resignedly left to rejoin her mother. Although the school began to prosper after a few months, Agnes still seemed weary and depressed, and she welcomed an invitation from Rosalie, now Lady Ashby, to visit Ashby Park. She found Rosalie disappointed in her marriage to a grumbling, boorish man who ignored her and who, after a honeymoon on the Continent, had forbidden her the frivolous pleasures of London and European society. Agnes also learned from Rosalie that Weston had left Horton a short time before.

A few days after Agnes returned to her mother and the school, she was walking along the water front one morning when she was surprised by Weston. He had secured a living in a nearby village. He promptly began calling on Agnes and her mother and as time passed gained Agnes' love and her mother's esteem. One day, while walking with Agnes to the top of a high hill, he proposed. As husband, father, clergyman, and manager of a limited income, he was in after years the perfect mate for virtuous and worthy Agnes.

AJAX

Type of work: Drama
Author: Sophocles (495?-406 B.C.)
Type of plot: Classical tragedy
Time of plot: The Trojan War
Locale: Phrygia, before Troy
First presented: c. 440 B.C.

Principal characters:
AJAX, a Greek warrior
ODYSSEUS, a Greek leader
TECMESSA, Ajax's female captive
TEUCER, Ajax's half-brother
EURYSACES, son of Ajax and Tecmessa

Critique:

The age-old problem of individual versus group prerogative is masterfully presented in this play. One finds it tempting to sympathize with Ajax for his devotion to his consort and his son, the love and admiration he commands from his followers, and the courage he displays before the walls of Troy. It is inevitable, however, that his ungovernable pride should bring about his ruin. His downfall, the tragic hero's dissolution as a man because of unbearable humiliation and shame, is one of the most touching and disturbing in literature. Sophocles achieved this terrible spectacle by unusual cogency of action, a remarkable delineation of character, and a judicious point of view.

The Story:

Odysseus, chosen by Greek leaders in the Trojan War to replace the dead Achilles as the chief warrior of the Greek forces, paced up and down before the tent of Ajax, who had been slighted by the selection of Odysseus. The goddess Athena, appearing above the tent, told Odysseus that Ajax, covered with blood, was in his tent. Her words confirmed Odysseus' suspicions that it had indeed been Ajax who had slaughtered all of the Greeks' livestock and their shepherd dogs. Athena explained that she had cast a spell over Ajax, who, in his hurt pride, had vowed to murder Menelaus and Agamemnon, the Greek commanders, as well as Odysseus. Under her spell Ajax had committed the horrible slaughter in the belief that the animals he slew were the hated

leaders who had opposed his election to the place of the late Achilles.

When Tecmessa, Ajax's Phrygian captive, revealed to his followers what the great warrior had done, they lamented his downfall and questioned the dark purposes of the gods. Certain that Ajax would be condemned to die for his transgressions, his warriors prepared to retire to their ships and return to Salamis, their homeland.

Ajax, recovered from the spell, emerged from his tent and clearly revealed to his friends that he was a shamed and broken man. Sick in mind at the thought of the taunts of Odysseus, he wished only to die. Even in his abject misery, however, he was sure that had Achilles personally chosen his successor he would have named Ajax. The despairing man tried to find some means of escape from the consequences of his deed. The alternative to death was to return to Salamis and his noble father, Telamon; but he knew that he could never shame Telamon by facing him. His friends, alarmed at his deep gloom and sensing tragedy, advised him to reflect; Tecmessa urged him to live for her sake and for the sake of their little son, Eurysaces. At the mention of the name of his beloved son, Ajax called for the boy. Solemnly he gave Eurysaces his great shield and directed that the child be taken to Salamis, so that he might grow up to avenge his father's disgrace. After dismissing Tecmessa and his son, he remained in his tent alone to clear his troubled thoughts. His followers, meanwhile, resumed their lament over their disgraced leader.

Apparently reconciled to his fate, Ajax emerged at last from his tent and declared that he was ready to recognize authority, to revere the gods, and to bury his sword with which he had brought disgrace and dishonor upon himself. His decision, he said, had been dictated by his affection for Tecmessa and Eurysaces. This apparent change brought forth cheers of rejoicing from his countrymen; they thanked the gods for what appeared to be Ajax's salvation.

In the meantime the Greeks taunted Teucer, Ajax's half-brother, for his kinship with one demented. Calchas, the Greek prophet, warned Teucer that unless Ajax were kept in his tent a full day, no one would again see Ajax alive, since the proud warrior had twice offended the goddess Athena in the past. But Ajax had already left his tent in order to bury his sword. Teucer and the men of Salamis, in alarm, hastened in search of their leader.

Ajax planted his sword, a gift from Hector, the great Trojan warrior, hilt-down in the earth. After he had asked the gods to inform Teucer of his whereabouts so that he might receive a proper burial, he fell upon his sword. Heavy underbrush partly concealed his body where it lay.

Tecmessa was the first to discover her dead lord; in sorrow she covered him with her mantle. Teucer was summoned. Tecmessa and the men of Salamis could not refrain from mentioning the dire part played by Athena in the tragedy of Ajax and the pleasure Menelaus and Agamemnon would feel when they heard of Ajax's death. Fearing foul play, Teucer ordered Tecmessa to bring Eurysaces immediately. Teucer himself was in a dilemma. He knew that the Greeks detested him because of his kinship with Ajax. He feared also that Telamon would suspect him of being responsible for Ajax's death, so that he might be Telamon's heir.

While Teucer pondered his own fate, Menelaus appeared and told him that Ajax could not receive proper burial because he had been a rebel, offensive to the gods. Teucer maintained that Ajax had not been subject to Spartan Menelaus, nor to anyone else, for he had come to Troy voluntarily at the head of his own men from Salamis; therefore he deserved burial. Seeing that Teucer held firm, Menelaus went away. Teucer dug a grave while Tecmessa and Eurysaces stood vigil over the body. The men of Salamis sang a dirge over their dead leader.

Agamemnon, King of Mycenae, appeared and rebuked Teucer, the son of a slave, for his audacity in defying the will of Menelaus. Agamemnon insulted the memory of Ajax by saying that he had been stronger than he was wise. Teucer, bitterly recalling Ajax's many heroic deeds in behalf of the Greek cause, reminded Agamemnon of the many blots on the escutcheon of the Atridae, Agamemnon's royal house. Teucer defended his own blood by pointing out that although his mother, Hesione, was a captive, she was nevertheless of noble birth.

Odysseus resolved the dispute by declaring that no Greek warrior should be denied burial. He himself had hated Ajax, but he admitted that Ajax had been both noble and courageous. He shook hands with Teucer in friendship, but Teucer, lest the gods be offended, refused his offer to assist in the burial. Thus Ajax, whose pride had brought him to an early death, received proper burial and the death ceremonies of a warrior hero.

AL FILO DEL AGUA

Type of work: Novel
Author: Agustín Yáñez (1904-   )
Time: Spring, 1909-spring, 1910
Locale: Near Guadalajara, Mexico
First published: 1947

Principal characters:

DON DIONISIO, the parish priest
MARÍA, and
MARTA, his nieces
PADRE ISLAS, and
PADRE REYES, assistant priests
DAMIÁN LIMÓN, a young man who had been to the United States
MICAELA RODRÍGUEZ, a spoiled girl
VICTORIA, a young widow, visiting from Guadalajara
GABRIEL, a young man reared by Don Dionisio
LUIS GONZAGA PÉREZ, a seminary student
MERCEDES TOLEDO, another young girl
LUCAS MACÍAS, a soothsayer

Al filo del agua is a Spanish phrase with two meanings, one literal, the other figurative. Literally, it signifies the moment that the rain begins. However, it is in its figurative sense that it takes on meaning as the title of this book: the imminence of something that is about to happen. The event about to take place was brought on by a growing dissatisfaction with the political situation and the unnaturalness of the environment imposed by the Church as reflected by life in a small town in Mexico.

In 1910, Porfirio Díaz had been dictator of Mexico for more than thirty years. He had ruled with an iron hand and only now had the dream of political freedom and social improvement begun to filter through to the many semi-isolated towns of Mexico. The same few families had always been the social leaders and political bosses in the communities and Díaz' thirty-odd years of rule had done nothing to lessen this strangle hold or to improve the lot of the common man. Education was nonexistent except for the privileged few, and superstition was rampant.

Another force which held the people in its grip was the Church, a circumstance especially true in rural areas where the long arm of Juarez' 1859 Reform Laws seldom reached. These laws had greatly reduced the political power of the Church, and such things as processions and public religious festivities were forbidden. In the small towns, however, with the ever-present threat of arrest hanging over their heads, the priests often continued their regular clerical activities in spite of the law.

Agustín Yáñez has painted against this background a series of character studies portraying the effects of a narrow and rigid as well as dull and conventional life on people of different ages, with varying degrees of education and exposure to outside influences. (These influences, being outside ones and therefore bad, make up a long and varied list, and include such things as Free Masonry, bright clothing, strangers, uncensored written material, fun, spiritualists, people who had been to the United States; the list could go on and on.) Yáñez creates a sense of monotonous semi-gloom with the sure hand of an artist who has experienced this kind of life himself at one time or another. The fictitious, but very typical, town in which the action takes place is set in the state of Jalisco, of which the author is a native.

Each morning the church bells in this town call the people out of their beds as early as four o'clock to begin another dreary, quiet, prayerful day. Life is very serious. The women wear dark somber colors and do not leave the house except to go to church or to do necessary errands. There is no visiting except in the case of extreme illness or a death in the house of a neighbor. There is little laughter, dancing, or singing. Strangers and strangeness are not only suspect, but already condemned. Nonconformity, even in small things, starts tongues wagging. At the end of each unvarying day, the church bells send the people to bed, an act which for many means the onset of sleepless hours or wrestling with guilty consciences and with wondering when and in what form God's wrath will be brought down upon their heads.

With this daily pattern providing the atmosphere, broken only by funerals, special fiesta days, and an occasional scandal, the action in the story begins as the people are preparing for their Lenten and Easter activities. The panorama of people and events proceeds on through the year, displaying the special religious days of June, the expected deaths, illnesses, and bad luck of August, the celebration of patriotic holidays in September, the scandalous pranks of the students home for vacation in November, the Christmas season with its festivities, and continues on into the New Year, at which time the people are awaiting the appearance of Halley's Comet. This event is being anticipated so intently by Lucas Macías, the soothsayer, that the rest of the people do well to prepare for trouble, for Lucas has from the start associated the appearance of this comet with the stepping onto the scene of Francisco Madero, the man who is to lead the revolution against the tyranny of Díaz.

The person who can most nearly be described as the main character is Don Dionisio, the stern and upright, but just and compassionate parish priest. He alone touches in some way upon the lives of all the other characters in the book. His main ecclesiastical help comes from two assistant priests who present a vivid contrast to each other, one, Padre Reyes, being liberal and forward-looking, the other, Padre Islas, narrow and conservative be-

yond belief. Although Padre Reyes is much more likable, it is Padre Islas, scurrying along the street from church to home so as to avoid meeting his parishioners on a personal basis, who wields more influence on the lives of the townspeople, for it is he who directs the organization to which all the unmarried girls belong. Into their minds he instills the urgent need to stay pure by remaining single, and he imbues them with a sense of guilt for even thinking wholesome thoughts connected with the opposite sex. This narrow man will never use the chapel of the Holy Family, but always the chapel of the Virgin Mary, and Padre Reyes, the other assistant, is not above teasing him by asking if he thinks María and Juan will make a nice couple, or if he is aware that Mercedes is just about ready to make someone a good wife. These questions are calculated to enrage Padre Islas. Padre Reyes, with his modern ideas about such things as life insurance—too far removed from the imaginations of the people to be noticed—is largely ignored, while Padre Islas is revered as a saint beyond the temptations and afflictions of ordinary man. Great is the disillusionment when the good Father Islas is found collapsed on the floor of the church in a fit of epilepsy, which results in his having to be removed permanently from the priesthood. The archbishop had chosen wisely when Don Dionisio was made head priest, with the authority for making final decisions, for he approaches the problems of his parishioners with the best elements of the philosophies of his two assistants—an urgent sense of responsibility for their souls accompanied by a forgiving and understanding heart.

Two other personalities who present a study in contrasts are María and Marta, the orphaned nieces of Don Dionisio, who has reared them since they were very small. At the time the story begins, they are in their twenties, unmarried, and on the verge of taking opposite paths in life. Marta, the contented, with her love for children, her work in the hospital, and other gentle occupations, is the ideal

50

end product of the social and religious forces at work in her environment. María, the rebellious, who has always read forbidden literature (*The Three Musketeers* and newspapers from the capital) behind her uncle's back, and who finally runs away with a woman of very questionable reputation to follow the revolutionary army, is a creature of reaction against this unnatural environment.

What happened to María happens, with variations, to nearly all the young people who have had contact in any way with the outside world. Luis Gonzaga Pérez, a young and talented seminary student, is unable to reconcile his inhibitions concerning the opposite sex with his natural desires, and at the end of the novel he is drawing lewd pictures on the walls of his room in the insane asylum.

Damián Limón, young son of a fairly prosperous landowner, leaves home, like the prodigal son, and goes to the United States to work. Upon his return home, when criticized for going to such a sinful place where Mexicans are treated like dogs, he counters by stating that at least they are paid in money instead of in promises, as in Mexico. Damián becomes scandalously involved in a flagrant love affair and kills the girl, after having just caused his father to have a fatal heart attack over an argument about his father's will. A corrupt political boss has a disgracefully light sentence placed upon him and, at the end of the story, he rides away to join the ranks of the revolutionaries.

The parents of Micaela Rodríguez, a spoiled only child, make the mistake of taking her to Mexico City for a few months. There she sees the parties, pretty clothes, and merriment of the capital's young people. Never again is she satisfied to stay in her dreary home town and, failing to force her parents to move away to a gayer place, she threatens vengeance on the environment that binds her and shocks the town to its roots with her shameless flirting and indecent dress. She ends up being stabbed by a jealous lover, but dies forgiving him and putting the blame for her death on her own actions.

Doubt seems to be the villain that causes the downfall of these unfortunate young people. They have tasted of the world, compared it with their narrow surroundings, and found them wanting. Being few in number, these unlucky ones have fallen under the weight of a relentless social system that brooks no questioning.

But the time is near at hand when many doubters will join together with enough force to make a crack in this teetering wall of hypocrisy, a crack which will ever become wider as education and enlightenment seep through. And in this thought is captured the essence of the title, *Al filo del agua*.

Agustín Yáñez has given us an unprejudiced and intricately detailed view of life in a Mexican town just after the turn of the century. The purpose of the book is not a call to arms to reform, but to present an understanding, not necessarily sympathetic, but always touching story.

ALCESTIS

Type of work: Drama
Author: Euripides (480-406 B.C.)
Type of plot: Classical tragedy
Time of plot: Remote antiquity
Locale: Pherae, in ancient Greece
First presented: 438 B.C.

Principal characters:
APOLLO, god of the sun
ADMETUS, King of Pherae
ALCESTIS, his wife
THANATOS, Death
HERCULES, son of Zeus and friend to Admetus

Critique:

Composed by Euripides as the fourth play of a tragic tetrology performed at the Feast of Dionysius in 438 B.C., *Alcestis* has characteristics of both the tragedy and the satyr play. Although this was a rare but not unique form among Attic playwrights, *Alcestis* is the only surviving example. Consistent with Euripidean technique, the conclusion of the drama results from the intervention of a heavenly power that resolves the conflict, in this case the character of Hercules.

The Story:

Phoebus Apollo had a son, Asclepius, who in time became a god of medicine and healing. Asclepius transgressed divine law by raising a mortal, Hippolytus, from the dead, and Zeus, in anger, killed Apollo's son with a thunderbolt forged by the Cyclops. Apollo then slew the Cyclops, a deed for which he was condemned by Zeus to leave Olympus and to serve for one year as herdsman to Admetus, King of Pherae in Thessaly.

Some time after Apollo had completed his term of service, Admetus married Alcestis, daughter of Pelias, King of Iolcus. But on his wedding day he offended the goddess Artemis and so was doomed to die. Apollo, grateful for the kindness Admetus had shown him in the past, prevailed upon the Fates to spare the king on the condition that when his hour of death should come, they should accept in ransom the life of whoever would consent to die in his place.

None of Admetus' kin, however, cared to offer themselves in his place. Then Alcestis, in wifely devotion, pledged herself to die for her husband. Finally the day arrived when she must give up her life.

Concerned for the wife of his mortal friend, Apollo appealed to Thanatos, who had come to take Alcestis to the underworld. But Thanatos rejected his pleas, warning the god not to transgress against eternal judgment or the will of the Fates. Apollo declared that there was one powerful enough to defy the Fates who was even then on his way to the palace of Admetus. Meanwhile Alcestis prepared for her approaching death. On the day she was to die she dressed herself in her rich funeral robes and prayed before the hearth fire to Vesta, goddess of the hearth, asking her to be a mother to the two children she was leaving behind, to find a helpmate for the boy, a gentle lord for the girl, and not to let them follow their mother's example and die before their time. After her prayers, she placed garlands of myrtle on each altar of the house and at each shrine prayed tearlessly, knowing that death was coming. Then in her own chamber she wept as she remembered the happy years she and Admetus had lived together. There her children found her, and she said her farewells to them. The house was filled also with the sound of weeping servants, grieving for the mistress they loved. Admetus also wept bitterly, begging Alcestis not to leave him. But the condition imposed by the Fates had to be met. While he watched, her breath grew fainter, and her cold hand fell languidly. Before she died, she asked him to promise that he would always care tenderly for their children and that he would never marry again.

At that moment Hercules arrived at the palace of Admetus, on his way to slay the wild horses of Diomedes in Thrace as the eighth of his twelve labors. Admetus concealed from Hercules the news of Alcestis' death so that he might keep the son of Zeus as a guest and carry out the proper rites of hospitality. Hercules, ignorant of what had taken place before his arrival in Pherae, spent the night carousing, drinking wine, and singing, only to awaken in the morning and discover that Alcestis had died hours before he came and that his host had purposely deluded him in order to make his stay in Pherae as comfortable as possible. In gratitude for Admetus' thoughtfulness and in remorse for having reveled while the home of his friend was deep in sorrow, he determined to ambush Thanatos and bring Alcestis back from the dead.

Since no labor was too arduous for the hero, he set out after Thanatos and Alcestis. Overtaking them, he wrestled with Thanatos and forced him to give up his victim. Then he brought Alcestis, heavily veiled, into the presence of sorrowing Admetus, and asked the king to protect her until Hercules returned from Thrace. When Admetus refused, Hercules insisted that the king at least peer beneath the woman's veil. Great was the joy of Admetus and his household when they learned that the woman was Alcestis, miraculously returned from the grave. Pleased with his efforts, doughty Hercules set out once more to face the perilous eighth labor which awaited him in Thrace, firm in the knowledge that with him went the undying gratitude of Admetus and the gentle Alcestis.

THE ALCHEMIST

Type of work: Drama
Author: Ben Jonson (1572?-1673)
Type of plot: Comedy of manners
Time of plot: Early seventeenth century
Locale: London
First presented: 1610

Principal characters:
FACE, a butler
SUBTLE, a swindler posing as an alchemist
DOL COMMON, their partner
LOVEWIT, owner of the house and Face's master
SIR EPICURE MAMMON, a greedy knight
DAME PLIANT, a young widow

Critique:

The Alchemist marked the peak of Ben Jonson's artistic career. Despite a somewhat huddled denouement, the play is a masterpiece of construction. As far as is known, the plot—which Samuel Taylor Coleridge declared one of the three most perfect in existence, the other two being Sophocles' *Oedipus the King* and Fielding's *Tom Jones*—was original with Jonson. In this play, Jonson, the artist superseded Jonson the moralist: as a highly entertaining and dramatic satire on human greed, *The Alchemist* displays none of the sermonizing which marks, more or less, Jonson's other plays.

The Story:

Master Lovewit having left the city because of plague, his butler, Jeremy, known as Face to his friends of the underworld, invited Subtle, a swindler posing as an alchemist, and Dol Common, a prostitute, to join him in using the house as a base of operations for their rascally activities. Matters fared well for the three until a dispute arose between Face and Subtle over authority. Dol, seeing their moneymaking projects doomed if this strife continued, rebuked the two men and cajoled them back to their senses.

No sooner had Face and Subtle become reconciled than Dapper, a gullible lawyer's clerk given to gambling, called, by previous arrangement with Face, to learn from the eminent astrologer, Doctor Subtle, how to win at all games of chance.

Dapper, in the hands of the two merciless rascals, was relieved of all his ready cash, in return for which Subtle predicted that Dapper would have good luck at the gaming tables. In order to gull Dapper further, Subtle told him to return later to confer with the Queen of Fairy, a mysterious benefactress who could promote Dapper's worldly success.

Abel Drugger, an ambitious young druggist who had been led on by Face, was the next victim to enter the house. To his delight, he learned from Subtle, who spoke in incomprehensible pharmaceutical and astrological jargon, that he would have a rich future.

Next arrived Sir Epicure Mammon, a greedy and lecherous knight, with his friend Pertinax Surly, a man versed in the ways of London confidence men. Having been promised the philosopher's stone by Subtle, Mammon had wild visions of transforming all of his possessions into gold and silver, but he was completely taken in by the duplicities of Subtle and Face. Subtle further aroused Mammon's greed by describing at length, in the pseudo-scientific gibberish of the alchemist-confidence man, the processes which led to his approximate achievement of the mythical philosopher's stone. Surly, quick to see what was afoot, scoffed at Subtle and at the folly of Mammon.

During the interview Mammon caught sight of Dol, who appeared inadvertently, and was fascinated. Thinking quickly,

Face told Mammon that Dol was an aristocratic lady who, being mad, was under the care of Doctor Subtle but who in her moments of sanity was most affable. Before he left the house Mammon promised to send to the unprincipled Subtle certain of his household objects of base metal for the purpose of having them transmuted into gold.

The parade of victims continued. Elder Ananias of the Amsterdam community of extreme Protestants came to negotiate for his group with Subtle for the philosopher's stone. Subtle, with Face as his assistant, repeated his extravagant jargon to the impressionable Ananias, who, in his greed, declared that the brethren were impatient with the slowness of the experiment. Subtle, feigning professional indignation, frightened Ananias with a threat to put out forever his alchemist's fire.

Drugger reappeared to be duped further. Subtle and Face were delighted when he told them that a wealthy young widow had taken lodgings near his and that her brother, just come into an inheritance, had journeyed to London to learn how to quarrel in rakish fashion. The two knaves plotted eagerly to get brother and sister into their clutches.

Ananias returned with his pastor, Tribulation Wholesome. Both Puritans managed to wink at moral considerations as Subtle glowingly described the near completion of the philosopher's stone. Prepared to go to any ends to procure the stone, Ananias and Tribulation contracted to purchase Mammon's household articles, which, Subtle explained, he needed for the experiment; the proceeds of the sale would go toward the care of orphans for whom Subtle said he was responsible.

Subtle and Face also plotted to sell these same household articles to the young widow, who, having just moved to London, was probably in need of such items. In the meantime Face met in the streets a Spanish Don—Surly in clever disguise—who expressed a desire to confer with Subtle on matters of business and health.

Dapper returned to meet the Queen of Fairy. At the same time Drugger brought to the house Master Kastril, the angry young man who would learn to quarrel. Kastril was completely taken in. Subtle, promising to make him a perfect London gallant, arranged to have him instructed by Face, who posed as a city captain. Kastril was so pleased with his new acquaintances that he sent Drugger to bring his sister to the house.

Kastril having departed, Dol, Subtle, and Face relieved Dapper of all of his money in a ridiculous ritual in which Dapper was to see and talk to the Queen of Fairy. During the shameless proceedings Mammon knocked. Dapper, who had been blindfolded, was gagged and hastily put into a water closet at the rear of the house. Mammon entered and began to woo Dol, whom he believed to be a distracted aristocratic lady. Face and Subtle, in order to have the front part of the house clear for further swindles, shunted the amorous pair to another part of the house.

Young Kastril returned with his widowed sister, Dame Pliant; both were deeply impressed by Subtle's manner and by his rhetoric. When the Spanish Don arrived, Subtle escorted Kastril and Dame Pliant to inspect his laboratory. By that time both Subtle and Face were determined to wed Dame Pliant.

Face introduced the Spaniard to Dame Pliant, who, in spite of her objections to Spaniards in general, consented to walk in the garden with the Don.

Meanwhile, in another part of the house, Dol assumed madness. Subtle, discovering the distraught Mammon with her, declared that Mammon's moral laxity would surely delay completion of the philosopher's stone. Following a loud explosion, Face reported that the laboratory was a shambles. Mammon despondently left the house, and Subtle simulated a fainting spell.

In the garden Surly revealed his true identity to Dame Pliant and warned the young widow against the swindlers. When, as Surly, he confronted the two rogues, Face, in desperation, told Kastril

55

that Surly was an impostor who was trying to steal Dame Pliant away. Drugger entered and, being Face's creature, insisted that he knew Surly to be a scoundrel. Then Ananias came to the house and all but wrecked Subtle's plot by talking indiscreetly of making counterfeit money. Unable to cope with the wily rascals, Surly departed, followed by Kastril.

Glad to be rid of his callers, Subtle placed Dame Pliant in Dol's care. But they were once more thrown into confusion when Lovewit, owner of the house, made an untimely appearance. Face, quickly reverting to his normal role of Jeremy, the butler, went to the door in an attempt to detain his master long enough to permit Subtle and Dol to escape.

Although warned by his butler that the house was infested, Lovewit suspected that something was amiss when Mammon and Surly returned to expose Subtle and Face. Kastril, Ananias, and Tribulation confirmed their account. Dapper, having managed to get rid of his gag, cried out inside the house. Deciding that honesty was the only policy, Face confessed everything to his master and promised to provide him with a wealthy young widow as his wife, if Lovewit would have mercy on his servant.

In the house, meanwhile, Subtle concluded the gulling of Dapper and sent the young clerk on his way, filled with the belief that he would win at all games of chance. Subtle and Dol then tried to abscond with the threesome's loot, but Face, back in Lovewit's good graces, thwarted them in their attempt. They were forced to escape empty-handed by the back gate.

Lovewit won the hand of Dame Pliant and in his good humor forgave his crafty butler. When those who had been swindled demanded retribution, they were finally convinced that they had been mulcted as a result of their own selfishness and greed.

ALECK MAURY, SPORTSMAN

Type of work: Novel
Author: Caroline Gordon (1895-   )
Type of plot: Fictional biography
Time of plot: Late nineteenth, early twentieth centuries
Locale: Virginia, Tennessee, Mississippi, Missouri
First published: 1934

Principal characters:
ALECK MAURY, a Southern sportsman
JAMES MORRIS, his uncle
VICTORIA, his aunt
JULIAN, his cousin
MR. FAYERLEE, owner of Merry Point
MRS. FAYERLEE, his wife
MOLLY FAYERLEE, their daughter, Aleck's wife
RICHARD, and
SARAH (SALLY), Aleck's and Molly's children
STEVE, Sarah's husband

Critique:

This novel tells of Aleck Maury, who devoted his life to his twin enthusiasms for gun and rod. To him, hunting and fishing were the very breath of life; everything else was secondary, including his career as a teacher of Latin and Greek. The book is a series of incidents which, when put together, describe Aleck Maury and make him seem real.

The Story:

Aleck Maury's love for hunting and fishing began in childhood. At the age of eight, Rafe, a Negro handyman at the Maury household, took Aleck coon hunting. Not long after, a mill owner named Jones took the boy fishing and encouraged his lifelong love for that sport. Aleck was always happiest when he was out in the fields. One of five children, he was reared by his oldest sister after his mother died. Until he was ten years old, he was educated at home by his father, who put great stress upon the classics and taught his children nothing else.

At the age of ten, Aleck went to live at Grassdale with his Uncle James and Aunt Victoria Morris and their son, Julian. There his education was to be broadened under the tutelage of Aunt Victoria, who was a learned woman. Aleck's life at Grassdale was pleasant, centering chiefly about sport.

When Aleck was graduated from the University of Virginia, he had a classical education but no plans for making a living. He tried several jobs. He cleared out a dogwood thicket for a set sum of money, worked on a construction project on the Missouri River, in the city engineer's office in Seattle, and as a day laborer on a ranch in California. While working at the ranch, he contracted typhoid fever and was sent back east as far as Kansas City, to stay with some relatives there. At last through the efforts of his family Aleck became a tutor at Merry Point, the home of Mr. Fayerlee, near Gloversville, Tennessee.

Aleck, living with the Fayerlees, became the local schoolmaster for the children of most of the landowners in the area. Aleck's first interest, however, was not in the school or the students he taught, but in the possibilities for fishing and hunting.

During his stay with the Fayerlees, Aleck fell in love with Molly Fayerlee, and in 1890 they were married. They continued to live on with the Fayerlees and Aleck continued to teach school. During his first year of marriage Aleck acquired the pup Gyges, a small but thoroughbred bird dog. He trained Gy from a pup and became greatly attached to him. The next fall Aleck's son Richard was born. Two years later a daughter Sarah, nicknamed Sally, was born. They all continued to live at Merry Point.

When Richard was seven, Aleck was offered the presidency of a small seminary in Mississippi, and over the protestations of the Fayerlee family the Maurys left Merry Point. On the way, while spending the night in Cairo, Aleck lost Gy. The dog was never heard of again. They continued their journey to Oakland and the seminary. When Aleck arrived, he found that the school was running smoothly under the able direction of Harry Morrow, his young assistant, who was interested in administration rather than teaching. A few months after arriving at Oakland, Aleck acquired an untrained two-year-old pointer named Trecho from his friend, William Mason. Once again Aleck started the slow, arduous training of a good hunting dog.

When Richard was fifteen, Aleck tried to interest him in the joys of his own life, hunting and fishing, but his son, although he was a splendid swimmer and wrestler, had little interest in his father's fondness for field and stream. That summer Richard, while swimming in the river with a group of his companions, was drowned. The boy had been Molly's favorite and his loss was almost more than she could bear. Aleck thought it would be best for all concerned to leave for different surroundings.

He decided after some correspondence with friends that he would start a school in Gloversville, and the family moved back there. Settled in the small Tennessee town, Aleck found much time for fishing and hunting. He met Colonel Wyndham and from him learned a great deal about casting, flies, and the techniques to be used for catching various fish. Finally he began to grow tired of the same pools and the same river, and it was with pleasure that he accepted Harry Morrow's offer of a job on the faculty of Rodman College at Poplar Bluff, Missouri, of which Morrow had just been made president.

Aleck's main reason for accepting the position was the possibility it offered for fishing in the Black River. Thus once again, after ten years in Gloversville, the Maury family was on the move to newer fishing grounds. Sally, however, did not accompany them, but went to a girls' school in Nashville. The faithful Trecho was also left behind, for he had been destroyed at the age of twelve because of his rheumatism.

At Rodman Aleck had only morning classes, a schedule which left him free to fish every afternoon. This pleasant life—teaching in the morning, fishing in the afternoon—continued for seven years. Then Molly died after an emergency operation. Mrs. Fayerlee and Sally arrived too late to see her alive. The three of them took her back to be buried in the family plot at Merry Point.

Aleck returned to Poplar Bluff and continued teaching there for a few years, but at last he resigned his position and went to live at Jim Buford's, near Gloversville, where he spent the next two years restocking Jim's lakes with bream and bass. Later he decided to go to Lake Harris in Florida to try the fishing; but he found it disappointing because of the eel grass which kept the fish from putting up a fight. About that time he received a letter from Sally, who had married and gone touring abroad with her husband. The letter informed him that she and her husband were soon to return home and that they hoped to find a quiet place in the country on some good fishing water, where Aleck would go to live with them. Aleck wrote and suggested that they start their search for a house near Elk River.

Four weeks later he meet Sally and Steve at Tullahoma, only to learn that Steve and Sally, who had arrived the day before, had already discovered the place they would like to have. They told him it was the old Potter house, close to the river. When Aleck saw the big, clapboard house, however, all his dreams

58

about a white cottage disappeared, and when he looked at the river he decided that it would probably be muddy about half the year. Seeing his disappointment, Steve and Sally promised to continue their attempt to find a more ideal house, but at the end of the day's search they decided that they still liked the old Potter house the best. That night Aleck boarded a bus bound for Caney Fork, the place where he really wanted to live, and he went to stay at a small inn located there. The fishing was always good at Caney Fork.

ALICE ADAMS

Type of work: Novel
Author: Booth Tarkington (1869-1946)
Type of plot: Social criticism
Time of plot: Early twentieth century
Locale: A small Midwestern town
First published: 1921

Principal characters:

ALICE ADAMS, a small-town girl
VIRGIL ADAMS, her father
MRS. ADAMS, his wife
WALTER ADAMS, his son
MILDRED PALMER, Alice's friend
ARTHUR RUSSELL, the Palmers' relative
MR. LAMB, of Lamb and Company

Critique:

Alice Adams is a rather simply told story containing one plot and concerning itself with one central character. The novel is the vehicle through which Tarkington expounds his philosophy of life and his gentle satire on small town manners and morals.

The Story:

Alice Adams had been reared in a town in which each person's business was everybody's business, sooner or later. Her father, Virgil Adams, worked for Lamb and Company, a wholesale drug factory in the town, where he also obtained a job for his son Walter. Alice had been one of the town's young smart set while she was in high school, but when the others of the group had gone to college Alice had remained behind because of economic reasons. As time passed she felt increasingly out of things. To compensate for a lack of attention, Alice often attracted notice to herself by affected mannerisms.

Alice had been invited to a dance given by Mildred Palmer, who, according to Alice, was her best friend. Walter had also been invited so as to provide her with an escort. Getting Walter to go out with Alice, however, was a process which took all the coaxing and cajoling that Mrs. Adams could muster. On the

night of the dance Alice departed in a made-over formal, carrying a homemade bouquet of wild violets, and with an unwilling escort who was driving a borrowed flivver. The party itself turned out no better than its inauspicious beginning. Alice was very much a wallflower except for the attentions of Frank Dowling, a fat, unpopular boy. Toward the end of the evening Mildred Palmer introduced Alice to a new young man, Arthur Russell, a distant relative of the Palmers. It was rumored that Mildred and Arthur would become engaged in the near future. Alice asked Arthur to find her brother, whom she had not seen since the second dance. When Arthur found Walter shooting dice with the Negro waiters in the cloakroom, Alice was mortified.

A week later Alice accidently met Arthur Russell and he walked home with her. During their walk Alice learned that Arthur had asked for an introduction to her at the dance. Flattered, Alice built up for herself a background which did not exist. Arthur asked for permission to call on her.

But Arthur failed to appear the next evening. Several nights later, after Alice had helped with the dishes, she was sitting on the front porch when Arthur finally came to call. To hold his interest, Alice asked him to promise not to listen to any gossip about her. As time went on, she repeated her fear that someone would talk about her. Her protestations were something Arthur could not understand.

For many years Mrs. Adams had been trying to convince her husband to leave his job at Lamb and Company and go into business for himself. Her idea was that he could start a factory to manufacture glue from a formula he and another young man at Lamb and Company had discovered years before. Meanwhile the other man had died and the only people who knew the formula were Mr. Lamb and Mr. Adams. Mr. Lamb had lost interest in the formula. Mr. Adams felt that his wife's scheme was dishonest, and in spite of her nagging he refused to do as she wished. But after Mr. Lamb's granddaughter failed to invite Alice to a dinner party she was giving, Mrs. Adams convinced her husband that the true reason was their own poor economic status. In that way she finally won his grudging agreement to her plan.

Without delay, Mr. Adams began to organize his new business. Walter refused to join him because Mr. Adams would not give him three hundred dollars immediately. But Mr. Adams needed all his money for his new project. He sent Mr. Lamb a letter of resignation, telling of his intention to start a glue factory. He expected some sort of action or at least an outburst on Mr. Lamb's part when he read the letter, but nothing was forthcoming. He went ahead with his arrangements and began to manufacture his glue.

Alice's mother decided the time had come to invite Arthur to dinner, and Alice agreed with great reluctance. An elaborate meal was prepared; a maid was hired to serve, and Mr. Adams was forced into his dress suit. But the dinner was a dismal failure, and everyone, including Arthur, was extremely uncomfortable. Arthur had more reason than the rest for being so, for he had heard Mr. Adam's venture discussed in the most unfavorable light. He had also heard some uncomplimentary remarks about Alice. Before dinner was over, a friend named Charley Lohr came to speak to Mr. Adams. When both her mother and father failed to return to the table, Alice and Arthur went out to the porch. She soon dismissed him, knowing that something had come between them. When she went into the house, Charley Lohr informed her that her brother had been caught short in his accounts and had skipped town.

Mr. Adams decided to get a loan from the bank the first thing in the morning in order to pay back what Walter had taken. However, when he went to his factory in the morning, he discovered that the building which had been erected across the street from his was in reality another glue factory, one started by Mr. Lamb. His hopes of obtaining money on his factory were shattered. Then Mr. Lamb rode up to gloat over his retaliation. Mr. Adams angrily accused Mr. Lamb of waiting until Walter got into trouble before announcing his new factory and thereby making Mr. Adams' property practically worthless. He worked himself into such a state that he had a stroke.

Mr. Lamb, feeling sorry for Mr. Adams, offered to buy him out, and Mr. Adams was forced to agree. Now there was no income in the family. Mrs. Adams decided to take in boarders, and Alice finally made up her mind to enroll in Frincke's Business College. She had lost more than Arthur Russell; she had lost her daydreams as well.

ALICE IN WONDERLAND

Type of work: Imaginative tale
Author: Lewis Carroll (Charles Lutwidge Dodgson, 1832-1898)
Type of plot: Fantasy
Time of plot: Victorian England
Locale: The dream world of an imaginative child
First published: 1865

Principal characters:
ALICE
THE WHITE RABBIT
THE DUCHESS
THE QUEEN OF HEARTS

Critique:

Adults will view this book as a gentle satire on education, politics, literature, and Victorian life in general, seen through the eyes of Alice, a child who is the product of a confusing environment. The book is written with charming simplicity. There are poetic parodies on Wordsworth and Southey which are amusing to the point of hilarity, as well as ingenuous observations on the status of powerful female rulers. Through all her puzzling adventures in the dream world, Alice remains the very essence of little girlhood. Children read this book with delight, finding in Alice a heroine who aptly represents their own thoughts and feelings about growing up.

The Story:

Alice was quietly reading over her sister's shoulder when she saw a White Rabbit dash across the lawn and disappear into its hole. She jumped up to rush after him and found herself falling down the rabbit hole. At the bottom she saw the White Rabbit hurrying along a corridor ahead of her and murmuring that he would be late. He disappeared around a corner, leaving Alice standing in front of several locked doors.

On a glass table she found a tiny golden key which unlocked a little door hidden behind a curtain. The door opened upon a lovely miniature garden, but she could not get through the doorway because it was too small. She sadly replaced the key on the table. A little bottle mysteriously appeared. Alice drank the contents and immediately began to grow smaller, so much so that she could no longer reach the key on the table. Next, she ate a piece of cake she found nearby and soon she began to grow to such enormous size that she could only squint through the door. In despair, she began to weep tears as big as raindrops. As she sat there crying, the White Rabbit appeared, bewailing the fact that the Duchess would be angry if he kept her waiting.

The White Rabbit dropped his fan and gloves. Alice picked them up and as she did so she began to grow smaller. Again she rushed to the garden door, but she found it shut and the golden key once more on the table out of reach.

Then she fell into a pool of her own tears! Splashing along, she encountered a mouse who had stumbled into the pool. Alice tactlessly began a conversation about her cat Dinah, and the mouse became speechless with terror. Soon the pool of tears was filled with living creatures, birds and animals of all kinds. An old Dodo suggested that they run a Caucus Race to get dry. Having asked what a Caucus Race was, Alice was told that the best way to explain it was to do it. Whereupon the animals ran themselves quite breathless and finally became dry.

Afterwards, the mouse told a "Tail" to match its own appendage. Alice was asked to tell something, but the only thing she could think of was her cat Dinah. Frightened, the other creatures went away, and Alice was left alone.

The White Rabbit appeared once

more, this time hunting for his gloves and fan. Catching sight of Alice, he sent her to his home to get him a fresh pair of gloves and another fan. In the Rabbit's house she found the fan and gloves and also took a drink from a bottle. Instantly she grew to a giant size, and was forced to put her leg up the chimney and her elbow out of the window in order to keep from being squeezed to death.

She managed to eat a little cake and shrink herself again. As soon as she was small enough to get through the door, she ran into a nearby wood where she found a caterpillar sitting on a mushroom. The caterpillar was very rude to Alice and he scornfully asked her to prove her worth by reciting "You Are Old, Father William." Alice did so, but the words sounded very strange. Disgusted, he left her after giving her some valuable information about increasing or decreasing her size. She broke off pieces of the mushroom and found to her delight that by eating from the piece in her left hand she could become taller, and from the piece in her right hand, smaller.

She came to a little house among the trees. There a footman, who looked very much like a fish, presented to another footman, who closely remembled a frog, an invitation for the Duchess to play croquet with the Queen. The two amphibians bowed to each other with great formality, tangling their wigs together. Alice opened the door and found herself in the chaotic house of the Duchess. The cook was stirring a large pot of soup and pouring plenty of pepper into the mixture. Everyone was sneezing except the cook and a Cheshire cat which sat on the hearth grinning. The Duchess herself held a sneezing, squalling baby, and sang to it a blaring lullaby. Alice, in sympathy with the poor child, picked it up and carried it out into the fresh air, whereupon the baby turned slowly into a pig, squirmed out of her arms, and waddled into the forest.

Standing in bewilderment, Alice saw the grinning Cheshire cat sitting in a tree. He was able to appear and disappear at will, and after exercising his talents, he advised Alice to go to a tea party given by the Mad Hatter. The cat vanished, all but the grin. Finally that, too, disappeared, and Alice left for the party.

There Alice found she had to deal with the strangest people she had ever seen— a March Hare, a Mad Hatter, and a sleepy Dormouse. All were too lazy to set the table properly; dirty dishes were everywhere. The Dormouse fell asleep in its teacup; the Mad Hatter told Alice her hair needed cutting; the March Hare offered her wine and then told her there was none. They asked her foolish riddles that had no answers. Then, worse, they ignored her completely and carried on a ridiculous conversation among themselves. She escaped after the Dormouse fell asleep in the middle of a story he was telling.

Next she found herself in a garden of talking flowers. Just as the conversation was beginning, some gardeners appeared with paint brushes and began to splash red paint on a rose bush. Alice learned that the Queen had ordered a red bush to be placed in that spot, and the gardeners had made a mistake and planted a white one. Now they were busily and fearfully trying to cover their error before the Queen arrived. But the poor gardeners were not swift enough. The Queen caught them in the act, and the wretched gardeners were led off to be decapitated. Alice saved them by shoving them down into a large flower pot, out of sight of the dreadful Queen.

A croquet game began. The mallets were live flamingoes, and the balls were hedgehogs which thought nothing of uncurling themselves and running rapidly over the field. The Duchess cornered Alice and led her away to the seaside to introduce her to the Mock Turtle and the Gryphon.

While engaged in a Lobster Quadrille, they heard the news of a trial. A thief had stolen some tarts. Rushing to the courtroom where a trial by jury was already in session, Alice was called upon to act as a witness before the King and Queen of Hearts. But the excited child upset the jury box and spilled out all its occupants. After replacing all the animals in the box, Alice said she knew nothing of the matter. Her speech infuriated the Queen, who ordered that Alice's head be cut off. The whole court rushed at her, and Alice defiantly called them nothing but a pack of cards. She awoke from her dream as her sister brushed away some dead leaves blowing over her face.

ALL FOOLS

Type of work: Drama
Author: George Chapman (c. 1559-1634)
Type of plot: Romantic comedy
Time of plot: Sixteenth century
Locale: Italy
First presented: c. 1604

Principal characters:
RINALDO, a young gentleman
VALERIO, his friend
GOSTANZO, Valerio's father
MARC ANTONIO, Rinaldo's father
FORTUNIO, Rinaldo's brother
CORNELIO, a jealous husband
GRATIANA, Valerio's wife
BELLANORA, Valerio's sister, loved by Fortunio
GAZETTA, Cornelio's wife

Critique:

All Fools is one of Chapman's best comedies. A successful adaptation to the English stage of material from two Terentian comedies, it lacks the weakness in plot construction that mars several of his plays. Delightful comic situations are developed through his deft handling of the complicated intrigue. The major characters, although based on traditional types, are individualized; and their actions, except in the final act, are skillfully motivated.

The Story:

Gostanzo fancied himself a man of true worldly wisdom. He loved money, relished his neighbor's misfortunes, and was unhampered by any petty scruples about honesty. Aware of the temptations that might lead a young man to become a waster, he had taken great care in rearing his son Valerio. He had lectured the boy on the importance of thrift and, to teach him responsibility, made him an overseer. But Valerio was also a man of worldly wisdom. Although he put on the appearance of industry and innocence in front of his father, he was well acquainted with the gentlemanly activities of dicing, drinking, and wenching. He had, as the result of these pursuits, accumulated a respectable number of debts. To cap his sins, he had now married Gratiana, a girl with beauty but no dowry.

Fortunio was a young man of quite different character. Without parading his virtue, he led an upright life and was a dutiful son. In love with Valerio's sister Bellanora, he was not permitted to court her because Gostanzo was seeking a wealthier son-in-law. Fortunio's brother Rinaldo, having experienced the fickleness of women, was through with love and now devoted himself exclusively to cozenage of others.

One day, when Rinaldo, Fortunio, Valerio, and Gratiana were together talking, they sighted Gostanzo coming their way, and all but Rinaldo rushed off. In answer to Gostanzo's questions, Rinaldo said that Gratiana was the wife of Fortunio, who dared not tell his father of the marriage; Gostanzo believed the lie. Although he promised to keep it secret, he nevertheless revealed it the minute he was alone with Marc Antonio, the father of Fortunio and Rinaldo. Acting on Rinaldo's suggestion, Gostanzo recommended that Fortunio and Gratiana be installed in his home. Marc Antonio accepted this offer, not because he was angry with his son, but because Gostanzo had convinced him that Fortunio was in danger of falling victim to greater evils. With the restraining influence of the strict Gostanzo and the good example of Valerio, he might still be saved.

Rinaldo's scheming thus enabled Valerio and his wife to live in the same house, and it also gave Fortunio a chance to pursue his courtship of Bellanora. When Gratiana was brought to Gostanzo's home, the old man told Valerio to kiss her, but the crafty youth feigned shyness. The father, gratified by this manifestation of a strict upbringing, congratulated himself on being a much better parent than the easy-going Marc Antonio.

Later, however, Gostanzo found Valerio embracing and kissing Gratiana. The old man, still not suspecting the true state of affairs, thought merely that his son was a fast learner. He decided that, to avoid mischief, Gratiana and Fortunio would have to leave his house. When he told Rinaldo of this development, Rinaldo suggested that his father be told that Gratiana was really Valerio's wife and that Marc Antonio now take her into his house. Rinaldo further advised that, in order to make the ruse effective, Valerio be permitted to visit her there. The plan met with the ready assent of Gostanzo, who, being innocently gulled, was happy in the thought that he would be gulling Marc Antonio.

Meanwhile, Rinaldo, encouraged by his success in this project, had been directing his genius to a new endeavor, a plan intended to gull Cornelio, an inordinately jealous husband who was an easy mark for a trickster and whose wife Gazetta complained that he brought home gallants and then upbraided her for being in their company. Rinaldo's accomplice in his scheme was Valerio, who had been angered at Cornelio for making fun of his singing. Valerio had little difficulty in awakening the jealousy in Cornelio. With the help of a page who defended Gazetta on the grounds that women's wantonness was a result of weakness and not design, he so infuriated Cornelio that the jealous husband attacked and wounded his wife's supposed lover.

When Marc Antonio was told that Valerio, not Fortunio, was married to Gratiana, he made merry with Gostanzo for his blind pride. The latter, unable to tolerate gloating other than his own, declared that the plot had been contrived for entertainment. When they met Valerio, Gostanzo feigned extreme anger with him and threatened to disown his son. Valerio, playing the penitent, protested his devotion to his father and avowed his love of Gratiana. Gostanzo, believing the whole affair a joke, dissembled an appearance of being softened and gave his blessing to the match.

Cornelio, meanwhile, had procured a notary and was proceeding with the divorce of his wife. A nosebleed, which he took as an omen, caused him to suspend action just as he was preparing to sign the final papers. After the notary left, a friend explained to him that he had been tricked into his jealousy by Rinaldo and Valerio. Cornelio resolved to repay them with a deception of his own.

When Cornelio found Rinaldo, he told this master trickster that Valerio had been arrested for debts. Since Valerio had been dodging the officials for some time, Rinaldo believed the lie and, having gone on bond for Valerio, he felt that some immediate action was unnecessary. At Cornelio's suggestion, he took Gostanzo with him to the Half Moon Tavern, where Cornelio said Valerio was being held before being taken to prison. Valerio was at the tavern, but not as a captive. Instead, he was engaged in his usual pursuits of drinking and playing dice.

When Gostanzo saw his son's true nature and also learned that Valerio really was married to Gratiana, he threatened, this time in earnest, to disown the boy and to settle his estate on his daughter. But this plan was rejected when he discovered that Bellanora had married Fortunio. The old man, frustrated in his efforts to control events, decided to accept them. Finally, when Cornelio revealed that his jealousy had been feigned in order to restrain his wife's high spirits, the reconciliations were complete and happiness reigned in the Half Moon Tavern.

ALL FOR LOVE

Type of work: Drama
Author: John Dryden (1631-1700)
Type of plot: Romantic tragedy
Time of plot: First century B.C.
Locale: Alexandria, Egypt
First presented: 1677

Principal characters:
MARK ANTONY, one of the Roman triumvirate
VENTIDIUS, his faithful general
DOLABELLA, Antony's friend
OCTAVIA, Antony's wife
CLEOPATRA, Queen of Egypt
ALEXAS, Cleopatra's eunuch

Critique:

Having written rhymed heroic dramatic verse with great success, Dryden turned to a study of Shakespeare and other great playwrights of the English Renaissance. He had only admiration for Shakespeare's great tragedies, but, influenced by the French neo-classicists, he felt that the Elizabethan playwrights had not shown sufficient discipline in construction or in the observance of the classical unities of time, place, and action. *All for Love, Or, The World Well Lost*, his answer as it were to these shortcomings, is an adaptation in the neo-classic manner—but not uncomfortably so—of Shakespeare's *Antony and Cleopatra*. Dryden's Antony occasionally slips into pompous rhetoric, however, and his Cleopatra never becomes the exciting personality of Shakespeare's Egyptian queen. Unity of action, unity of place, dignity of expression, and well-conceived characters especially mark this play as a great piece of dramatic literature. The difference between *All for Love* and *Antony and Cleopatra* is not simply the difference between Dryden and Shakespeare; Dryden excelled himself here.

The Story:

After his humiliating defeat at Actium, Mark Antony retired to Alexandria, Egypt, where he remained in seclusion for some time in the temple of Isis. He avoided meeting his mistress, Cleopatra, the Queen of Egypt, whose cowardice had largely caused the defeat. Meanwhile the Romans, under Octavius, Maecenas, and Agrippa, had invaded Egypt, where, having laid siege to Alexandria, they calmly awaited Antony's next move.

Serapion, a patriot and a priest of Isis, became alarmed at a sudden rising of the Nile and by prodigious disturbances among the royal tombs; these events seemed to presage disaster for Egypt.

Ventidius, Antony's trusted and highly successful general in the Middle East, came at this time to Alexandria to aid his commander. Serapion and Alexas, Cleopatra's loyal, scheming eunuch, tried to encourage citizens and troops with a splendid birthday festival in Antony's honor. Ventidius, in Roman fashion, scorned the celebration. He told Antony's Roman soldiers not to rejoice, but to prepare to defend Antony in his peril.

Antony, clearly a ruined man, at last came out of his seclusion. While he cursed his fate and lamented the day that he was born, Ventidius, in concealment, overheard the pitiful words of his emperor. Revealing his presence, he attempted to console Antony. Both men wept; Antony marveled that Ventidius could remain faithful to a leader who had brought a large part of the Roman Empire to ruin through his love for Cleopatra.

Ventidius offered to Antony his twelve legions, which were stationed in Lower Syria, but his stipulation that these legions would not fight for Cleopatra plunged doting Antony into renewed gloom. When Ventidius mentioned the name of Cleopatra lightly, Antony took offense and cursed the general as a traitor. After this insult Antony, his mind filled with misgivings, guilt, and indecision, hastened to assure Ventidius of his love for him. He promised to leave Cleopatra to join the legions in Syria.

The word that Antony was preparing to desert her left Cleopatra in a mood of anger and despair. Meanwhile Charmion, her maid, went to Antony and begged the Roman to say farewell to her mistress. Antony refused, saying that he did not dare trust himself in Cleopatra's presence.

Not daunted by Antony's refusal, Alexas then intercepted him as he marched out of Alexandria. The eunuch flattered the Romans and presented them with rich jewels from Cleopatra. As Antony was with difficulty clasping a bracelet around his arm, Cleopatra made her prepared appearance. Antony bitterly accused her of falseness and of being the cause of his downfall. The two argued. In desperation, Cleopatra told Antony that as her friend he must go to Syria, but that as her lover he must stay in Alexandria to share her fate. Antony wavered in his determination to leave when Cleopatra told him that she had spurned Octavius' offer of all Egypt and Syria if she would join his forces, and he elected to stay when she represented herself as a weak woman left to the mercy of the cruel invaders. Antony declared, in surrendering again to Cleopatra's charms, that Octavius could have the world as long as he had Cleopatra's love. Ventidius was overcome with shame and pity at Antony's submission.

Cleopatra was triumphant in her renewed power over Antony, and Antony himself seemed to have recovered some of his former magnificence when he was successful in minor engagements against the troops of Octavius. While Octavius, biding his time, held his main forces in check, Ventidius, still hopeful of saving Antony, suggested that a compromise might be arranged with Maecenas or with Agrippa.

Dolabella, the friend whom Antony had banished because he feared that Cleopatra might grow to love the young Roman, came from Octavius' camp to remind Antony that he had obligations toward his wife and two daughters. Then Octavia and her two young daughters were brought before Antony, Octavia, in spite of Antony's desertion, still hoping for reconciliation with her husband. When Antony accused her of bargaining with her brother Octavius, Octavia, undismayed, admitted that Octavius was prepared to withdraw from Egypt at the news that a reconciliation had been effected between his sister and Antony. Octavia's calm dignity affected Antony greatly, and when his two small daughters embraced him, he declared himself ready to submit to the will of Octavia. Cleopatra, entering upon this family reunion, exchanged insults with the momentarily triumphant Octavia.

Still afraid to face Cleopatra for the last time, Antony prevailed upon Dolabella to speak his farewell to Cleopatra. Dolabella, aspiring to Cleopatra's favors, accepted the mission with pleasure. But Alexas, knowing of Dolabella's weakness and ever solicitous of the welfare of Egypt, advised Cleopatra to excite Antony's jealousy by pretending to be interested in Dolabella. After Ventidius and Octavia had secretly overheard the conversation between Dolabella and Cleopatra, Ventidius, now unwittingly a tool of Alexas, reported to Antony Cleopatra's apparent interest in the young Dolabella. Octavia confirmed his report, and Alexas suggested to the raging Antony that Cleopatra was capable of perfidy. Antony's passionate reaction to this information convinced Octavia that her mission was a failure and she returned to the Roman camp. Antony meanwhile, accused Cleopatra and Dolabella of treachery. Ignoring their earnest denials, he banished them from his presence.

Cleopatra, cursing the eunuch's ill advice, attempted unsuccessfully to take her own life with a dagger. Antony ascended a tower in Alexandria harbor to watch an impending naval engagement between the Egyptian and Roman fleets. To his horror he saw the two fleets join and the entire force advance to attack the city. Antony realized now that his end was near; furthermore, his heart was broken by the belief that Cleopatra was responsible for the treachery of the Egyptian fleet. When Alexas brought false word that Cleopatra had retired to her tomb and had taken her life, Antony, no longer desiring to live, fell on his own sword. The faithful Ventidius killed himself. Cleopatra came to the dying Antony and convinced him, before he died, that she had remained steadfast in her love for him. Then, to cheat Octavius of a final triumph, she dressed herself in her royal robes and permitted herself to be bitten by a poisonous asp. Her maids, Iras and Charmion, killed themselves in the same manner. Serapion entered to find that Cleopatra had joined her Antony in death.

ALL MEN ARE BROTHERS

Type of work: Novel
Author: Shih Nai-an (fl. fourteenth century)
Type of plot: Picaresque romance
Time of plot: Thirteenth century or earlier
Locale: China
First transcribed: Possibly the fourteenth or fifteenth century

Principal characters:
SHIH CHIN, The Nine Dragoned
LU TA, later LU CHI SHEN, The Tattooed Priest
LING CH'UNG, The Leopard Headed
CH'AI CHIN, The Little Whirlwind
YANG CHI, The Blue-Faced Beast
CHU T'UNG, The Beautiful Bearded
LEI HENG, The Winged Tiger
CH'AO KAI, The Heavenly King
WU YUNG, The Great Intelligence
KUNG SUN SHENG, Dragon in the Clouds
SUNG CHIANG, The Opportune Rain
WU SUNG, The Hairy Priest
WANG THE DWARF TIGER
TAI CHUNG, The Magic Messenger
LI K'UEI, The Black Whirlwind
LU CHÜN I, The Jade Ch' Lin

Critique:

All Men Are Brothers translated by Pearl Buck, was published in the United States in 1933. She supplied the present English title, which is a translation of a saying by Confucius because she felt that the Chinese title, the *Shui Hu Chuan* (literally, "water margins novel"), conveyed little meaning. The stories which make up the plot originated many years before the novel as a whole was composed and probably have some basis in fact. The version chosen by the translator is the shortest, omitting the spurious chapters telling of the robbers' downfall. It runs to well over 1,200 eventful pages, and the reader is likely to be appalled by the enormous number of characters he must keep in mind; 108 named chieftains form the band at the close of the book. The plot outline which follows can convey very little of the extraordinary bloodthirstiness of these "good fellows," who slaughter entire households of their enemies, who occasionally indulge in cannibalism, and whose reasons for becoming outlaws are not always noble. But the characters are vividly portrayed; the story is always interesting, and all is presented with the greatest realism and vigor. Long attributed to Shih Nai-an, many scholars now claim that Lo Kuan-chung may well be the author, or that the real author is unknown.

The Story:

To escape the persecution of evil Commander Kao, a military instructor fled to the borders. On the way he instructed a village lord's son, Shih Chin, in warlike skills. Later Shih Chin became friendly with the robbers of Little Hua Mountain. Discovery of this alliance forced Shih Chin to flee.

He fell in with Captain Lu Ta and Li Chung. Lu Ta, after killing a pig butcher who was persecuting a girl, escaped capture by becoming priest Lu Chi Shen. But his violence and intemperance forced the abbot to send him to another temple.

On the way he made peace between a village lord and the robbers of Peach Blossom Mountain, now led by Li Chung.

Shih Chin joined the robbers of Little Hua Mountain. Lu Chi Shen went on to his temple, where he became a friend of military instructor Ling Ch'ung. Because Commander Kao's son lusted for Ling Ch'ung's wife, Ling Ch'ung was falsely accused of murder, branded, and exiled to Ch'ang Chou. His guards were prevented by Lu Chi Shen from carrying out their secret orders to kill Ling Ch'ung. Again on his way, Ling Ch'ung was hospitably received by Lord Ch'ai Chin.

In Ch'ang Chou, Ling Ch'ung accidentally escaped a death trap and killed his three would-be assassins. Again he encountered Ch'ai Chin, who sent him to take refuge in Liang Shan P'o, a robbers' lair headed by ungracious Wang Lun.

Warrior Yang Chi, after killing a bully, was branded and sent to be a border guard. His skill delighted Governor Liang of Peking, who kept and promoted him and even selected him to transport rich birthday gifts to Liang's father-in-law. To rid the way of robbers, Chu T'ung and Lei Heng were sent out ahead of the party carrying the treasures. Lei Heng captured drunken Liu T'ang and took him to Lord Ch'ao Kai, but the lord arranged his release on privately discovering that Lei Heng had come to seek him; Lei Heng brought the news of the birthday gifts, which he, Ch'ao Kai and a teacher, Wu Yung, then plotted to steal. Magician Kung Sun Sheng and the three Juan brothers joined them.

The plotters cleverly drugged Yang Chi and his disguised soldiers and stole the treasure. Yang Chi in despair left the others, who resolved to throw the guilt on him. Yang Chi fell in with Lu Chi Shen; they went to Double Dragon Mountain and, overcoming the robber chief who refused to admit them, became the leaders of the band.

When Ch'ao Kai was discovered to have been one of the robbers, plans were made to catch him; but with the aid of scribe Sung Chiang and of robber-catcher Chu T'ung, Ch'ao Kai and the others escaped to Liang Shan P'o. Ling Ch'ung killed the ungracious Wang Lun, and Ch'ao Kai was made the chief. Ling Ch'ung discovered that his wife had killed herself to escape the advances of Commander Kao's son. The robbers vanquished two groups sent against them.

Sung Chiang's connection with the robbers was discovered by his unfaithful mistress. Enraged at her blackmail threats, he killed her and escaped to Ch'ai Chin's village. There he met Wu Sung, who was on his way to see his older brother after a long absence.

Wu Sung killed a tiger and was greatly fêted. He was of heroic size; his brother was puny and small. The latter's wife tried unsuccessfully to seduce Wu Sung. In Wu Sung's absence, she took a lover and with his help killed her husband. Wu Sung returned, and killed the pair. Though generally pitied, he was branded and exiled.

After an eventful journey, Wu Sung defended his jailer's son against a usurper and so offended the tyrant that he plotted with General Chang to accuse Wu Sung falsely of a crime. Wu Sung killed the plotters and joined those at Double Dragon Mountain.

Sung Chiang, going to visit a military magistrate, Hua Yung, was captured by the robbers of the Mountain of Clear Winds, but they recognized and welcomed him. One of them, lustful Wang The Dwarf Tiger, captured the wife of a civil magistrate, Liu Kao. Thinking to please Hua Yung, Sung Chiang persuaded Wang to release her. Later the woman, a troublemaker, identified Sung Chiang as one of the robbers. Sung Chiang and Hua Yung escaped to the Mountain of Clear Winds, and Liu Kao was killed.

General Ch'ing Ming came against these robbers and was captured. Their plot to force him to join their band was successful. Liu Kao's wife, recaptured, was executed. Sung Chiang promised to get a wife for the disappointed Wang

The Dwarf Tiger. The whole band decided to join those at Liang Shan P'o, but Sung Chiang was summoned home for the burial of his father. The report of his father's death turned out to be, however, a trick to keep Sung Chiang from turning outlaw. Persuaded to stand trial for his mistress' murder, he was branded and exiled. The trip was very eventful, involving many near escapes in encounters with robbers who later proved friendly. At his destination Sung Chiang became a friend of his gaoler, Tai Chung, who possessed magic enabling him to walk three hundred miles a day. Another friend, violent but loyal Li K'uei, caused much trouble which Sung Chiang was able to smooth over. One day Sung Chiang became drunk and wrote revolutionary verses on a wall. Tai Chung, sent to a distant city to get execution orders, went instead to Liang Shan P'o, where a letter was forged, freeing Sung Chiang. But a mistake made in the seal resulted in Tai Chung's death sentence also. Both were freed from the execution grounds by the robbers. All went back to Liang Shan P'o, enlarging their group with additional robbers recruited along the way.

Sung Chiang set out to bring his father and brother to the robbers' lair. He was miraculously saved from capture by a temple goddess who gave great prophecies. The robbers took the Sung family to the lair. Kung Sun Sheng and Li K'uei went out to get their old mothers.

On his journey Li K'uei killed a false robber who pretended to be himself, but the impostor's wife escaped. Li K'uei's mother, on the return journey, was killed by tigers. Li K'uei killed the tigers but when he went to receive the reward money, the impostor's wife identified him and he was captured. Another of the band freed him, however, and they returned to Liang Shan P'o.

Shih Hsiu opened a meat shop with the help of Official Yang Hsiung. Shih Hsiu discovered adultery between Yang Hsiung's wife and a priest. They killed the adulterers and escaped. Later they fell in with a thief, Shih Ch'ien, who caused a row and was captured in the village of Chu. In Liang Shan P'o the robbers planned warfare against the Chu village; the others were at last victorious. Li K'uei, ignoring a pact between the robbers and the Hu village, killed all the members of the Hu household except the female warrior, The Ten-Foot Green Snake, who had previously been captured by the robbers. Later she joined the robbers and married Wang The Dwarf Tiger.

Robber-catcher Lei Heng, after killing a courtesan, was allowed to escape to Liang Shan P'o by Robber-catcher Chu T'ung, who was, consequently, exiled. However, he pleased the magistrate, who liked to have Chu T'ung look after his little son. By killing the little boy the robbers forced Chu T'ung to join them.

Li K'uei and Ch'ai Chin went to right a wrong; Ch'ai Chin was captured and the robbers attempting to free him were repelled by their enemies' magic. Kung Sun Sheng, now a hermit, was sent for; his magic finally enabled the robbers to overcome the enemy and free Ch'ai Chin.

A fresh advance planned by Commander Kao against the robbers resulted in many useful additions to Liang Shan P'o when enemy leaders were captured and persuaded to change allegiance. The robbers of Double Dragon, Peach Blossom, and Little Hua Mountains, after some difficulties of capture and escape, joined those at Liang Shan P'o.

A stolen horse intended for Sung Chiang had been stolen again by the Chun family. Instructor Shi Wen Kung, now possessor of the horse, boasted that he would destroy the robbers. Chief Ch'ao Kai, while leading his men, was mortally wounded. Dying, he asked that whoever should capture Shi Wen Kung be named the new chief. A long period of mourning followed.

Rich and respected Lu Chün I was enticed to Liang Shan P'o in hopes that he would join them. Returning, he was arrested and imprisoned as a robber. His steward, now in possession of his wife and goods, plotted to have Lu Chün I killed. Many events followed, including the near death of Sung Chiang, but finally the city was taken. The prisoners were freed and the adulterers killed. Lu Chün I refused Sung Chiang's offer to make him the chief.

The robbers captured additional soldiers sent against them and added many of the leaders to their ranks. Ch'ao Kai's death was finally avenged in the conquest of the Chun family and of Shi Wen Kung, whose actual captor was Lu Chün I, who still refused to become the chief. Since all the robbers wished Sung Chiang to remain the leader, he prepared a test. He and Lu Chün I each led a group against one of the two cities remaining to be taken. The first to take his city would be the chief. After some reverses, Sung Chiang was successful. He then went to the aid of Lu Chün I, who had been twice vanquished by warrior Chang Ch'ing. This general, finally overcome, was persuaded to join the outlaws. Sung Chiang received a heavenly message in the form of a miraculous stone tablet which listed all thirty-six greater and seventy-two lesser chieftains who made up the robber band. All swore undying loyalty, wishing to be united forever, life after life.

ALL QUIET ON THE WESTERN FRONT

Type of work: Novel
Author: Erich Maria Remarque (1897-
Type of plot: Social criticism
Time of plot: World War I
Locale: Germany and France
First published: 1928

Principal characters:
PAUL BÄUMER,
ALBERT KROPP,
MÜLLER,
TJADEN,
HAIE WESTHUS, and
STANISLAUS KATCZINSKY (KAT), German soldiers

Critique:

All Quiet on the Western Front is a powerful novel reflecting the disillusionment that followed World War I. Written in the first person with short, simple sentences, this outstanding book makes clear the common soldier's reactions to shellfire, hunger, fear, sickness, and danger. There is no show of heroism in the story. Yet the hero, Paul Bäumer, engenders the essence of heroism. He is symbolic of any boy who must become a soldier.

The Story:

Just out of school, little more than nineteen years old, Paul Bäumer and his companions were in the front lines of the army. Albert Kropp, Müller, Leer, Tjaden, Haie Westhus, the farmer Detering, and Stanislaus Katczinsky, called Kat, the forty-year-old food plunderer, were part of the second company in the front lines, where Corporal Himmelstoss contrived cruel and inhuman assignments and punishments for his men. Tjaden hated him a little more than the others did. Kemmerich had his leg shot off. When he died, Müller got his boots.

The boys wanted to get back at Himmelstoss, but they knew that it would do them no good to complain about him. One night, when they caught Himmelstoss alone, they threw a sheet over his head and gave him a sound thrashing. Tjaden never forgot his own satisfaction

in that accomplishment.

During the bombardments Paul saw men cry like babies or do other things for which they were later ashamed. When the trenches were quiet the men sat in groups talking about what they would do when the war ended. Paul always felt bewildered during such discussions because, having been drafted so young, he had no occupation to which he could return.

Himmelstoss was reprimanded for his treatment of the men, and they knew about it. They could not directly disobey him because that would be insubordination, but they could jeer at him and insult him. Tjaden was called before a court-martial for his insults, and given a three-day open confinement. He thought his punishment worth the pleasure of insulting the corporal.

The company moved closer to the front. At first the men sat in the trench and waited, fighting rats and playing cards. The recruits were frightened, and Paul and the old-timers kept an eye on them. One young recruit went mad and climbed out of the trench; he had to be tied down to keep him from committing suicide. There was a retreat and then another attack, with the trenches nearly flattened under the bombardment. After one attack a man lay dying somewhere on the field. They could hear his cries but could not find him. When the second company was relieved, there were only thirty-two men left from the original company of two hundred.

Relief came to Paul and the others. Good food and rest was all they needed. They met some friendly French girls. At night they took food with them for a bribe and sneaked across the river to the girls' house. The girls helped them to forget the war.

Paul was given a fourteen-day leave. He went home to see his sister Erna and his mother, who was sick in bed. His mother had saved from her own small rations his favorite food. He felt strange there in his home. Erna told him that their mother had cancer. One day he met in the street an officer who demanded a salute. Paul went home and took off his uniform. People asked too many questions about the war, questions which he could not answer.

At the end of his leave Paul went to a training camp for four weeks. On his last Sunday in the camp Paul's father and sister came to see him. They told him that his mother was in the hospital.

Finding his old company, Paul anxiously looked for his comrades. He found Kat, Tjaden, and Kropp. Haie had been killed. Paul shared with his friends the moldy cake he had brought from home. The men were given new uniforms. They had periods of extra drill. It was rumored that they were going to Russia. Then they heard that the kaiser was coming. After he inspected them and had watched a review, the new uniforms were taken from the men.

During an attack Paul found himself alone in a shell hole. Panicky and lonely, he crawled out of the hole to find his friends. Caught by machine-gun fire, he crawled into another hole. When a French soldier leaped into the hole, Paul stabbed him. After what seemed many hours Paul noticed that the man was still alive. He tried to relieve the dying man's pain. After the man died, Paul's conscience tormented him. When he was able to crawl from the shell hole, he found Müller and Kat, who fed him and comforted him by telling him that he had committed no crime.

Paul, Kat, Müller, Albert, and Tjaden were detailed to guard a heavily bombarded village where an important supply dump was located. They spent three weeks eating, drinking, and wandering about. Enemy fire continued to molest them. Albert and Paul were wounded. In the hospital they bribed a doctor to let them stay together. They were taken to a Catholic hospital, where the cleanliness almost made Paul sick. His broken leg refused to heal. Albert lost his leg. After a while Paul was able to hobble around on crutches, but he could not bear Albert's jealous gaze. Paul recovered and went home for a short while. His mother was still living. Soon he returned to his company.

The war dragged on. Müller was killed and Paul inherited Kemmerich's boots. Dysentery, typhus, influenza, and violent death dogged them constantly. Kat was wounded while he and Paul were in a trench together. Paul carried his friend through the lines. Just as he brought him to safety, Kat was killed when a piece of shrapnel struck him in the head.

The summer of 1918 passed. Paul was lonely and philosophical. He stayed in a convalescent ward after he had been slightly gassed. The meaning of the war loomed dismally before him. No one will ever know, he thought, what the war had done to him and the other soldiers.

In October, 1918, on a day when the army communiqué reported that all was quiet on the western front, a stray bullet hit Paul, and he died.

75

ALL THE KING'S MEN

Type of work: Novel
Author: Robert Penn Warren (1905-   )
Type of plot: Social criticism
Time of plot: Late 1920's and early 1930's
Locale: Southern U.S.A.
First published: 1946

Principal characters:
>JACK BURDEN, a journalist and political lackey
>WILLIE STARK, a political boss
>SADIE BURKE, his mistress
>ANNE STANTON, a social worker
>ADAM STANTON, her brother
>JUDGE IRWIN

Critique:

All the King's Men, after a sluggish beginning, races smoothly to its inevitable ending. Warren's literary style is excellent. It is so good that the reader is likely to regret reaching the final pages of the book. Although the rise of Willie Stark is ostensibly the theme of the novel, the real issue is the character of Jack Burden, a caustic-tongued, brilliant journalist, whose self-examination becomes a symbol of the era that is treated in the book. From the opening description of Sugar Boy's drive through the country highway until the last pages when Jack Burden realizes his self-destruction and, phoenix-like, rises from the ruins of his past to make a new life with Anne Stanton, the plot is gripping and real.

The Story:

When Governor Willie Stark tried to intimidate old Judge Irwin of Burden's Landing, the judge stood firm against the demagogue's threats. As a result, Willie ordered Jack Burden to find some scandal in the judge's past that could ruin the elderly man.

Jack had met Willie back in 1922, when Willie, the county treasurer, and Lucy Stark, his schoolteacher wife, were fighting against a corrupt building contractor who was constructing the new schoolhouse. Sent by his newspaper, the *Chronicle,* to investigate, Jack found

Willie and Lucy both out of jobs but still fighting against graft. Two years later the fire escape of the school collapsed during a fire drill and Willie became a hero.

Willie then ran in the Democratic primary race for governor. There were two factions, those of Harrison and MacMurfee. Because it was to be a close election, someone proposed that Willie be used as a dummy candidate to split the rural MacMurfee followers. Tiny Duffy and some other men convinced Willie that he could save the state. By then Willie had become a lawyer and politically ambitious man. Jack covered the campaign.

Aiding Willie was Sadie Burke, a clever, energetic woman with political skill. Inadvertently she revealed Harrison's plan to Willie. Crushed and gloomy at this news, Willie rallied his spirits and offered to campaign for MacMurfee, who was elected.

Willie practiced law for a few years until 1930 when he ran for governor with the assistance of Sadie Burke, who became his mistress, and Tiny Duffy, who was Willie's political jackal.

Meanwhile Jack had quit his job on the *Chronicle.* Reared by a mother who had remarried since Ellis Burden had deserted her, Jack had become a faithless, homeless cynic whose journalism career meant nothing to him as an ideal. He had, in his youth, played with Anne and Adam Stanton. Adam was now a famous surgeon, and Anne, still unmarried, had become a welfare worker.

Jack was in love with Anne, but time had placed a barrier between him and the girl with whom he had fallen in love during the summer after he had come home to Burden's Landing from college. He had been twenty-one then, she seventeen. But Jack's youthful cynicism, which later took possession of him completely, spoiled him in Anne's eyes.

When Jack went to work for Governor Willie Stark, Jack's mother was deeply pained and Judge Irwin was disgusted, but Jack cared little for their opinions.

By 1933 Willie was on the verge of losing his wife, who could not stand her husband's political maneuvers and his treatment of their son Tom. Willie assured Jack that Lucy knew nothing abcut Sadie Burke. Lucy remained with Willie through his reëlection in 1934 and then retired to her sister's farm. She appeared with Willie in public only for the sake of his reputation.

Jack began to dig into Judge Irwin's past. Delving into the judge's financial transactions during the time when he was attorney general under Governor Stanton, Jack learned that a power company had been sued by the government for a large sum. As a bribe to the attorney general the company fired one of its men to give a highly paid job to Irwin. Later this man, Littlepaugh, committed suicide after writing the facts in a letter to his sister. Still living, Miss Littlepaugh told Jack the story.

The issue of the Willie Stark six-million-dollar hospital demanded use of this scandal which Jack had uncovered. Willie told Jack that he wanted Adam Stanton to head the new hospital. It would, Jack knew, be a ridiculous offer to the aloof and unworldly young doctor, but he made an effort to convince Adam to take the post. Adam flatly refused. A few days later Anne sent for Jack. She wanted Adam to take the position. Jack showed Anne the documents proving Judge Irwin's ac-

ceptance of a bribe and Governor Stanton's attempt to cover up for his friend. Knowing that Adam would want to protect his father's good name, Anne showed the evidence to him. He then said he would head the hospital. Later Jack wondered how Anne had known about the plans for the hospital because neither he nor Adam had told her.

Jack's suspicions were confirmed when Sadie Burke, in a torrent of rage, told him that Willie had been betraying her. Jack knew then that Anne Stanton was the cause.

Disillusioned, he packed a suitcase and drove to California. This journey to the West and back completed, Jack, his torment under control, went back to work for Willie.

One of MacMurfee's men tried to bribe Adam to use influence in selecting a man named Larson as the builder of the medical center. When Adam, outraged, decided to resign, Anne phoned Jack for the first time since he had learned of her affair with Willie. Anne and Jack decided to get Adam to sign a warrant against the man who had tried to bribe him. Jack also warned Anne that as a witness she would be subject to public scrutiny of her relationship with Willie, but she said she did not care. Jack asked her why she was associating with Willie. She said that after what Jack had told her about Governor Stanton's dishonesty in the past she did not care what happened to her. Later, Jack persuaded Adam not to bring suit.

After Willie's political enemy, MacMurfee, tried to blackmail him because of a scandal concerning Tom Stark, Willie ordered Jack to use his knowledge to make Judge Irwin throw his weight against MacMurfee's blackmail attempt. When Jack went to Burden's Landing to confront Judge Irwin with the evidence that Jack had obtained from Miss Littlepaugh, the old man shot himself.

In the excitement following the suicide, Jack's mother told him that he had caused his father's death. Belatedly, Jack discovered the reason for Ellis Burden's desertion. In his will Judge Irwin left his estate to his son, Jack Burden.

Only one way seemed left to handle MacMurfee. Willie decided to give the building contract for the hospital to Mac-Murfee's man, Larson, who in turn would suppress the scandal about Tom. Duffy made the arrangements.

Tom Stark was a football hero. One Saturday during a game his neck was broken. Adam reported that Tom would remain paralyzed. This news had its effect on Willie. He told Duffy that the hospital deal was off. Turning to Lucy once more, he dismissed Sadie Burke and Anne Stanton.

Duffy, driven too far by Willie, phoned Adam and told him that Anne had been responsible for his appointment. Adam, having known nothing of his sister's relationship with the governor, went to her apartment to denounce her. Then, in the hall of the state building, Adam shot Willie and was killed immediately afterward by Willie's bodyguard.

Piece by piece the tangled mess of Jack's life began to take new meaning. He separated himself from every particle of his past with the exception of two people: his mother, whose devotion to Judge Irwin over all the years had given her a new personality in Jack's eyes, and Anne Stanton, whom he married.

ALL'S WELL THAT ENDS WELL

Type of work: Drama
Author: William Shakespeare (1564-1616)
Type of plot: Romantic comedy
Time of plot: Sixteenth century
Locale: France and Italy
First presented: c. 1602

Principal characters:
THE KING OF FRANCE
BERTRAM, Count of Rousillon
THE COUNTESS OF ROUSILLON, his mother
HELENA, the Countess' ward
PAROLLES, a scoundrel, Bertram's follower
A WIDOW OF FLORENCE
DIANA, her daughter

Critique:

More serious and dramatic than most of the Shakespearian comedies, *All's Well That Ends Well* is thought to have been revised several times before its first publication in the Folio of 1623. It is not a smooth piece of work. Parts of it are farce-comedy; other parts are marked by a seriousness of insight that is not always compatible with the general tone. Shakespeare's purpose was to portray the blindness brought about by prejudices formed without reason. Yet he gave sound basis for Bertram's refusal to see the good in Helena. Twice she humiliated him and forced him into unwanted situations. It took all of Shakespeare's skill to bring about a happy ending in the face of such odds.

The Story:

Bertram, the Count of Rousillon, had been called to the court to serve the King of France, who was ill of a disease that all the royal physicians had failed to cure. In the entire country the only doctor who might have cured the king was now dead. On his deathbed he had bequeathed to his daughter Helena his books and papers describing cures for all common and rare diseases, among them the one suffered by the king.

Helena was now the ward of the Countess of Rousillon, who thought of her as a daughter. Helena loved young Count Bertram and wanted him for a husband, not a brother. Bertram considered Helena only slightly above a servant, however, and would not consider her for a wife. Through her knowledge of the king's illness, Helena at last hit upon a plot to gain the spoiled young man for her mate, in such fashion as to leave him no choice in the decision. She journeyed to the court and, offering her life as forfeit if she failed, gained the king's consent to try her father's cure on him. If she won, the young lord of her choice was to be given to her in marriage.

Her sincerity won the king's confidence. She cured him by means of her father's prescription and as her boon asked for Bertram for her husband. That young man protested to the king, but the ruler kept his promise, not only because he had given his word but also because Helena had won him over completely.

When the king ordered the marriage to be performed at once, Bertram, although bowing to the king's will, would not have Helena for a wife in any but a legal way. Pleading the excuse of urgent business elsewhere, he deserted her after the ceremony and sent messages to her and to his mother saying he would never belong to a wife forced upon him. He told Helena that she

79

would not really be his wife until she wore on her finger a ring he now wore on his and carried in her body a child that was his. And these two things would never come to pass, for he would never see Helena again. He was encouraged in his hatred for Helena by his follower, Parolles, a scoundrel and a coward who would as soon betray one person as another. Helena had reproached him for his vulgar ways and he wanted vengeance on her.

Helena returned to the Countess of Rousillon, as Bertram had commanded. The countess heard of her son's actions with horror, and when she read the letter he had written her, restating his hatred for Helena, she disowned her son, for she loved Helena like her own child. When Helena learned that Bertram had said he would never return to France until he no longer had a wife there, she sadly decided to leave the home of her benefactress. Loving Bertram, she vowed that she would not keep him from his home.

Disguising herself as a religious pilgrim, Helena followed Bertram to Italy, where he had gone to fight for the Duke of Florence. While lodging with a widow and her daughter, a beautiful young girl named Diana, Helena learned that Bertram had seduced a number of young Florentine girls. Lately he had turned his attention to Diana, but she, a pure and virtuous girl, would not accept his attentions. Then Helena told the widow and Diana that she was Bertram's wife, and by bribery and a show of friendliness she persuaded them to join her in a plot against Bertram. Diana listened again to his vows of love for her and agreed to let him come to her rooms, provided he first gave her a ring from his finger to prove the constancy of his love. Bertram, overcome with passion, gave her the ring, and that night, as he kept the appointment in her room, the girl he thought Diana slipped a ring on his finger as they lay in bed together.

News came to the countess in France and to Bertram in Italy that Helena had died of grief and love for Bertram. Bertram returned to France to face his mother's and the king's displeasure, but first he discovered that Parolles was the knave everyone else knew him to be. When Bertram held him up to public ridicule, Parolles vowed he would be revenged on his former benefactor.

When the king visited the Countess of Rousillon, she begged him to restore her son to favor. Bertram protested that he really loved Helena, though he had not recognized that love until after he had lost her forever through death. His humility so pleased the king that his confession of love, coupled with his exploits in the Italian wars, won him a royal pardon for his offense against his wife. Then the king, about to betroth him to another wife, the lovely and wealthy daughter of a favorite lord, noticed the ring Bertram was wearing. It was the ring given to him the night he went to Diana's rooms; the king in turn recognized it as a jewel he had given to Helena. Bertram tried to pretend that it had been thrown to him in Florence by a high-born lady who loved him. He said that he had told the lady he was not free to wed, but that she had refused to take back her gift.

At that moment Diana appeared as a petitioner to the king and demanded that Bertram fulfill his pledge to recognize her as his wife. When Bertram tried to pretend that she was no more than a prostitute he had visited, she produced the ring he had given her. That ring convinced everyone present, especially his mother, that Diana was really Bertram's wife. Parolles added to the evidence against Bertram by testifying that he had heard his former master promise to marry the girl. Bertram persisted in his denials. Diana then asked for the ring she had given to him, the ring which the king thought to be Helena's. The king asked Diana where she had gotten the ring. When she refused to tell on penalty of her life, he ordered her taken to prison. Diana then declared that she would send for her bail. Her bail was Helena, now carrying Bertram's child within her, for it was she, of course, who had received him in Diana's rooms that fateful night. To her Diana gave the ring. The two requirements for becoming his real wife being now fulfilled, Bertram promised to love Helena as a true and faithful husband. Diana received from the king a promise to give her any young man of her choice for her husband, the king to provide the dowry. And so the bitter events of the past made sweeter the happiness of all.

ALMAYER'S FOLLY

Type of work: Novel
Author: Joseph Conrad (Teodor Józef Konrad Korzeniowski, 1857-1924)
Type of plot: Romantic realism
Time of plot: Late nineteenth century
Locale: Dutch East Indies
First published: 1895

Principal characters:

ALMAYER, an unsuccessful trader of Dutch ancestry
MRS. ALMAYER, his Malay wife
NINA, his half-caste daughter
DAIN MAROOLA, Nina's Malay lover
LAKAMBA, Rajah of Sambir, Almayer's enemy

Critique:

Almayer's Folly is a good example of Conrad's carefully constructed stories. Laid in the Far East, as many of his novels are, the story is played out against the inscrutable mystery of nature. The theme of the meeting of East and West has long found varied treatment in English literature.

The Story:

By marrying Lingard's adopted daughter, a Malay, Almayer had inherited that prosperous merchant's business and his plans for amassing a huge fortune in gold from rich mines up the Pantai River. Almayer and his wife had one daughter, Nina, a beautiful girl, who had been sent to Singapore, where for ten years she was educated as a European. She returned home to Sambir unexpectedly at the end of that time, for she could not bear to be treated as a half-caste in a white community. Unsuccessful in business, Almayer nursed dim hopes that he could find a gold mine and, his fortune made, take Nina to Amsterdam to spend his last days in prosperous retirement.

News that the English were to have control of the Pantai River caused Almayer to start building a new house in his compound, not far removed from the one in which he was living. He wanted a house fine enough to receive the British. When the project was abandoned and the Dutch were left in nominal power, Almayer stopped work on his new house. A company of Dutch seamen christened the structure "Almayer's Folly."

The native rajah, named Lakamba, had a compound across the river from Almayer's home. There he lived with his women and his slaves and his principal aide, Babalatchi. Lakamba kept close watch on Almayer when he would leave for several days at a time with a few of his men. But Almayer gave up his trips after a time and settled down to empty daydreams on his rotten wharf. His native wife despised him.

Nina's presence in Sambir offered another problem for Almayer, for the young men of the settlement were eyeing her with interest.

One day the handsome son of a Malayan rajah came sailing up the river in a brig and wanted to trade with Almayer. His name was Dain Maroola. At length, after conversations with Lakamba and long conferences with Almayer, Dain got what he was after, gunpowder. Meanwhile he had fallen passionately in love with Nina. One night she came into the women's room in her father's house and discovered her mother counting out the money Dain had been giving her in payment for Nina. Mrs. Almayer had been arranging meetings between Nina and Dain, and giving them warning at the approach of Almayer. Mrs. Almayer wished her daughter to remain native. She had a deep distrust of white men and their ways.

Dain went away, promising that he would return to help Almayer in locating the hidden gold mine. When he did return, he saw Almayer for just a moment and then hurried to see Lakamba. He told the rajah that his brig had fallen into the hands of the Dutch and that he had narrowly escaped with one slave. Most of his men had been killed. And in a day or two the Dutch would be up the Pantai looking for him.

After this interview Lakamba told Babalatchi he must poison Almayer before the Dutch arrived. Now that Dain knew where the gold treasure was, Almayer was no longer needed. If allowed to live, he might reveal his secret to the white men.

Next morning the body of a Malay was found floating in the river. The head was smashed beyond recognition, but it wore an anklet and a ring that had belonged to Dain. Almayer was overcome with grief, for Dain was his last hope of finding the gold. The Dutch officers who came looking for Dain told how he had escaped from his brig and how, as the Dutch approached it, the gunpowder it carried ignited and blew up the boat, killing two of the Dutch. Almayer promised his visitors that after they had dined he would deliver Dain into their hands.

Meanwhile Babalatchi was telling Lakamba the true story of Dain. Nina had been waiting for the young Malay on the night of his conference with Lakamba, and she had taken him to a secluded clearing farther up the river. There he was now hiding. The corpse that had floated down the river was that of his slave, who had died when the canoe overturned. Mrs. Almayer had suggested that Dain put his anklet and ring on the body and let it float down the river. Lakamba and Babalatchi planned Dain's escape from his Dutch enemies. Knowing that Dain would not leave without Nina, Babalatchi and Mrs. Almayer plotted to get her away from Almayer, who was drinking with the Dutch. After some persuasion Almayer did lead his guests to the grave of the man recovered from the river. The Dutch took the anklet and ring as proof that Dain was dead. Then they left for the night.

Nina, willing to go with Dain, felt an urge to see her father once more before she left, but her mother would not let her go into the house where her father lay in a drunken sleep. Nina went to the clearing where Dain was hiding. Soon afterward a slave girl awakened Almayer and told him where Nina was. Almayer was panic-stricken. He traced Nina to Dain's enclosure and begged her to come back to him, but she would not. She did not want to run the risk of insults from white people. With Dain she would be a ranee, and she would be married to a Malay, a brave warrior, not a lying, cowardly white man. Almayer threatened to send his servant to tell the Dutch where Dain was.

While they argued, Babalatchi came up and cried out that the slave girl had revealed Dain's hiding place to the Dutch, who were now on their way to capture the young Malay. Babalatchi, astounded when Dain announced that he would stay with Nina, left them to their fate. After he had gone, Almayer said he would never forgive Nina, but he offered to take the two to the mouth of the river. So in heavy darkness the fugitive lovers escaped their pursuers.

On an island at the mouth of the river Dain, Nina, and Almayer awaited the canoe that would take the lovers to Lakamba's hidden boat. After the two had gone, Almayer covered up Nina's footprints and returned to his house up the river. His compound was deserted. Mrs. Almayer with her women had gone to Lakamba for protection, taking Dain's gift of money with her. Almayer found the old rusty key to his unused office. He went inside, broke up the furniture, and piled it in the middle of the room. When he came out he threw the key into the river and sat on his porch until the flames began to billow from his office. He was burning down his old house.

He lived out the rest of his days in "Almayer's Folly." Finally he began the practice of smoking opium in an effort

83

to forget his daughter Nina. When he died, the opium had given his eyes the look of one who indeed had succeeded in forgetting.

AMADÍS DE GAUL

Type of work: Novel
Author: Vasco de Lobeira (c. 1360-c. 1403)
Type of plot: Chivalric romance
Time of plot: First century
Locale: France, England, and the rest of Europe
First published: 1508

Principal characters:
AMADÍS OF GAUL
KING PERIÓN, his father
PRINCESS ELISENA, his mother
GALAOR, another son of King Perión
LISUARTE, King of Great Britain
BRISENA, his queen
ORIANA, their daughter
URGANDA, an enchantress
ARCALAUS, a magician

Critique:

"The best of all books of this kind and unique in its art" was the description of *Amadís de Gaul* put by Cervantes into the mouth of Don Quixote. It had many competitors. Besides thirteen other versions in fifty years, dozens of other romantic tales of knights-errant were written after the fifteenth-century Garci Ordóñez (or Rodríguez) de Montalvo, Mayor of Medina del Campo, found a three-volume novel in Portuguese by Lobeira, and, according to his testimony, "corrected the original—corrupt and composed in old style—and took out superfluous words and substituted others more polished and elegant," thus producing a piece of effulgent Renaissance prose. Scholars have disputed the identity of the Lobeira who wrote the version found by Montalvo, a manuscript reportedly seen in the library of the Duke of Alveiro as late as 1750, but destroyed, perhaps, along with the library, in the Lisbon earthquake of 1755. João de Lobeira flourished between 1258 and 1285. Vasco de Lobeira, knighted in the battle of Aljubarrota in 1385, could not have been born until after 1350, the year in which a book containing a reference to Amadís was circulated in Seville. If Vasco de Lobeira was the author of Montalvo's source, he must have based the work on an earlier story. But regardless of who wrote the first long prose novel with a single hero in modern European literature, Montalvo rewrote it and, adding a fourth part, produced the only surviving version of this long-drawn-out tale with an unreal plot believable only to those who lived in a rapidly expanding and newly explored world where anything might be credible. Certainly the Montalvo version is superior to its many sequels in which giants became taller, wild beasts fiercer, and magicians more powerful. Glorifying the ideals of chivalry, the story had great influence on the manners and thinking, and of course the literature, of its time.

The Story:

Not many years after the passion of Christ there lived in Lesser Britain a Christian king named Garinter. His older daughter was married to the King of Scotland. The younger daughter, Elisena, found none of her suitors attractive until the day her father brought home King Perión of Gaul, whom Garinter had watched defeat two powerful knights and kill a lion. The scheming of Elisena's attendant, Darioleta, allowed the young people to meet secretly in the royal garden. King Perión departed ten days later without knowing the results of their nights of love.

When Elisena's son was born, Darioleta concealed her mistress' indiscretion by putting him into an ark, along with his father's sword and ring, and a parchment declaring the boy to be "the timeless Amadís, son of a king." She set the ark afloat in the river beside the palace; it drifted out to sea where it was found by a knight, Gandales, who was on a voyage to Scotland. Gandales, who brought up the foundling with his son Gandalín, called the boy "Child of the Sea."

Gandales, riding through the woods when the boy was three, rescued Urganda, an enchantress who was being pursued by a knight. The grateful witch, after prophesying that the adopted boy would become the flower of knighthood, the most honorable warrior in the world, promised to aid him should he ever need her help.

When the boy was seven, King Languines of Scotland and his queen saw him and offered to bring him up at court. Five years later King Lisuarte and Queen Brisena paused in Scotland on their way to claim the throne of England. Until all was safe, they asked permission to leave behind their daughter Oriana. King Languines appointed the "Child of the Sea" to be her squire.

The two children fell so deeply in love with each other that never again did they fall out of love, but they dared not let others know of their feelings. To be worthy of Oriana, Amadís determined to be knighted, and when King Perión visited Scotland to seek help against his enemy, King Abies of Ireland, Oriana asked her father's old friend to knight Amadís. The young knight then rode away in search of fame through adventures.

Urganda met him in the forest and gave him a lance with which he rescued King Perión from Irish knights. Though neither was aware of the blood relationship between them, Amadís swore always to aid King Perión in time of danger. Then followed a series of fantastic and extraordinary adventures, among them the encounter with haughty Galpano, whose custom was to stop and rob all who passed through his realm. Amadís defeated the bully and his two brothers, though in the battles he was so severely wounded that he had to be nursed back to health by a friendly noble.

Meanwhile, King Perión had married Elisena. Although they lamented their lost son, they took pleasure in a second son, Galaor. When King Abies sent an expedition against Gaul, Amadís overcame the Irish champion. In the celebration festivities at King Perión's court, the identity of Amadís was discovered through the ring he wore and King Perión proudly acknowledged his long-lost son.

Amadís remained melancholy, thinking himself unworthy to aspire to the daughter of the King of England. He did briefly visit her at Vindilisora (Windsor), only to be called away to rescue his brother Galaor. That summons was a trick of the enchanter Arcalaus, who cast a spell over the knight and disarmed him. When the villain appeared in the armor of Amadís and riding his horse, Oriana almost died. Only the timely news of further feats of arms by Amadís told her he was still alive, and so she was restored to health.

Tireless in his villainy, Arcalaus caused King Lisuarte to disappear and abducted Oriana. Amadís and his brother, knighted by Amadís, rescued the princess, but in the absence of the king, the traitor Barsinan tried to seize Brisena and usurp the throne. Amadís, dressed in rusty armor, defeated the rebel; and when Oriana's father reappeared twelve days of feasting followed. Amadís, however, was no nearer to winning the hand of his beloved in spite of his great service to the king.

Continuing to seek knightly fame, Amadís and his friends sailed for the Firm Island, settled by Apolidón, son of the King of Greece, who had taken refuge there after eloping with the daughter of Emperor Siudan of Rome. Here was an enchanted arch through which only faithful lovers could pass. Beyond it was a marriage chamber guarded by invisible knights. After his arrival in that land Amadís received a note from Oriana, who had believed the lying charges of unfaithfulness made against him by a malignant dwarf. She had signed herself as a damsel pierced through the heart by the sword of Amadís.

His ecstasy of grief upon reading the note and his withdrawal, under the name of Beltenebros (The Fair Forlorn One) to the hermitage at the Poor Rock, convinced Oriana that she had wronged him. However, there was nothing she could do to right matters, for King Lisuarte had given her in marriage to the Emperor of Rome.

When a fleet from Rome took her away, Amadís, calling himself The Greek Knight, defeated it and returned Oriana to her father, asking only that she be protected against further misalliances. King Lisuarte decided to punish such effrontery by an attack on Firm Island, a decision that ranged the knights of the world on two sides. King Lisuarte enlisted the help of the Emperor of Rome.

Amadís visited the Emperor of Constantinople and sent a messenger to the King of Bohemia. Arcalaus, hating both Amadís and King Lisuarte, encouraged King Aravigo to march with his army and prey on both sides.

When the hosts assembled for the battle, King Gasquilán of Sweden sent a personal challenge to Amadís to meet him in single combat between the lines. The king's overthrow was the signal for a general onslaught that lasted for two days, until at last the death of the Emperor of Rome disheartened and routed his army.

Out of affection for Oriana, Amadís did not pursue the defeated host, but King Aravigo took this opportunity to plunder the followers of King Lisuarte. A hermit, who had been trying to bring about peace among the combatants, sent the youthful Esplandián to take the news of King Lisuarte's distress to Amadís. The hero marched at once to the rescue of King Lisuarte, a kindness that wiped out the enmity between them. The marriage of Oriana and Amadís was solemnized on Firm Island. Afterward the couple passed under the Arch of True Love into the magic bridal chamber.

THE AMBASSADORS

Type of work: Novel
Author: Henry James (1843-1916)
Type of plot: Psychological realism
Time of plot: About 1900
Locale: Paris, France
First published: 1903

Principal characters:
CHADWICK NEWSOME (CHAD), an American expatriate
LAMBERT STRETHER, his friend
MARIA GOSTREY, an acquaintance of Strether
COMTESSE DE VIONNET, in love with Chadwick Newsome
MRS. POCOCK, Chadwick's married sister
MAMIE POCOCK, Mrs. Pocock's husband's sister

Critique:

Henry James put great emphasis on the construction and form of his novels, and *The Ambassadors* is one of his best in point of construction. There are no loose ends; the entire story is neatly gathered together. The importance of this novel in Henry James' work is that in it he at last conquered his embarrassment over people from America. His earlier novels had displayed the people of his native land as rather barbaric in their appreciation of Europe. But in Lambert Strether and Chadwick Newsome, James portrayed two Americans who had the intelligence to realize in Paris what they had missed in the bleak and narrowed existence of their earlier lives in New England.

The Story:

Lambert Strether was engaged to marry Mrs. Newsome, a widow. Mrs. Newsome had a son Chadwick, whom she wanted to return home from Paris and take over the family business in Woollett, Massachusetts. She was especially concerned for his future after she had heard that he was seriously involved with a Frenchwoman. In her anxiety she asked Strether to go to Paris and persuade her son to return to the respectable life she had planned for him.

Strether did not look forward to his task, for the young man had ignored all his mother's written requests to return home. Nor did Strether know what hold Chadwick's mistress might have over him or what sort of woman she might be. He strongly suspected that she was a young girl of unsavory reputation. Strether realized, however, that his hopes of marrying Mrs. Newsome depended upon his success in bringing Chad back to America, where his mother could see him married to Mamie Pocock.

Leaving his ship at Liverpool, Strether journeyed across England to London. On the way he met Miss Gostrey, a young woman who was acquainted with some of Strether's American friends, and she promised to aid Strether in getting acquainted with Europe before he left for home again. Strether met another old friend, Mr. Waymarsh, an American lawyer living in England, whom he asked to go with him to Paris.

A few days after arriving in Paris, Strether went to Chad's house. The young man was not in Paris, and he had temporarily given the house over to a friend, Mr. Bilham. Through Bilham, Strether got in touch with Chad at Cannes. Strether was surprised to learn of his whereabouts, for he knew that

Chad would not have dared to take an ordinary mistress to such a fashionable resort.

About a week later Strether, Miss Gostrey, and Waymarsh went to the theater. Between the acts of the play, the door of their box was opened and Chad entered. He was much changed from the adolescent college boy Strether remembered. He was slightly gray, although only twenty-eight.

Both Strether and Chad Newsome pleased each other on sight. Over coffee after the theater, the older man told Chad why he had come to Europe. Chad answered that all he asked was an opportunity to be convinced that he should return.

A few days later Chad took Strether and his friends to a tea where they met Mme. and Mlle. de Vionnet. The former, who had married a French count, turned out to be an old school friend of Miss Gostrey. Strether was at a loss to understand whether Chad was in love with the comtesse or with her daughter Jeanne. Since the older woman was only a few years the senior of the young man and as beautiful as her daughter, either was possibly the object of his affections.

As the days slipped by it became apparent to Strether that he himself wanted to stay in Paris. The French city and its life were much calmer and more beautiful than the provincial existence he had known in Woollett, and he began to understand why Chad was unwilling to go back to his mother and the Newsome mills.

Strether learned that Chad was in love with Mme. de Vionnet, rather than with her daughter. The comtesse had been separated from her husband for many years, but their position and religion made divorce impossible. Strether, who was often in the company of the Frenchwoman, soon fell under her charm. Miss Gostrey, who had known Mme. de Vionnet for many years, had only praise for her and questioned Strether as to the advisability of removing Chad from the woman's continued influence.

One morning Chad announced to Strether that he was ready to return immediately to America. The young man was puzzled when Strether replied that he was not sure it was wise for either of them to return, that it would be wiser for them both to reconsider whether they would not be better off in Paris than in New England.

When Mrs. Newsome, back in America, received word of that decision on the part of her ambassador, she immediately sent the Pococks, her daughter and son-in-law, to Paris along with Mamie Pocock, the girl she hoped her son would marry. They were to bring back both Strether and her son.

Mrs. Newsome's daughter and her relatives did not come to Paris with an obvious ill-will. Their attitude seemed to be that Chad and Strether had somehow drifted astray, and it was their duty to set them right. At least that was the attitude of Mrs. Pocock. Her husband, however, was not at all interested in having Chad return, for in the young man's absence Mr. Pocock controlled the Newsome mills. Mr. Pocock further saw that his visit was probably the last opportunity he would have for a gay time in the European city, and so he was quite willing to spend his holiday going to theaters and cafés. His younger sister, Mamie, seemed to take little interest in the recall of her supposed fiancé, for she had become interested in Chad's friend, Mr. Bilham.

The more Strether saw of Mme. de Vionnet after the arrival of the Pococks, the more he was convinced that the Frenchwoman was both noble and sincere in her attempts to make friends with her lover's family. Mrs. Pocock found it difficult to reconcile Mme. de Vionnet's aristocratic background with the fact that she was Chad's mistress. After several weeks of hints and genteel pleading, the Pococks and Mamie went to Switzerland, leaving Chad to make a decision whether to return to America. As for Mr. Strether, Mrs. Newsome had advised that he be left alone to make his own decision, for the widow wanted to avoid the appearance of having lost her dignity or her sense of propriety.

While the Pococks were gone, Strether and Chad discussed the course they should follow. Chad was uncertain of his attitude toward Mamie Pocock. Strether assured him that the girl was already happy with her new love, Mr. Bilham, who had told Strether that he intended to marry the American girl. His advice, contrary to what he had thought when he had sailed from America, was that Chadwick Newsome should remain in France with the comtesse, despite the fact that the young man could not marry her and would, by remaining in Europe, lose the opportunity to make himself an extremely rich man. Chad decided to take his older friend's counsel.

Waymarsh, who had promised his help in persuading Chad to return to America, was outraged at Strether's changed attitude. Miss Gostrey, however, remained loyal, for she had fallen deeply in love with Strether during their time together in Paris. But Strether, realizing her feelings, told her that he had to go back to America alone. His object in Europe had been to return Chad Newsome to his mother. Because he had failed in that mission and would never marry Mrs. Newsome, he could not justify himself by marrying another woman whom he had met on a journey financed by the woman he had at one time intended to marry. Only Mme. Vionnet, he felt, could truly appreciate the irony of his position.

AMELIA

Type of work: Novel
Author: Henry Fielding (1707-1754)
Type of plot: Domestic realism
Time of plot: 1740's
Locale: England
First published: 1751

Principal characters:
CAPTAIN BOOTH, a soldier
AMELIA, his wife
ELIZABETH HARRIS, her sister
SERGEANT ATKINSON, her foster brother
DR. HARRISON, Booth's benefactor
MISS MATTHEWS, a woman of the town
COLONEL JAMES, Booth's former officer

Critique:

As Fielding declared in his introduction to *The History of Amelia*, he satirized nobody in the novel. Amelia, the long-suffering wife of every generation, is charming and attractive. The foibles of her husband still ring true. Dr. Harrison is a man each reader would like to know. Some of the interest of the novel lies in Fielding's accurate presentation of prison life and the courts. Having been a magistrate for many years, he was able to present these scenes in a most modern and realistic way, for aside from presenting the virtuous character of Amelia, Fielding wanted his novel to interest people in prison and legal reform. Although the novel lacks the extravagant humor of his earlier novels, the plot presents many amusing characters and complex situations.

The Story:

One night the watchmen of Westminster arrested Captain William Booth, seizing him during his attempt to rescue a stranger who was being attacked by two ruffians. The footpads secured their own liberty by bribing the constables, but Booth, in spite of his protests, was hailed before an unjust magistrate. The story he told was a straightforward one, but because he was penniless and shabbily dressed the judge dismissed his tale and sentenced him to prison. Booth was desperate, for there was no one he knew in London to whom he could turn for aid. His plight was made worse by his reception at the prison. His fellow prisoners stripped him of his coat, and a pickpocket made off with his snuffbox.

While he was smarting from these indignities, a fashionably dressed young woman was brought through the gates. Flourishing a bag of gold in the face of her keepers, she demanded a private room in the prison. Her appearance and manner reminded Booth of an old friend of questionable background, a Miss Matthews whom he had not seen for several years. But when the woman passed him without a sign of recognition, he believed himself mistaken.

Shortly afterward a guard brought him a guinea in a small parcel, and with the money Booth was able to redeem his coat and snuffbox. The rest of the windfall he lost in a card game. Booth was penniless once more when a keeper came to conduct him to Miss Matthews, for the woman was indeed she. Seeing his wretched condition as he stood by the prison gate, she had sent him the mysterious guinea.

Reunited under these distressing circumstances, they proceeded to relate the stories of their experiences. Miss Matthews told how she had been committed to await sentence for a penknife attack on a soldier who had seduced her under false promises of marriage.

Booth, in turn, told this story. He had met a Miss Amelia Harris, a beautiful

91

girl whose mother at first opposed her daughter's marriage to a penniless soldier. The young couple eloped but were later, through the efforts of Dr. Harrison, a wise and kindly curate, reconciled with Amelia's mother. Booth's regiment was ordered to Gibraltar, shortly before a child was to be born to Amelia. He left reluctantly, leaving Amelia in the care of her mother and her older sister, Elizabeth. At Gibraltar Booth earned the good opinion of his officers by his bravery. Wounded in one of the battles of the campaign, he was very ill, and Amelia, learning of his condition, left her child with her mother and sister and went to Gibraltar to nurse her sick husband. Then Amelia, in her turn, fell sick. Wishing to take her to a milder climate, Booth wrote to Mrs. Harris for money, but in reply received only a rude note from Elizabeth. He hoped to get the money from his army friend, Major James, but that gentleman was away at the time. Finally he borrowed the money from Sergeant Atkinson, his friend and Amelia's foster brother, and went with his wife to Montpelier. There the couple made friends with an amusing English officer named Colonel Bath and his sister.

Joy at the birth of a second child, a girl, was dampened by a letter from Dr. Harrison, who wrote to tell them that old Mrs. Harris was dead, and that she had left her property to Amelia's sister. The Booths returned home, to be greeted so rudely by Elizabeth that they withdrew from the house. But for the help of Dr. Harrison, they would have been destitute. Harrison set Booth up as a gentleman farmer and tried to help him make the best of his half-pay from the Army. But because of several small mistakes, Booth made enemies among the surrounding farmers. Dr. Harrison was traveling on the continent at the time and in his absence Booth was reduced almost to bankruptcy. He came to London to try his fortunes anew. He preceded Amelia, found modest lodgings, and wrote her where they were. It was at this point that another misfortune

landed him in prison. At the end of Booth's story, Miss Matthews sympathized with his unfortunate situation, congratulated him on his wife and children, and paid the jailer to let Booth spend the next few nights with her in her cell.

Booth and Miss Matthews were shortly released from prison. The soldier wounded by Miss Matthews having completely recovered, charges against her were dropped. Miss Matthews also secured the release of Booth, and the two were preparing to leave prison when Amelia arrived. She had come up from the country to save him, and his release was a welcome surprise for the distressed wife. The Booths set themselves up in London. Shortly afterward, Booth met his former officer, now Colonel James, who in the meanwhile had married Miss Bath and grown quickly tired of her. Mrs. James and Amelia resumed their old friendship. Booth, afraid that Miss Matthews would inform Amelia of their affair in prison, told Colonel James of his difficulties and fears. The colonel gave him a loan and told him not to worry. Colonel James was himself interested in Miss Matthews, but he was unable to help Booth by his intercession. Miss Matthews continued to send Booth reproachful and revealing letters which might at any time have been intercepted by Amelia.

While walking in the park one day, the Booths met Sergeant Atkinson. He joined their household to help care for the children, and soon he started a half flirtation with a Mrs. Ellison, Booth's landlady.

Mrs. Ellison proved useful to the Booths, for a lord who came also to visit her advanced money to pay some of Booth's debts. Meanwhile Miss Matthews had spitefully turned Colonel James against Booth. Colonel Bath, hearing his brother-in-law's poor opinion of Booth, decided that Booth was neither an officer nor a gentleman, and challenged him to a duel. Colonel Bath believed in nothing so much as a code of honor, and when, in the duel, Booth had run him through, without serious injury, the colonel was so much impressed by Booth's gallantry that he forgave him and brought about a reconciliation between James and Booth.

During this time Mrs. Ellison had been trying to arrange an assignation between Amelia and the nobleman who had given Booth money to pay his gambling debts. Amelia was innocently misled by her false friends. But the nobleman's plan to meet Amelia secretly at a masquerade was thwarted by another neighbor, Mrs. Bennet. This woman, who had been a boarder in Mrs. Ellison's house, had also met the noble lord, had encountered him at a masquerade, and had drunk the drugged wine he provided. To prevent Amelia's ruin in the same manner, Mrs. Bennet came to warn her friend. Then she informed Amelia that she had recently married Sergeant Atkinson, whom Amelia had thought in love with Mrs. Ellison. But Amelia's joy at learning of both the plot, which she now planned to escape, and of the marriage, was marred by the news that Booth had again been put into prison for debt, this time on a warrant of their old friend Dr. Harrison.

Amelia soon discovered that Dr. Harrison had been misled by false rumors of Booth's extravagance, and had put him in jail in order to stop his rash spending of money. Learning the truth, Dr. Harrison had Booth released from prison.

On the night of the masquerade Amelia remained at home but sent Mrs. Atkinson dressed in her costume. At the dance Mrs. Atkinson was able to fool not only the lord but also Colonel James. The complications of the affair were many, almost every relationship being misunderstood. Booth fell in with an old friend and lost a large sum of money to him. Again he became worried about being put in jail. Then he became involved in a duel with Colonel James over Miss Matthews, whom Booth had visited only at her insistence. Before the duel could take place, Booth was again imprisoned for debt, and Dr. Harrison was forced to clear his name with Colonel James. Finally James forgave Booth, and Miss Matthews promised never to bother him again.

Called by chance into a strange house to hear the deathbed confession of a man named Robinson, Dr. Harrison learned that Robinson had at one time been a clerk to a lawyer named Murphy who had made Mrs. Harris' will. He learned also that the will which had left Amelia penniless was a false one prepared by Elizabeth and Murphy. Dr. Harrison had Robinson write a confession so that Amelia could get the money that was rightfully hers. The lawyer Murphy was quickly brought to trial and convicted of forgery.

Booth's troubles were now almost at an end. With Dr. Harrison he and Amelia returned home to confront Elizabeth with their knowledge of her scheme. Elizabeth fled to France, where Amelia, relenting, sent her an annual allowance. Booth's adventures had finally taught him not to gamble, and with his faithful Amelia he settled down to a quiet and prosperous life blessed with many children and the invaluable friendship of Dr. Harrison and the Atkinsons.

THE AMERICAN

Type of work: Novel
Author: Henry James (1843-1916)
Type of plot: Psychological realism
Time of plot: Mid-nineteenth century
Locale: Paris, France
First published: 1877

Principal characters:
CHRISTOPHER NEWMAN, an American
MR. TRISTRAM, a friend
MRS. TRISTRAM, his wife
M. NIOCHE, a shopkeeper
MLLE. NIOCHE, his daughter
MADAME DE BELLEGARDE, a French aristocrat
CLAIRE DE CINTRÉ, Madame de Bellegarde's daughter
MARQUIS DE BELLEGARDE, Madame de Bellegarde's older son
VALENTIN DE BELLEGARDE, Madame de Bellegarde's younger son
MRS. BREAD, Madame de Bellegarde's servant

Critique:

In this novel Henry James shows the interreaction of two cultures, the American and the French. His primary interest is not in the action; his aim is to analyze the various psychological situations created by the events of the plot. The author scrutinizes the inner lives of his characters and writes about them in an urbane and polished style uniquely his own.

The Story:

In 1868 Christopher Newman, a young American millionaire, withdrew from business and sailed for Paris. He wanted to loaf, to develop his aesthetic sense, and to find a wife for himself. One day, as he wandered in the Louvre, he made the acquaintance of Mlle. Nioche, a young copyist. She introduced him to her father, an unsuccessful shopkeeper. Newman bought a picture from Mlle. Nioche and contracted to take French lessons from her father.

Later, through the French wife of an American friend named Tristram, he met Claire de Cintré, a young widow, daughter of an English mother and a French father. As a young girl, Claire had been married to Monsieur de Cintré, an evil old man. He had soon died, leaving Claire with a distaste for mar-

riage. In spite of her attitude, Newman saw in her the woman he wished for his wife. But an American businessman was not the person to associate with French aristocracy. On his first call, Newman was kept from entering Claire's house by her elder brother, the Marquis de Bellegarde.

True to his promise, M. Nioche appeared one morning to give Newman his first lesson in French. Newman enjoyed talking to the old man. He learned that Mlle. Nioche dominated her father and that he lived in fear that she would leave him and become the mistress of some rich man. M. Nioche assured Newman that he would shoot her if she did. Newman took pity on the old man and promised him enough money for Mlle. Nioche's dowry if she would paint some more copies for him.

Newman left Paris and traveled through Europe during the summer. When he returned to Paris in the autumn he learned that the Tristrams had been helpful; the Bellegardes were willing to receive him. One evening Claire's younger brother, Valentin, called on Newman and the two men found their opposite points of view a basis for friendship. Valentin envied Newman's liberty to do as he pleased; Newman wished himself acceptable to the society in which the Bellegardes moved. After they had become good friends, Newman told Valentin that he wished to marry his sister and asked Valentin to plead his cause. Warning Newman that his social position was against him, Valentin promised to help the American as much as he could.

Newman confessed his wish to Claire, and asked Madame de Bellegarde, Claire's mother, and the marquis for permission to be her suitor. The permission was given, grudgingly. The Bellegardes needed money in the family.

Newman went to the Louvre to see how Mlle. Nioche was progressing with her copying. There he met Valentin and introduced him to the young lady.

Mrs. Bread, an old English servant of the Bellegardes, assured Newman that he was making progress with his suit. He asked Claire to marry him and she accepted. Meanwhile, Valentin had challenged another man to a duel in a quarrel over Mlle. Nioche. Valentin left for Switzerland with his seconds. The next morning Newman went to see Claire. Mrs. Bread met him at the door and said that Claire was leaving town. Newman demanded an explanation. He was told that the Bellegardes could not allow a commercial person in the family. When he arrived home, he found a telegram from Valentin stating that he had been badly wounded and asking Newman to come at once to Switzerland.

With this double burden of sorrow, Newman arrived in Switzerland and found Valentin near death. Valentin guessed what his family had done and told Newman that Mrs. Bread knew a family secret. If he could get the secret from her, he could make them return Claire to him. Valentin died the next morning.

Newman attended the funeral. Three days later he again called on Claire, who told him that she intended to enter a convent. Newman begged her not to take this step. Desperate, he called on the Bellegardes again and told them that he would uncover their secret. Newman arranged to see Mrs. Bread that night. She told him that Madame de Bellegarde had killed her invalid husband because he had opposed Claire's marriage to M. de Cintré. The death had been judged natural, but Mrs. Bread had in her possession a document which proved that Madame de Bellegarde had murdered her husband. She gave this paper to Newman.

Mrs. Bread left the employ of the Bellegardes and came to keep house for Newman. She told him that Claire had gone to the convent and refused to see anyone, even her own family. The next Sunday Newman went to mass at the convent. After the service he met the Bellegardes walking in the park and showed them a copy of the paper Mrs. Bread had given him.

The next day the marquis called on Newman and offered to pay for the document. Newman refused to sell. He offered, however, to accept Claire in exchange for it. The marquis refused.

Newman found he could not bring himself to reveal the Bellegardes' secret. On the advice of the Tristrams he traveled through the English countryside and in a melancholy mood went to some of the places he had planned to visit on his honeymoon. Then he went to America. Restless, he returned to Paris and learned from Mrs. Tristram that Claire had become a nun.

The next time he went to see Mrs. Tristram, he dropped the secret document on the glowing logs in her fireplace and told her that to expose the Bellegardes now seemed a useless and empty gesture. He intended to leave Paris forever. Mrs. Tristram told him that he probably had not frightened the Bellegardes with his threat, because they knew that they could count on his good nature never to reveal their secret. Newman instinctively looked toward the fireplace. The paper had burned to ashes.

AN AMERICAN TRAGEDY

Type of work: Novel
Author: Theodore Dreiser (1871-1945)
Type of plot: Social criticism
Time of plot: Early twentieth century
Locale: Kansas City, Chicago, and Lycurgus, New York
First published: 1925

Principal characters:
CLYDE GRIFFITHS
ROBERTA ALDEN, his mistress
SAMUEL GRIFFITHS, Clyde's wealthy uncle
SONDRA FINCHLEY, society girl whom Clyde loves

Critique:

An American Tragedy is probably Dreiser's best novel. The title itself is, of course, significant. Dreiser believed that Clyde's downfall was due to the American economic system and he presents a strong indictment against that system. If Clyde had had the privileges of wealth and social position, he would never have been tempted to a moral decision and his consequent ruin. The novel is a powerful document on the theme of social inequality and lack of privilege.

The Story:

When Clyde Griffiths was still a child, his religious-minded parents took him and his brothers and sisters around the streets of various cities, where they prayed and sang in public. The family was always very poor, but the fundamentalist faith of the Griffiths was their hope and mainstay throughout the storms and troubles of life.

Young Clyde was never religious, however, and he always felt ashamed of the existence his parents were living. As soon as he was old enough to make decisions for himself, he decided to go his own way. At sixteen he got a job as a bellboy in a Kansas City hotel. There the salary and the tips he received astonished him. For the first time in his life he had money in his pocket, and he could dress well and enjoy himself. Then a tragedy overwhelmed the family.

Clyde's sister ran away, supposedly to be married. Her elopement was a great blow to the parents, but Clyde himself did not brood over the matter. Life was too pleasant for him; more and more he enjoyed the luxuries which his job provided. He made friends with the other bellhops and joined them in parties that centered around liquor and women. Clyde soon became familiar with drink and brothels.

One day he discovered that his sister was back in town. The man with whom she had run away had deserted her, and she was penniless and pregnant. Knowing his sister needed money, Clyde gave his mother a few dollars for her. He promised to give her more; instead he bought an expensive coat for a girl in the hope that she would yield herself to him. One night he and his friends went on a party in a car that did not belong to them. Coming back from their outing, they ran over a little girl. In their attempt to escape, they wrecked the car. Clyde fled to Chicago.

In Chicago he got work at the Union League Club, where he eventually met his wealthy uncle, Samuel Griffiths. The uncle, who owned a factory in Lycurgus, New York, took a fancy to Clyde and offered him work in the factory. Clyde went to Lycurgus. There his cousin, Gilbert, resented this cousin from the Middle West. The whole family, with the exception of his uncle, considered

Clyde beneath them socially, and would not accept him into their circle. Clyde was given a job at the very bottom of the business, but his uncle soon made him a supervisor.

In the meantime Sondra Finchley, who disliked Gilbert, began to invite Clyde to parties she and her friends often gave. Her main purpose was to annoy Gilbert. Clyde's growing popularity forced the Griffiths to receive him socially, much to Gilbert's disgust.

In the course of his work at the factory Clyde met Roberta Alden, with whom he soon fell in love. Since it was forbidden for a supervisor to mix socially with an employee, they had to meet secretly. Clyde attempted to persuade Roberta to give herself to him, but the girl refused. At last, rather than lose him, she consented and became his mistress.

At the same time Clyde was becoming fascinated by Sondra. He came to love her and hoped to marry her, and thus acquire the wealth and social position for which he yearned. Gradually he began breaking dates with Roberta in order to be with Sondra every moment that she could spare him. Roberta began to be suspicious and eventually found out the truth.

By that time she was pregnant. Clyde went to drug stores for medicine that did not work. He attempted to find a doctor of questionable reputation. Roberta went to see one physician who refused to perform an operation. Clyde and Roberta were both becoming desperate, and Clyde saw his possible marriage to the girl as a dismal ending to all his hopes for a bright future. He told himself that he did not love Roberta, that it was Sondra whom he wished to marry. Roberta asked him to marry her for the sake of her child, saying she would go away afterward, if he wished, so that he could be free of her. Clyde would not agree to her proposal and grew more irritable and worried.

One day he read in the newspaper an item about the accidental drowning of a couple who had gone boating. Slowly a plan began to form in his mind. He told Roberta he would marry her and persuaded her to accompany him to an isolated lake resort. There, as though accidentally, he lunged toward her. She was hit by his camera and fell into the water. Clyde escaped, confident that her drowning would look like an accident, even though he had planned it all carefully.

But he had been clumsy. Letters that he and Roberta had written were found, and when her condition became known he was arrested. His uncle obtained an attorney for him. At his trial, the defense built up an elaborate case in his favor. But in spite of his lawyer's efforts, he was found guilty and sentenced to be electrocuted. His mother came to see him and urged him to save his soul. A clergyman finally succeeded in getting Clyde to write a statement—a declaration that he repented of his sins. It is doubtful whether he did. He died in the electric chair, a young man tempted by his desire for luxury and wealth.

AMPHITRYON

Type of work: Drama
Author: Titus Maccius Plautus (c. 254-184 B.C.)
Type of plot: Farce
Time of plot: The Heroic Age
Locale: Thebes
First presented: c. 185 B.C.

Principal characters:
AMPHITRYON, a Theban general
ALCMENA, his wife
JUPITER, and
MERCURY, Roman gods
SOSIA, Amphitryon's slave

Critique:

Amphitryon is closely akin to many of the other Plautine plays in that it is a comedy of mistaken identity. It has long been believed that a lost Greek play was the original of Plautus' comedy, but no definite proof is available. Amphitryon has had a great influence on modern drama throughout the Western world, and there have been numerous translations, adaptations, and imitations. Such great dramatists as John Dryden, in England, and Molière, in France, made use of its theme and structure. Shakespeare's Comedy of Errors, taken largely from Plautus' The Menaechmi, owes something also to Amphitryon. In very recent times a production of the story as adapted by Jean Giraudoux was successful as a stage play under the title Amphitryon 38.

The Story:

Amphitryon, a Theban, joined the army of Thebes to fight against the Teloboans. When he left for the wars, his wife Alcmena, daughter of Electryon, was pregnant. Nevertheless, in the absence of Amphitryon, Jupiter fell in love with Alcmena and decided that he must enjoy her favors. Disguising himself as Amphitryon, Jupiter appeared to Alcmena as her husband, just returned from a battle with the Teloboans. Alcmena was unable to penetrate the disguise of the impostor and welcomed Jupiter as her husband. Because Jupiter wished to enjoy Alcmena as long as possible, he had the sun, moon, and stars remain fixed, and so the night he spent with Alcmena was long enough for her to conceive and be ready to bring forth a child by Jupiter at the same time she gave birth to the child by her husband.

In the meantime Amphitryon's ship returned to Thebes. Because it was still night Amphitryon's slave, Sosia, fearfully walking the streets of the sleeping town, tried to console himself with the pleasantness of the news he was bringing to its citizens. He thought how well his master, Amphitryon, had handled the war with the Teloboans, how the enemy had refused to arbitrate the dispute over lands, how the battle had been joined, and how Amphitryon had been awarded the golden cup of Pterela as a token of the valor displayed in the battle.

While Sosia soliloquized, Mercury, disguised as Sosia, was listening to every word. Mercury had assumed the disguise to aid his father, Jupiter, in the latter's scheme to make love to Alcmena. As Sosia came through the streets to Amphitryon's house, Mercury, in the guise of Sosia, was guarding the house and the inmates against any disturbance. When Sosia saw Mercury he was afraid, but he went up to the door and tried to enter. Mercury, as Sosia, told him to be gone and beat him with his fists. When Sosia cried out that he was a slave named Sosia who belonged to the household, he received another drubbing.

Sosia, confused, then asked the stranger who he was. Merucry replied that he was

Sosia, a slave of the household. Looking closely, Sosia saw that the person in front of him was dressed and looked exactly like himself. When Sosia went on to ask questions about the household, Mercury answered each one satisfactorily. Sosia asked about his own conduct during the battle; Mercury replied that he had been drinking. Knowing that the answer was correct and sure that someone had stolen his very identity, Sosia ran off to the ship, leaving Mercury to chuckle over the ruse which would prevent Amphitryon from spoiling Jupiter's night with Alcmena.

Eventually Jupiter took leave of Alcmena, after telling her that he had to return to his army, lest the men become bitter because their leader absented himself while they could not. When she grew sad at the thought of his departure, the god, to propitiate her, gave her the golden cup of Pterela which Amphitryon had received as a token of merit in the war. As he left, Jupiter ordered the night to move on in its regular course.

Amphitryon was furious when Sosia returned to the ship. He thought that the slave must be mad or, at the very least, drunk, and he refused to believe that anyone could have stolen the identity of Sosia, as the slave declared. Amphitryon, anxious to discover what was happening, set out for his home immediately, taking Sosia with him. By the time the real Amphitryon and Sosia arrived at the house Jupiter and Mercury had departed. Alcmena was surprised to see her husband return in so short a time. She feared that he was simply testing her fidelity.

Amphitryon, greeting his wife as a husband would after an absence of months, was unable to understand what Alcmena meant when she rebuked him for leaving her a short time before on a pretext of returning to his army. When she told Amphitryon that he had spent the night with her, Amphitryon became suddenly and decidedly angry. Then she mentioned the golden cup of Pterela, which she had received from Jupiter during his visit in disguise. Amphitryon declared she could

not have the cup, for he had it under seal in his possession. But when he opened the chest in which he had put the cup, it was missing; the gods had stolen it to give to Alcmena.

In spite of the evidence produced to show that it was he who had been with his wife, Amphitryon was exceedingly angry and accused his wife of losing her honor by breaking her marriage vows. Alcmena, entirely innocent of any such intent and still believing that her husband had visited her earlier, was hurt and furious at the charges he made. Amphitryon, wishing to be fair but wanting to get to the bottom of the matter, went to get Alcmena's kinsman, Naucrates, who had been with him all night on board the ship. He also told Alcmena that he would divorce her unless she could prove her innocence.

Alcmena was upset at the charges heaped upon her by Amphitryon and made plans to leave the house. Jupiter, sorry for the trouble he had caused, prepared to help her. He appeared to Alcmena in disguise and softened somewhat her anger against Amphitryon. Speaking as Amphitryon, he apologized for the charges made against Alcmena's honesty and virtue.

Amphitryon was unable to find Naucrates and returned to his home. Warned by Mercury, Jupiter appeared as Amphitryon, and a riotous scene, with both men seeming to be Amphitryon, followed, an argument broken off when word came that Alcmena was about to give birth to a child. As Amphitryon prepared to leave, Jupiter struck him unconscious with a thunderbolt. With Jupiter's aid Alcmena painlessly gave birth to two sons, one by Amphitryon and the other by Jupiter. One child was so active that he could hardly be held on his cot to be bathed, and the waiting-women reported that within a few minutes of his birth the baby had strangled two large snakes that entered the room. The voice of Jupiter called out to Alcmena and told her that the lusty lad, Hercules, was his and the other child

99

Amphitryon's.

After the waiting-women had gone, Jupiter himself appeared to Amphitryon and told the husband what had happened. When he warned Amphitryon not to be harsh toward his wife for producing a child by a god, Amphitryon, faced with no other choice, promised to obey all that the god commanded.

AMPHITRYON 38

Type of work: Drama
Author: Jean Giraudoux (1882-1944)
Time: The Heroic Age
Locale: In and about Amphitryon's palace, Thebes
First presented: 1929

Principal characters:
JUPITER, master of the gods
MERCURY, his half-son
AMPHITRYON, a general of Thebes
ALKMENA, his wife
SOSIE, their servant

It is a fact that much influence was exerted on the written works of Jean Giraudoux by the physical productions of all but two of his plays in the theater of actor-director Louis Jouvet. Such a close and mutually advantageous association of managers or directors with a favorite playwright (or vice versa) has become an established pattern in the modern theater. Where highly personal directorial techniques and positive artifice exist in director and author, the published product is likely to contain much that the playwright never conceived in the original manuscript. The result is as it should be, not only living theater, but an art form embodying a power of ideas. In the partnership between Jouvet and Giraudoux, the actor respected and hallowed the poet. The happy circumstance of complete understanding between the writer's temperament and spirit and the actor's interpretative powers insured a rarity in the theater; Giraudoux wrote in a prose style that is practically verse, and the words roll from the tongues of actors with an ease and fluency that many writers strive for but few attain. *Amphitryon 38*, the second production of the Giraudoux-Jouvet collaboration, conclusively established Giraudoux as a playwright of great wit and dexterity.

The recasting of Greek myths into modern molds has long fascinated playwrights. Giraudoux's *Amphitryon 38* may or may not be the thirty-eighth version of that legend. The whimsical title, implying that legends and myths belong to time, sets the mood for the capricious events of the play.

The Amphitryon legend tells us that Jupiter impersonated Amphitryon and gained admission to the bed of his wife Alkmena. From this encounter Hercules was born. On this familiar framework Giraudoux draws fresh character, weaves new plot structure, and imbues the play with wit and ideas impossible in the original. The result is a mixture of theology, high comedy, satire, farce, and matrimonial and political commentary.

Basking on a cloud and spying on their victim, Jupiter and Mercury lay plans for the seduction of Alkmena as if preparing for a tasty banquet. In order to remove Amphitryon from his bedchamber, Mercury suggests that Jupiter have the friendly Athenians declare war on Thebes. Amphitryon, a stalwart general of the Theban army, will hurry to engage the enemy. Mercury will then take the place of Sosie, a servant, and tell Alkmena that Amphitryon will momentarily desert the battle and return to her bed that very night. Jupiter, of course, will impersonate Amphitryon and partake of the delectable Alkmena.

Giraudoux's writings have long been concerned with the causes of war; opportunities for comment on the high level planning of war appear early in *Amphitryon 38* and in most of his other plays. Giraudoux leaves the sordid, clinical reporting of battle for his colleagues; he himself, in play after play, shows us the causes of conflict, frequently a startlingly inhuman cause which frighteningly illustrates the workings of political power.

101

Jupiter arrives before the palace of Alkmena amidst a great clanging noise, for he has forgotten the laws of gravity in his descent. With the help of Mercury he goes through some difficulty in transforming himself from the guise of a god to that of a mortal. Giraudoux sets for himself the difficult task of showing Jupiter the god and Jupiter the mortal simultaneously, a device of dual identity he uses in many of his works.

Mercury has already prepared the faithful wife for the return of Amphitryon, to whom she has promised fidelity or suicide if she knowingly deceives him Jupiter whets his appetite for love by demanding admission to her bed as a lover, not as a huband. It is not enough to love within the union of marriage—the added fillip is to be the tantalizingly illegal husband-seducer. With guileless logic, Alkmena swears fidelity to her husband-wife vows and refuses to open her gates and admit the false husband Jupiter to her chambers as a lover. As her husband, however, he gains easy entry through the gates which had been unlocked all the while.

Mercury thoughtfully holds back the dawn until Jupiter consummates the union, but he takes the precaution of informing the universe that Jupiter has made another mortal conquest so that the proper celestial eruptions will signify the seduction. He also practices a caprice of his own and has the real Amphitryon leave the battle and return to Alkmena the next day. This is only fair, for Jupiter, as has been his practice, will reveal his true identity to Alkmena with the coming of dawn and take leave of her in a burst of ego-satisfying, celestial glory.

But Mercury and Jupiter have underestimated the power of Alkmena. Giraudoux shows us here, as he does in other plays, his strong conviction that the female possesses a brand of intellect of an extraordinary nature; mere feminine wiles and physical beauty are but a means to an end, for the true power of logic and incisiveness belong in the female mind. Alkmena, without deliberation, but because she is a woman, is more than a match for Jupiter. When dawn finally arrives, she is found on her patio placidly eating breakfast fruit, while Jupiter, the traditional ravisher of innocent womanhood, lolls in the drowsy sensuality of her bed. When he joins her, he tries to reveal his true identity, but he is thwarted at every turn by Alkmena's charming and unclouded humanistic approach to divinity. There is a clarity and lack of religious fervency here that might pass for naïveté. But Giraudoux has more in mind than mere flippancy; Alkmena's childlike reasoning is the embodiment of utter simplicity and faithfulness in the kind, matter, and form of the gods. It is a perfectly satisfying and workable theology, uncluttered by the implementalia of animistic practices.

Jupiter, having satisfied his desires, and knowing that if his true identity is revealed Alkmena will kill herself and his unborn seed, now wishes to whet his holy ego by paying a formal celestial visit to Alkmena, thereby legalizing their secret union. Mercury makes the official proclamation of the impending visit, and Leda, Queen of Sparta, who has had some previous knowledge of heavenly unions, pays a duty call on Alkmena. In the scene between the two women Giraudoux epitomizes his own simplicity and clarity of style. With wit and candor, Leda describes her encounter with the heavenly swan. There is no pretense or pomposity here, only statement of fact which becomes a kind of understatement that runs through all of Giraudoux's plays and is particularly apparent in his female characterizations. The expected is avoided, humor for its own sake and wit as a result of syntax. The comedy is the result of character rather than situation, but the situation produces the character.

Alkmena, having discovered that Leda longs for another encounter with Jupiter, persuades the queen to take her place in the bedchamber. Jupiter will visit her in the form of Amphitryon, for he has a habit of appearing in the form most desired by his earthly mates. Leda agrees, and the real

Amphitryon arrives, is mistaken for Jupiter masquerading, and is sent into the palace. Only when Jupiter himself appears to Alkmena does she realize her mistake.

The resolution of the provocative situation is brought about by the resourceful Alkmena. Will Jupiter forego the celestial visit for which she is so evidently unprepared, and remain only friends with her? Jupiter quickly agrees to this strange relationship and assures the suspicious Alkmena that he has never visited her before—as her lover. Jupiter then gives his blessing to Alkmena and Amphitryon and bids them name their unborn child Hercules. As a twinkling afterthought, he offers to be godfather to the child.

Amphitryon 38 may appear to the casual reader or spectator to be comedy that is witty, satirical, and playfully suggestive. In order to appreciate Giraudoux fully, it is necessary to look further for the social and political playwright. Giraudoux does not obscure his point, nor does he burden his audience with a message. Rather, he tantalizes with ideas craftily derived from situation, character, and language that joins the comedy of manners and the comedy of ideas.

ANABASIS

Type of work: Poem
Author: St.-John Perse (Alexis St.-Léger Léger, 1887-   )
Time: The past
Locale: The East
First published: 1924

Principal characters:
The Conqueror-Prince
A Woman
The Mariner

If the distinction between traditional poetry and modern poetry is that the traditional attempts to tell about experiences and emotions (*has* its own subject matter) whereas the modern attempts to present experiences and emotions directly (*is* its own subject matter), then St.-John Perse can be said to be both a traditional and a modern poet at the same time. His five long works—*Éloges, Anabasis, Exile, Winds*, and the recent and magnificent *Seamarks*—have been called "epics of the soul." But each has a more definite, a more tangible, subject matter than the soul itself. *Éloges,* for example, is about childhood; *Seamarks* is a poem in praise of the sea, a majestic symbol enclosing the beginning, perhaps the end, of life.

There is always a coherent system of solid reality behind what T. S. Eliot calls Perse's "logic of the imagination." The modernist surface of the poems may present what seem at first glance to be fascinatingly juxtaposed but apparently disconnected images, brilliantly phrased but completely gratuitous declamations, catalogues of wonderful but bewilderingly selected things. Below the surface, however, is a firm foundation of experience, as systematized and coherent as that of *The Knight's Tale* or *Madame Bovary*.

In Perse's *Anabasis* this concreteness is perhaps more clearly seen, more palpably felt, than in any of his other poems. *Anabasis* is, first of all, a modern poem, reminiscent in its technique of Rimbaud and of the French Symbolist school in general. Relying on the "logic of imagination" rather than on the logic of discourse, it attempts to present experience directly. But as we discover (through the impact of the images and through our resultant awareness of their symbolic meanings) the nature of the experience being presented, we realize that we are being told *about* an experience, as well. Something is happening in an epic more than in the figurative sense of the word, and it is happening somewhere—in time and in a certain place.

The place is important for at least two reasons. It is the East, not the romanticized Orient, not specifically the Far East or the Near East, but the wide expansive East of the great conquerors like Alexander, Tamerlane, Genghis Khan; the East of ancient ceremony, the age-old source of knowledge. As such, it is important symbolically, for the experience presented is in one sense the experience of knowledge—of awareness, of contact with (or, perhaps more accurately, of a return to) reality. A theme that runs through the poem is the theme of power, the power of knowledge—

> The Sun is unmentioned but his power is amongst us
> and the sea at morning like a presumption of the mind.

> Et le soleil n'est point nommé, mais sa puissance est parmi nous
> et la mer au matin comme une présomption de l'esprit.

There is also a recurrence of ceremony.

The language is important for the clarity and immediacy of imagery that it al-

ANABASIS by St.-John Perse. The translation by T. S. Eliot is used with the permission of the American publisher. Copyright, 1938, 1949, by Harcourt, Brace & Co., Inc.

lows the poet. His scene is not the romantic East in any vague or misty sense. For the East is familiar to St.-John Perse as fact. It must be remembered that Perse the poet is also Alexis St.-Léger Léger, a leading French diplomat until the time of the German occupation during World War II. As a diplomat he had spent the early part of his career in China. There, undoubtedly, the keen senses of the poet Perse took in the sights, sounds, and ceremonial ways of that ancient land, the poet's sensibilities transmuting them into images that make up the texture of *Anabasis* and give the poem its strong feeling of reality of the East that underlines its theme of contact with the real:

Milch camels, gentle beneath the
    shears, sewn with mauve
scars, let the hills march forth under
    the facts of the harvest sky
—let them march in silence over the
    pale incandescence of the
plain;

Chamelles douces sous la tonte,
    cousues de mauves
cicatrices, que les collines s'acheminent
    sous les données
du ciel agraire—qu'elles cheminent
    en silence sur les in-
candescences pâles de la plaine;

or

                                    Through
the gate of living chalk we see the
things of the plain: living
    things,
        excellent things!

                            Par la
porte de craie vive on voit les choses
de la plaine: choses
    vivantes, ô choses
        excellentes!

sacrifice of colts on the tombs of chil-
    dren, purification of
widows among the roses and consign-
    ments of green birds in the
courtyards to do honour to the old men;

des sacrifices de poulains sur des
    tombes d'enfants,

des purifications de veuves dans les
    roses et des rassemble-
ments d'oiseaux verts dans les cours en
    l'honneur des vieil-
lards;

many things on the earth to hear and
    to see, living
things among us!

beaucoup de choses sur la terre à
    entendre et à voir,
choses vivantes parmi nous!

Anabasis stands firmly on the substrata of the poet's life in still another way; and again these facts work themselves up to the symbolic surface of the poem. It is a story of a quest and of conquest and of the continuing cycle of these things, for after two conquests the poem ends at the beginning of a new search. The quest, the military advance into the new country, from which the poem derives its name, is at its basic level the search for reality. (Eliot's note, that the title is not an allusion to Xenophon but is used in a literal sense, bears repetition.) The quest is the Rimbaudian search, but with a significant difference: For Perse, there is no descent into hell; there is sufficient reality for him above ground. To capture it, he must return to ancient ways and ceremonies; but the reality is there.

In this princeliness the essential difference between Perse and Rimbaud can be found. The poem begins, "Sur trois grandes saisons m'établissant avec honneur,/j'augure bien du sol où j'ai fondé ma loi":

I have built myself, with honor and
    dignity have I
built myself on three great seasons,
    and it
promises well, the soil whereon I
    have established my Law.

The poet is the Prince, the lawgiver, the conqueror, the founder of cities. As the Prince, Perse can do in this poem the very things that Rimbaud had to leave his poetry to do. Just as there need be no descent, so there need be no flight from poetry into action. Perse's life has been a life of action; for him there has been only the necessity of distilling the experience of the action into poetry. Born on a family-owned Caribbean island, he had been educated as an aristocrat whose destiny was to serve his state. His diplomatic career had been one of authority and responsibility, of power, decision, and restraint. These also go into the distillation. The poem is powerful yet restrained and it is about power, the conquest of those "living things, excellent things."

Thus, while Rimbaud had to descend into hell to find himself and had then to fly to primitivism to find reality, Perse knows himself already as the Prince and knows from experience, not so much the primitive, but the ceremonial and ancient. With these he turns to poetry to find the reality of that experience. Aside from obvious technical similarities—and in technique Perse owes much to Rimbaud, particularly in his use of "poetic prose," which is really poetry measured in terms of paragraphs rather than in terms of lines—the two are alike in their search but different in their means of searching. In this respect, it is Perse who is the true poet: the maker, serene, detached, anonymous.

In this sense, *Anabasis* is a poem by the Prince and is about the quest and conquest by the poet as the Prince. It is divided into ten parts. These parts were indicated in the original merely by Roman numerals, but later they were given titles (actually brief synopses) by Lucien Fabre. Part I, following the beautiful introductory "Song" ("Under the bronze leaves a colt was foaled") ("Il naissait un poulain sous les feuilles de bronze") deals with the "arrival of the Conqueror at the site of the city which he is about to build." The dominating symbols here are those of power, knowledge, and humanity: the Sun, salt, and thirst:

> "Him who has not praised thirst and
> drunk the water of
> the sands from a sallet
> I trust him little in the commerce of

the soul. . . ."

> "Qui n'a, louant la soif, bu l'eau
> des sables dans un
> casque,
> je lui fais peu crédit au commerce
> de l'âme. . . ."

The next three parts—"Tracing the plan of the city," "Consultation of augurs," and "Foundation of the city"—are quieter: ceremony and the business of living take the place of power:

> Come, we are amazed at you, Sun!
> You have told us such
> lies!

> Va! nous nous étonnons de toi, Soleil!
> Tu nous as
> dit de tels mensonges!

Gradually blended with the ceremony are discontentment and lust. The city is good, and it has its own beauty,

> . . . more beauty
> than a ram's skin painted red!

> . . . plus beau
> qu'une peau de belier peinte en rouge!

But the sense of reality is dulled by its busyness and shoddy ways.

In Part V, "Restlessness towards further explorations and conquests," the symbols of knowledge and power begin to serve as counterpoint to those of city and ceremony. They reassert themselves more in Parts VI and VII—"Schemes for foundation and conquest" and "Decision to fare forth"—in which a new, erotic theme is added. Now the lust felt in the second part assumes new meaning. Love joins power, knowledge, humanity; the

> "scented girls, who shall soothe us
> with a breath, silken
> webs"

> "parfumées, qui nous apaiseront d'un
> souffle, ces
> tissus"

join the Sun, the Law, and Salt as dominant symbols. These symbols give way for a time to those of desolation and dryness in Part VIII, "March through the desert"; but they rise with new strength in the penultimate section, "Arrival at the threshold of a great new country." Here the erotic theme reaches its climax in a song reminiscent of the Song of Solomon in its voluptuous grandeur. It is spoken by one of the women (perhaps the Princess) of the city which the Prince is about to capture, and with its note of physical union the triumphant union of all the themes and symbols is announced. The poet-prince, victorious over reality, sees the "living things, excellent things" in a state of full awareness in the final section of the poem. Ceremony, the occupations of the men of the city, serve with love, law, power to make awareness of reality complete, triumph unconditional.

The first half of the final section is called "Acclamation, festivities, repose." The second adds, "Yet the urge towards departure, this time with the mariner." There is still more "out in the vast spaces" where the mariner plots the way. This is the reality of the earth, but there is one more conquest to be made.

There is more for the Prince, but the poem, with its look to the heavens, is complete. The reader has watched the conquest and participated in it; he has been told about an experience and has had it presented directly, thanks to the Prince's knowledge and power.

THE ANABASIS

Type of work: History
Author: Xenophon (c. 430-c. 354 B.C.)
Time: 401-399 B.C.
Locale: Persia, Babylon, Armenia, Paphlagonia, Thrace
First transcribed: Fourth century B.C.

Principal personages:
XENOPHON, the narrator
CYRUS, son of King Darius of Persia
ARTAXERXES, the older son of Darius
TISSAPHERNES, a Persian general
CLEARCHUS, a Spartan exile, a general under Cyrus
CHIRISOPHUS, a Spartan mercenary captain
AGASIAS, a Stymphalian captain in the Greek army
PROXENUS, a Theban mercenary captain under Cyrus

The *Anabasis* is Xenophon's personal account of one of the most amazing marches in history, the march of a Greek army numbering ten thousand men from Babylon to the Black Sea. Xenophon played a leading role in the march and was, in effect, supreme commander of the army, although he refused the actual title. This account of the Persian expedition begins with the recital of Cyrus' effort to wrest the Persian throne from his brother Artaxerxes, but its principal part is concerned with the march from Babylon after the death of Cyrus at the battle of Cunaxa. The narrative is lively and vivid; it presents a great historical event from the perspective of a humane leader who organized his troops and maintained discipline by combining intelligence with the methods of Greek democratic leadership.

After the death of King Darius of Persia, his son Artaxerxes took possession of the throne. Cyrus, the younger son, with the support of his mother, Parysatis, began to build up an army to wrest control of Persia from his brother. By pretending to need troops to fight the Persian general Tissaphernes and the Pisidians, Cyrus acquired armies from the Peloponnese, the Chersonese (under the Spartan exile Clearchus), the Thessalians (under Aristippus), the Boeotians (under Proxenus), the Stymphalians (under Sophaenetus), and the Achaeans (under Socrates, the mercenary).

Cyrus marched from Sardis to Tarsus, gathering the elements of his army. At Tarsus the troops under Clearchus refused to move forward, arguing that they had not been hired to fight against the king. Clearchus dealt with the mutiny by first enlisting the loyalty of the men to himself (by pretending he would stay with them and not with Cyrus) and then by supporting Cyrus' claim that the enemy was not the king, but Abrocomas, one of the king's commanders.

By marches averaging fifteen miles a day Cyrus brought his army from Tarsus to Issus, the last city in Cilicia, where he was joined by ships from the Peloponnese. The march continued through the gates of Cilicia and Syria without opposition.

When Cyrus arrived at the city of Myriandrus, Xenias the Arcadian and Pasion the Megarian deserted the army. Cyrus refused to pursue or punish them, declaring that they had served him well in the past.

The army moved on to the Euphrates and the city of Thapsacus. Here the word was finally given to the Greek soldiers that the campaign was to be against King Artaxerxes. At first the soldiers refused to go further without more pay, but when Menon led his forces across the Euphrates in order to set a good example and to win Cyrus' favor, and when Cyrus promised to give each soldier additional pay, the Greeks crossed the river in force,

108

making the crossing on foot. Since the Euphrates was usually too high for such a passage, the army was encouraged by this good sign.

When they reached the Arabian desert, Cyrus forced the troops to long marches in order to bring them to water and fodder. He kept discipline by ordering important Persians to help with the wagons when the road was difficult. A quarrel between the soldiers of Menon and Clearchus was halted by Cyrus' warning that they would all be destroyed if they fought among themselves.

Orontas, a Persian under Cyrus, attempted to transfer his army to the king's forces, but Cyrus learned of the plan by intercepting a letter from Orontas to the king. At a trial held in Cyrus' tent Orontas was condemned to death. He was never seen again.

Cyrus moved through Babylonia and prepared for battle with King Artaxerxes, but when the king's forces failed to take a stand at a defensive ditch which had been dug, Cyrus proceeded with less caution.

The two armies met at Cunaxa, and the Greeks put the opposing Persian forces to flight. Cyrus, with six hundred Persian cavalry, charged the center of the Persian line in order to reach the king; but after wounding King Artaxerxes, Cyrus was himself killed by a javelin blow. The cavalrymen with Cyrus were killed, except for the forces under Ariaeus, who hastily retreated.

While the main Greek armies under Clearchus and Proxenus were pursuing the Persians, the king's troops broke into Cyrus' camp and seized his mistresses, money, and property. Tissaphernes then joined the king's force and attacked the Greeks, but again the Greeks put the Persians to flight.

Phalinus, a messenger from King Artaxerxes, attempted to force Clearchus to surrender, but the Spartan, regarding the Greeks as victors, refused. The Greeks then allied themselves again with Ariaeus, who had been second to Cyrus,

and pledged their support of him. When Ariaeus refused to attempt further battle against the king, the joint decision was to take a longer route back, putting as much distance as possible between their forces and the king's army.

The Greeks began their march and by accident came close to the king's army, frightening it into retreat. A truce was then arranged, and the king transferred supplies to the Greeks. Finally a treaty was made which provided safe conduct for the Greek army, with Tissaphernes as escort.

Many of the Greek leaders suspected Tissaphernes of treachery, but Clearchus, reassured by a conference with the Persian general, went to Tissaphernes with four of his generals and twenty of his captains in order that those who had been slandering the Persian commander could be named. Then, at a signal from the treacherous Tissaphernes, the Persians massacred the captains and took the generals as prisoners. The generals—Clearchus, Proxenus, Menon, Agias, and Socrates—were taken to the king and beheaded. Ariaeus was discovered to have been involved with Tissaphernes in this act of treachery.

After the capture of the generals, Xenophon, who had accompanied the Greek army at the urging of his friend Proxenus, bolstered the courage of the Greeks and urged that new generals and captains be appointed. The army responded to this decisive act of leadership.

Mithridates, a Persian commander who had been with Cyrus, returned to the Greeks and pretended to be friendly, but he suddenly attacked them and had to be driven back. The Greeks were then pursued by Tissaphernes and harassed by attacks from the Carduchi as they crossed the mountains to Armenia. Hearing that Tiribazus, the governor of Western Armenia who had promised the Greeks safe passage, planned to attack them, the Greek generals ordered a raid on Tiribazus' camp and then quickly resumed the march across snow-covered plains. The soldiers suffered from snow-blindness, frostbite, and bulimia.

To encourage the soldiers, Xenophon often worked and marched with the men. He arranged to procure guides from the Armenians and conceived the idea of capturing the mountain pass beyond the Phasis River by climbing it at night. Chirisophus and Xenophon were the principal leaders of the march.

In the country of the Taochi the Greeks were delayed by an attack from a fortification out of which large boulders were rolled down a hill, but when the stones were exhausted and as the opposing forces—including women and children—began to leap from the walls, the Greeks took possession. Finally, after fighting the Chalybes, the Greeks came within sight of the sea on their arrival at Trapezus.

Chirisophus was sent to secure ships, and the Greeks, now numbering eighty-six hundred troops of their original ten thousand, went on plundering expeditions for supplies. When Chirisophus was delayed, the available ships were loaded with the sick and wounded and with women, children, and baggage, while the rest of the army continued by land. After battling their way through the country of the barbarous Mossynoici, the Greeks arrived in the Euxine. There Xenophon considered founding a city, but he rejected the idea when the others opposed him. Some of the generals were critical of Xenophon's disciplinary measures, but he was able to defend himself against their charges.

The Greeks bought food and also plundered supplies from the Paphlagonians. During their stay in that territory the captains went to Xenophon and asked him to be commander-in-chief of the army, but after reflection and sacrifices to the gods he decided that it would be better both for himself and the army if the command were either kept divided or given to some other man. When Chirisophus was elected commander-in-chief,

Xenophon willingly accepted a subordinate position.

By this time the Greeks had enough ships to carry all their men, and they sailed along the Paphlagonian coast from Harmene, the port of Sinope, to Heraclea, a Greek city in the country of the Maryandyni. The army then split into three parts because of a disagreement about demanding supplies from Heraclea. The Arcadians and Achaeans, who favored the demand, formed one body; Chirisophus, no longer in supreme command, headed a second body of troops; and Xenophon commanded the remainder. The Arcadians landed in Thrace and attacked some villages. When they got into difficulties, they were rescued by Xenophon and his force. At Port Calpe the three armies were reunited.

Many Greeks were killed by the Bithynians while hunting for supplies, but the Greek forces finally achieved victory over them. A quarrel involving Cleander, the Spartan governor of Byzantium, and Agasias, a Greek captain who had rescued one of his men from arrest by Dexippus, a traitorous Greek acting by Cleander's order, was settled by Xenophon's diplomacy.

Eventually the army crossed the straits from Asia to Byzantium. After some difficulty with Anaxibius, a Spartan admiral at Byzantium, the Greeks joined forces with King Seuthes of Thrace and participated in numerous raids on Thracian villages for supplies. When King Seuthes withheld pay from the Greeks, Xenophon was blamed but after a long inquiry, during which Xenophon was accused of being too much concerned with the welfare of the ordinary soldier, King Seuthes finally gave the Greeks the money due them.

Xenophon then led the army out of Thrace by sailing to Lampsacus, marching through the Troad, and crossing Mount Idea to the plain of Thebe. When the army reached Pergamon in Mysia, Xenophon conducted a partially successful raid against the Persian Asidates. He then turned the Greek army over to Thi- bron, the Spartan commander, who used the Greeks to war against Tissaphernes and Pharnabazus, a Persian governor.

THE ANATOMY OF MELANCHOLY

Type of work: Philosophical and scientific treatise
Author: Robert Burton (1577-1640)
First published: 1621

The seventeenth century found men beset by intellectual ferment, even intellectual confusion. Ideas and theories, old and new, clamored for attention and consideration because science had not yet begun to classify, assimilate, accept, and reject what man found in the world about him. More than that, each man attempted, in an age before specialization, to master all, or as much as he could, of human knowledge. Such was the age in which Robert Burton, who styled himself Democritus, Jr., wrote *The Anatomy of Melancholy*, which in many ways exemplifies the times in which it was written.

Burton was more than an educated man; he was a learned man who gave his life to learning, and much of his vast hoard of erudition found its way into his book. Ostensibly a study on melancholy, his work, before it was finished, absorbed into its pages most of the learning of Burton's time, either through his examination of everything he could associate with melancholy or through his many digressions.

The Anatomy of Melancholy is difficult to categorize. Its organization is complex, almost incoherent. An outline for each of the three "partitions" of the book, complicated though each is, does not indicate all that Burton managed to cram into the pages. The device seems really to be Burton's way of following a "scientific" convention of the times. Perhaps the best way to categorize the book is to regard it as an informal and heterogeneous collection of essays on man's dissatisfaction with the universe, as the seventeenth century saw it, and on ways in which that dissatisfaction could be cured. In that sense, at least, the book is a treatise on psychology, although the digressions Burton made are so numerous and involved that the reader sometimes wonders whether the author may not have lost his way.

Burton assuredly had no special theme or thesis he was attempting to prove. One critic has said that all *The Anatomy of Melancholy* proves is that a seventeenth-century classical education could produce an astounding amount of recondite learning. While Burton presented no set of principles, scientific or otherwise, to be proved, he did bring to his work a tremendous zest for learning as he found it in the books he read. This sense of gusto often puts the modern reader at a disadvantage, for Burton larded his paragraphs heavily, perhaps no English writer more so, with tags of Latin prose and poetry, and nowadays too few readers have a knowledge of Latin which enables them to read even tags in that language. The quotations are from countless authorities, many of them long since almost forgotten. A typical page, for example, cites Leo Afer, Lipsius, Zuinger, Seneca, Tully, Livy, Rhasis, Montaltus, Celsus, and Comesius. It is the host of references, allusions, and quotations that makes Burton's style seem heavy. Actually, he wrote in the tradition of Francis Bacon, studiously striving for a plain, even colloquial and racy, style. Like Bacon, too, he frequently begins a topic with an allusion, an anecdote, or a quotation as a springboard and from such a start often moves to whimsy and humor.

Sections of *The Anatomy of Melancholy* are famous for various reasons. The opening letter, a foreword to the reader, is well known for its satirical tone and its catalogue of the follies of mankind. Humor and whimsy account for the popularity of the sections on marriage and bachelorhood, on the "love of learning or overmuch study," and on the nature of spirits. The last "partition," ostensibly on melancholy growing out of love and religion, has many short synopses of world-famous stories. One contemporary critic has shown that if Elizabethan literature had somehow been lost during the intervening centuries, we could reconstruct a good bit of its nature from a study of *The Anatomy of Melancholy* alone.

The pervading tone of the book is satirical, but Burton's satire is always realistic, reflecting the point of view of an objective, even detached, observer of human folly. He begins the first "partition" with a contrast between man as he was in the Garden of Eden and man as he has been since the Fall. The result of man's transgression, according to Burton, is that mankind has since suffered a universal malady, a melancholy that affects both mind and body. Since he regards man as a whole, from a humanistic point of view, he proceeds to mingle sympathetically both religion and science. Much of the learning and many of the notions and theories which found their way into the book are nowadays of historical interest only, such as the analysis of the four humors, the discussion of the understanding and the will (as the seventeenth century used those terms), and the discussion of the nature of angels and devils. Still amusing, however, are his discussions of old age, diet, heredity, exercise, and constipation. While admitting that none is a panacea, Burton offers various cures for melancholy, including prayer, practice of the arts, the study of geography, coffee, traditional games, and moderate amounts of wine and other drink.

Like many another learned man in history, the writer often found himself discoursing on subjects on which there is perhaps no answer. Thus it is in his critique on marriage, which he delivers under the heading of "Cure of Love-Melancholy," that Burton, who himself never married, first quotes twelve reasons in favor of marriage, taking them from Jacobus de Voragine. Those arguments in favor of marriage include statements that a wife is a comfort and assistance in adversity, that she will drive away melancholy at home, that she brings an additional supply of the "sweet company of kinsmen," and that she enables a man to have fair and happy children. Immediately following these arguments, Burton himself adds an equal number as an Antiparodia. He suggests that a wife will aggravate a man's misery in adversity, will scold a man at home, bring a host of needy relatives, and make him a cuckold to rear another man's child. At the last, all Burton can say is that marriage, like much of life, is filled with chance: " 'Tis a hazard both ways I confess, to live single or to marry."

A sound observer of human nature, Burton also showed sympathetic understanding for his fellow beings. Living in an age when religious beliefs held a strong hold on men's and women's emotions, reinforced by fears of a physical Satan and Calvinistic doctrines of predestination and the depravity of man, he advocated that people afflicted by religious melancholy turn from contemplation of the more awful aspects of God and religion to such aspects of God as His infinite mercy and love. He even advocated recreation of an honest sort as an antidote to too much religion. In this, as in other ways, Burton was a man who stood out as being ahead of his time, a rare tribute to a man in any age.

AND QUIET FLOWS THE DON

Type of work: Novel
Author: Mikhail Sholokhov (1905-   )
Type of plot: Historical chronicle
Time of plot: 1913-1918
Locale: Tatarsk, Russia
First published: 1928

Principal characters:
GREGOR MELEKHOV, a Cossack
PIOTRA, Gregor's brother
NATALIA, Gregor's wife
AKSINIA ASTAKHOVA, Gregor's mistress
BUNCHUK, a revolutionary leader

Critique:

Inasmuch as this novel has been so frequently mentioned by the Russians as proof that great art can be produced under their form of government, the book deserves careful consideration. The Russians are quite right in being proud of Sholokhov. *And Quiet Flows the Don* is a good book, free of any propaganda and standing on its own merit as a novel. The book is doubly successful, both as historical narrative and as an interesting story of people living during a difficult period in history.

The Story:

The Melekhov family lived in the small village of Tatarsk, in the Don basin of Tsarist Russia. Gregor, the oldest son, had a love affair with Aksinia, wife of his neighbor, Stepan Astakhova. Stepan was away serving a term in the army. In an effort to make his son settle down, Gregor's father arranged a marriage with Natalia Korshunov. Because Gregor never loved Natalia, their relationship was a cold one. Soon Gregor went openly to Aksinia and the affair became the village scandal.

When he heard the gossip, Gregor's father whipped him. Humiliated and angry, Gregor left home. With Aksinia he became the servant of the Listnitsky family, well-to-do landowners who lived outside the village of Tatarsk. When Aksinia bore him a daughter, Gregor's

father relented enough to pay a visit before Gregor left for the army.

In the meantime, Gregor's wife, Natalia, tried to commit suicide because Gregor did not return her love. She went back to her own home, but the Melekhovs asked her to come to them. She was glad to do so. When Gregor returned to Aksinia, on his first leave from the army, he discovered that she had been unfaithful to him with Eugene Listnitsky, the young officer-son of his employer. Aksinia's daughter had died, and Gregor felt nothing but anger at his mistress. He fought with Eugene and whipped Aksinia as well. Then he returned to his own home, and there he and Natalia became reconciled. During the time he served in the army, Natalia bore him twins, a boy and a girl.

In the war against the Central Powers, Gregor distinguished himself. Wounded, he was awarded the Cross of St. George and so he became the first Chevalier in the village. While in the army, he met his brother, Piotra, and his enemy, Stepan Astakhova, who had sworn to kill him. Nevertheless, on one occasion he saved Stepan's life during an attack.

Discontent was growing among the soldiers. Bolshevik agitators began to talk against the government and against a continuance of the war. In Eugene Listnitsky's company an officer named Bunchuk was the chief agitator. He deserted before Listnitsky could hand him over to the authorities.

Then the provisional government of Kerensky was overthrown and a Soviet Socialist Republic was established. Civil war broke out. The Cossacks, proud of their free heritage, were strongly nationalistic and wanted an autonomous government for the Don region. Many of them joined the counter-revolutionists, under such men as Kornilov. Many returned to their homes in the Don basin. Gregor, joining the revolutionary forces, was made an officer of the Red Army.

Meanwhile the revolutionary troops in Rostov were under attack. Bunchuk, the machine gunner, was prominent in the battle and in the administration of the local revolutionary government. He fell in love with a woman machine gunner, Anna Poodko, who was killed during an attack. The counter-revolutionary troops were successful, and the Red Army troops had to retreat.

Gregor returned to the village and resumed the ordinary life he had led before the war. Soon news came that revolutionary troops were advancing on the village. When his neighbors prepared to flee, Gregor refused to do so. Stories of burning, looting, and rape spread through the countryside. A counter-revolutionary officer attempted to organize the villagers against the approaching enemy troops. He named Gregor as commander, but the nomination was turned down in anger because all the village knew that Gregor sympathized with the Reds, had fought with them. Instead, Gregor's brother Piotra was named commander.

The village forces marched out, Gregor going with them. When they arrived at their destination, they found that the revolutionary troops had already been defeated and that the leaders had been captured. Gregor asked what would happen to them. He was told they would be shot. Then Gregor came face to face with Podtielkov, his old revolutionary leader. When the latter accused him of being a traitor and opportunist, all of Gregor's suppressed feelings of disgust and nationalism burst forth. He reminded Podtielkov that he and other Red leaders had ordered plenty of executions, and he charged that Podtielkov had sold out the Don Cossacks. The revolutionists died prophesying that the revolution would live. Gregor went back to his Cossack village.

ANDERSEN'S FAIRY TALES

(SELECTIONS)

Type of work: Tales
Author: Hans Christian Andersen (1805-1875)
Type of plots: Folk tradition
Time of plots: Indeterminate
Locale: Denmark
First published: At intervals, 1835-1872

Principal characters:
KAREN, who owned the red shoes
THE UGLY DUCKLING
THE SNOW QUEEN
KAY, a little boy
GERDA, a little girl
THE SHEPHERDESS, a china figure
THE CHIMNEYSWEEP, her lover
THE EMPEROR
A TIN SOLDIER
A POOR SOLDIER

Critique:

Hans Christian was a dreamy little boy whose thoughts were very much like those of many of the characters in his fairy tales. When his father died and his mother remarried, he asked to go to Copenhagen to make his fortune. Because a soothsayer had told his mother that Hans would be Denmark's pride, she let him go. When he tried to enter the theater, he had little success. However, influential men realized he was a poet and befriended him until his publications began to attract attention. By the time Hans Christian Andersen died, he was Denmark's most beloved countryman. His tales may be fantastic, running through many moods, but they merely reflect his own character which was equally fantastic, though lovable.

The Stories:

THE RED SHOES

Karen was a little girl so poor that she had to go barefoot in winter. An old mother shoemaker felt sorry for her and made Karen a clumsy pair of shoes out of pieces of red felt. When Karen's mother died, the girl had to wear the red shoes to the funeral. An old lady, seeing Karen walking forlornly behind her mother's coffin, pitied her and took the child home. The old lady thought the red shoes ugly and burned them.

One day Karen saw the queen and the little princess. The princess was dressed all in white, with beautiful red morocco shoes.

When the time came for Karen's confirmation, she needed new shoes. The old lady, almost blind, did not know that the shoes Karen picked out were red ones just like those the princess had worn. During the confirmation Karen could think of nothing but her red shoes.

The next Sunday, as Karen went to her first communion, she met an old soldier with a crutch. After admiring the red shoes, he struck them on the soles and told them to stick fast when Karen danced. During the service she could think only of her shoes. After church she started to dance. The footman had to pick her up and take off her shoes before the old lady could take her home.

At a ball in town Karen could not stop dancing. She danced out through the fields and up to the church. There an angel with a broad sword stopped her and told her she would dance until she became a skeleton, a warning to all other vain children.

She danced day and night until she came to the executioner's house. There she tapped on the window and begged him to come out and cut off her feet. When he chopped off the feet, they and the little red shoes danced off into the forest. The executioner made Karen wooden feet and crutches and taught her a psalm, and the parson gave her a home.

Karen thought she had suffered enough to go to church, but each time she tried she saw the red shoes dancing ahead of her and was afraid. One Sunday she stayed at home. As she heard the organ music, she read her prayer book humbly and begged help from God. Then she saw the angel again, not with a sword but with a green branch covered with roses. As the angel moved the branch, Karen felt that she was being carried off to the church. There she was so thankful that her heart broke and her soul flew up to heaven.

THE UGLY DUCKLING

A mother duck was sitting on a clutch of eggs. When the largest egg did not crack with the rest, an old matriarchal duck warned the setting fowl that she might as well let that egg alone; it would probably turn out to be a turkey. But the egg finally cracked, and out of it came the biggest, ugliest duckling ever seen in the barnyard. The other ducklings pecked it and chased it and made it so unhappy that it felt comfortable only when it was paddling in the pond. The mother duck was proud only of the very fine paddling the ugly duckling did.

The scorn heaped on his head was so bitter that the duckling ran away from home. He spent a miserable winter in the marsh.

When spring came he saw some beautiful white swans settle down on the water. He moved out to admire them as they came toward him with ruffled feathers. He bent down to await their attack, but as he looked in the water he saw that he was no longer a gray ugly duckling but another graceful swan. He was so glad then that he never thought to be proud, but smiled when he heard some children say that he was the handsomest swan they had ever seen.

THE SNOW QUEEN

A very wicked hobgoblin once invented a mirror that reflected everything good as trivial and everything bad as monstrous; a good thought turned into a grin in the mirror. His cohorts carried it all over the earth and finally up to heaven to test the angels. There many good thoughts made the mirror grin so much that it fell out of their hands and splintered as it hit the earth. Each tiny piece could distort as the whole mirror had done.

A tiny piece pierced Kay through the heart and a tiny grain lodged in his eye. Kay had been a happy little boy before that. He used to play with Gerda in their rooms high above the street, and they both admired some rose bushes their parents had planted in boxes spanning the space between their houses. With the glass in his eye and heart, however, Kay saw nothing beautiful and nothing pleased him.

One night he went sledding in the town square. When a lady all in white drove by, he thought her so beautiful that he hitched his sled behind her sleigh as she drove slowly around the square. Suddenly her horses galloped out of the town. The lady looked back at Kay and smiled each time he tried to loosen his sled. Then she stopped the sleigh and told Kay to get in with her. There she wrapped him in her fur coat. She was the Snow Queen. He was nearly frozen, but he did not feel cold after she kissed him, nor did he remember Gerda.

Gerda did not forget Kay, and at last she ran away from home to look for him. She went to the garden of a woman learned in magic and asked all the flowers if they had seen Kay, but the flowers knew only their own stories.

She met a crow who led her to the prince and princess, but they had not heard of Kay. They gave her boots and a muff, and a golden coach to ride in when they sent her on her way.

Robbers stopped the golden coach. At the insistence of a little robber girl, Gerda was left alive, a prisoner in the robber's house. Some wood pigeons in the loft told Gerda that Kay had gone with the Snow Queen to Lapland. Since the reindeer tethered inside the house knew the way to Lapland, the robber girl unloosed him to take Gerda on her way.

The Lapp and the Finn women gave Gerda directions to the Snow Queen's palace and told her that it was only through the goodness of her heart that Kay could be released. When Gerda found Kay, she wept so hard that she melted the piece of mirror out of his heart. Then he wept the splinter from his eye and realized what a vast and empty place he had been in. With thankfulness in her heart, Gerda led Kay out of the snow palace and home.

THE SHEPHERDESS AND THE SWEEP

In the middle of the door of an old wooden parlor cupboard was carved a ridiculous little man with goat's legs, horns on his head, and a beard. The children called him Major-general-field-sergeant-commander-Billy-goat's-legs. He always looked at the china figure of a Shepherdess. Finally he asked the china figure of a Chinaman, who claimed to be her grandfather, if he could marry the Shepherdess. The Chinaman, who could nod his head when he chose, nodded his consent.

The Shepherdess had been engaged to the china figure of a Chimneysweep. She begged him to take her away. That night he used his ladder to help her get off the table. The Chinaman saw them leave and started after them.

Through the stove and up the chimney went the Shepherdess and the Chimneysweep. When she saw how big the world was, the Shepherdess began to cry, and the Chimneysweep had to take her back to the parlor. There they saw the Chinaman broken on the floor. The Shepherdess was distressed, but the Chimneysweep said the Chinaman could be mended and riveted.

The family had the Chinaman riveted so that he was whole again, but he could no longer nod his head. When the Major-general-field-sergeant-commander-Billy-goat's-legs asked again for the Shepherdess, the Chinaman could not nod, and so the Shepherdess and the Chimneysweep stayed together and loved each other until they were broken to pieces.

THE EMPEROR'S NEW CLOTHES

Once there was a foolish Emperor who loved clothes so well that he spent all of the kingdom's money to buy new ones. Two swindlers, who knew the Emperor's weakness, came to town with big looms. They told the people they wove the most beautiful cloth in the world but that it had a magical property. If someone unworthy of his post looked at it, the cloth became invisible.

The Emperor gave them much gold and thread to make him a new outfit. The swindlers set up their looms and worked far into the night. Becoming curious about the materials, the Emperor sent his most trusted minister to see them. When the minister looked at the looms, he saw nothing; but, thinking of the magical property of the cloth, he decided that he was unworthy of his post. Saying nothing to the swindlers, he reported to the Emperor, praising the colors and pattern of the cloth as the swindlers had described it.

Others, looking at the looms, saw nothing and said nothing. Even the Emperor saw nothing when the material was finished and made into clothes, but he also kept silent. He wore his new clothes in a fine procession. All the people called out that his new clothes were beautiful, all except one little boy who said that the Emperor did not have on any clothes at all.

Then there was a buzzing along the line of march. Soon everyone was saying that the Emperor wore no clothes. The Emperor, realizing the truth, held himself stiffer than ever until the procession ended.

THE STEADFAST TIN SOLDIER

A little boy had a set of twenty-five tin soldiers made out of the same tin spoon. Since there was not quite enough tin, one soldier had only one leg, but he stood as solidly as those with two legs.

The one-legged soldier stood on a table and looked longingly at a paper castle, at the door of which stood a paper dancer who wore a gauze dress. A ribbon over her shoulder was held in position by a spangle as big as her face.

One morning the little boy put the one-legged soldier on a window sill. When the window opened, the soldier fell three stories to the ground. There he stuck, head down between two stones, until some boys found him. They made a paper boat for the soldier and sailed it down the gutter. After a time the boat entered a sewer. Beginning to get limp, it settled deeper into the water. Just as the soldier thought he would fall into the water, a fish swallowed him.

When the fish was opened, the soldier found himself in the same house out of which he had fallen. Soon he was back on his table looking at the dancer. For no reason the boy threw him into a roaring fire. Suddenly a draft in the room whisked the dancer off the table and straight to the soldier in the fire. When the fire burned down, the soldier had melted to a small tin heart. All that was left of the dancer was her spangle, burned black.

THE TINDER BOX

A soldier was walking along the highroad one day when a witch stopped him and told him that he could have a lot of money if he would climb down a hollow tree and bring her up a tinder box. Thinking that was an easy way to get money,

he tied a rope around his waist and the witch helped him to climb down inside the tree.

He took along the witch's apron, for on it he had to place the dogs that guarded the chests of money. The first dog, with eyes as big as saucers, guarded a chest full of coppers. The soldier placed the dog on the apron, filled his pockets with coppers, and walked on.

The next dog, with eyes as big as millstones, guarded silver. The soldier placed the dog on the apron, emptied his pockets of coppers, and filled them with silver.

The third dog had eyes as big as the Round Tower. He guarded gold. When the soldier had placed the dog on the apron, he emptied his pockets of silver and filled them, his knapsack, his cap and his boots with gold. Then he called to the witch to pull him up.

When she refused to tell him why she wanted the tinder box, he cut off her head and started for town. There he lived in splendor and gave alms to the poor, for he was good-hearted.

He heard of a beautiful princess who was kept locked up because of a prophecy that she would marry a common soldier. Idly he thought of ways to see her.

When his money ran out, and he had no candle, he remembered that there was a piece of candle in the tinder box. As he struck the box to light the candle, the door flew open and the dog with eyes like saucers burst in, asking what the soldier wanted. When he asked for money, the dog brought it back immediately. Then he found that he could call the second dog by striking the box twice, and the third dog by striking it three times. When he asked the dogs to bring the princess, she was brought to his room.

The king and queen had him thrown into prison when they caught him. There he was helpless until a little boy to whom he called brought the tinder box to him.

When the soldier was about to be hanged, he asked permission to smoke a last pipe. Then he pulled out his tinder box and hit once, twice, three times. All three dogs came to rout the king's men and free the soldier. The people were so impressed that they made the soldier king and the princess his queen.

ANDRIA

Type of work: Drama
Author: Terence (Publius Terentius Afer, c. 190-159 B.C.)
Type of plot: Comedy
Time of plot: Second century B.C.
Locale: Athens
First presented: 166 B.C.

Principal characters:
SIMO, a wealthy Athenian
PAMPHILUS, Simo's son
GLYCERIUM, beloved of Pamphilus
DAVUS, slave of Pamphilus
CHREMES, another wealthy Athenian, friend of Simo
CRITO, a traveler from Andros
CHARINUS, a suitor for the daughter of Chremes

Critique:

Although *Andria* was Terence's first play, it shows those characteristics for which this dramatist was noted throughout his career. As in all his plays, the action is closely knit, with no digressions, and the comedy is of a more serious turn than the popular slapstick humor. The language is natural. Actually, the plot was not new. Terence admitted that he had adapted his drama from two plays by Menander, the Greek dramatist who wrote *The Lady of Andros* and *The Lady of Perinthos.* The whole story turns, like so many Greek and Latin comedies, on the theme of mistaken identity. The modern reader will undoubtedly compare it to Shakespeare's *Comedy of Errors,* which in turn was freely adapted from *The Menaechmi* of Plautus. Nor have modern authors ceased to adapt from Terence's *Andria.* It was the basis of Baron's *L'Andrienne,* Sir Richard Steele's *The Conscious Lovers,* and Thornton Wilder's novel, *The Woman of Andros.*

The Story:

One day Simo confided in a servant that he had been pleased with his son Pamphilus until that very afternoon, when he had discovered that his son was in love with Glycerium, the sister of a courtesan who had recently died. Simo, who wished to marry his son to the daughter of his friend Chremes, saw in his son's love for Glycerium a threat to his plans.

Later Simo encountered his son's slave, Davus, and threatened him with severe punishment. Simo was afraid that Davus, a clever fellow, would help Pamphilus thwart his father's plans for his future. Davus immediately saw that some scheme would have to be put into action quickly if the love between Pamphilus and Glycerium were to end in marriage, even though Glycerium was already pregnant by Pamphilus.

Pamphilus' own scheme was to acknowledge the expected infant and then claim that Glycerium was actually an Athenian whose father had been shipwrecked on Andros and who had been reared by the family of the courtesan as a foster child. But Davus laughed at the story and felt that no one would believe it.

Pamphilus, warned that his father wanted him to marry that very day, was greatly troubled. He was put at ease, however, when Davus heard that the approaching marriage to Chremes' daughter had been refused by the girl's father, for Chremes had also learned of the affair between Pamphilus and the courtesan's sister. Davus told Pamphilus to agree to the marriage for the time being. Before long, he added, some way out of the predicament might be found.

Charinus met Davus and Pamphilus and told them that he was in love with Chremes' daughter. Pamphilus said he had no desire to marry the girl and that Charinus was welcome to her. Not knowing the true reason for Pamphilus' assent,

121

Charinus was thrown into despair within the hour, when he heard Pamphilus agree to marry Chremes' daughter.

Later, while Simo, the father, and Davus stood before the door of Glycerium's residence, they heard the servants send for a midwife. Simo was angry, thinking that Davus was trying to trick him into believing that Glycerium was having a child by his son. A short time later Glycerium was delivered of a baby boy. When Simo heard the news, he still thought Davus was trying to trick him and refused to believe what he heard.

Meanwhile Pamphilus waited patiently, believing that no marriage with Chremes' daughter had been arranged. While he waited, however, his father met Chremes on the street, and they agreed once more to marry their children to one another.

When Davus reported the latest development to Pamphilus, the young man was furious, for it now seemed certain he would never be able to marry the woman he loved. Glycerium, from her confinement bed, sent for Pamphilus to learn what progress he was making in his plans to marry her.

Davus, to prevent the marriage between Pamphilus and Chremes' daughter, had Glycerium's maidservant lay the infant on a bed of verbena in front of Simo's door. Chremes came up the street and saw the child. Davus, pretending that he did not see Chremes, began to argue with Glycerium's servant. During the argument the fact that the child was the son of Pamphilus and Glycerium was shouted aloud. Chremes stormed into Simo's house to withdraw again his offer of marriage between Pamphilus and his daughter.

Soon afterward Crito, a cousin of the dead courtesan, came looking for the house of his dead cousin. As soon as he found it, he asked the maidservant if Glycerium had found her parents in Athens. Davus, looking after Pamphilus' interests, overheard the conversation and entered the house after them.

When Davus left the house a few minutes later, he met Simo, who ordered the slave chained and thrown into a dungeon. While Chremes and Simo were talking over the delayed wedding, Pamphilus also left the house. After some argument the young man convinced his father that Crito had proof that Glycerium was an Athenian and Pamphilus would have to marry her because they had had a child. Pamphilus re-entered the house where Glycerium was lodged and emerged presently with Crito.

Chremes immediately recognized Crito as an acquaintance from Andros. Simo was finally convinced that Crito was an honorable man from that island. Crito then told how Phania, a citizen of Athens, had been shipwrecked on Andros and had died there. With the man had been a little girl, whom the dying man said was his brother's daughter. Chremes then broke into the story to exclaim that Glycerium must be his own daughter, because Phania had been his brother. When Chremes asked what the girl's name had been, Crito said that her name had been changed to Glycerium from Pasibula, the name of Chremes' daughter.

Everyone congratulated Chremes on finding his long-lost child. Pamphilus reminded his father that there could be no barrier to the marriage since Glycerium, too, was a daughter of Chremes and, according to the law, Pamphilus would have to marry her as her seducer. Chremes, overjoyed, declared that he would give a dower of ten talents to the bride.

Davus was freed from the dungeon, and Pamphilus told him all that had occurred. While they spoke, Charinus entered, happy that the other daughter of Chremes was now free to be his bride. The father gave ready consent to Charinus' suit and said that his only objection had been a desire to have his family united with Simo's. In addition, he promised that Charinus would receive a large dowry as well as a wife.

ANDROMACHE

Type of work: Drama
Author: Euripides (c. 485-c. 406 B.C.)
Type of plot: Tragedy of intrigue
Time of plot: About a decade after the Trojan War
Locale: The temple of Thetis in Thessaly
First presented: c. 426 B.C.

Principal characters:
ANDROMACHE, Hector's widow, slave to Neoptolemus
HERMIONE, wife of Neoptolemus and daughter of Menelaus
MENELAUS, King of Sparta
PELEUS, Neoptolemus' grandfather
MOLOSSUS, son of Andromache and Neoptolemus
ORESTES, Agamemnon's son
THETIS, goddess and dead wife of Peleus
CHORUS OF PYTHIAN MAIDENS

Critique:

Andromache is one of Euripides' most poorly constructed plays; both the plot line and the focus on personalities undergo a radical shift in the middle. It moves, not by development out of the original situation, but by accretion, and new characters are introduced with no preparation whatsoever. The first half of the play concerns Hermione's foiled plot against her rival, Andromache; the second deals with Orestes' treacherous murder of his rival, Neoptolemus; and there is only a very tenuous connection between the two. Written shortly after the outbreak of the war between Athens and Sparta, the play seems to be strongly motivated by Euripides' intense hatred of Spartan characteristics as they are shown in the arrogance of Hermione, the treachery of Orestes, and the criminal brutality of Menelaus. Although flawed, *Andromache* nevertheless has a certain hardness and brilliance that are fascinating.

The Story:

After the death of Hector and the fall of Troy, Andromache had been given as a special prize to Neoptolemus, son of Achilles. As his slave and concubine, she had borne a son, Molossus, thereby arousing the jealous wrath of Hermione, the barren wife of Neoptolemus. Fearing Hermione's hatred and sensing impend-

ing doom, Andromache sought sanctuary in the sacred grounds of the temple of Thetis, after secretly sending her son to a neighbor for safekeeping.

Hermione appeared at the temple and accused Andromache of seeking to oust her, taunted her for bearing a son to Hector's slayer, and threatened her with death. Andromache protested that as an aging woman and a helpless slave she would be mad to compete with Hermione and that she herself had gracefully accepted Hector's illegitimate children rather than let herself be corrupted by jealousy. Hermione, unmoved by these arguments, left the temple after threatening that she would find bait that would lure Andromache from her sanctuary.

She was true to her word, for soon afterward Menelaus arrived leading Molossus by the hand. The Spartan king warned that he would kill the boy on the spot if Andromache would not emerge and offer up her own life instead. Once again Andromache argued with a Spartan, pointing out that murder would surely pollute his reputation and that Neoptolemus would never condone the death of his only son. But Menelaus was adamant, and Andromache emerged from the sanctuary to learn that both she and her son were marked for slaughter. But before the order for execution could be

123

carried out, the aged Peleus appeared and in response to her supplication commanded that her bonds be loosened. Furious with Menelaus, Peleus denounced Spartan cowardice and treachery and ordered the king to leave Thessaly at once and to take his barren daughter with him. Menelaus, however, announced that he was leaving with his army only in order to vanquish a city hostile to Sparta, after which he would return to confront Neoptolemus himself and settle the matter of his daughter's status in Thessaly.

After everyone had left the temple, a terribly distraught Hermione entered carrying a sword with which she intended to commit suicide. After her nurse had wrested the sword from her, Hermione, in great anguish, lamented the horrible deed she had plotted and chanted her fear that Neoptolemus would banish her. Suddenly Orestes appeared, claiming that he was merely passing through on his way to the oracle at Dodona, and Hermione threw herself at his feet. Because Orestes had once been betrothed to Hermione and had always loved her, he revealed that he had actually come to carry her off; he was prepared to murder her husband even if the deed involved sacrilegious treachery. Hermione's taunts at Andromache were now ironically being fulfilled upon herself.

After the desperate pair had fled, Peleus appeared. Before he could question the chorus about the fearful rumors he had heard, a messenger brought sad news. Peleus' grandson, Neoptolemus, was dead; he had been horribly murdered and mutilated by Orestes and his brigands while praying to the gods in the temple of Phoebus. The body of Neoptolemus was then carried in on a bier and bereaved old Peleus lamented the end of his line, for the only son of his only son was now dead. Throwing his scepter on the ground, the distraught king resolved to grovel in the dust until his death. At that moment the dim form of the divine Thetis, the goddess who had once been his wife, appeared hovering in mid-air. She commanded her husband to cease his mourning and take the body of Neoptolemus to be buried at the Pythian altar as a reproach to the Spartans. She further commanded that he take Andromache and Neoptolemus' son to Helenus, whom Andromache would marry so that the line of Peleus could continue. After this mission Peleus himself would be converted into a god and live with Thetis in the halls of Nereus forever. Peleus consented, moralizing that every prudent man should take heed to marry a wife of noble stock and give his daughter to a good husband.

ANDROMACHE

Type of work: Drama
Author: Jean Baptiste Racine (1639-1699)
Type of plot: Neo-classical tragedy
Time of plot: Shortly after the close of the Trojan War
Locale: Epirus
First presented: 1667

Principal characters:
ANDROMACHE, widow of Hector and captive of Pyrrhus
PYRRHUS, King of Epirus and son of Achilles
ORESTES, son of Agamemnon and spurned suitor of Hermione
HERMIONE, daughter of Helen and affianced bride of Pyrrhus
PYLADES, Orestes' friend and companion

Critique:

The appearance of *Andromache* on the stage was one of the great events of the French theater for 1667 and for all time. This play has been acted more times than any other drama by Racine. Its dramatic simplicity is outstanding. Each of the four leading characters is dominated by a single emotion. Orestes loves Hermione to distraction; Hermione is overwhelmed by Pyrrhus; Pyrrhus is madly in love with Andromache; Andromache can think only of the dead Hector and their child, Astyanax. Suffering of an emotional kind drives the four characters into a maze of spite, love, hate, and vengeance. At the end only Andromache is left—Pyrrhus and Hermione are dead, and Orestes has gone mad. The distinction is important, for Racine killed off the three who were led by their personal passions, but he saved the sole character whose unselfish grief was for others.

The Story:

Orestes, son of the Greek leader, Agamemnon, journeyed to Epirus to tell Pyrrhus, King of Epirus, that the Greeks were fearful of Astyanax, the young son of Hector and Andromache, who might someday try to avenge the fall of Troy. Because of their fear, they had sent Orestes to request that Pyrrhus put Astyanax to death.

Pyrrhus had fallen in love with Andromache, however, and at first, afraid of losing her love, he refused to grant the request. To Orestes, who had long loved Hermione, betrothed of Pyrrhus, the news of Pyrrhus' love for Andromache was welcome. Orestes thought he saw in the situation a chance for him to win Hermione for his wife. Orestes' friend Pylades was amazed, for Orestes had previously sworn that his love for Hermione had degenerated into hate because she spurned him.

When Pyrrhus refused to kill Astyanax or turn the child over to the Greeks, Orestes threatened him. Pyrrhus swore that he would make Epirus a second Troy before he permitted the death of Astyanax. Pyrrhus, hoping that his decision would lead her to forget her dead husband, told Andromache what he had done, but she made no response to his overtures. Angered, Pyrrhus told her that unless she married him the child would die.

Meanwhile Hermione, spurned by Pyrrhus, was trying to decide whether she loved or hated the king, and whether she wanted to flee with Orestes. When Pyrrhus, rebuffed by Andromache, went to her, they decided that they were still in love. Reconciled to Hermione, Pyrrhus promised to love only her and to give Astyanax to the Greeks.

But Hermione, changing her mind, prepared to flee with Orestes to inflict punishment on Pyrrhus, after Orestes told her that Pyrrhus had renewed his suit of Andromache. Pyrrhus returned while they spoke and announced that he was ready to give over the boy to the Greeks because Andromache had again spurned his love and aid.

Convinced that Pyrrhus had decided to

marry Hermione only to keep her from her Greek lover, Orestes plotted to carry off the girl. Pylades, his friend, agreed to help in the abduction. When Hermione met Orestes, she spoke only of her approaching marriage to Pyrrhus, whom she still loved. While they talked, Andromache entered the room and begged Hermione to protect Astyanax, whom Pyrrhus had determined to kill. Andromache reminded Hermione that Hector had championed Helen, Hermione's mother, when the Trojans had wished to murder her. Hermione refused to listen and scorned Andromache's request.

Andromache then pleaded with Pyrrhus, but he told her that her plea came too late. At last, when Andromache vowed to kill herself, her vow and tears moved the vacillating Pyrrhus, who once again told her that he would marry her instead of Hermione and champion the boy against the Greeks. But Andromache refused to save her son by marrying her captor and former enemy. After a conference with her waiting-woman, she decided to consult her husband's ghost. The result of that conference was a decision to marry Pyrrhus, thus bringing Astyanax under Pyrrhus' protection, and then to kill herself.

Hermione, furious when she learned that on the following day Pyrrhus intended to marry Andromache, sent for Orestes and told him that she wanted his help in avenging herself on the king. Without promising herself to Orestes, she asked him to kill Pyrrhus during the wedding ceremony.

At first Orestes demurred. Not wishing to become an assassin, he wanted to declare war on Pyrrhus and earn glory on the battlefield. But at Hermione's urging he finally agreed to the murder. She told

him that it would be easy to commit the crime, because the king's guards had been sent to watch over Astyanax and none had been ordered to guard the nuptial ceremonies. She finally added that after the murder she would become Orestes' bride.

After Orestes left, Pyrrhus came once more to Hermione. Hoping that the king had changed his mind again, she sent her serving-woman to tell Orestes not to act until he had further word from her. But Pyrrhus had come to tell her only that he intended to marry Andromache, come what would. Hermione vowed she would have revenge.

This was her message to Orestes. Finally Orestes arrived to inform her that the deed was done; Pyrrhus had died at the hands of Orestes' soldiers.

Hermione, turning on Orestes, declared that she disowned such savagery and would have no more to do with him because he had killed the man she loved. When Orestes argued with her that she had persuaded him to commit the murder for her sake, her only defense was that she had been distraught at having her love spurned by Pyrrhus and that Orestes should not have listened to her. When she rushed out of the room, Pylades came with the Greek warriors to warn Orestes that if they were to escape the wrath of Pyrrhus' subjects they must take ship and sail away from Epirus at once. The people, they said, were obeying Andromache as their queen. And Hermione was dead; she had run into the temple and thrown herself on Pyrrhus' body, after stabbing herself with mortal wounds.

Hearing that news, Orestes turned mad and fainted in his agony. His men quickly took him away and made their escape from Epirus.

ÁNGEL GUERRA

Type of work: Novel
Author: Benito Pérez Galdós (1843-1920)
Type of plot: Political and religious tragedy
Time of plot: Late nineteenth century
Locale: Madrid and Toledo
First published: 1890-1891

Principal characters:
ÁNGEL GUERRA, a widower
DOÑA SALES, his mother
ENCARNACIÓN ("CIÓN"), his seven-year-old daughter
LORENZA ("LERÉ"), Doña Sales' nurse
ARÍSTIDES GARCÍA BABEL, an embezzler
FAUSTO GARCÍA BABEL, his dishonest brother
DULCENOMBRE ("DULCE") BABEL, Ángel's sometime mistress
PADRE CASADO, a priest

Critique:

Pérez Galdós, a great figure in Spanish literature of the late nineteenth century, wrote thirty novels in addition to the forty-six in his series called National Episodes. *Ángel Guerra* belongs to a group of about eight that present a picture of religious faith and the results of fanaticism on Spanish life. This group includes some of his best, *Doña Perfecta* (1876), *Gloria* (1876-1877), *The Family of León Roch* (1879), and *The Crazy Woman in the House* (1892). *Ángel Guerra* is the story of a politician and a mystic, a character whose names, "Angel" and "War," were intended to present his dual personality. By environment he was made a rebel who hated his mother, yet received from her the wealth that meant his personal freedom. Not only does the novel depict the working of fate, but it also presents a philosophy of religion and the influence of a deeply religious atmosphere on a man who was essentially destructive and modern. Besides the intermingling of human and religious love, the novel contains a realistic touch in having violence and crime cure idealism. As always, in the novels of this great local color artist, the painting of the background is unforgettable: the summer houses in the suburbs of Toledo, the narrow cobbled streets of the city, and the noble, austere cathedral.

The Story:

Ángel Guerra, thirty and a widower, father of an adored daughter Encarnación, had spent an unhappy childhood. An idealist, he had turned to the revolutionists, thinking that if everything were overthrown life could be improved in the rebuilding. His mother, Doña Sales, disapproved of him and treated him like a child, even after he was married. An extremely rich woman, she tried to starve her liberal-minded son into submission to her wishes, but she managed only to drive him into the company of advocates of violence, the Babels.

The Babel household contained an unsavory group. With Babel lived his brother, Captain Agapito, an ex-slaver, and his children, drunken Matías and slippery Policarpo. Babel's family was as bad. Arístides, an embezzler, had fled from Cuba; Fausto had been dismissed from the post office for peculation; and Dulcenombre had love affairs from which the whole family profited. She became attracted to Ángel and lived with him for a year in order to escape her family, but he was too poor to marry her.

At last the crimes of the Babels sent Ángel also into hiding, with a wounded hand that Dulce bandaged. After a month of skulking he went home to find his mother, Doña Sales, dying. Leré, the twenty-year-old tutor of "Ción," was nursing her. At first she and Dr. Maquis re-

127

fused to let Ángel see the sick woman, but finally he was allowed to be with her during her dying moments. She left him a comfortable fortune, but when he tried to use it selfishly the convent-trained Leré shamed him into carrying out his mother's desires with it.

Troubles mounted for Ángel. Dulce, his mistress, became ill. Ción died. Leré announced she was entering a convent in Toledo. In his loneliness, Ángel followed her, and when Dulce came looking for him he had already gone. Following the advice of her uncle, Captain Agapito, she sought solace in alcohol.

Ángel had both rich and poor relatives in Toledo. He became a boarder at the home of Teresa Pantoja, along with two priests. Leré was already working for one of the nursing orders. Discussing life with her, and moved by his loneliness, his affection for her, and the religious atmosphere of Toledo, Ángel also found himself seeking the comfort of the Church.

The appointment of one Babel to a government post in Toledo brought the whole family, including Dulce, to that city. To escape them, Ángel went to live with wealthy relatives in the outskirts of Toledo. Leré demanded that he marry Dulce or never see her again. Going to discuss the situation with Dulce, Ángel found her disgustingly drunk. In a quarrel that followed, he almost killed Arístides. Again, at Leré's bidding, he went to Arístides to ask forgiveness. He learned that Dulce's illness had cured her of her liking for alcohol and that she was planning to enter a convent.

Ángel's many conversations with Leré caused considerable gossip, with the result that the Mother Superior called the girl in for questioning. Although she was declared innocent, the lack of trust so angered Ángel that he declared his intention of founding a convent to be put in Leré's charge. She declared that she would accept his plan only if he became a priest. Ángel agreed.

Padre Casado, a clear-sighted priest, whose preference for farming instead of books had prevented his advance in the Church, prepared Ángel for taking holy orders. One night, while he and Leré were nursing an ailing priest, Ángel felt desire for the girl. Later he confessed his carnal thoughts to Padre Casado, who could not understand any sexual attraction to a woman in plain nun's clothing. They also discussed Ángel's plans for the convent, and his philosophy for improving mankind by a Christian revolution.

Ángel tried to prove his theories when Arístides, again caught in crime, and Fausto, also fleeing justice, begged him for help and he hid them. Joined by Policarpo, they demanded money for a flight to Portugal. Ángel was stabbed during a quarrel over his refusal. Although badly wounded, he would not give the police the name of his assailant.

Leré came to nurse Ángel. The dying man had no regrets. Like Don Quixote, he felt that the approach of death restored his reason and also solved his problems. He would not have made a good priest, he declared. He apportioned his wealth, designating most for Leré's project, some for relatives and servants, before he died. Leré, stifling her sorrow, returned to the convent where she was assigned to nurse another patient.

ANNA CHRISTIE

Type of work: Drama
Author: Eugene O'Neill (1888-1953)
Type of plot: Social realism
Time of plot: Early twentieth century
Locale: Johnny the Priest's saloon, New York City, and Provincetown harbor
First presented: 1921

Principal characters:
CHRIS CHRISTOPHERSON, captain of the barge, *Simeon Winthrop*
ANNA, his daughter
MAT BURKE, a stoker
MARTHY OWEN, a prostitute

Critique:

O'Neill claims rightfully that the ending of his play was not intended to be a happy one. The play illustrates O'Neill's idea that the forces which control our destinies and which seemingly lie outside ourselves are really within. O'Neill agrees with Galsworthy in maintaining that man's character is his fate and in *Anna Christie* he proves it.

The Story:

Old Chris Christopherson looked upon the sea as the symbol of a malignant fate. True, he was now skipper of the coal barge, *Simeon Winthrop*, but in his younger days he had been an able seaman and bosun on the old windjammers and had visited every port in the world. As far back as he knew, the men of his family in Sweden had followed the sea. His father died aboard ship in the Indian Ocean, and two of his brothers were drowned. Nor was the curse of the sea confined to the men in the family. After the news of her husband's and her sons' deaths, Chris' mother had died of a broken heart. Unable to bear the loneliness of being a sailor's wife, his own wife had brought their young daughter, Anna, to America to live with some cousins on a farm in Minnesota. Here Anna's mother had died, and the girl was brought up by her relatives.

Chris had not seen his daughter for almost twenty years. One day while he was having a drink at Johnny the Priest's saloon near South Street in New York City, he received a postcard from St. Louis telling him that Anna was on her way to New York.

This news threw Chris into something of a panic, for living on the barge with him was an ancient prostitute named Marthy. Chris decided to get rid of the woman. Being a kind-hearted soul and genuinely fond of Marthy, he disliked the idea of turning her out. But Marthy said that Chris had always treated her decently, and she would move on to someone else.

When Marthy caught a glimpse of Chris's daughter, she was shocked. Anna was twenty years old and pretty in a buxom sort of way. But her painted face and cheap showy clothes were tell-tale evidence of what she was—a prostitute. Marthy wondered what Chris' reaction was going to be.

In his eyes, however, Anna was the innocent child he had always imagined her to be, and he was even hesitant about ordering wine to celebrate their reunion. Life on the barge was an entirely new experience for Anna Christopherson. She came to love the sea and to respond to its beauty with the same intensity with which her father responded to its malignance. With the soothing effect of her new environment, and the presence of her father's gentleness and simplicity, Anna began to lose some of her hardness and to build up some faith in men.

One night, while the *Simeon Winthrop* was anchored in the outer harbor of Provincetown, Massachusetts, Chris heard cries for help. He pulled aboard the barge four men from a boat which had been drifting for five days after the wreck of their ship. One of the men, an Irishman named Mat Burke, took an immediate fancy to Anna, and even in his weakened condition he made it clear that he intended to have Anna for his own.

Mat Burke represented everything in life that Chris hated. In the first place, he was a stoker on a steamship, an occupation the old windjammer sailor regarded as beneath contempt. Secondly, Burke followed the sea and so was connected in the old Swede's mind with inevitable tragedy. But lastly, and most important from Chris' viewpoint, Mat was obviously in love with Anna and wanted to take her away from him. But to Anna Mat represented all that she had always wanted in life. At first she was naturally suspicious of his Irish glibness, but she soon began to see that underneath his voluble exterior there were some genuine convictions, a basic core of integrity which gave her as a woman a sense of security, as well as, in the light of her own past, a gnawing fear.

Her father and Mat were mortal enemies from the start. This conflict reached its climax one day in the cabin when Chris, goaded on by the Irishman's taunts, came at Mat with a knife, intending to kill him. Anna came in as Mat overpowered the old man. She realized that they were fighting over her as if she were a piece of property which must belong to one or the other.

This situation was so close to her previous experience with men that she made them both listen to a confession of the truth about herself, of which apparently neither of them had been aware. She informed her father that his romantic picture of her idyllic life on the Minnesota farm was untrue from beginning to end, that she had been worked relentlessly by her relatives, and that at sixteen she had been seduced by one of her cousins. At last she had gone to St. Louis and entered a bawdy house, where her experience with men did not differ greatly from what she had known on the farm. She informed Mat that for the first time in her life she had realized what love might be. But Mat, having neither intelligence nor imagination enough to appreciate Anna's sincerity, angrily called her names and left the barge in disgust. Chris followed him, and the two men proceeded to get drunk. Anna waited on the *Simeon Winthrop* for two days, hoping that Mat would return. Finally she prepared to go to New York and resume her old profession.

Her father was the first to return with the news that to save her from going back to the old life he had signed on the *Londonderry,* a steamer to Capetown, Africa, and had made arrangements for his pay to be turned over to Anna. When Mat returned, Anna felt sure he had come back merely to kill her. He was bruised and bloody from waterfront fights. He too had signed on the *Londonderry,* and the irony of her father and Mat on the same boat struck Anna as funny. Finally she made Mat see that she had hated the men who had bought her and that all she wanted was the assurance of one man's love.

Chris was glad that Anna and Mat were reconciled, were going to be married and be happy, for he now realized that much of Anna's past misery was his own fault. But at the same time he wondered what tricks the malignant sea would play on Anna and Mat in the future.

ANNA KARÉNINA

Type of work: Novel
Author: Count Leo Tolstoy (1828-1910)
Type of plot: Social criticism
Time of plot: Nineteenth century
Locale: Russia
First published: 1875-1877

Principal characters:
ANNA KARÉNINA
ALEXEI KARÉNIN, her husband
COUNT VRONSKY, her lover
STEPAN OBLONSKY, her brother
KITTY SHTCHERBATSKY, Stepan's sister-in-law
KONSTANTINE LEVIN, in love with Kitty

Critique:

Anna Karénina, one of Tolstoy's masterpieces, is distinguished by its realism. The novel contains two plots: the tragedy of Madame Karénina, in love with a man who is not her husband, and the story of Konstantine Levin, a sensitive man whose personal philosophy is Tolstoy's reason for writing about him. The story of Anna is an absorbing one and true; the person of Levin reflects Tolstoy's own ideas about the Russian society in which he lived. Thus the book is a closely knit plot of a woman bound in the fetters of the Russian social system and a philosophy of life which attempts to untangle the maze of incongruities present in this society.

The Story:

Anna Karénina, the sister of Stepan Oblonsky, came to Moscow in an attempt to patch up a quarrel between her brother and his wife, Dolly. There she met the handsome young Count Vronsky, who was rumored to be in love with Dolly's younger sister, Kitty.

But Konstantine Levin, of an old Muscovite family, was also in love with Kitty, and his visit to Moscow coincided with Anna's. Kitty refused Levin, but to her chagrin she received no proposal from the count. Indeed, Vronsky had no intention of proposing to Kitty. His heart went out to Anna the first time he laid eyes on her, and when Anna returned to her home in St. Petersburg, he followed her.

Soon they began to be seen together at soirees and at the theater, apparently unaware of gossip which circulated about them. Karénin, Anna's husband, became concerned. A coldly ambitious and dispassionate man, he felt that his social position was at stake. One night he discussed these rumors with Anna and pointed out the danger of her flirtation, as he called it. He forbade her to entertain Vronsky at home, and cautioned her to be more careful. He was not jealous of his wife, only worried over the social consequences of her behavior. He reminded her of her duty to her young son, Seryozha. Anna said she would obey him, and there the matter rested.

But Anna was unable to conceal her true feelings when Vronsky was injured in a race-track accident. Karénin upbraided her for her indiscreet behavior in public. He considered a duel, separation, divorce, but rejected all of these courses. When he finally decided to keep Anna under his roof, he reflected that he was acting in accordance with the laws of religion. Anna continued to meet Vronsky in secret.

Levin had returned to his country estate after Kitty had refused him, and there he busied himself in problems of agriculture and peasant labor. One day he went into the fields and worked with a scythe along with the serfs. He felt that he was beginning to understand the old primitive philosophy of their lives. He planned new developments, among them a cooperative enterprise system. When he heard that Kitty was not married after all, and that she had been ill but was soon returning to Moscow, he resolved to seek her hand once more. Secretly, he knew she loved him. His pride, as well as hers, had kept them apart.

Accordingly, Levin made the journey to Moscow with new hope that soon Kitty would be his wife.

Against her husband's orders, Anna Karénina sent for Vronsky and told him that she was with child. Aware of his responsibilities to Anna, he begged her to petition Karénin for a divorce so that she would be free to marry him. Karénin informed her coldly that he would consider the child his and accept it so that the world should never know his wife's disgrace, but he refused to think of going through shameful divorce proceedings. Karénin reduced Anna to submission by warning her that he would take Seryozha away if she persisted in making a fool of herself.

The strained family relationship continued unbroken. One night Karénin had planned to go out, and Anna persuaded Vronsky to come to the house. As he was leaving, Karénin met Vronsky on the front steps. Enraged, Karénin told Anna that he had decided to get a divorce and that he would keep Seryozha in his custody. But divorce proceedings were so intricate, the scandal so great, the whole aspect of the step so disgusting to Karénin that he could not bring himself to go through with the process. As Anna's confinement drew near, he was still undecided. After winning an important political seat, he became even more unwilling to risk his public reputation.

At the birth of her child, Anna became deathly ill. Vronsky, overcome with guilt, attempted suicide, but failed. Karénin was reduced to a state of such confusion that he determined to grant his wife any request, since he thought her to be on her deathbed. The sight of Vronsky seemed to be the only thing that restored her. After many months

of illness, she went with her lover and baby daughter to Italy, where they lived under strained circumstances. Meanwhile, Levin proposed once more to Kitty, and after a flurry of preparations they were married.

Anna Karénina and Vronsky returned to Russia and went to live on his estate. It was now impossible for Anna to return home. Although Karénin had not gone through with divorce proceedings, he considered himself separated from Anna and was everywhere thought to be a man of fine loyalty and unswerving honor, unjustly imposed upon by an unfaithful wife. Sometimes Anna stole into town to see Seryozha but her fear of being discovered there by her husband cut these visits short. After each visit she returned bitter and sad. She became more and more demanding toward Vronsky, with the result that he spent less time with her. She took little interest in her child. Before long she convinced herself that Vronsky was in love with another woman. One day she could not stay alone in the house. She found herself at the railway station. She bought a ticket. As she stood on the platform gazing at the tracks below, the thunder of an approaching train roared in her ears. Suddenly she remembered a man run over in the Moscow railroad station on the day she and Vronsky met. Carefully measuring the distance, she threw herself in front of the approaching train.

After her death, Vronsky joined the army. He had changed from a handsome, cheerful man to one who welcomed death; his only reason for living had been Anna.

For Levin and Kitty life became an increasing round of daily work and everyday routine, which they shared with each other. Levin knew at last the responsibility wealth imposed upon him in his dealings with the peasants. Kitty helped him to share his responsibility. Although there were many questions he could never answer satisfactorily to himself, he was nevertheless aware of the satisfying beauty of life, its toil, leisure, pain, and happiness.

ANNA OF THE FIVE TOWNS

Type of work: Novel
Author: Arnold Bennett (1867-1931)
Type of plot: Domestic realism
Time of plot: Late nineteenth century
Locale: Rural England
First published: 1902

Principal characters:
EPHRAIM TELLWRIGHT, a miser
ANNA, his older daughter
AGNES, his younger daughter
HENRY MYNORS, Anna's suitor
WILLIE PRICE, in love with Anna
BEATRICE SUTTON, Anna's friend

Critique:

Anna of the Five Towns was the first of Bennett's novels dealing with the pottery region of the Five Towns. It is primarily a novel of character, but Anna changes so slightly that the reader is hardly aware of any development in her attitudes or actions. In fact, her tragedy occurs because she cannot change her original nature. But in spite of certain weaknesses, the story has touches of Bennett's great writing skill and human insight and is worth the time of all Bennett lovers. The novel is also Bennett's most detailed study of the repressive effects of Wesleyanism, which affects all his characters in one degree or another.

The Story:

Ephraim Tellwright was a miser, one of the wealthiest men in any of the Five Towns, a group of separate villages joined by a single road. He was a former preacher, concerned more with getting congregations in good financial shape, however, than with the souls of his parishioners. Although he had made money from rentals and foreclosures, in addition to marrying money, he lived in the most frugal way possible and gave his two daughters nothing but the barest essentials. Both of his wives had died, the first giving him his daughter Anna and the second producing Agnes before her death. Mr. Tellwright was usually amiable. As long as his meals were on time, no money was wasted, and the house was never left alone and unguarded, he paid little attention to his daughters.

Anna loved her father even though she could never feel close to him. Agnes, much younger, followed her sister's lead. The two girls were especially close, since their father ignored them most of the time.

On Anna's twenty-first birthday her father called her into his office and told her that she would that day inherit almost fifty thousand pounds from her mother's estate. He had invested the original sum wisely until it had grown to a fortune. Anna, who had never owned one pound to call her own, could not comprehend an amount so large. Accustomed to letting her father handle all business affairs, she willingly gave him control of her fortune. The income from the stocks and rentals was deposited in the bank in her name, but she gave her father her checkbook and signed only when he told her to. The money made little difference in Anna's life; it simply lay in the bank until her father told her to invest it.

One result of the money, however, was unhappy for Anna. Among her properties was a run-down factory owned by Titus Price. Because Price was continually behind in his rent, Mr. Tellwright forced Anna to keep demanding something on account. Knowing that the property would never rent to anyone else, the old miser never put Price out but kept hounding him for as much as the man could pay. Anna usually had to deal with Willie Price, the son, and she always left the interview with a feeling of guilt. Although the sight of Willie's embarrassment left her unhappy, she always demanded his money because she was afraid to face her father without it.

A teacher in the Sunday School in which Anna taught was Henry Mynors, a pillar in the church and a successful man in the community. Anna, attracted to him, tried to join in his religious fervor, but she could not quite bring herself to repent and to accept God publicly. She felt repentance to be a private matter, not one to be dragged out in meeting. Henry was patient with her, however. When the townspeople said that he was interested mainly in her money, Anna refused to believe the gossip. Henry began to call on her occasionally, combining his courtship with business with Mr. Tellwright. The miser persuaded Anna to invest some of her money in Henry's business, after arranging first for a large share of the profits and a high interest. Anna, caring little for the money, liked to be associated with Henry and spent much time with him.

After Anna had received her fortune, she was invited for the first time to the house of Mrs. Sutton, the social leader of the town. Mrs. Sutton's daughter Beatrice and Anna became friends. There was talk that Beatrice and Henry Mynors had once been engaged. The Suttons took Anna and Henry to the Isle of Man on a vacation, and Anna thought there could never again be such luxurious living. She had had to take ten pounds of her own money without her father's

knowledge in order to get clothes for the trip, and the miser had berated her viciously when she told him what she had done. Being with Henry and the Suttons, however, helped her forget his anger. When the vacation was marred by Beatrice's serious illness, Anna won a permanent place in the Suttons' affection by her unselfish and competent nursing.

After Beatrice had recovered, Anna and Henry returned home. Before they left the island Henry proposed to Anna and she accepted. Later her father gave his consent because Henry knew the value of money. Young Agnes was enchanted by the romantic aspects of the courtship, and Anna was happy in her quiet love for Henry. But her joy at being engaged was soon clouded by the news that old Mr. Price, Willie's father, had hanged himself. Anna felt that she and her father were to blame because they had hounded him for his rent. Henry assured her that Mr. Price was in debt to many people and that she need not feel guilty. Nevertheless, Anna worried a great deal about the suicide and about Willie.

Later Willie confessed to her that a bank note he had given in payment had been forged. The confession seemed to reduce Willie to nothing. Anna, realizing that he and his father had been driven to desperation, tried to protect Willie and his father's reputation by taking the forged note from her father's office. When she told Mr. Tellwright that she had burned the note, he was so furious with her that he never forgave her.

Because Willie was planning to make a fresh start in Australia, Henry arranged to buy the Price house for them to live in after he and Anna were married. Although Anna was sure she could never be happy in a house the miserable Prices had owned, she was docile and let Henry make all the arrangements.

When Anna told her father that she needed one hundred pounds to pay for her linens and her wedding clothes, Mr. Tellwright denounced her for a spendthrift. Handing over the checkbook, he told her not to bother him again about her money. Henry, pleased at the turn of events, was full of plans for the use of Anna's fortune. Then there was more bad news about Mr. Price. Before his death he had defrauded the church of fifty pounds. Anna tried to cover up for him so that Willie would never know, but someone told the secret. Willie, ready to leave for Australia, heard of the theft. When he told Anna goodbye, he was like a whipped child. As Anna looked into his eyes for the last time, she knew suddenly that he loved her and that she loved him. She let him go, however, because she felt bound by her promise to Henry. She had been dutiful all her life; it was too late for her to change.

Willie was never heard from again. Had anyone in Five Towns happened to look into an abandoned pitshaft, the mystery of Willie would have been solved. The meek lad had found his only way to peace.

THE ANNALS OF TACITUS

Type of work: History
Author: Cornelius Tacitus (c. 55-c. 120)
Time: 14-69
Locale: The Roman Empire
First transcribed: c. 119

Principal personages:

TIBERIUS, Augustus Caesar's stepson and successor
GERMANICUS (NERO CLAUDIUS DRUSUS),Tiberius' brother
AGRIPPINA (MAJOR), Germanicus' wife and Caligula's mother
DRUSUS, Tiberius' son
DRUSUS, Germanicus' son
CALIGULA, Tiberius' successor
CLAUDIUS, Caligula's uncle and his successor
MESSALINA, Claudius' first wife
AGRIPPINA (MINOR), Claudius' niece and second wife
BRITANNICUS, Claudius' son, killed by Nero
NERO, Agrippina's son and Claudius' successor
POPPAEA, Nero's wife
AELIUS SEJANUS, Tiberius' favorite
PISO, leader of a conspiracy against Nero

Cornelius Tacitus is by an accident of fate the sole surviving historian of his day; all the writings of his contemporaries and immediate predecessors are lost. It may be that the fates were guided by standards of literary aesthetics rather than scientific accuracy, for though Tacitus' facts and interpretations have from time to time been severely criticized, he has always been admired for his lucid, morally-charged narrative style. The *Annals* are not merely a skillful prose account of a half-century of Roman history, but also a compassionate evaluation of the horrors of imperial despotism. In fact, the earliest extant manuscript is entitled *Ab excessu divi Augusti* (although in Book IV, the writer refers to his work as *Annals*).

Obviously, Tacitus saw in Roman history a gradual decline from a primitive Golden Age when no laws were necessary to times when laws became a necessity and, finally, an abominable evil. As the *Annals* proceed from the reign of Tiberius to those of Claudius and Nero (a section dealing with Caligula is lost, as are the last books) the tyranny becomes more cruel, the populace and patricians grow more submissive, the opportunists and informers become more despicable, and the dwindling number of virtuous men find themselves more helpless.

In these matters, Tacitus is by no means taciturn; in fact, so great are the horrors depicted in the *Annals* that until the atrocities of twentieth-century politics and war recapitulated them on a horrendously magnified scale, civilized men were inclined to view Tacitus' account as grossly exaggerated, beyond the possible depths of human nature.

Tacitus is modest about his aims, though the grave irony of his remarks should not go unnoticed:

The matter upon which I am occupied is circumscribed, and unproductive of renown to the author—a state of undisturbed peace, or only interrupted in limited degree, the sad condition of affairs in the city, and a prince indifferent about extending the bounds of the empire. Not unprofitable, however, will it be to investigate matters which, though unimportant in a superficial view, frequently give the first impulse to events of magnitude. . . . I have only to record the mandates of despotism, incessant accusations, faithless friendships, the ruin of innocence; the one unvarying repetition of causes terminating in the same event, and presenting no novelty from their similarity and tiresome repetition. (IV, 32-33)

In general, Tacitus presents not a sustained history, but a chronological depiction of selected events—some thoroughly detailed over several chapters and others sketched in lightly, continually referred to but not described extensively in any one place. It has been conjectured that the original *Annals* consisted of three hexads, the pattern employed by Vergil, Statius, Polynus, and Cicero; but there is no concrete evidence that there were two books written after XVI, and the loss of Books VII-X prevents us from being absolutely certain they fitted with Books XI-XII to constitute a middle hexad. At any rate, the *Annals,* as they now stand, can be conveniently arranged by subject matter—the reign of Tiberius is the concern of the first six books, of Claudius in books XI-XII, and of Nero in the final four books. This is not to say that the focus of attention is concentrated on the three emperors. In dealing with Tiberius, for example, Tacitus devotes the opening forty-nine chapters to the first year (more space than to any other year of the entire history), beginning with the jockeying for power after the death of Augustus. Since Tiberius never led troops in battle after he became emperor, the narrative shifts to Tiberius' son Drusus (Chapters 16-30) quelling the Pannonian mutiny and to Germanicus (most of Chapters 31-71) campaigning on the Rhine. These two men, logical heirs to the throne, were the objects of the intrigues of the utterly unscrupulous Aelius Sejanus, Tiberius' favorite. Jealous of Germanicus' successes, Tiberius had him recalled and sent to the East as king in Armenia, where he died in A.D. 19, probably at the hands of Piso under orders from Tiberius. Piso's trial ended abruptly with his unexplained murder, though Tacitus hints that Tiberius arranged that as well. Drusus, then, dominated the sons of Germanicus (Nero, another Drusus, and Caligula) as heir-apparent, but Tiberius openly preferred Sejanus—"a stranger was called in as co-adjutor in the government; nay, how little was wanting to his being declared col-

league." This Sejanus, "whose heart insatiably lusted for supreme domination," then dispatched Drusus with a slow poison that made him appear a victim of disease, and set out to marry Livia, his widow and the sister of Germanicus. There remained, however, Agrippina, widow of Germanicus, and her three sons. Sejanus contrived open enmity between Agrippina and Tiberius and skillfully arranged for the emperor to retire to Capri from Rome in A.D. 27. There, while Sejanus plotted his rise to power, the ruler "indulged his cruel and libidinous disposition . . . in the secrecy of a retired situation." One of the most tantalizing lacunae of the *Annals* deals with Agrippina's hopeless struggle for the rights of her sons and the final conflict between Sejanus and the emperor, a struggle leading to Sejanus' execution.

The first hexad ends with Tiberius at the age of seventy-eight, when he had outlived all the intriguers who surrounded him and relinquished "nothing of his libidinous excesses." His end was dramatic, and Tacitus relishes the irony. Assured by Tiberius' physician that his death was imminent,

Caligula in the midst of a great throng of persons, paying their gratulations, was already going forth to make a solemn entrance on the sovereignty, when suddenly a notice came, "that Tiberius had recovered his sight and voice, and had called for some persons to give him food to restore him." The consternation was universal: the concourse about Caligula dispersed in all directions . . . Caligula himself stood fixed in silence —fallen from the highest hopes, he now expected the worst. Macro [Caligula's right hand man], undismayed, ordered the old man to be smothered with a quantity of clothes. . . . (VI, 51)

The dramatic technique is magnificent. Caligula is left as a monstrous legacy to Rome. However, the extant history resumes in Book XI with Claudius' succession to the purple. The new emperor is depicted as a cut above his predecessors: he dignified the theater, augmented the alphabet, restrained predatory creditors, increased the Senate, and incorporated new provinces into the Empire. But the intrigues flourished, centering upon Claudius' wife Messalina, who was concerned at the way in which freedmen (especially Narcissus and Pallas) had gained the actual power. Messalina, knowing she was about to be murdered by Claudius' agents, committed suicide: "Tidings were then carried to Claudius 'that Messalina was no more'; without inquiring whether by her own or another's hand, [he] called for a cup of wine and proceeded in the feast." Tacitus brilliantly achieves a sense of horror at the moral corruption of the Empire with just such detail and understatement. Book XII opens with the contest among the freedmen concerning the choice of a new wife for Claudius. Pallas prevailed with his suggestion of Agrippina, despite the fact that she was the daughter of Claudius' brother Germanicus. The horrendous narrative continues to delineate debauchery and chaos. Nero destroyed the emperor's son Britannicus, and Agrippina afterward poisoned Claudius in order to secure the succession for her own son, Nero. Book XIII tells of Agrippina's struggles for power, first against the freedwoman Acte and then against Poppaea, Nero's wife—murders and counter-murders and abortive palace revolts that went on while Nero engaged in his orgiastic debauches. Book XIV opens with Poppaea's vigorously dramatic reproach against Nero for his cowardice in not destroying his mother, who had desperately clung to life and power by incestuously lavishing her own body on her son. Tacitus handles Nero's attempts on Agrippina's life with almost grotesque comedy. First, she was put to sea in a faulty vessel, but she swam ashore while another woman, hoping to save herself by claiming to be the emperor's mother, was slain. Finally, brute force was resorted to and she was slain in bed: ". . . to the centurion, as he was drawing his sword to dispatch her, she presented her womb, and with a loud voice, 'Strike your sword into my belly,'

she cried, and was instantly dispatched." Thus, Tacitus vivifies an important dramatic scene with a stroke of realism.

Nero, struck with remorse and apparently unaware of the extent to which Roman society had degenerated to his own low level, feared to return to the capital. Matricide during the Republic would have seemed the destruction of morality's basis, the family. But Nero's entry into Rome was triumphant and he thenceforth "abandoned himself to all his inordinate passions which, though insufficiently controlled, had been somewhat checked by his reverence for his mother, such as it was." Throughout his career "Nero wallowed in all sorts of defilements, lawful and unlawful: and seemed to leave no atrocity which could add to his pollution," including one which Tacitus describes with great disgust—a mock-marriage "with all the solemnities of wedlock" to a homosexual. The height of his inhuman cruelty was the great fire of Rome, in which he madly reveled and from which he gained enormous profits. The most sustained episode of the final books concerns the conspiracy in A.D. 65 of Piso and eighteen other leaders to assassinate Nero and set up Piso as emperor.

Piso gave no promise of better government, since he was almost as addicted to sensuous pleasure as Nero himself, but some change was obviously necessary. The conspiracy had difficulty settling on a method, and before it could get under way the plot was inadvertently revealed when Epicharis, a freedwoman, attempted to solicit one of Nero's naval officers, Volusius Proculus, who alerted Nero. One of the rare cases of personal virtue was Epicharis' refusal to betray the conspirators, despite the horrible torture she endured. In their haste the conspirators betrayed themselves, and in panic Nero began wholesale slaughters. Chapters 37-70 constitute a steady series of death scenes—Epicharis, Seneca, Subrius Flavus, Lucan (who died reciting his verses), and others—each presented with vivid detail. Piso, himself, though urged to stir up a popular revolt, chose to sever his veins and "left a will full of odious flattery to Nero, in tenderness to his wife, a depraved woman and void of every recommendation but personal beauty."

The deaths of those close to Nero continued. Poppaea died "by a fit of passion in her husband, who gave her a violent blow with his foot when she was pregnant; for I cannot believe he poisoned her as some have stated." Her funeral was sumptuous; she was embalmed with spices rather than cremated as was the custom, but her death was "rejoiced at by those who recollected her . . . lewdness and cruelty." An account of the last two years of Nero's life is missing, and the *Annals,* ending in mid-sentence, suggest that this section was lost.

Such are the main lines of Tacitus' history, but the text abounds in frequent digressions tracing in close detail the fortunes of the Roman Empire and its provinces and outposts so vividly that some authorities suggest that he must have had a host of reliable sources in the form of autobiographies and diaries. However, the *Annals* are clearly the personal document of a writer with sincerity, intelligence, courage, and enormous artistry. In a very real sense, Tacitus was an Existentialist in his view of social corruption replacing traditional morality. Convinced that human effort is absurd, he was sustained, however, by a faith in human solidarity and unity in suffering. The gravity of his tragic vision is relieved by a deeply felt compassion for suffering mankind, and he has left in the *Annals* one of the greatest histories of all time.

ANNALS OF THE PARISH

Type of work: Novel
Author: John Galt (1779-1839)
Type of plot: Social chronicle
Time of plot: 1760-1810
Locale: Scotland
First published: 1821

Principal characters:
THE REVEREND MICAH BALWHIDDER, minister at Dalmailing
LORD EAGLESHAM, the minister's friend and patron
BETTY LANSHAW, the first Mrs. Balwhidder
LIZY KIBBOCK, the second Mrs. Balwhidder
MRS. NUGENT, a widow, the third Mrs. Balwhidder
MR. CAYENNE, an industrialist
LADY MACADAM, a high-spirited old lady in the parish

Critique:

John Galt was important to his own time both as a settler in Canada and as a novelist who presented Scottish life in fiction. As both a novelist and a leader in the Canada Company, he has, however, been largely forgotten. In the field of fiction Galt was so far overshadowed by Sir Walter Scott in his own time that he never became widely known outside of Britain, and the neglect has continued, unfortunately, to this time. A Scot himself, Galt wrote in the *Annals of the Parish* about the Scotland he and his parents had known, and he wrote lovingly. His humane feeling and the love he gave to his own country can be marked on almost every page he wrote. In this novel the strongest and most sympathetically portrayed character is of the Scottish Presbyterian clergyman of strict Calvinist persuasion. Hardly less important are the descriptions of the new class of industrialists.

The Story:

As a young man just out of divinity school at the University of Glasgow, and but recently accepted for the ministry, the Reverend Micah Balwhidder was appointed to the charge of the established Presbyterian church in the village of Dalmailing, in western Scotland. Because he had been appointed by a great landowner, without their approval, the people of Dalmailing tried to prevent Mr. Balwhidder from taking his post. On the Sunday Mr.

Balwhidder was installed, the ministers officiating had to enter the church through a window, because the door had been nailed fast. Nor did they try to go to the church without a guard of soldiers.

Immediately after being installed, Mr. Balwhidder began a series of visits to his parishioners, as he believed a good Calvinistic clergyman should do. He was rebuffed at door after door, until Thomas Thorl, the minister's most outspoken opponent, relented and accepted him. The rest of the parish followed within a matter of weeks. Soon after the excitement died down, Mr. Balwhidder married his first wife, Betty Lanshaw, a cousin with whom he had grown up; he believed strongly that a minister should be married to accomplish his best work.

During the first few years of his ministry, during the 1760's, Mr. Balwhidder fought earnestly against two habits among his parishioners, smuggling and drinking. He felt that both were sinful. In the end, however, he became reconciled to tea as a beverage, for he thought it better for his people to drink that instead of spirituous liquors. His main objection to smuggling was that it encouraged lawlessness among his people and resulted in the appearance of illegitimate children.

One of the chief problems in Dalmailing, so far as the minister was concerned, was the Malcolm family, composed of Mrs. Malcolm, a widow, and her five children. The minister always tried to help them succeed, for they were hard-working folk who had known better days. The first ray of success for them came when Charles Malcolm was made an officer in the merchant marine, an event which gladdened Mr. Balwhidder's heart. In that same year the first Mrs. Balwhidder died. Her death saddened the whole parish, for everyone had come to love her.

In the following year, 1764, Mr. Balwhidder tried to write a doctrinal book. He found, however, that he had too much to do to keep his house and servants in order and so he decided to look about for another wife, and none too soon, for one of his maidservants was with child. Some of the village gossips blamed the minister, although the actual father admitted his part in the affair. As soon as a year and a day had passed after his first wife's death, Mr. Balwhidder married Lizy Kibbock, the daughter of a very successful farmer in the parish.

The second Mrs. Balwhidder immediately set out to augment her husband's stipend. She purchased cattle and hogs and set up a regular dairy. Within a year she had sufficient income from her projects so that the minister's pay could be put into the bank. Her husband approved heartily of her industry, not only because he himself was made comfortable but because the industry of his wife encouraged greater efforts on the part of other women in the parish. In that year three coal mines were opened in the parish, bringing new prosperity to the people.

In 1767 a great event occurred in the village's history. Lord Eaglesham, after being thrown in a muddy road which ran through the village, resolved to have a fine highway built to prevent a second occurrence. The new road made transportation much easier for the villagers. The event also caused the lord and Mr. Balwhidder to become friends, for at the time of the accident the clergyman had lent Lord Eaglesham some dry clothes. Through the nobleman's influence Mr. Balwhidder was on many occasions able to help the people of his village.

Scandal threatened the pulpit in 1772, when a visitor from another parish, Mr. Heckletext, was invited to speak. Shortly after his sermon the church session learned that he was the father of an illegitimate child by one of the village girls. It was a bitter lesson for Mr. Balwhidder, who resolved never again to permit a man to speak from his pulpit until he had thoroughly investigated the stranger's habits and character.

The 1770's were disturbing times for the minister of Dalmailing. Mr. Balwhidder was a peace-loving man who hated to see his young parishioners enlist to fight against the rebellious colonists in America. More especially, he hated to hear of the battles in which some of them were killed. The greatest blow given him by the war was the death of the widow Malcolm's son, who died a hero in a naval battle with the French. Mr. Balwhidder, who looked upon the fatherless Malcolm family as his particular charge, grieved as much as if the boy had been his own son.

He was also in difficulties with Lady MacAdam, an older woman who had been at court in England and France in her youth. A spirited woman who wanted to have a good time in life and to dictate to other people, she was beside herself when she learned that her son, an officer in the Royal Scots regiment, was in love with the oldest Malcolm girl. She mistreated the girl shamefully, refusing even to listen to the minister's remonstrations. Using his own judgment, he finally had to marry the young people against her wishes. She soon became reconciled, however, after the marriage had taken place.

After the close of the American Revolution, a loyal American who had returned to Britain settled in Dalmailing. This man, Mr. Cayenne, had a temper as fiery as his name. The weaving mill he set up near the village brought prosperity to the parish, but it also brought troubles. During the 1790's the weavers who settled there were in favor of the French Revolution, while Mr. Balwhidder and his more conservative parishioners were all against it. Aside from their political differences, the weavers also belonged to different faiths, a fact which gave the minister grave concern, for he disliked any other church to set itself up as long as the Presbyterian Church was the official church of the land. He fought a lengthy but losing battle against churches which preached other doctrines than his own. It was the one problem which he felt he could not solve, for the tide of history was against him.

In 1796, Mr. Balwhidder again became a widower. Still of the opinion that to serve his people best he ought to be a married man, he took another wife a year later. His third wife was Mrs. Nugent, a widow of good reputation.

As the years passed the minister's two children, a son and a daughter, grew up and were married. Finally, in 1810, the church authorities decided that Mr. Balwhidder who had served his parish for fifty years, should have some help. But he had become so deaf and so forgetful that he himself decided to retire. He preached a farewell sermon to his crowded church and then set himself to write into a book the annals of the parish he had served so long.

Type of work: History
Author: Livy (Titus Livius, 59 B.C.-A.D. 17)
Time: 753-9 B.C.
Locale: Rome, Spain, Carthage, Greece, Macedonia
First transcribed: c. 26 B.C.-A.D. 14

Livy undertook a great task. In his *Ab urbe condita libri,* he was attempting to narrate the history of nearly eight centuries, from the time of Romulus and Remus to the reign of Tiberius. The work occupied 142 books, of which barely a quarter have been preserved: Books I-X and XXI-XLV, along with some fragments of several others. Even so, this material is enough to fill six volumes in one English translation and thirteen in another.

Titus Livius Patavinus (from his birthplace, Padua), was originally a teacher of rhetoric and apparently, from casual references in his writing, a friend of the Emperor Augustus. Perhaps the emperor, as part of his program to glorify Rome, suggested that Livy stop teaching and write a history of the city. The project represented a challenge. His only sources were traditions, the official temple annals listing the consuls and the chief events of each year, and personal records, frequently exaggerated, kept by the famous families. Like Herodotus, however, Livy was always attracted to a colorful story. Macaulay declared in disgust: "No historian with whom we are acquainted has shown so complete indifference to the truth."

But probably a truthful chronicle was not what Livy set out to produce. In addition to his patriotic duty, he wanted by his dramatic power and the charm of his style to impress the sophisticated readers of Rome. Accuracy came second. He was no soldier in his battles, no statesman in recording the problems of government; even as a geographer he was most hazy. In an epoch when research was unknown, he was no critical historian. When he found two conflicting accounts, he was likely to chose the more colorful, or include both and let the reader be the judge.

The *Annals* were issued in "decades," or units of ten, a volume at a time, the first between 27 and 25 B.C., at the time Vergil was writing his *Aeneid.* The work did what the author intended: painted vividly the grandeur of Rome, even though, like an artist, he sometimes changed details for better composition. Whatever his faults as a historian, Livy the novelist, the dramatist, the orator, left unforgettable pages for readers of later generations.

It is a wonder that so much of his work has come down to us, for he had many enemies. Pope Gregory I, for example, ordered all available copies burned because of the superstitions they contained, and other Church fathers were also to blame for the hundred books that have disappeared, including those about Livy's own times. More than one modern historian has wished he could exchange the first ten books for those in which Livy set down what he had seen. Few, however, would willingly give up the books dealing with the sixteen years of the Punic Wars, the story of the life and death struggle between Rome and Carthage.

"It would be a satisfaction to me," declared Livy in the preface to the first decade of his *Annals,* "that I have contributed my share to perpetuate the achievements of a people, the lords of the world." He determined "neither to affirm nor refute" the traditions antedating the founding of Rome, even though they were "more suited to the fiction of poetry than to the genuine record of history." In writing them down, however, his aim was to acquaint the Romans of his day with the lives and customs of ancestors who might serve as examples in the present low moral status of Rome, "when we can neither endure our vices nor their remedies."

He began by repeating the legend of Aeneas, who led the Trojans to Latium and married Lavinia. He listed the petty chiefs who followed, making no changes in the story of Romulus and Remus and their wolf nurse. He related briefly the account of the founding of Rome, April 21, 753 B.C., when the ceremonies ended with the quarrel between the brothers and the death of Remus. By inviting in the discontented from the neighboring tribes, Romulus populated the city, then provided wives by kidnaping the Sabine women who came as guests to a feast.

In the remaining books of the first decade, which carries the story through 460 years, Livy paid special attention to Rome's virtuous and exemplary citizens: Cincinnatus, summoned from his plow to drive back the Aequians; Virginius, protecting his daughter Virginia from lustful decemvir Appius Claudius; Camillus, returning from exile to fight the Gauls; Manlius, defending the capitol; and the patriotic Curtius, riding his horse into a chasm in the Forum to preserve his city. The decade ends when the defeat of the Samnites left Rome the master of Italy.

The next ten books have been lost. Only because they were summarized in an epitome does the world know Livy's account of what happened between 294 and 219 B.C.

At the beginning of the next decade, Books XXI-XXX, Livy declared: "I am about to relate the most memorable of all wars that were ever waged, the war which the Carthaginians under Hannibal maintained against the Roman people." As far as ancient history goes, he was undoubtedly right. It was a war between the Indo-Germanic and the Semitic races for world dominion. The two were not only equally matched, but they were also familiar with the enemy's war tactics and potential power; and their hatred for each other, as the historian pointed out, was as strong as their armies.

Livy never minimized the exploits of twenty-six-year-old Hannibal, who became the outstanding figure in his book. What details he could not find recorded of the crossing of the Alps by ninety thousand infantry, twelve thousand cavalry, and thirty-seven elephants, he made up from his imagination.

Scipio the father, having failed to stop the Carthaginians in Gaul, tried again on the plains of Italy, but one defeat after another brought terror to the imperial city. After Trebia and Lake Trasimene, the delaying tactics of Fabius Maximus succeeded in holding back the invaders for a time, but the impatience of another consul, Varro, resulted in the culminating Roman disaster at Cannae (216 B.C.). Had Hannibal taken advantage of his victory, he could easily have entered Rome.

Book XXV deals with another phase of the struggle. Marcellus, besieging Syracuse, was held at bay for three years by the craft of a seventy-four-year-old mathematician, Archimedes, with his invention of the catapult and the grappling hooks that lifted the prows of Roman ships trying to attack the breakwater, and sank them. Ultimately, however, the Romans found the weak spot in the defenses and captured the island.

On another battlefront, a second Scipio, later to be called Africanus, was trying to keep Spain from being used as the Carthaginians' European headquarters. A comparison of the version by Livy with another by Polybius shows the superiority of Livy's technique. Though Scipio could not immobilize Hasdrubal entirely or prevent his departure with reinforcements for his brother in Italy, the delay did contribute to the Carthaginian defeat on the Metaurus River, a Roman victory that was quickly neutralized by the death of Marcellus in a clash with Hannibal. Eventually, however, Roman might prevailed when Scipio carried the war into Africa. Although Hannibal was recalled for the defense of Carthage, his veterans were no match for the Roman legionaries at the Battle of Zama (202 B.C.), and defeated Carthage was literally wiped from the map.

An additional fifteen books of Livy's history survive, dealing with Roman expansion in Greece and Asia and ending when Macedonia became a Roman province. But this story is an anticlimax. No longer were the soldiers fighting for the life of Rome, but the plunder they hoped to acquire, so that the reader does not follow the story with the same interest. But even in these pages, the storytelling ability of Livy is still apparent. It is easy to understand why he was called the greatest prose writer of the Augustine Age.

ANTHONY ADVERSE

Type of work: Novel
Author: Hervey Allen (1889-1949)
Type of plot: Picaresque romance
Time of plot: Late eighteenth and early nineteenth centuries
Locale: Western Europe, Africa, North America
First published: 1933

Principal characters:
ANTHONY ADVERSE
DON LUIS, MARQUIS DA VINCITATA, husband of Anthony's mother
MARIA, Anthony's mother
MR. BONNYFEATHER, Anthony's grandfather
FAITH PALEOLOGUS, Mr. Bonnyfeather's housekeeper
ANGELA GUISEPPE, Anthony's mistress
FLORENCE UDNEY, Anthony's first wife
DOLORES DE LA FUENTE, Anthony's second wife
VINCENT NOLTE, Anthony's friend, a banker

Critique:

Anthony Adverse is the story of a soldier of fortune whose ramblings carry him over a large part of Europe, to Africa, and to North America. The book contains a wealth of incident, as well as mention of historical personages. The characters, however, are subordinate to the plot. The novel is also interesting because its various sections represent different types of romantic fiction.

The Story:

The pretty young Marquise Maria da Vincitata, daughter of a Scottish merchant of Leghorn, fell in love with young Denis Moore within a year of her marriage and met with him secretly in France while her husband was taking a cure for his gout. Don Luis, the arrogant Marquis da Vincitata, discovering the intrigue, spirited his wife away and killed her gallant, luckless lover when he started out in pursuit. Maria's baby was born high up in the Alps. After his wife had died in childbirth, Don Luis took the child to Leghorn, where he stealthily deposited the infant at the Convent of Jesus the Child. The only tokens of its parentage were a cape and a statue of the Madonna which had belonged to Maria.

The boy, christened Anthony by the nuns, lived at the convent until he was ten. Then he was delivered to a prominent merchant of the town, Mr. Bonnyfeather, to become his apprentice.

Bonnyfeather and his housekeeper had no trouble recognizing the cape and the doll as possessions of the merchant's daughter, Maria. Although Anthony was given the surname Adverse and was not told of his relationship to his benefactor, he was carefully educated with the tacit understanding that he would one day inherit the flourishing Bonnyfeather business.

Anthony matured early. Seduced by the housekeeper, Faith Paleologus, he also had a brief affair with the cook's daughter, Angela. He was attracted, too, by the English consul's daughter, Florence Udney, but was not encouraged by her mother, who was unaware that Anthony had any expectations.

Anticipating the eventual arrival of Napoleon's army in Leghorn, Mr. Bonnyfeather quietly liquidated his business, sent his money abroad, and made plans to retire. He arranged passage for his grandson on the American ship *Wampanoag*, under Captain Jorham. Anthony was to sail to Cuba to collect some money on a long-overdue account.

The *Wampanoag* stopped first at Genoa. There Anthony visited Father Xavier, a Jesuit, who had been his guardian at the convent. Mr. Bonnyfeather had given the priest the right to decide whether the time had come to tell Anthony he was the merchant's heir. It was from the priest's lips that Anthony learned of his origin and prospects.

When the *Wampanoag* reached Havana Anthony discovered that his creditor, Gallego, was in Africa as a slave trader. With the aid of the captain-general, Don Luis de la Casas, a plan was devised whereby Anthony would sail to Africa as a government agent. There he would impound a cargo of Gallego's slaves, bring them to Cuba for sale, and split the proceeds with the captain-general, thus satisfying the Bonnyfeather debt. Strongly attracted by Don Luis' young relation, Dolores de la Fuente, the young man finally agreed to stay in Africa and to ship several additional cargoes of slaves, for the enrichment of the captain-general and the increase of his own hopes that he might one day marry Dolores.

The trip aboard the *Ariostatica* was a trying one. Father François, a monk who was being shipped to Africa because he had tried to give aid and comfort to the slaves, fell ill of yellow fever and nearly died. Anthony, forced to rule the crew and its captain with an iron hand, was able to put down a mutiny as the ship sailed up the Rio Pongo to the Gallego establishment. There he learned that Gallego had died a few months before, leaving his factor, Ferdinando, in charge.

Anthony took over the trade station and for three years shipped cargoes of human freight to Cuba to be sold there. To the sorrow of Father François, he took the half-breed Neleta, Ferdinando's sister, as his mistress. But he was not able completely to reconcile himself to trading in human bodies.

While Anthony was absent from the trading station, Father François was captured by a native witch doctor, Mnombibi, and crucified. Upon his return, Anthony found the priest pinioned to his own cross. With the knowledge that Mr. Bonnyfeather was dead, and that Captain Bittern of the *Unicorn* was waiting in the Rio Pongo to bear him back to Leghorn, Anthony decided to leave the trading station. He left Neleta behind.

Don Luis, Marquis da Vincitata, arrived in Leghorn at the same time. They were both there on business, the marquis to close up the Casa Bonnyfeather, of which he was landlord, and Anthony to receive the merchant's will from Vincent Nolte, a banker with whom he had been friendly in his youth. Vincent suggested that Anthony take advantage of an offer made by M. Ouvrard, a French financier who was planning to supply the bankrupt Spanish government with French food and money, in return for silver from Mexican mines. Anthony was to take charge of the shipments, which would arrive at New Orleans from Vera Cruz, and to reinvest profitably as much of the money as he could. The rest was to be shipped to Florence Udney's husband, David Parish, in Philadelphia, and from there on to Europe.

Traveling to Paris to make arrangements, Vincent and Anthony were waylaid in the Alps by Don Luis, who tried to force their coach over a cliff. His plans were thwarted, however, and his own carriage and coachman plunged into the deep gorge. At the time Don Luis was traveling with Faith Paleologus, whom he had made his mistress. The two had dismounted to watch the destruction of Anthony and his friend. After their plot failed, they were left to descend the mountain on foot.

In Paris Anthony met Angela for the first time in many years. She had borne him a son, and had become a famous singer and the mistress of Napoleon. She refused to marry Anthony and follow him to America, but she did give him his son. At her entreaty, Anthony left the child with Vincent's childless cousin, Anna.

Anthony's affairs prospered in New Orleans. He was able to invest the silver profitably, to form a bank, and to build a handsome plantation for himself. When David Parish died of heart failure, Anthony married Florence. Their daughter, Maria, was three, when the plantation house caught fire one night while Anthony was away. His wife and daughter were burned to death.

Burdened by his sorrow, Anthony started west. Captured by a tribe of Indians, he escaped, only to fall into the hands of soldiers from Santa Fé. There he was brought before the governor, Don Luis, and sentenced to go to Mexico City in a prison train. That same day Don Luis had a stroke and died. Faith, his wife by that time, prepared to return to Spain.

Anthony spent two years in the Hospital of St. Lazaro before Dolores, widow of a wealthy landowner, found him and arranged for his freedom. Later they were married and went to live in the village of San Luz. Dolores bore him two children. All went well until an ax slipped one day and caught Anthony in the groin while he was felling a tree. He bled to death before he was found.

Many years later, long after the village had been deserted by Dolores and her people, a group of migrants on their way to Santa Fé came to its site. The little Madonna, which Anthony had carried with him through life, still stood in a chapel in the ruins of San Luz. Mary Jorham, the young niece of a Captain Jorham, found the image, but she was not allowed to keep it because her parents thought it a heathen idol. Instead, it served as a fine target for a shooting match. It was splintered into a thousand pieces.

ANTIGONE

Type of work: Drama
Author: Sophocles (495?-406 B.C.)
Type of plot: Classical tragedy
Time of plot: Remote antiquity
Locale: The city of Thebes
First presented: 440 B.C.

Principal characters:
CREON, tyrant of Thebes
ANTIGONE, daughter of Oedipus
ISMENE, her sister
HAEMON, son of Creon
TIRESIAS, a prophet

Critique:

Although the main problem of this play would be unimportant today, the discussions of the responsibilities of a ruler are as pertinent now as in ancient Greece. The characters of the play move to their tragic ends with highly dramatic speeches, while the moral and philosophical problems of the plot are displayed through the chorus and soliloquies. When first presented, the play was so successful with Athenian audiences that Sophocles was made a general in the war against Samos. Recent presentations of the play have been well received by both audience and critic.

The Story:

Polynices and Eteocles, sons of the cursed family of King Oedipus, led two armies against each other before the gates of Thebes, and both brothers were killed in single combat with each other. Creon, their uncle, and now the tyrant ruler of the city, ordered that Eteocles be given full funeral rites, but that Polynices, who had attacked the city, be left unburied and unmourned. Anyone who broke this decree would be punished with death.

Antigone and Ismene, the sisters of Polynices and Eteocles, discussed this order, and with grief for the unburied brother tearing at her heart, Antigone asked Ismene to aid her in giving him burial. When Ismene refused to help in so dangerous a task, Antigone went defiantly to bury Polynices.

Shortly afterward, Creon learned from a sentry that the body had been buried. Angrily he ordered the sentry to find the perpetrator of the deed. The sentry returned to the grave and uncovered the body. During a dust storm Antigone came to look at the grave and, finding it open, filled the air with lamentation. Her cries attracted the attention of the guard, who captured her and took her to Creon.

Questioned by Creon, she said that to bury a man was to obey the laws of the gods, even if it were against the laws of a man. Her reply angered Creon. Antigone must die. Ismene tried to soften Creon's heart toward her sister by reminding him that Antigone was engaged to his son, Haemon. But Creon remained firm.

Haemon incurred his father's anger by arguments that Creon should soften his cruel decree because of popular sympathy for Antigone. Creon said that he cared nothing for the ideas of the town, and Haemon called his answer foolish. As a punishment, Creon ordered that Antigone be killed before Haemon's eyes. Haemon fled with threats of revenge. Creon ordered that Antigone be walled up in a cave outside Thebes and left there to die for her crime against his law.

When Antigone was led out of the city, the people of Thebes followed her, lamenting her fate. She was thrust into the cave. All this while, Polynices' body lay unburied outside the walls. The prophet Tiresias warned Creon that the gods had not been pleased with his action, and that the body should be buried. He foretold that before long Haemon would die if his father did not bury Polynices and rescue Antigone from the cave.

Creon, realizing that Tiresias' prophesies had never proved false, hurried to avert the fate the prophet had foretold. Quickly he ordered a tomb prepared for Polynices, and he himself set off to release Antigone. But the will of the gods could not be changed so easily. When he reached the cave, he heard his son's voice within, crying out in grief. Creon entered and saw that Antigone had hanged herself with a rope made from her own dress. Haemon, sword in hand, rushed at his father as if to attack him, but instead he spat on the old man. He then fell on his sword and killed himself in sorrow over Antigone's death. The news of these events quickly traveled back to the city, and Creon's wife, hearing of so many misfortunes, died by her own hand.

On returning to Thebes with the body of his son, Creon learned of his wife's death. Seeing that his life could no longer have meaning, he had himself led out of the city into exile. He was, himself, the final victim of his harsh tyranny.

THE ANTIQUARY

Type of work: Novel
Author: Sir Walter Scott (1771-1832)
Type of plot: Domestic romance
Time of plot: Late eighteenth century
Locale: Scotland
First published: 1816

Principal characters:
JONATHAN OLDBUCK OF MONKBARNS, the antiquary
LOVEL, an illegitimate son of unknown parents
SIR ARTHUR WARDOUR, a baronet, Oldbuck's friend
MISS ISABELLA WARDOUR, his daughter
EDIE OCHILTREE, a beggar
HECTOR M'INTYRE, Oldbuck's nephew
THE EARL OF GLENALLAN, present head of a powerful family
DOUSTERSWIVEL, a magician

Critique:

Not one of the most popular of Scott's novels, *The Antiquary* is nevertheless a respected member of the Waverley group and the novel most nearly contemporary to Scott's own time. Although it is a romance, it is also a novel of manners. Scott admitted that when necessary he sacrificed the plot in order to describe more clearly the manners of the characters, particularly those of the lower social classes. His characterizations of the Scottish peasants are much more vivid than are those of the upper classes. But the touch of magic that was Scott's is evident everywhere in this novel, as it is in all he wrote.

The Story:

When old Jonathan Oldbuck of Monkbarns first met young Lovel, he was impressed by the young man's good manners and conduct; but he was also mystified by the little he could learn of Lovel's past. It was obvious that Lovel was not the boy's real name and that there was something in his history of which he was ashamed.

From his good friend Sir Arthur Wardour, Oldbuck at last learned something of Lovel's history. The young man was the illegitimate son of unknown parents. Although a benefactor had settled a large estate on him, he lived in solitude and disgrace because of his questionable ancestry. To make matters worse, he was in love with Sir Arthur's daughter, Isabella. Though the girl loved him, she would not accept him because she knew her father would not permit an alliance with a man of unknown and illegitimate origins. Even after Lovel had saved her life and that of her father, when they were trapped by the tides, she gave him no more than the thanks due him for his bravery.

Sir Arthur was in serious financial straits, in debt to dozens of tradesmen and friends, among them Oldbuck. In order to restore his fortune, he had fallen into a plot prepared by one Dousterswivel, an evil magician who had promised his aid in finding valuable minerals on Sir Arthur's property. Sir Arthur, forced to put up money before Dousterswivel would work his magic, had already borrowed one hundred pounds from Oldbuck, who suspected that Dousterswivel was the crook that he was.

Before the magician could attempt to work his magic, Oldbuck's nephew, Captain Hector M'Intyre, came home for a visit. A hot-headed young man, he accused Lovel of lying about the little he told of his past. Hector challenged Lovel to a duel, and although Lovel did everything he could to prevent it the duel was fought. Lovel wounded Hector fatally, or so it appeared, and was forced to flee the country on a boat provided by a friend. Hector did recover, but Lovel did not hear the news until much later. He had been aided in his flight by Edie Ochiltree, a beggar who knew all the secrets of the countryside. While Edie hid Lovel in a cave, they overheard Dousterswivel trying to convince Sir Arthur that he could find buried treasure in that cave, if Sir Arthur would put up the necessary money. Edie used that knowledge to good account.

When Sir Arthur asked Oldbuck for another hundred pounds to give to Dousterswivel so that he would get the treasure from the cave, Oldbuck insisted that they go to the cave and dig for the treasure. Although the magician tried to prevent the excursion, Oldbuck would not be denied. Everyone present was completely surprised when, after much digging, old Edie the beggar stuck a pick into the ground and hit a chest. When the chest was opened, the bewildered spectators found a fortune in coin; Sir Arthur was saved from disaster. Edie, in an attempt to pay back Dousterswivel, tricked him into digging for hours for more treasure that Edie said was also buried in the cave. He also arranged with a friend to have a specter appear and frighten the magician half to death.

About the same time there occurred another event which was to have great influence upon Oldbuck, Sir Arthur, and their friends. An old woman in the neighborhood sent for the Earl of Glenallan, head of a wealthy and powerful family. Before she died, the old woman wanted to clear her conscience of a terrible wrong she had done the earl when he was a young man. The earl had been in love with a girl whom his mother hated, primarily because of her family. The earl had secretly married the girl before his mother, in a spiteful attempt to break up the romance, told her son that the girl was his own sister. Because of certain letters and the perjured testimony of servants, including the old woman telling the story, the earl had believed his mother's story.

His wife had taken her own life, but before she died she had given birth to a male child. A servant had whisked the child away, and the old woman did not know whether he had lived or died. The earl, who had lived a life of misery because of the horrible crime he thought he had committed in marrying his own sister, was joyful at the news given him by the old crone, even though he grieved at the useless death of the girl he loved. He told the story to Oldbuck and asked his help in determining whether the child had lived.

While Oldbuck and the Earl of Glenallan were conducting their investigation, news came that the French were about to raid the Scottish coast. Hector, who was now fully recovered from the wound suffered at Lovel's hands, prepared to gather troops and meet Major Neville, an officer in charge of local defense. Lovel had not been heard from since the duel, and there were rumors that he had died at sea. Then old Edie brought the joyful news that the ship carrying Lovel had put in to shore and that all aboard were safe. From his remarks to Oldbuck, the old gentlemen learned that the money found in the cave on Sir Arthur's land had been buried there by Lovel and Edie after they had overheard the conversation between Dousterswivel and Sir Arthur. Lovel, hearing of Sir Arthur's financial difficulties, had taken that way of helping Isabella's father without embarrassing the old gentleman by offering him money outright.

When Major Neville appeared to take charge of the garrison, everyone was amazed to see that he was in reality Lovel. Lovel, or rather Major Neville, brought word that there would be no battle. A watchman had mistaken a bonfire for a signal that the French were coming. As they all stood talking, the Earl of Glenallan noted the young man's marked resemblance to his dead wife. Then the mystery was solved. Through old papers and the words of old servants of the Glenallan family, the earl learned that without doubt Lovel was his son. While a baby, the boy had been cared for by the earl's brother and, unknown to the earl, had inherited his uncle's fortune.

Lovel was restored to his rightful place, and within a month he and Isabella Wardour were married. From that time on all the friends lived in peace and prosperity and joy.

ANTONY AND CLEOPATRA

Type of work: Drama
Author: William Shakespeare (1564-1616)
Type of plot: Romantic tragedy
Time of plot: About 30 B.C.
Locale: Egypt and various parts of the Roman Empire
First presented: 1606-1607

Principal characters:
MARK ANTONY,
OCTAVIUS CAESAR, and
LEPIDUS, triumvirs, ruling Rome
ENOBARBUS, and
EROS, Antony's friends
SEXTUS POMPEIUS, leader of the party opposed to Octavius Caesar
CLEOPATRA, Queen of Egypt
OCTAVIA, Caesar's sister and Antony's wife
CHARMIAN, and
IRAS, Cleopatra's attendants

Critique:

In his tragedies Shakespeare rose to dramatic heights seldom equaled. Although critics may argue to determine the greatest of his tragedies, surely *Antony and Cleopatra* is among the top few. Its scope is staggering; it covers the whole Roman Empire and the men who ruled it. Only a genius could match the greatness of the scenes with such beauty of poetry and philosophy. Here a man born to rule the world is brought to ruin by his weaknesses and lusts. Deserted by friends and subjects, he is denied even a noble death, but must attempt suicide. Even that he bungles. The tragedy is grimly played out; honor and nobility die, as well as the man.

The Story:

After the murder of Julius Caesar, the Roman Empire was ruled by three men, the noble triumvirs, Mark Antony, Lepidus, and Octavius, Caesar's nephew. Antony, having been given the Eastern sphere to rule, had gone to Alexandria and there he had seen and fallen passionately in love with Cleopatra, Queen of Egypt. She was the flower of the Nile, but a wanton who had been the mistress of Julius Caesar and of many others. Antony was so filled with lust for her that he ignored his own counsel and the warnings of his friends, and

as long as possible he ignored also a request from Octavius Caesar that he return to Rome. Sextus Pompeius, son of Pompey the Great, and a powerful leader, was gathering troops to seize Rome from the rule of the triumvirs, and Octavius Caesar wished to confer with the other two, Antony and Lepidus. At last the danger of a victory by Sextus Pompeius, coupled with the news that his wife Fulvia was dead, forced Antony to leave Egypt and Cleopatra and journey to Rome.

Pompeius was confident of victory so long as Antony stayed in Egypt, for Antony was a better general than either Lepidus or Octavius. When Pompeius heard that Antony was headed toward Rome, his hope was that Octavius and Antony would not mend their quarrels but would continue to fight each other as they had in the past. Lepidus did not matter; he sided with neither of the other two, and cared little for conquest and glory. Pompeius faced disappointment, however, for Antony and Octavius mended their quarrels in the face of common danger. To seal their renewed friendship, Antony married Octavia, the sister of Octavius; through her, each general would be bound to the other. Thus it seemed that Pompeius' scheme to separate Antony and Octavius would fail. His last hope was that Antony's lust would send him back to Cleopatra; then he and Octavius would battle each other and Pompeius would conquer Rome. To stall for time, he sealed a treaty with the triumvirs. Antony, with his wife, went to Athens on business for the Empire. There word reached him that Lepidus and Octavius had waged war in spite of the treaty they had signed, and Pompeius had been killed. Octavius' next move was to seize Lepidus on the pretext that he had aided Pompeius. Now the Roman world had but two rulers, Octavius and Antony.

But Antony could not resist the lure of Cleopatra. Sending Octavia, his wife, home from Athens, he hurried back to Egypt. His return ended all pretense of friendship between him and Octavius. Each man prepared for battle, the winner to be the sole ruler of the world. Cleopatra joined her forces with those of Antony. At first Antony was supreme on the land, but Octavius ruled the sea and lured Antony to fight him there. Antony's friends and captains, particularly loyal Enobarbus, begged him not to risk his forces on the sea, but Antony, confident of victory, prepared to match his ships with those of Octavius at Actium. But in the decisive hour of the great sea fight Cleopatra ordered her fleet to leave the battle, and sail for home. Antony, leaving the battle and his honor and his glory, followed her. Because he had set the example for desertion, many of his men left his forces and joined the standard of Octavius.

Antony was sunk in gloom at the folly of his own actions, but his lust had made him drunk with desire, and everything, even honor, must bow to Cleopatra. She protested that she did not know that Antony would follow her when she sailed away. Antony had reason enough to know she lied, but he still wanted the fickle wanton at any cost.

Octavius sent word to Cleopatra that she might have all her wishes granted if she would surrender Antony to Octavius. Knowing that Octavius was likely to be the victor in the struggle, she sent him a message of loyalty and of admiration for his greatness. Although Antony had seen her receive the addresses of Octavius' messenger, and even though he ranted and stormed at her for her faithlessness, she was easily able to dispel his fears and jealousy and make him hers again. After a failure to sue for peace, Antony decided to march again against his enemy. At this decision even the faithful Enobarbus left him and went over to Octavius, for he thought Antony had lost his reason as well as his honor. But Enobarbus too was an honorable man who shortly afterward died of shame for deserting his general.

On the day of the battle victory was in sight for Antony, in spite of overwhelming odds. But once more the flight of the Egyptian fleet betrayed him. His defeat left Octavius master of the world. Antony was like a madman, seeking nothing but revenge on treacherous Cleopatra. When the queen heard of his rage, she had word sent to him that she was dead, killed by her own hand out of love for him. Convinced once more that Cleopatra had been true to him, Antony called on Eros, his one remaining follower, to kill him so that he could join Cleopatra in death. But faithful Eros killed himself rather than stab his beloved general. Determined to die, Antony fell on his own sword. Even that desperate act was without dignity or honor, for he did not die immediately and he could find no one who loved him enough to end his pain and misery. While he lay there, a messenger brought word that Cleopatra still lived. He ordered his servants to carry him to her. There he died in her arms, each proclaiming eternal love for the other.

When Octavius Caesar heard the news of Antony's death, he grieved. Although he had fought and conquered

Antony, he lamented the sorry fate of a great man turned weakling, ruined by his own lust. He sent a messenger to assure Cleopatra that she would be treated royally, that she should be ruler of her own fate. But the queen learned, as Antony had warned her, that Octavius would take her to Rome to march behind him in his triumphant procession, where she, a queen and mistress to two former rulers of the world, would be pinched and spat upon by rabble and slaves. To cheat him of his triumph, she put on her crown and all her royal garb, placed a poisonous asp on her breast, and lay down to die. Charmian and Iras, her loyal attendants, died the same death. Octavius Caesar, entering her chamber, saw her dead, but as beautiful and desirable as in life. There was only one thing he could do for his one-time friend and the dead queen: he ordered their burial in a common grave, together in death as they had wished to be in life.

APOLOGIA PRO VITA SUA

Type of work: Autobiography
Author: John Henry Newman (1801-1890)
First published: 1864.

This long essay, also known as *History of My Religious Opinions,* is the famous reply written by John Henry Newman in answer to the attack made upon him by Charles Kingsley (1819-1875). The years 1833 to 1841 had seen the publication of the *Tracts for the Times,* to which Newman had been a contributor; these tracts, which gave their name to the "Tractarian Movement" or "Oxford Movement," were the spearhead of the great theological controversy of the middle years of the century. Newman and his friends were eager to return the Anglican Church to something like its position during past centuries; they valued tradition and hierarchy; they wished to go back to the severe, authoritarian faith of the past, from which they believed the Church of England had lapsed. In a word, they were the "High Church" party; and some idea of the rift that was created within the Church can be gleaned from Trollope's Barchester novels. In 1845, Newman left the Anglican Church for the Roman; two years later he was ordained priest in that communion.

In January, 1864, Kingsley, an Anglican clergyman of what was known as the "Broad Church" party and a popular novelist, attacked Newman in a magazine article, in which he stated that "Truth, for its own sake, has never been a virtue with the Roman clergy. Father Newman informs us that it need not, and on the whole ought not to be. . . ." To this article, Newman replied in a pamphlet in February of that year, whereupon Kingsley wrote still another pamphlet entitled "What, then, does Dr. Newman mean?" in which he accused Newman of having "gambled away" his reason, of having a "morbid" mind, and of not caring about "truth for its own sake." It was in answer to this pamphlet that *Apologia pro Vita Sua* was written.

Newman divided his work into chapters, each dealing with a crucial period

in his life. The first gives the story of his youth and his education up to his thirty-second year, by which time he was a Fellow of Oriel College, Oxford, and had been ordained in the Anglican Church. By his own account, he emerges as an extraordinarily precocious lad, preoccupied at a very early age with religious questions. He resembled, indeed, the hero of his own novel *Loss and Gain*—which phrase might be applied as a description of his career. The modern reader will smile at Newman's decision, reached at the age of fifteen, that celibacy was the only course for him; yet his prodigious intellect shines through his very modest account of his youth. He tells us of his reading; but the real influences were his friends Hurrell Froude and the older John Keble (1792-1866). It was Froude, with his love for tradition and for the external beauty of the Roman Church, who began to soften Newman's insular dislike of that institution.

The year 1830 was a momentous one for Newman. The revolution that deposed Charles X of France distressed him; the Whig victory in England distressed him even more. He had a violent hatred of Liberalism, and everywhere it seemed triumphant. The "Tractarian Movement" was largely a counterattack. Newman himself claimed that the movement had begun to stir as far back as 1828, when he was Vicar of St. Mary's, Oxford; but the date of its beginning is usually set in July of 1833, when Keble preached a famous sermon at Oxford against the errors of the Whig government in Church policy. The *Tracts for the Times,* written by Newman and his friends, stated their position. As Newman saw it, the Whigs must be opposed and the Church of England returned to the position of authority it had held during the early seventeenth century. He considered himself as belonging to neither the "High" nor the "Low" Church party; he was merely anti-

Liberal. He explained his position as based on: (1) dogma (he had no use for "religion as a mere sentiment"; there must be positive beliefs); (2) a visible Church with sacraments and rites and the Episcopal system; (3) anti-Romanism. Such was the general point of view of the Oxford Movement. Newman, incidentally, had very little to say about ritual, usually associated with the High Church position. He was interested in theology, not liturgics.

Newman admitted frankly that in the vast amount of writing he did during these years he had attempted to refute many of the tenets of Romanism. What he was seeking for himself was a basis in reason for his beliefs; for the Anglican Church, he was seeking a theology of its own that would make it more than a *via media*. These investigations led him to a consideration of the common heritage of Romanism and Anglicanism and to the question of how much of the Roman belief could be accepted by an Anglican. He began to be convinced that in English history the real objection to Rome had been political rather than theological; that Romanism and Anglicanism had, after all, not been so far apart as was generally believed. Inevitably, he began to find a difference between Roman dogmas, which he could accept, and Roman practice, which he often could not. He confessed that, for a long time, the stumbling block had been the Roman veneration of the Virgin and prayers to the saints. But he was obviously drawing closer to Rome.

It was Tract XC, published in 1841, that brought the storm on Newman's head and led to his final break with the Church of England. In this tract he examined the question of how far the Thirty-Nine Articles, on which the Church rests, were capable of a Roman interpretation. Immediately he was accused of everything from "traducing the Reformation" to planning to build a monastery near Oxford. He himself was feeling grave doubts about Anglicanism, derived mainly from his reading on the abstruse doctrines of the Monophysites. When he

could no longer conscientiously maintain his clerical position, he resigned his living of St. Mary's in September of 1843. As he explained, he had spent the years from 1835 to 1839 trying, in his writings, to benefit the Church of England at the expense of the Church of Rome and the years from 1839 to 1843 trying to benefit the Church of England without prejudice to the Church of Rome. In 1843 he began to despair of the Church of England.

The years between 1843 and 1845 were spent, according to Newman, in retirement. He had now reached the crossroads but was as yet unable to make his final decision. He had already retracted the "hard things" he had said against Rome, the things he had felt compelled to say in defense of the Anglican Church. He made a point of seeing no Roman Catholics; his struggle was purely an inward one. Though he still felt that the Church of England was a branch of the true Church, though he still deplored the "Mariolatry" of Rome, he was convinced that Rome was more in accord with the early Church. His horror of Liberalism also played its part; he very genuinely felt that the spirit of Liberalism was the spirit of Antichrist. As he now saw the situation, on the one hand there was Liberalism leading inevitably to atheism; on the other, Anglicanism leading to Rome. He still remained in lay communion with the Church of England during this difficult period, but more and more often he found himself asking this question: "Can I be saved in the English Church?" When he was compelled to answer in the negative, he made the great decision and was received into the Roman Communion in 1845. Two years later he was ordained priest.

In the concluding section of the essay Newman defended himself against the jibes that were hurled at him after his conversion. It was said that by submitting to Rome he had abdicated his power of personal judgment and that he was now compelled to accept dogmas which might, at any moment, be changed. His reply was that the Roman doctrines were not difficult for him, that historically the Church had not suppressed freedom of intellect. He felt that an infallible Church had been intended by the Creator to preserve religion—especially in an age of increasing skepticism. Lastly—and this is the most famous part of the essay—he advanced the idea that a conflict between authority and private judgment is beneficial to the man whose ideas are being tested.

Though the *Apologia* won Newman a resounding victory over Kingsley, the work is not easy reading. The difficulty does not lie in the style, for no one has written more clearly and simply than he. But he wrote for readers who were familiar with Church history and with theological problems, so that most readers in our age of religious ignorance and indifference lack the knowledge to grasp many of his arguments. It is difficult today to understand his dilemma. Yet the *Apologia* remains a powerful and sincere work. Some, naturally, have seen in Newman, as Kingsley must have done, only a man whose habit of mind made him take refuge in an authoritarian Church which would solve his spiritual problems for him. Others, taking the opposite view, would agree with Ramon Fernandez that "In him intelligence and faith act as mutual brakes and yet no attentive reader can accuse him of the slightest artifice."

AN APOLOGY FOR THE LIFE OF COLLEY CIBBER, COMEDIAN

Type of work: Autobiography
Author: Colley Cibber (1671-1757)
Time: Late seventeenth and early eighteenth centuries
Locale: England
First published: 1740

Principal personages:
COLLEY CIBBER, actor, playwright, producer
WILLIAM CONGREVE, playwright
SIR JOHN VANBRUGH, architect and playwright
JOHN GAY, poet, author of *The Beggar's Opera*
JOSEPH ADDISON, essayist and author of the successful *Cato*
SIR RICHARD STEELE, essayist and playwright
ALEXANDER POPE, author of *The Dunciad*

To read Colley Cibber's *Apology* is to recapture intimate views of London theatrical, social, and literary life during the last decade of the seventeenth and the first quarter of the following century, as observed by a successful actor and theatrical manager, a playwright of sorts, and a man of shrewd insight into his own foibles and those of his fellows.

Published ten years after his retirement from the stage (1730) and his acceptance of the poet laureateship, this autobiography is a frank and engaging account of his childhood experiences as the son of a well-known sculptor, his schoolboy activities, his early days as a stage-struck youth, his long career in the theater, and his candid and unprejudiced observations of people and events. For this is an *apology*, not in the sense of an acknowledgment of wrongdoing, mistake, or regrettable circumstance, but as an explanation of the life of a man who was regularly and closely connected with the theater; who knew and talked with many of the most influential people of his day; who was acquainted with political actions, backstage gossip, and the infinite variety of public life and private in his time. Cibber was attempting, as he expressed it in the first chapter, to present "as true a picture of myself as natural vanity will permit me to draw," since "a man who has pass'd above forty years of his life upon a theatre, where he has never appear'd to be himself, may have naturally excited the curiosity of his spec-

tators to know what he really was, when in no body's shape but his own. . . ." He also proposed to include "the theatrical history of my own time, from my first appearance on the stage to my last exit."

Following a simple chronological pattern of development, Cibber devotes the first three chapters of his autobiography to matters of his parents and family. His father had emigrated from Holstein many years before the Restoration in 1660; his mother was a member of the Colley family, formerly of some prominence in Rutlandshire. His education was regrettably limited to a few years in a free school. Early in life, he says he was possessed of a "giddy negligence," an inconsistency of character, and these qualities persisted, he admits, frequently to his own embarrassment. But Cibber notes that Pope's selection of him as the heir to the throne of folly in *The Dunciad* was done not so much to satirize Cibber as it was to give publicity to the poem, for an attack on the laureate was likely to gain increased sales for any publication. Thus, with remarkable good nature, Cibber transforms Pope's malicious defamation into a device for "profit to himself." This was both a successful and extraordinary outcome for any controversy with Alexander Pope, "the wasp of Twickenham."

Cibber's attempts to gain entrance to Winchester proving fruitless, he next tried the life of a trooper in the Revolution of 1688. His father sought preferment for his lively and mercurial son in

161

various ways, but by 1690, Cibber succumbed to the "allurements of a theatre," and so his long stage career began.

In the remaining portion of the book, chapters IV through XVI, Cibber intermingles autobiographical details and anecdotes with factual accounts of the history of the London stage from its restoration in 1660 until his retirement in the 1730's; with personal reminiscences and valuable word-portraits of actors and actresses, playwrights, managers; with first-hand experiences with the licensing acts and Masters of Revels. For example, before recounting his early days in the theater, Cibber sets forth, swiftly but convincingly, his own "short view of the stage" from its rebirth in 1660 until the time he became an actor in 1690. To this he adds an account of the greatest players of the time, describing them in vivid and satisfying detail, evaluating their performances, enumerating their best roles. His highest praise goes to Betterton and Mrs. Bracegirdle, for Cibber knew them all, regarded them closely as a student of acting, and valued their talents shrewdly as a stage manager. He writes of his own first appearance in a significant acting role as the chaplain in Otway's *The Orphan,* of the first prologue he composed, of his first play, the successful *Love's Last Shift.* This play led to his long acquaintance-ship with Sir John Vanbrugh, an architect turned playwright. Cibber frankly admits that Gay's *The Beggar's Opera* was a "vast success" and that his attempt to offset this portrayal of highwaymen, thieves, and receivers of stolen goods with a comedy in praise of virtue, *Love in a Riddle,* was a resounding failure. In this instance, his middle-class morality seems to have blurred Cibber's judgment, for the charm and delightful raciness of Gay's ballad-opera have made it a favorite for countless generations, while no one but an avid student of the history of English comedy has ever heard of *Love in a Riddle.*

Cibber traces the complex and curious history of the rival acting companies, of the rise to great popularity of Italian opera, of his ultimate assumption of a position of authority as actor-manager. He pauses to comment upon the building of a new theater, the Hay Market, and its weaknesses acoustically. He remarks upon the actor-manager's difficulties with gentlemen who sought to master the intricacies of theater operation, of the intense rivalries and jealousies of actors and actresses, of the origin of actor's benefits. He admits freely his own inadequacies as a tragic actor, for his voice was unsuited to heavy roles; however, he does assert his success as a villain. He comments on the unfortunate public attitude toward the profession of acting; he even offers good advice to would-be playwrights, suggesting that they always pay particular attention to their plotting.

No doubt it is this union of the frank appraisal of a man who recognizes his own mistakes and strong points with his shrewd observations of personages and events that gives Cibber's book its continuing vigor, its essential charm. He can look upon the self-seeking defections of actors with charity, for he realizes intimately the insecurity of their profession and excuses their failure to fulfill certain obligations as understandable. He perceives that well-meaning patrons of the theater could not possibly understand all the implications of their amateurish decisions, and so he deals with them gently, despite all the trouble they caused him as an actor-manager. In short, Cibber is both a professional in the theater and a devoted, though not always gifted, master craftsman in the art of the drama. His youthful passion for the stage and acting and writing plays and refurbishing old dramas seems never to have left him. His lifelong interest in matters theatrical seldom wavers; hence his desire to record important happenings in dramatic history, his awareness of the significance of minor occurrences, and his appraisal of the people concerned with these events large and small combine to give this account remarkable value.

If the test of excellence in autobiographical writing is the author's ability not only to set down his views of people, events, and circumstances accurately and with satisfying detail, but also to portray his own qualities with rich revealing honesty, then Colley Cibber's *Apology* deserves recognition. For Cibber's enthusiasm for the stage and its people is intensely absorbing; his zeal to make his readers understand the development of English acting, the facts of play production during his time, and the history of the theater in those lively years is genuine and almost incomparable. Moreover, his sincerity, his good humor, his vanity, his strong armor against insult and vitriolic attack, his keen sense of justice, and his wholesome absorption in the "allurements of a theatre," make this autobiography a record unique in theatrical writings. Cibber the playwright, manager, actor, play-doctor, poet laureate is dead long since save for specialists in theatrical matters. But Colley Cibber the apologist and commentator on dramatic history is still intensely human, vivid, and readable.

THE APOSTLE

Type of work: Novel
Author: Sholem Asch (1880-   )
Type of plot: Religious chronicle
Time of plot: Shortly after the Crucifixion
Locale: The Roman Empire
First published: 1943

Principal characters:

SAUL OF TARSHISH, afterwards known as Paul
JOSEPH BAR NABA OF CYPRUS, Saul's friend, an early convert
REB ISTEPHAN, a famous Jewish preacher
SIMON BAR JONAH, called Peter
REB JACOB, Joseph's son

Critique:

The Apostle is a faithful attempt to chronicle the life of the two great apostles, Peter and Paul. Adhering carefully to the history of the period, the author has presented a sympathetic portrait of the struggles of the early Christians. His knowledge of contemporary events gives the reader a vivid picture of the life of the period shortly after the Crucifixion.

The Story:

It was seven weeks after the crucifixion of Yeshua of Nazareth by Pontius Pilate. All the poor of Jerusalem, who had found in Jeshua their Messiah, had gone into hiding; but the word was spreading. Little by little the story was told, of Yeshua who had come back after his death, of the Messiah who had appeared to his disciples. The matter was hotly argued on all sides. The pious Jews could not believe in a Messiah who had been killed; the Messianists devoutly affirmed their faith.

Saul of Tarshish and Joseph bar Naba came upon a street preacher, a rustic Galilean, who told with great conviction of Yeshua's return after he had been entombed. Cries of belief and of repugnance interrupted his talk. Saul himself spoke with great bitterness against this Messiah, for he had no patience with the gentle Yeshua who was hanged.

The agitation rapidly spread. One of the most vigorous upholders of Yeshua was Reb Istephan. He had a gift for moving men's souls, and more and more Jews became persuaded. Joseph bar Naba himself had known Yeshua in his lifetime, and when Joseph heard Reb Istephan he was convinced. Joseph became a Messianist. This conversion disgusted Saul, and in sorrow and bitterness he turned away from his friend Joseph.

Then a dramatic incident took place. Simon, the first of Yeshua's disciples, healed Nehemiah the cripple in the name of the Nazarene. Many were much impressed by the cure, but others resented Simon's use of the Messiah's name. As a result his enemies had their way, and Simon was imprisoned by the High Priest to await trial. Then another miracle happened! Simon and his follower Jochanan had been securely locked in a dungeon, but in the morning they were walking the streets again. It was said that they had passed directly through the stone walls — with the help of Yeshua.

The resentment against the wild Galileans grew among the rulers, while the humble folk followed Simon with trust. The High Priest again brought Simon to trial; but Simon spoke so well in defense of his doctrine that he was freed. And now the tumult increased. The ignorant folk, seeing Simon released, concluded that there was official sanction for the

THE APOSTLE by Sholem Asch. Translated by Maurice Samuel. By permission of the author and the publishers, G. P. Putnam's Sons. Copyright, 1943, by Sholem Asch.

new cult; hence more joined the followers of Yeshua.

Saul was greatly incensed. He believed that the Messiah was yet to come, that the disciples were corrupting Jerusalem. He went to the High Priest and secured appointment as official spy. In his new job Saul tracked down the humble Messianists and sentenced them to the lash. Growing in power, Saul the Zealot finally took Reb Istephan prisoner for preaching the new faith. With grim pleasure Saul led the way to the stoning pit and watched Istephan sink beneath the flung rocks. As he died, the preacher murmured a prayer for the forgiveness of his tormentors. Saul was vaguely troubled.

Then the Messianists were much heartened. Reb Jacob ben Joseph, Yeshua's younger brother, came to Jerusalem to head the humble cult, and Saul could do little against this pious and strict Jew. By chance the High Priest heard of more Messianists in Damascus Saul volunteered to investigate and hurried to his new field. But on the way a vision appeared to him and said, "Saul, Saul, why dost thou persecute me?" Saul then recognized Yeshua for his Lord and as he was commanded he went on to Damascus, although he was still blinded by the heavenly apparition. A follower of the new religion baptized him and restored his sight. The penitent Saul hurried away from the haunts of man. In all he waited seven years for his mission.

Finally as he prayed in his mother's house, the call came. Joseph bar Naba asked Saul to go with him to Antioch to strengthen the congregation there. At last Saul was on the way to bring the word of the Messiah to others. He left for Antioch with Joseph and the Greek Titus, Saul's first convert.

Now Simon had founded the church at Antioch among the Greeks. The perplexing question was, could a devout Jew even eat with the gentiles, let alone accept them into the church? In Jerusalem Jacob held firmly to the law of the Torah: salvation was only for the circumcised. Simon vacillated. In Jerusalem he followed Jacob; among the Greeks he accepted gentiles fully. Joseph had been sent by the elders of Jerusalem to Antioch to apply the stricter rule to the growing Messianic church.

Saul at first met with much suspicion. The Messianists remembered too well Saul the Zealot who had persecuted them. But little by little the apostle won them over. Yeshua appeared to Saul several times, and he was much strengthened in the faith. At last Saul found his true mission in the conviction that he was divinely appointed to bring the word of Yeshua to the gentiles. He worked wonders at Antioch and built a strong church there, but his acceptance of gentiles cost him Joseph's friendship. As a symbol of his new mission Saul became Paul and began his years of missionary work.

To Corinth, to Ephesus, to Cyprus— to all the gentiles went Paul. Everywhere he founded a church, sometimes small but always zealous. With him much of the time went Lukas, the Greek physician. Lukas was an able minister and a scholar who was writing the life of Yeshua.

The devout Jews in Jerusalem were greatly troubled by this strange preacher who accepted the gentiles. Finally they brought him up for trial. Paul escaped only by standing on his rights as a Roman citizen. As such he could demand a trial before Caesar himself. Paul went to Rome as a captive, but he rejoiced, for he knew the real test of Christianity would be in Rome. Already Simon was there, preaching to the orthodox Jews.

The evil Nero made Paul wait in prison for two years without a hearing, and even then only the intervention of Seneca freed the apostle. For a short time Simon and Paul worked together, one among the Jews and the other among the gentiles. They converted many, and the lowly fervently embraced the promise of salvation.

To give himself an outlet for his

fancied talents as an architect, Nero burned Rome and planned to rebuild a beautiful city. But the crime was too much even for the Romans. To divert suspicion from himself, Nero blamed the Christians. He arrested thousands of them, and on the appointed day opened the royal carnage. Jews and Christians hour after hour were gored by oxen, torn by tigers, chewed by crocodiles. At the end of the third day many Romans could no longer bear the sight, but still Nero sat on. It was so strange: the Christians died well, and with their last breath they forgave their persecutors.

Simon, only a Jew, was crucified afterward; Paul, born a Roman citizen, was beheaded. With them to the execution went Gabelus the gladiator, who had accepted Christianity. But the deaths of Simon and Paul were in reality the beginning. The martyrdom of the early Christians was the foundation stone of the Christian church.

THE APPLE OF THE EYE

Type of work: Novel
Author: Glenway Wescott (1901-   )
Type of plot: Regional romance
Time of plot: Twentieth century
Locale: Rural Wisconsin
First published: 1924

Principal characters:
HANNAH MADOC, a primitive
JULE BIER, Hannah's lover
SELMA, Jule's wife
ROSALIA, Jule's and Selma's daughter
MIKE, Rosalia's lover
DAN STRANE, Rosalia's cousin

Critique:

This novel tells of the background and youth of Dan Strane in rural Wisconsin, and the story of Hannah Madoc reveals the set of values against which the author measures his characters. Jule himself believed in Hannah's goodness, but he was too weak to break away from his own social ties to marry the girl he really loved. The emphasis upon sex in the story is typical of a young boy's wonder at the difference between religious doctrines and the natural functions of man's true personality.

The Story:

When her drunken father came home one night and swung at her with a broom handle, patient, hard-working Hannah Madoc pushed him off the porch in self-defense. He died a few days later, leaving his daughter orphaned and penniless, and Hannah went to work in Mrs. Boyle's store. There she waited on customers during the day and served the men liquor in the evening.

One night Jule Bier saw her behind the store counter. Ever since the death of his wife and the piling up of debts, old Mr. Bier had struggled to make enough money from his farm to give Jule a chance in life. Cold and calculating, the elder Bier had sent Jule to work as a hired hand on the neighborhood farms. Jule began to court Hannah during long walks at night; he took her to

neighborhood dances, and they went for rides in his buggy. Hannah soon tired of the attentions of other men. When Mr. Boyle attempted to make love to her, she quit her job to go to work on a farm near Jule's home.

Old Mr. Bier sent Jule to court Selma Duncan, the oldest daughter of a wealthy farmer. Blindly obeying his father, Jule proposed to the girl and was accepted. Then he realized what he had done. Facing Hannah, he was bewildered by her grief, only half aware of his own.

Leaving the neighborhood of Sheboygan, Hannah went to Fond du Lac, where she became a prostitute and lost in a few years her beauty and vitality. At last Jule went to Fond du Lac to bring his former sweetheart back to her home. Hannah ended her years in bitter sterility, answering a call for help from a neighbor, nursing a sick calf, or taking care of someone's children when their mother became ill. She died, prematurely aged and broken, as the result of a fall.

Jule and Selma had one daughter, Rosalia. Selma's sister, Mrs. Strane, had a son, Dan, who was a boy of fourteen when Rosalia was in her early twenties. Mike, a young man with a keen zest for life, worked on Jule's farm. Because his mother was so tight-lipped and because she tried to instill in him a chastity of ignorance and abstinence, Dan had developed an adolescent feeling of frustration and curiosity. He longed to know what sex was, how it affected people, but at the same time he was overcome by an inbred feeling of shame. It was Mike who cleared the way for Dan after they became friends. Mike, who believed that life should be full of experience both physical and mental, made life's processes a wonderful thing, not obscene and dirty, as Dan's mother had led the boy to believe. Breaking away from the mother who had been his idol, Dan replaced her with his new friend, Mike. Mike, in love with Rosalia, shared his deeper feelings with his young friend. Dan had grown up.

Mike loved Rosalia and he desired her, but at first Rosalia resisted his love-making. One afternoon he seduced her. Rosalia's subsequent tears frightened him, but soon she learned to hide her terror of love. She told Mike that they ought .o get married to redeem their sin, but Mike's suggestion that Selma might not approve quieted the frightened girl. Mike was not certain that he wanted to marry Rosalia. When Jule quietly told Mike that he had noticed Rosalia's and Mike's love and that he would not object to the marriage if Mike wanted it, Mike felt trapped. He quit his job with Jule and left the Bier farm.

Dan was inconsolable. Having looked upon his cousin and Mike as perfect lovers, he could not understand why Mike should leave. Rosalia brooded, her sense of guilt increasing after Mike's departure. Although she hid her feelings from her parents, Dan knew enough of her affair with Mike to be curious about Rosalia's feelings. But he could learn nothing from her. Rosalia herself was not as calm as she appeared to be. The punishment for love was a child. She felt a surge of emotion within her, and it seemed permanently a part of her. She concluded that she must be with child. It was inevitable; she had sinned and this was to be her harvest. Deserted by her lover-husband, she could not bear to

think of her shame. She told some neighbors that she was going to run off to meet Mike, and one night during a snowstorm she left her home.

No one had heard from Rosalia or Mike. Dan and Selma waited through the winter. Once, when Dan went to visit his aunt in Milwaukee, he looked for Mike, but he did not find him. In the spring a neighbor brought the news to Jule that Rosalia's body had been found in the swamp. Fearing that the news would kill the already ailing Selma, Jule made the neighbor and Dan promised to tell no one about Rosalia's body. They buried the girl in the swamp.

All summer Dan worked on his father's farm. He had begun to hate the memory of Mike ever since he had helped Jule bury the body of Rosalia. A hundred times over Dan killed Mike in effigy. In the fall Selma died, and Dan went to live with Jule. The kindly, patient man, who had seen so much of life, won Dan's affections.

Jule wanted Dan to tell him all he knew about Rosalia and Mike. The wonderful understanding of the old man impressed his nephew. Mike had done the best he knew how, Jule maintained. In turn, he told Dan about Hannah Madoc. If Hannah had been Rosalia's mother instead of Selma, Jule said, Rosalia would not have been destroyed through fear. Hannah knew how to handle life. Religious people were always trying to make life better than it was, but life should be accepted at its simple, natural values. Dan accepted his uncle's views.

Dan's father had never understood his son. Having completed his high school education, Dan was becoming restless. His father, realizing that Dan was not cut out for farm work, suggested that he go to college. With high hopes that he would find more answers to his questioning of life, Dan prepared to enter the state university.

APPOINTMENT IN SAMARRA

Type of work: Novel
Author: John O'Hara (1905-   )
Type of plot: Naturalism
Time of plot: 1930
Locale: Pennsylvania
First published: 1934

Principal characters:
JULIAN ENGLISH, a car dealer
CAROLINE, his wife
HARRY REILLY, a rich man
AL GRECCO, the bootlegger's handyman

Critique:

This novel is in the tradition of the roaring twenties; it deals with prohibition, bootleggers, easy morals. In style it recalls F. Scott Fitzgerald, who is mentioned in the book. The character analysis is somewhat in the manner of Lewis' *Babbitt*. *Appointment in Samarra* goes beyond mere pandering to sensationalism, however, in that it sustains a theme of moral judgment, as implied by the title. The lives led by these people can have no fruitful or important end.

The Story:

Julian English was thirty, a congenial seller of cars, popular with the country club set. He had the right connections with Ed Charney, the local bootlegger, and consequently was always well supplied with liquor. He and Caroline had been married four years. They were both natives of Gibbsville and had an assured social position. They had no children.

Just before Christmas they went to a party at the country club. As usual, Julian had had too much to drink. He sat idly twirling his highball and listening to Harry Reilly's stories. Harry was a rich Irish Catholic and definitely a social climber. Actually, Julian hated Harry, although Harry had lent him twenty thousand dollars the previous summer to bolster his Cadillac agency. But that loan did not give Harry the right to make passes at Caroline, Julian thought darkly.

Harry told stories in paragraphs. He always paused at the right time. Julian kept thinking how fitting it would be if he stopped the stories by throwing his drink in Harry's face. Julian grew bored. On impulse he did throw his drink in Harry's face. A big lump of ice hit Harry in the eye.

On the way home Julian and Caroline quarreled furiously. Julian accused his wife of infidelity with Harry, among other people. Caroline said that Julian always drank too much and chased women as well. More important, Harry had a mortgage on the car agency and a good deal of influence with the Catholics, and he was a man who could hold a grudge.

Al Grecco was a little man who as Ed Charney's handyman had a certain standing in the town. He liked Julian because Julian was the only one of the social set who was really friendly. Al grew up on the wrong side of the tracks. Before he was finally sentenced to a year in prison he had been arrested several times. When he got out he worked in a poolroom for a while until his boss died. The widow wanted Al to stay on as manager, but he went to work for Charney. Now he delivered bootleg booze, ran errands, and kept an eye on the torch singer at the Stage Coach, a country inn owned by Charney. Helene Holman, the singer, was Charney's girl, and if she were not carefully watched, she might out of sheer good-heartedness extend her favors to other men.

On Christmas Day Julian woke up with a hangover. As was his custom, he quarreled with the cook. At Caroline's suggestion he went to Harry Reilly's house to apologize. Although Reilly's sister was sympathetic, she brought down word that Harry would not see him; he had a black eye and still nursed a grouch.

Julian's father and mother came for Christmas dinner. The father, a staid, successful surgeon, was suspicious of his son. He always looked for evidence of moral weakness in Julian, for his own father had committed suicide after embezzling a fortune. He was afraid that the English inheritance was stained. Dinner was a trying time.

Caroline and Julian had supper at the club. The usual crowd was there. Julian was unmercifully ribbed in the locker room. In a dismal mood he sat drinking by himself while he waited for a chance to see Father Creedon and ask him to patch up his affair with Harry. The old priest was sympathetic and made light of the incident. After agreeing that Harry was a bore, he promised to send Julian some good Irish whiskey.

Ed Charney was a good family man who spent Christmas Day with his wife and son. He intended to go out to the Stage Coach only in the evening. Then his son became suddenly ill. It looked as if he would have to stay home. Mindful of Helene's weaknesses, he telephoned Al Grecco to go out to the inn and keep watch on her. It was Christmas night and she would be drinking too much. Al did not care for the assignment, but he dutifully went out to the inn and sat down with Helene.

The country club set began to drift in. Froggy Ogden, who was Caroline's one-armed cousin, was the oldest man there; he seemed to feel a responsibility for Julian, who was still drinking. In a spirit of bravado Julian danced several times with Helene, even though Al warned him of Charney's anger. Finally, carried away by the music and too many drinks, Julian and Helene left the dance floor. Caroline and Froggy found Julian in a stupor in the back of a sedan and took him home.

The day after Christmas Caroline went to her mother and announced her intention to divorce Julian. Her mother found it difficult to listen to her daughter; she believed herself above the foibles of the younger generation. Caroline thought herself a heroine in an old-fashioned melodrama. But she was determined not to go back to Julian. After meeting him on the street and quarreling again, she canceled the big party they were to have given that evening.

Al Grecco, as he backed out of the garage with a case of Scotch, had decided to kill Ed Charney. When Charney had phoned him, he had tried to excuse his lack of vigilance: he protested that he had only let Helene dance. But Ed in a rage had said some things that Al could not accept.

Determined to look businesslike, Julian went to his office at the auto agency. He sat importantly at his desk and wrote figures on a piece of scratch paper. The only conclusion he could reach was that he needed more money. One of his salesmen came in to try to lay down the law. He asserted that Julian's difficulties were gossiped about strenuously in the little town of Gibbsville. The offense to Charney was particularly grave: he had been a good friend to the agency and had helped them sell cars to other bootleggers.

Julian left the office in no cheerful mood. He wandered into his club for lunch. Since it was the day after Christmas, the dining-room was deserted except for some elderly lawyers and Froggy. Avoiding his wife's cousin, Julian sat down in a far corner of the room. After picking up his plate, Froggy followed him and began to reproach him for his conduct with the torch singer. He told Julian he had always distrusted him and had warned Caroline about his conduct many times. When Froggy invited him outside to fight, Julian refused because he could not hit a one-armed man. Froggy became more insulting, so that the lawyers came to their table to interfere. Julian was intensely angered when they seemed to side with Froggy. Turning quickly, he hit one of the lawyers full in the mouth and dislodged his false teeth.

Julian went home and fell asleep. About ten o'clock a society reporter awoke him when she came to get a story about the canceled party. After several drinks, he tried to seduce her but with no success. As soon as she left, Julian went to the garage, closed the door, and started the motor. He was pronounced a suicide by the coroner.

THE ARABIAN NIGHTS' ENTERTAINMENTS
(SELECTIONS)

Type of work: Tales
Author: Unknown
Type of plots: Adventure romances
Time of plots: The legendary past
Locale: India, China, Persia, Arabia
First transcribed: Fifteenth century

Principal characters:
SHAHRIAR, Emperor of Persia and India
SCHEHERAZADE, his bride
THE FISHERMAN
THE KING OF THE BLACK ISLES, half man, half marble
SINDBAD THE SAILOR, a wanderer from Baghdad
THE SULTAN OF INDIA
HOUSSAIN,
ALI, and
AHMED, his sons
PERIEBANOU, Ahmed's wife
ALI BABA, a woodcutter in Persia
CASSIM, his brother
MORGIANA, his slave
ALADDIN, a good-for-nothing boy in China

Critique:

The Arabian Nights' Entertainments is the title usually used in English to designate a group of tales more properly called *The Thousand and One Nights.* These stories, adapted and formalized by bazaar storytellers, had their origins in many lands throughout the East and were handed down by word of mouth for hundreds of years. Some present interesting parallels. In the story of "The Three Sisters" a baby is put in a basket to float down a river, a circumstance reminiscent of the Biblical account of Moses in the bulrushes. In Sindbad's various journeys by sea there are similarities to the wanderings of Ulysses as related by Homer, in one instance a close parallel to the Cyclops story. Some of the characters have been drawn from history. But whether the source is folklore, religious tradition, or history, the tales have a timeless quality appealing, from legendary times to the present, to authors of every sort. Stories of Robin Hood have the same flavor. More recently, Gilbert and Sullivan used the "sisters and the cousins and the aunts" grouping such as Aladdin employed to impress the sultan that he had plenty of followers to back his cause as suitor for the hand of the princess. Most scholars believe that the collection took its present form in Cairo in the fifteenth century; it was introduced to the Western World in a translation by Antoine Galland, published in Paris in 1704. Traditionally there were a thousand and one stories told by Scheherazade to her emperor-husband, but in extant manuscripts the tales are not always the same. Practically all modern editions contain only a small portion of the complete collection. Those most frequently reprinted have become minor classics of the world's literature.

The Stories:

Convinced by the treachery of his brother's wife and his own that all women were unfaithful, Shahriar, Emperor of Persia and India, vowed that he would marry a new wife every day and have her executed the next morning. Only Scheherazade, wise as well as beautiful, had the courage to try to save the young women of Persia. On the night of her marriage to Shahriar, she began to tell him a tale which fascinated him so much that he stayed her death for one more night so that he could learn the end of the story. Scheherazade told him stories for one thousand and one nights. At that time, convinced of her worthiness and goodness, he bade her live and made her his consort.

One tale Scheherazade told was "The History of the Fisherman and the Genie": A poor Mussulman fisherman drew from the sea in his nets a strange box with a seal on top. When he pried off the top, a huge genie appeared and threatened him with death, offering the poor man no more than his choice in the manner of his death. The fisherman begged for his life because he had done the genie a favor by releasing him, but the genie declared that he had vowed death to the man who opened the box. Finally the fisherman exclaimed that he could not believe anything as huge and terrible as the genie could ever have been in a space so small. Dissolving into a cloud of smoke, the genie shrank until he could slip back into the box, whereupon the fisherman clamped on the lid. Throwing the box back into the sea, he warned all other fishermen to beware if it should ever fall into their nets.

Another story was "The History of the Young King of the Black Isles": A fisherman caught four beautiful fish, one white, one red, one blue, and one yellow. They were so choice that he took them to the sultan's palace. While the fish were being cooked, a beautiful girl suddenly appeared and talked to the fish, after which they were too charred to take to the sultan. When the same thing happened two days in a row, the sultan was called. After asking where the fish came from, he decided to visit the lake. Nearby he found a beautiful, apparently deserted palace. As he walked through the beautiful halls, he found one in which a king was sitting on a throne. The king apologized for not rising, explaining that

his lower half was marble.

He was the King of the Black Isles. When he had learned that his queen was unfaithful to him, he had nearly killed her blackamoor lover. In revenge the queen had cast a spell over her husband, making him half marble. Daily she whipped him, then had him dressed in coarse goat's hair over which his royal robes were placed. In the meantime, while she had kept her lover barely alive, she had changed her husband's town and all its inhabitants into the lake full of fish.

The king told the sultan where the queen's lover was kept. There the sultan went, killed the lover, and put himself in the blackamoor's place. The queen, overjoyed to hear speaking the one she had kept from the edge of death so long, hastened to do all the voice commanded. She restored the king to his human form and the lake to its previous state as a populous town. The four colors of fish indicated the four different religions of the inhabitants.

When the queen returned to the sultan, whom she mistook for her lover, he killed her for her treachery. Thereafter he took home with him the King of the Black Isles, and rewarded the fisherman who had led him to the magic lake.

Shahriar was vastly entertained by "The History of Sindbad the Sailor": A poor porter in Baghdad, resting before the house of Sindbad, bewailed the fact that his lot was harder than that of Sindbad. Overhearing him, Sindbad invited the porter to dine with him. During the meal he told of the hardships he had suffered in order to make his fortune.

On his first voyage, to India by way of the Persian Gulf, Sindbad's ship was becalmed near a small green island. The sailors climbed upon the island, only to find that it was really a sea monster which heaved itself up and swam away. Sindbad was the only man who did not get back to the ship. After days of clinging to a piece of driftwood, he landed on an island where some men were gathered. They led him to a maharajah who treated Sindbad graciously.

When he had been there some time his own ship came into port, and he claimed his bales of goods, to the astonishment of the captain, who thought he had seen Sindbad killed at sea. Then Sindbad sailed home in the ship in which he had set out.

The porter was so impressed with the first tale that he came again to hear a second. On his second voyage Sindbad was left asleep on an island where the sailors had rested. There he found a huge roc's egg. Knowing that the parent bird would return to the nest at dusk, he waited. When it came, he used his turban to tie himself to the bird's leg. In the morning the bird flew to a place surrounded by mountains. There Sindbad freed himself when the bird descended to pick up a serpent. The place seemed deserted, except for large serpents. Diamonds of great size were scattered throughout the valley.

Sindbad remembered that merchants were said to throw joints of meat into the diamond valley, from which big eagles carried the joints to their nests close to shore. At the nests the merchants frightened away the birds and recovered diamonds which had stuck to the meat. Sindbad collected some large diamonds. Then with his turban he fastened a piece of meat to his back and lay down. An eagle picked him up and carried him to its nest. When he was dropped into a nest, the merchant who claimed the nest was indignant and accused Sindbad of stealing his property. Sindbad offered him some choice diamonds. In return the merchant was glad to take the adventurer back to civilization.

On his third voyage Sindbad was wrecked on an island inhabited by cannibal dwarfs and huge black creatures with only one eye in the middle of their foreheads. Sindbad and his friends blinded one black giant, but two others helped the blind one to chase the sailors. By the time the giants and a large serpent had overtaken them, only Sindbad was lucky enough to escape.

Sindbad sailed from a port in Persia on his fourth voyage. He and his friends were shipwrecked on an island inhabited by black cannibals who fattened the sailors before killing them. Sindbad refused the food, grew too thin to interest the black men, and finally found his way to the shore. There he met white men who took him to their kingdom. To please the king, Sindbad made a fine saddle. In appreciation the king married Sindbad to a beautiful girl. In that country a man or woman was buried alive if the spouse died. When Sindbad's wife died, he was put in a tomb with a small amount of bread and water. As he ate the last of his food he heard an animal snuffling, then running away. Following the sound, he found himself on the shore and hailed a ship which carried him home.

Sindbad used his own ship on his fifth voyage. After his sailors had broken open a roc's egg, the parent rocs hurled tremendous stones on the ship and broke it to pieces. Sindbad came under the power of the Old Man of the Sea and escaped only after making the old man so intoxicated that he loosed his death grip on Sindbad. Again Sindbad found a ship to take him home; he did much profitable trading on the way.

All his companions on the sixth voyage succumbed on a beautiful but lifeless coast. Sindbad, expecting to die, built a raft which he put in an underground river to drift where it would. When he reached the kingdom of Serendib, he had to be revived. He found the country exceedingly rich and the people kind. When he asked to be allowed to go home, the king sent him there with rich presents for Sindbad's ruler, the Caliph Harun-al-Rashid of Baghdad.

Sindbad made his seventh and final voyage to take gifts from the caliph to the King of Serendib. He carried them safely, but his return trip was delayed when corsairs seized his ship and sold the sailors into slavery. Sindbad, sold to an ivory merchant, was ordered to shoot an elephant a day. Annoyed at Sindbad's persistence, an elephant picked him up and took him to an elephant burial ground, to which Sindbad and his owner returned many times to gather ivory. As a reward, the merchant sent Sindbad home with rich goods.

Another diverting tale was "The History of Prince Ahmed": Houssain, Ali, and Ahmed, sons of the Sultan of India, were all in love with the Princess Nouronnihar, their father's ward. To determine who should be the bridegroom, the sultan sent them out to find the most extraordinary things they could. Whoever brought back the rarest object would win the hand of the princess.

Houssain found a magic carpet which would transport him wherever he wished. Ali found an ivory tube containing a glass which would show any object he wished to see. Ahmed found an artificial apple, the odor of which would cure any illness. The three princes met before they journeyed home. As they displayed their gifts, Houssain, looking through the tube, saw the princess apparently at the point of death. They all jumped on his magic carpet and were whisked to her bedroom, where Ahmed used his magic apple to revive her. The sultan could not determine which article was the most unusual, for all had been of use to effect the princess' recovery. He suggested an archery contest. Prince Ali shot farther than Houssain, but Ahmed's arrow could not be found. The sultan decided in favor of Ali. Houssain retired to become a dervish. Ahmed, instead of attending the wedding, went in search of his arrow, which he found at the foot of a mountain, much farther away than he could have shot. Looking around, he found a door into the mountain. When he passed through the door, he found a fairy called Periebanou, who pleased him so much that he married her.

When Ahmed went to visit his father, he refused to discuss where or how he lived, but he appeared to be so rich that the courtiers grew jealous and persuaded the sultan that it was dangerous to have

his son so powerful a neighbor. The sultan asked Ahmed to perform unreasonable tasks, made possible only by Periebanou's help; but while fulfilling one request her brother became so annoyed with the sultan that he killed him. Ahmed became sultan and afterward dealt kindly with his brothers.

Scheherazade pleased her lord also with "The History of Ali Baba and the Forty Thieves": Ali Baba was a Persian woodcutter. One day, to hide from a band of strange horsemen, he climbed a tree under which they halted. When the leader cried, "Open, Sesame!" to a rock nearby, a door opened through which the men carried their heavy packs. After the men left, Ali Baba used the secret word to investigate the cave. He found such riches there that the gold he took could never be missed.

He and his wife were content with that amount, but his brother Cassim, to whom he had told his story, was greedy for more wealth. Without telling Ali Baba, Cassim went to the cave. He was so excited by the gold that he forgot the password and could not get out. The robbers found and murdered him.

The robbers tried to find Ali Baba in order to kill him and so keep the secret of their hoard. The leader brought his men, hidden in oil jars, to Ali Baba's house, but a beautiful slave, Morgiana, went in search of oil, discovered the ruse, and killed the bandits. Again the captain, disguised as a merchant, entered the house, but Morgiana saw through his disguise and killed him.

To reward Morgiana, Ali Baba not only made her a free woman, but he also gave her to his son in marriage. Ali Baba was then the only one who knew the secret of the cave. He used the hidden wealth in moderation and passed the secret on to his posterity.

No less pleasing was "The History of Aladdin, or the Wonderful Lamp": Aladdin was a youthful vagabond who lived in China. An African magician, sensing that Aladdin would suit his plans, and pretending to be the boy's rich uncle, took him to a secret place to get a magic lamp. Passing through halls stored with treasures, Aladdin filled his gown with so many things that he could not give the magician the lamp at the moment he wanted it, and the magician sealed him up in the earth. By chance Aladdin rubbed a ring which the magician had given him. A genie appeared and escorted him home.

When Aladdin showed his mother the lamp, she tried to clean it to sell. As she rubbed, another genie appeared from whom Aladdin asked food. The food appeared on silver trays that Aladdin sold one by one to a Jewish chapman. When an honest jeweler stopped Aladdin one day and asked to buy the silver, Aladdin began to realize the great riches he had at his finger tips, enough to win him the sultan's daughter as his wife.

Because the grand vizier wanted his own son to marry the princess, he suggested many outrageous demands which the sultan made upon Aladdin before he could be considered a suitor. The genies produced slaves, costumes, jewelry, gold, and chargers in such profusion that the sultan gladly accepted Aladdin's suit. Overnight Aladdin had the genie build a magnificent palace next to the sultan's.

Life went smoothly until the African magician, while Aladdin was away, persuaded the princess to trade the old lamp for a new one. Then the magician transported the great palace to Africa. When Aladdin came home, the sultan threatened him with arrest, but allowed him forty days in which to find the palace with the princess therein. Rubbing his ring by chance and summoning its genie, Aladdin asked to be carried wherever his palace was. The princess was overjoyed to see him. After he had killed the magician by a ruse, he ordered the genie of the lamp to transport the palace back to China. There, after disposing of the magician's brother, who had followed them, Aladdin and the princess lived happily ever after.

THE ARBITRATION

Type of work: Drama
Author: Menander (342-291 B.C.)
Type of plot: Comedy of manners
Time of plot: Fourth century B.C.
Locale: A suburb of Athens
First presented: c. 310 B.C.

Principal characters:
CHARISIUS, a young Athenian
PAMPHILA, his wife
SMICRINES, miserly father of Pamphila
ONESIMUS, Charisius' slave
CHAERESTRATUS, Charisius' friend and neighbor
SYRISCUS, a charcoal burner
DAVUS, a goatherd
HABROTONON, a pretty harp-playing slave
SOPHRONA, a nurse

Critique:

What Aristophanes was to the great age of Greek comedy, Menander was to New Comedy, that form characterized by the abandonment of the chorus and the intervention of the gods and by its concern with domestic problems of ordinary mortals. Tradition made Menander author of a hundred plays, of which about eighty titles are still known, but for centuries all trace of his writings, except for a few fragments, was lost. In the late nineteenth century papyri recovered from Egyptian tombs enabled students to get a better idea of Menander's writing. Still more recent discoveries provided almost complete versions of two of his comedies: *The Girl with the Shorn Locks,* about a soldier-lover who mistreated his mistress and almost lost her, but won her back by marrying her, and the *Arbitration.* Actually, the title refers only to one amusing scene in this comedy of a harsh father, a knavish slave, and a slave girl with a heart of gold. The play contains stock material and situations. The nurse, even to her name, is a type, as are the servant and the avaricious father. But Menander's clever plotting is shown in his use of the miser as the arbitrator whose decision regarding the fate of his own grandson brings trouble to him and provides material for the picaresque servant's amusing insults. The action is lively and the dialogue amusing, especially in the

scene in which the two slaves, Onesimus and Habrotonon, outmaneuver each other.

The Story:

Pamphila, the daughter of a respected but miserly Athenian citizen, had been ravished by a drunken young man of ordinarily good behavior during the night festival of the Tauropolia. The only clue she had to his identity was a signet ring which he had left in her possession. A short time later Pamphila was married to her ravisher, a young Athenian named Charisius, and Smicrines, her father, provided a good dowry for his idealistic but rather priggish son-in-law. Pamphila, who soon learned to love her husband, gave birth to her child during his absence and, acting on the advice of her nurse Sophrona, exposed the infant and with the baby a pouch containing assorted tokens, including the ring. Charisius, learning of the birth from his prying servant Onesimus, decided that the child could not be his. Instead of repudiating Pamphila, however, he left home and began to waste his substance in rich feasts given at the home of his friend Chaerestratus, who lived next door. Pamphila was distracted because the husband she loved had deserted her for the company of hired dancing girls and harp players.

177

So matters stood when Smicrines came to investigate reports of Charisius' conduct; he had heard that his son-in-law was spending every night for a hired harp player a sum sufficient to feed a slave for a month. Just before his arrival a conceited, loud-mouthed cook, Carion, on his way to prepare a meal in the house of Chaerestratus, vainly questioned Charisius' servant Onesimus about his master; the cook also wanted to know why Charisius neglected his wife and paid twelve drachmas a night to be entertained by the lovely, harp-playing slave, Habrotonon. While Carion and Onesimus were talking, the musician was delivered by her master. The slave dealer managed to persuade bemused Charisius that he owed money for several previous nights' entertainment. Charisius paid, but wily Onesimus recovered the overpayments for himself.

When Smicrines appeared, Onesimus managed to befuddle the anxious, angry father with the story that it was Chaerestratus who was giving the parties and that Charisius attended only to protect his friend's possessions and good name.

After Smicrines had gone into his son-in-law's house, two of Chaerestratus' tenants appeared to pay their rent. They were Davus, a goatherd, and Syriscus, a charcoal burner accompanied by his wife carrying a baby. While they waited they argued over another matter. A month earlier Davus had come upon a baby exposed in the hills. His first impulse had been to adopt the foundling, but later, having calculated the cost of rearing a child, he was returning the infant to the place where he had found it when Syriscus offered to adopt the baby in place of his own child who had just died. Now Syriscus, having learned that Davus had kept the trinkets left beside the baby, claimed them because they might some day help to identify the child's parents. Davus had refused to give up the tokens, but he had agreed to let someone else decide the matter. Smicrines, reappearing from the house of Charisius, was per-

suaded to listen to the story and give his decision. Deciding that the trinkets ought to go with the baby, he ordered Davus to give Syriscus the pouch containing them.

While Syriscus and his wife were looking over the contents of the pouch, Onesimus recognized the signet ring that his master had lost at the time of the Tauropolia festival a year before. The slave borrowed it to show his master, then hesitated because to return it would be to accuse Charisius of having fathered the abandoned baby. Habrotonon came came along about that time, saw the ring, heard the story, and concocted a scheme of her own. She would learn the truth by wearing the ring and seeing if Charisius recognized it. In that case, she would claim that she had been the girl he had ravished and so rescue the child from the life of a slave. Onesimus knew very well that her chief purpose was to win her own freedom.

Smicrines reappeared, determined to demand the return of his daughter and her dowry. The neighbors tried to dissuade him by saying that everything would turn out all right. As the party ended, broken up by Habrotonon and her claim that the child was hers, Onesimus infuriated the miser by congratulating him on bringing happiness to everybody by his arbitration.

Pamphila begged her father not to meddle with her marriage; she had no desire for another husband, she declared. If Charisius was infatuated with a harpist, that was only a temporary estrangement. At her father's announcement that his current love was the mother of his child, Pamphila fainted.

Regaining consciousness, she accused her nurse Sophrona of causing all the trouble by preventing her confession to Charisius after the birth of the child. While they argued, Habrotonon happened by and recognized Pamphila as the girl who had been Charisius' companion of a year earlier. She told the patrician so when he came to keep his promise to arrange for her freedom. At first he regarded the story as another of her lies. To save himself, Onesimus also accused her of having invented the story. Habrotonon maintained stoutly that it was true, and she declared that she would rather see the child looked after properly than win her own freedom.

Chaerestratus, who had always admired the lovely slave, began questioning her about her own early history, but she remembered nothing of her infancy, not even her name. Then the sight of a small silver cup with an indecipherable inscription among the trinkets of Syriscus caused her to comment that she had once possessed a similar cup. Smicrines, seeing the cup for the first time, identified it as having once belonged to his oldest daughter, who had been kidnapped by the slave traders during the siege of the city some years before. Sophrona, recognizing the harp player as Smicrines' long-lost daughter Clearista, stirred the girl's recollection by using her baby name of "grasshopper."

Chaerestratus, who had loved the girl from the first, now asked to marry her, and when he showed miserly Smicrines how he could get his daughter back without spending money in court trials, he got both the girl and her father's blessing. Rascally Onesimus, instead of getting the beating he deserved, was probably given his freedom.

ARCADIA

Type of work: Novel
Author: Sir Philip Sidney (1554-1586)
Type of plot: Pastoral romance
Time of plot: Classical antiquity
Locale: Arcadia, in Greece
First published: 1590

Principal characters:
PRINCE PYROCLES (ZELMANE), son of Evarchus, King of Macedon
PRINCE MUSIDORUS (DORUS), Duke of Thessalia, Pyrocles' friend, Evarchus' nephew
BASILIUS, Duke of Arcadia
GYNECIA, his wife
PAMELA, his older daughter
PHILOCLEA, his younger daughter
PHILANAX, Arcadian general, Basilius' friend
DAMETAS, Basilius' chief herdsman
MISO, his wife
MOPSA, his daughter
EVARCHUS, King of Macedon

Critique:

Although the original version of this work was intended by Sidney as an entertainment for his sister Mary, Countess of Pembroke, and her friends (the tale was originally titled *The Countess of Pembroke's Arcadia*), this light pastoral story holds a significant place in the development of the English novel, for it serves as a bridge between the delicately written Italian romances and the more sturdy prose tales of the later Elizabethan period in England. The original *Arcadia* was revised and considerably enlarged by Sidney into an unfinished version which was published in 1590. The "old" *Arcadia*, although not published in its complete and original form until 1926, clearly shows the complete primary intention of its author. It has a rustic charm and coherence of plot not nearly so evident in the more ambitious later version. The presence of occasional passages of poetry and of the four eclogues, largely in the form of poetry, which are inserted among the five "books" of the romance is a carry-over from the earlier continental romances; but the plot, skillfully handled for its time, and the philosophical asides of the author pointed the way toward a more serious genre of fiction to follow.

The Story:

Basilius, the powerful Duke of Arcadia, a quiet and peaceful province of Greece, ruled his faithful subjects happily and well. Being overcome by an ungovernable curiosity to learn what the future held for him, his wife Gynecia, and his beautiful daughters Pamela and Philoclea, he went to consult the Oracle at Delphos. There he was told that his older daughter, Pamela, would be stolen from him; his younger daughter would engage in an unsuitable love affair; his wife would commit adultery; and a foreign ruler would sit upon his throne—all within a year.

Basilius told the prophecy to his friend Philanax, whom he left in charge of the country while he, in an effort to escape the destiny foretold by the Oracle, took his wife and daughters into a secluded part of the country to live for the year. Basilius lived in one of two lodges with his wife and Philoclea; in the other he put Pamela under the care of Dametas, a rude shepherd of whose honesty Basilius had a high opinion.

Shortly after the duke's retirement, two young princes, Pyrocles and Musidorus, arrived in Arcadia. Young men of great courage, personal beauty, and integrity, who had been reared together in close friendship, they had been swept ashore at Lydia after experiencing a shipwreck and many strange adventures as well as performing many acts of daring and honor.

Pyrocles saw a picture of Philoclea, learned of her enforced retirement, and fell in love with her. Determined to see the princess face to face, he told Musidorus of his love and of his plan to disguise himself as a chivalric Amazon and in woman's guise to approach Philoclea. For a name, he took that of his lost lady, Zelmane.

After a lengthy debate, in which Musidorus attempted to convince his friend of the folly of love, Pyrocles still remained firm in his intention; and the two princes traveled to the place of the duke's retirement, Pyrocles in his disguise as an Amazon. While Musidorus waited in a nearby wood, Pyrocles, now Zelmane, sat down and sang a melancholy song which awakened Dametas, who hastened to the duke's lodge to tell him of a strange woman who had arrived in the vicinity.

Basilius, upon seeing Pyrocles in his disguise, fell in love with the supposed Amazon. His true identity still unsuspected, he was introduced to the duke's family and invited to remain with them for a while. Soon a young shepherd appeared. He was Musidorus, who had fallen in love with Pamela on sight and assumed a disguise of his own. After telling his contrived tale of being sent by a friend to serve Dametas, Musidorus, under the name Dorus, was taken by the chief herdsman as a servant.

Zelmane saved Philoclea from a savage lion, but in doing so he was discovered by Gynecia, the duke's wife, to be a man; she immediately fell in love with him. Dorus, meanwhile, saved Pamela from a bear. Before long both princesses began to become enamored of the disguised princes.

The Arcadian shepherds, as was their custom, met and exchanged poetic songs for their own entertainment and that of the duke's family and his guests. The songs, often accompanied by dancing, chiefly concerned the gods and the human passions. This occasion only increased the intensity of the tangle of love relationships that had so rapidly developed.

After the pastoral festival, Gynecia and Basilius both declared their love for Zelmane, and Philoclea was puzzled greatly by the strange passion she felt for the person she thought a woman. In the meantime Dorus pretended to be in love with Mopsa in order to be near Pamela, who in this manner became aware of his affection for her. He also managed, by subtle stories and poems, to reveal his true station to her.

Pyrocles, distressed by the advances of Basilius, revealed his true identity to Philoclea, who at first embraced him joyously but then became ashamed of her sudden show of affection. Gynecia, suspecting this attachment, was overcome with jealousy.

While Gynecia, having sent Philoclea home from a meeting with Pyrocles, was starting to tell the disguised prince of the depth of her love, they were attacked by some roving ruffians. Pyrocles, Basilius, and then Dorus with the aid of some shepherds drove off the attackers. This was only the prelude to an uprising by the citizens of a nearby Arcadian village, who had become enraged by the duke's seeming unconcern about his country. In an impassioned speech, however, Pyrocles convinced them of their error and stirred in them a renewed loyalty to Basilius. This triumph was celebrated by another pastoral entertainment, largely taken up with a poetic debate between Reason and Passion. Once more, the poems, dances, and stories served to increase the depth of the emotions felt by the royal party.

Dorus then told his friend of his moderate success with Pamela, whom he had urged to flee with him to Thessalia. Pyrocles, sharing Dorus' sorrow over their separation, decided to press his suit of Philoclea and to rid himself of the importunate demands of Basilius and Gynecia. When they renewed their entreaties, Pyrocles, still in his disguise and fearing to deny them outright, gave them hopeful but obscure answers.

Meanwhile, Dorus, having tricked Dametas and his family into leaving the lodge, had escaped with Pamela to a forest on the way to Thessalia. There they were set upon by a band of ruffians.

The false Zelmane, hard pressed by Gynecia's declarations, was forced to pretend a deep passion for her, a situation which so distressed Philoclea that she kept to her room in the lodge, in profound sorrow. In order to be free to execute a plan to be alone with Philoclea, Pyrocles moved from the lodge to a dark cave not far away. He then took the duke and his wife aside separately and made an assignation with each at the same time in the cave.

When Basilius met Gynecia, who had dressed like Zelmane, in the cave, he failed to recognize his wife. Gynecia, ashamed of her actions, embraced him lovingly. Back at the lodge, Pyrocles, now in his own person, crept into Philoclea's room and, after a brief time, won her over and stayed the night.

Dametas, realizing that he had been tricked, began a search for Pamela. Entering the duke's lodge by a secret entrance, he discovered Philoclea and Pyrocles asleep. He left hastily to inform the local citizens of the treachery.

In the cave Gynecia, angered at her husband's praise of Zelmane, revealed her identity. Basilius, ashamed, repented his weakness, pledged renewed love to his wife, and drank a long draught from a cup of a mysterious beverage standing close by. The liquid was a potion, believed by Gynecia to be a love philter, which the duchess had brought to give to Zelmane. After drinking it, Basilius fell to the ground and appeared to die.

The duke's death being discovered, Philanax, with a troop of soldiers, imprisoned Gynecia, Pyrocles, and Philoclea.

The rogues who had attacked Dorus and Pamela, the remnant of the rebellious band which had earlier caused much trouble, overwhelmed the lovers and captured them. While in captivity, Musidorus revealed his actual name and rank. A short time later some of Philanax's soldiers, sent to search for Pamela, came upon the band and their prisoners. Recognizing the princess, the soldiers returned the entire group to Philanax, who put the lovers under restraint.

There was now a great turmoil, and many opinions and beliefs were exchanged as to the real guilt in the death of the duke and the disgrace of the princesses.

Hearing that Evarchus, King of Macedon, had arrived in Arcadia to visit the duke, Philanax persuaded him to be the judge in the trial of the five people involved. Gynecia admitted her guilt and begged to be executed. Then Evarchus, not recognizing his son and his nephew because they had been away for such a long time, condemned the two princes to death and the princesses to milder punishments. Even after learning the true identity of the young men, Evarchus refused, from a deep sense of justice, to alter his verdict.

At that point Basilius, who had swallowed only a powerful sleeping potion, awoke. The young lovers and the duchess were promptly forgiven. Basilius pondered on how accurately the Oracle's prophecy had been fulfilled and how happily events had turned out. The princes and their loves, soon wed, assumed the high stations for which their rank fitted them.

ARGENIS

Type of work: Prose romance
Author: John Barclay (1582-1621)
Type of plot: Pseudo-classical heroic allegory
Time of plot: The Hellenistic era
Locale: Sicily and the Western Mediterranean
First published: 1621

Principal characters:

POLIARCHUS, the name assumed by Astioristes, Prince of France
ARGENIS, Princess of Sicily
MELEANDER, King of Sicily, her father
ARCHOMBROTUS, the name assumed by Hyempsal, Prince of Mauritania, during his sojourn in Sicily
HYANISBE, Queen of Mauritania
RADIROBANES, King of Sardinia
LYCOGENES, a Sicilian noble, leader of the rebellion against Meleander
ARSIDAS, a Sicilian noble, Governor of Messana, a friend to Poliarchus
GELANORUS, a French noble sojourning in Sicily in the guise of Poliarchus' servant
SELENISSA, a Sicilian matron, Argenis' nurse and companion
TIMOCLEA, a Sicilian matron, a friend to Poliarchus and, later, Argenis' companion
NICOPOMPUS, a Sicilian courtier-poet of pro-monarchial sentiments

Critique:

John Barclay, the son of a Scot, was born in France, died in Italy, and wrote in Latin. His last work, *Argenis*, finished only a month before his death, became immediately popular and remained so for two centuries. Seven years after its publication it had been honored by three translations into English (the first, by Ben Jonson, in 1623, is, unfortunately, not extant), and as late as the nineteenth century it received the high praise of Samuel Taylor Coleridge. Its original popularity was not due entirely to its artistic merits, however, for it was as satire that it first caught the fancy of readers on both sides of the Channel. Barclay had already a reputation as a satirist, but in *Argenis* the objects of his attacks are generalized behind a screen of allegory. The story of the love of Poliarchus and Argenis is supposed to represent the wars and intrigues in France before the Concordat under Henry IV. As revealed by the *Clovis* published in the edition of 1623, Sicily, the scene of the action, stands for France, with Argenis a personified symbol of the throne contested during the religious wars and Poliarchus and Archombrotus representing different aspects of Henry of Navarre (later Henry IV). Meleander is Henry III; Mauritania is England; Hyanisbe, Elizabeth; and Radirobanes, the rapacious and deceitful Philip of Spain. The whole work is aimed at opponents of the monarchical system. Although interest in the work as satire lasted only as long as the controversy over the divine right of kings remained a vital issue, *Argenis* was long praised for the grandeur of its expression, the nobility of its theme, the heroic stature of its characters. Today, however, only its historical interest remains; it stands with Honoré d'Urfé's *L'Astrée* as an interesting transitional work between the Greek-influenced prose romances of the sixteenth century on the one hand, and the interminable French romances of La Calprenède and Mlle. de Scudéry on the other.

The Story:

Before the Mediterranean world had ever come under the dominance of Rome, a young adventurer from Africa landed on the shores of Sicily and was met by a distraught lady who begged him to assist her friend, who was being attacked by thieves. The young man, who gave his name as Archombrotus, sped to the rescue only to find that his help was not needed: the lady's friend had dispatched the thieves singlehanded. The three returned to the lady's house where Archombrotus learned that the lady was Timoclea, a respected Sicilian matron, and that her friend was young Poliarchus, also a stranger to Sicily, who had distinguished himself in the service of King Meleander against a rebel army led by the traitorous noble, Lycogenes. Poliarchus, having urged more forceful resistance to the rebellion, had been banished when the over-cautious king declared a truce. Meleander, Archombrotus learned, had a beautiful daughter, Argenis; Archombrotus concluded immediately that Poliarchus was in love with her.

While engaged in their discussion, they noticed signal fires blazing on the surrounding hilltops. Timoclea explained that these were beacons fired to warn the people that a traitor was at large. Presently a servant entered with word that Poliarchus was the one accused of treachery; the "thieves" had been Lycogenes' ambassadors, and the king had interpreted his defense as an attempt to break the truce. Timoclea, loyal to her guest, hid him immediately in a cave on her estate and then sent for his friend Arsidas, the Governor of Messana. Arsidas arrived promptly, and he and Poliarchus' servant, Gelanorus, devised a plan whereby it was given out that Poliarchus had been drowned after a fall from his horse. Arsidas hastened to Argenis to tell her, secretly, the truth so that she should not be distracted by false news of Poliarchus' death.

Meanwhile, rustics on Timoclea's estate mistook Archombrotus for Poliarchus, seized him, and carried him off to the king. Meleander, realizing their mistake, took Archombrotus into his council but praised the peasants for their loyalty. At the same time, Arsidas arranged to have Argenis see Poliarchus. As a priestess of Pallas presiding over the sacrifice to celebrate the truce, she was to insist that the common people be allowed to worship the goddess beforehand, and Poliarchus was to come before her in the dress of a peasant. Thus the lovers were briefly united. Poliarchus then fled with Arsidas to Italy. Argenis, throwing herself into a frenzy, claimed that the goddess would not honor the sacrifice or the truce.

Enraged, Lycogenes resumed the war, and Meleander fled with his train to the fortified seaport of Epercte. On the way he was almost drowned when his coach, driven by a rebel spy, plunged into the river, but he was saved by Archombrotus, who was thus made secure in his favor.

The war going badly for the king, Archombrotus convinced him that their only hope lay in the return of the champion Poliarchus. The king sent a precious brooch to Poliarchus as a peace offering; however, spies of Lycogenes poisoned the brooch, and the rebel sent his own messenger with a letter warning Poliarchus that the brooch was fatal. If the king's messenger arrived first, Poliarchus would be dead; if Lycogenes', he would become an enemy of the king—either way, Lycogenes would no longer have to fear him.

But Poliarchus and his servant Gelanorus had already left for Sicily. Shipwrecked off the coast, they were rudely hauled aboard a pirate craft. The two routed the pirates and turned the ship over to its rightful owner.

Discovering among the pirate treasure jewels and letters belonging to Queen Hyanisbe of Mauritania, Poliarchus immediately ordered the ship to Mauritania so that he could return the royal property. The queen was delighted, for the letters concerned the whereabouts of her knight-errant son. She ordered a celebration which would have continued indefinitely had not Poliarchus been anxious to return to his beloved. But in spite of his anxiety, he was forced to stay when smitten by an attack of the ague. Gelanorus was dispatched with letters in his stead.

In the meantime, at Epercte, Meleander's situation was becoming untenable.

184

When matters seemed hopeless, the tremendous fleet of Radirobanes, King of Sardinia, arrived to help defend the rights of the monarch against rebel upstarts. The combined forces of Meleander and Radirobanes routed the army of Lycogenes, and Archombrotus slew the rebel leader in single combat.

The rebellion ended, Archombrotus became the king's favorite. Having fallen in love with Argenis, during the siege, and with Poliarchus gone, he thought himself the foremost claimant for her hand. But Radirobanes also announced his claim to the hand of the princess. Meleander was in a quandary. Archombrotus was his favorite, but both gratitude and the armed fleet in the harbor lent weight to Radirobanes' cause. Meleander solved the problem by leaving the decision up to Argenis. The Sardinian ruler advanced his plea; the Sicilian princess rebuffed him. Radirobanes then gained the confidence of Argenis' nurse and companion, Selenissa, who in nightly installments told him the following story:

Lycogenes had also demanded Argenis and, being refused, had threatened to abduct her. To forestall his design, Meleander had his daughter, along with Selenissa and certain young ladies of her court, placed in an inaccessible and heavily guarded castle. While they were thus secluded, a beautiful stranger who gave her name as Theocrine came to Selenissa and begged sanctuary. Admitted to the castle, she shared the chamber of the princess. When Lycogenes' men stormed the castle, Theocrine seized a sword and put the attackers to flight. The supposed Theocrine was in reality Poliarchus, who, having heard of the beauty of Argenis, had used that disguise to be near her. When he begged forgiveness, Argenis immediately fell in love with him. He had then disappeared, to return later in Meleander's service. The king, convinced that Theocrine was warlike Pallas, had dedicated his daughter to the service of that beautiful, austere goddess.

Despairing of winning the princess by fair means, Radirobanes planned to blackmail her into acceptance of his proposal, but Selenissa persuaded him that abduction would be the better course. But Argenis, having overheard part of Selenissa's betrayal, feigned an illness that kept her inaccessible, thereby frustrating Radirobanes' plans. Thwarted, Radirobanes returned with his fleet to Sardinia, leaving with Meleander a letter informing him of the true identity of Theocrine and demanding payment of three hundred talents for his aid. When Meleander confronted his daughter with the information he had received, she denied any untoward dealings in the affair. Meleander, only half believing her, demanded that she marry Archombrotus. Selenissa, seeing the damage she had done, killed herself, and Timoclea succeeded her as chief lady of the household.

Meanwhile, Poliarchus, having recovered from his illness, had returned in disguise to Sicily. Seeing no chance of amicable dealings with Meleander, he asked Argenis to delay her marriage to Archombrotus while he found some means to settle the matter. Then he sailed away. Weeks passed and he failed to return. Finally Argenis sent Arsidas to find him, with letters pleading for his return.

Arsidas' ship was wrecked, however, and he was rescued and taken aboard the leading ship of a great war fleet. Gobrias, the captain, received Arsidas hospitably and informed him that the fleet belonged to the King of France, who was preparing to attack Sicily. The king himself was commanding the flagship, which was leading the second half of the fleet.

To entertain his guest, Gobrias told him the strange history of the French ruler, King Astioristes—how his mother had kept his birth a secret so that he would not be murdered in a rebellion that was going on at the time, how he had been reared by foster parents, had proved himself a hero in battle, and had finally been revealed as the true prince; how he had heard of the beauty of the Sicilian princess, Argenis, and had sojourned in Sicily under the name of Poliarchus to win her, and how now—as king, the old king having died in his absence—he was sailing to claim her.

Arsidas immediately identified himself as Poliarchus' friend and offered his assistance. Gobrias was delighted, but before the two halves of the fleet could establish a rendezvous, a terrible storm came up, driving each part to a different point on the African coast. The flotilla commanded by the French king found safety in the harbor of Mauritania, and once again Astioristes, the one-time Poliarchus, was entertained by Hyanisbe. His arrival was most fortunate, for Radirobanes was threatening Mauritania. Hyanisbe had sent for her son, Hyempsal, who was at the court of King Meleander in Sicily, but he had not yet returned. When the Sardinian troops arrived, they were repulsed by the French. Poliarchus and Radirobanes met in single combat, and the Sardinian ruler was slain. Disheartened, his followers were routed, but Poliarchus was injured and again confined in Mauritania.

Returning belatedly to his mother's defense, Hyempsal turned out to be Archombrotus. Hyanisbe was dismayed when she found that her son and her protector were enemies; but when she learned the cause of their quarrel she was relieved and she wrote to Meleander a letter which, she promised, would end their difficulties.

While Astioristes was recovering from his wounds, Hyempsal led a successful expedition to Sardinia. Then the two returned to Sicily and presented Hyanisbe's sealed letter to Meleander. The message proved as effective as Hyanisbe had promised. Hyempsal, it was revealed, was the son of Meleander and the king's secret first wife, Hyanisbe's sister. Thus he was both the heir to the Sicilian throne and Argenis' half-brother. Since there was now no obstacle to the marriage of Argenis and Astioristes, Meleander gave them his blessing, the wedding took place at once, and an epithalamium was written by the courtier-poet Nicopompus.

DER ARME HEINRICH

Type of work: Poem
Author: Hartmann von Aue (c. 1170—between 1210 and 1220)
Type of plot: Didactic romance
Time of plot: Late twelfth century
Locale: Germany
First transcribed: Between 1192 and 1202

Principal characters:
HEINRICH VON AUE, a Swabian knight
A PEASANT GIRL

Critique:

Hartmann von Aue, a knight in the service of a Swabian nobleman and one of the first truly German writers, received his education in monastery schools. Later he traveled in France and translated many French poems into Middle High German. The death of his much admired master in 1195 was the chief reason for his participation in a crusade in Palestine, possibly in 1197. This experience revealed the basic conflict of his life, the struggle to choose between the pen and the sword. The presence of secular and religious elements in *Der arme Heinrich* mirrors the author's dilemma as knight and poet in one person. Regardless of the existence of other legends embodied in the story, *Der arme Heinrich* is considered one of the earliest forms of original German literature. The poem shows the influence of martyr legends popular at the time, especially in the inspired speech of the heroine, a simple peasant girl. The writer also displays remarkable ability for characterization and gives the reader a vivid picture of medieval life and thinking. Hartmann von Aue is regarded as the founder of the German court epic, surpassed only by that master of the chivalric romance, Wolfram von Eschenbach (c. 1170-c. 1220).

The Story:

Heinrich von Aue, a Swabian knight, was a fortunate man. Wealthy and of noble birth, he was known throughout the land for his high standard of honor. Fulfillment of his obligations as a knight was his goal; nothing but purest virtue and upright truth marked his life.

Suddenly, however, all his happiness was blighted by a terrible disaster: Heinrich became leprous. As in the case of Job in ancient times, his physical appearance deteriorated rapidly; but he did not have the patience of Job. All his life seemed a curse to him, and his pride left him without friends. His cheerful nature vanished; he detested even the light of day. Only one thing kept him alive, the hope of a cure for his terrible disease.

Trying to find a cure for his malady, he searched out the most famous doctors in all Europe. The school of Montpellier was known for its able doctors and so he went hopefully to that place, only to learn that there was no medicine to heal him. Disappointed, he traveled to Salerno, where he talked to many skilled physicians. At last he met a master who told him that he could be healed, yet the cure itself would be of such a nature that it would be impossible to achieve it; therefore the doctor preferred not to talk about it.

Desperately, Heinrich begged the doctor to reveal his remedy. After some hesitation the physician yielded and told the knight that he could be cured only by the heart's blood of a virgin who would submit willingly, out of love, to a fatal operation.

Heinrich, realizing the hopelessness of his situation, returned sadly to Swabia. All his worldly belongings he gave to the poor and to the monks. Of his land and estates, he kept no more than a clearing in a wood where a poor but contented peasant lived. When Heinrich decided to

187

live in his house in the wood, the peasant and his family did all they could to ease the suffering of the leprous man. Loving the knight, they were concerned for his health because they realized that they would never find such a good master again. The young daughter of the peasant was, in particular, deeply moved by Heinrich's suffering.

One day the peasant asked why the doctors had been unable to help his master. Heinrich told him of the visit to Salerno and described the impossible cure of which the doctor had spoken. The young girl overheard this tale. Late that same evening she told her parents that she wanted to be the virgin who could save their master's life. Her parents were horrified when they heard her request, and her father threatened physical punishment if she dared to mention the subject again. But the next evening the girl began to talk once more of her desire to help the leprous knight. She spoke in such a convincing manner that her parents did not interrupt her but listened in amazement as their daughter begged with heart-moving words to be allowed to gain the eternal life which would be assured her. She spoke also of the uncertainty her earthly life offered, of the catastrophe which could befall the whole family if their master should die and a harsh ruler scourge the countryside. At last she was able to convince her parents that her service to God and her master would be the only honorable thing to do, and sorrowfully they gave their consent to her intended sacrifice.

Very early the next morning she told the unbelieving Heinrich of her willingness to offer herself for his cure. He warned her that she should not talk lightly about such a subject and assured her that she would soon forget her impulsive idea. After the parents confirmed the seriousness of their daughter's wish, Heinrich took a long time to consider her offer. Finally he too yielded to her pleas. Beautiful clothes and furs and a fine horse were bought for the girl, and at last she and Heinrich set out on their journey to Salerno. When the doctor there heard from Heinrich that the girl was willing to sacrifice herself in that fashion, he doubted the knight's words and took the girl aside to implore her to speak the truth by telling him whether she was ready of her own free will to face so horrible a fate. Impressed by her sincerity and beauty, the doctor declared that he would be much happier not to take her heart's blood. Still the girl remained steadfast and begged the doctor to proceed with the operation at once.

Sitting in a neighboring room, Heinrich heard the doctor sharpening his knife. The knight peered through a small hole in the wall and saw the girl tied to a table. For the first time he realized how beautiful she was, and he bitterly accused himself of trying to circumvent the judgment of God by sacrificing the girl's beauty to his ugliness. At the very last moment he was able to stop the doctor before an incision had been made. Although the girl implored him not to become weak and called him a coward, a man without the courage of a true knight, Heinrich disregarded her insults and left with her for home.

During the journey back the grace of God touched Heinrich and rapidly his leprosy disappeared; he and the girl had passed the test given to them by God. Heinrich looked younger and handsomer than ever before. The rumor of his miraculous cure having spread throughout the countryside, Heinrich's vassals came to meet the travelers two days before they arrived at their destination. The happy parents of the girl were the first to meet them, and all thanked God for her deliverance and the knight's cure.

In spite of the peasant girl's low birth, the council of knights agreed that the hand of God had surely chosen her to become Heinrich's wife. All in the land, rich and poor, rejoiced when Heinrich and the girl were wed.

ARNE

Type of work: Novel
Author: Björnstjerne Björnson (1832-1910)
Type of plot: Pastoral romance
Time of plot: Early nineteenth century
Locale: Norway
First published: 1858

Principal characters:
NILS, a tailor
MARGIT, his wife
ARNE, their son
BAARD BÖEN, Nils' enemy
ELI, Baard's daughter

Critique:

Arne is best described as a pastoral story, but the discerning reader will find it also an allegory of the life of Norse peasants. He will read of their devotion to personal honor, their ability to translate memory into action of word or deed. He will read of a man as wicked as Nils and feel that Nils was in a sense a martyr to evil spirits. He will leave the story of Arne with a sense of completion, for the restless and tragic searching of Nils' life is in a sense fulfilled when the daughter of his enemy marries his son.

The Story:

Arne was born on the hillside farm of Kampen. He was the son of Margit, betrayed one night when she attended a dance. The man said to be the child's father was Nils, the tailor, who in his free time fiddled for country dances. Arne's grandmother was a frugal widow who saved what she earned so that her daughter and her grandson might not want for lack of a man to look after them. In the meantime the fiddler-tailor, Nils, drank more and tailored less so that his business fell off.

By the time Arne was six he knew a local song written about the wild behavior of his father. His grandmother insisted that Arne be taught his origin. Not long afterward Nils suffered a broken back in a barn fight with Baard Böen. About the same time the old grandmother, who felt that her days were numbered, warned her daughter against wasting the money saved for her use.

When the grandmother died, Arne's mother brought Nils home to be nursed. The next spring Margit and Nils were married and Nils recovered enough to help with some of the farm work. At first Nils was gloomy and morose because he was no longer able to join the fiddlers and the dancers at weddings, and he drank heavily. As his strength returned he began to fiddle once more. Arne went along to merry-makings to carry his fiddle case. By this companionship Nils weaned Arne away from Margit by degrees. Occasionally the boy was remorseful, but his father's hold grew stronger as time passed.

Finally, during a scene of drunken violence, Nils died. Arne and his mother took the blame for his death partly upon themselves. Arne became aloof from the villagers; he tended his cattle and wrote a few songs.

He became more and more shy. At a wedding, interpreting one of the folk tales as referring to him, he told a wild story, part truth, part fancy, about his father's death. Then he rushed from the house. He had had too much brandy, and while he lay in the barn recovering, his mother told him she had once found Nils there in the same condition—on the occasion of Arne's christening.

Arne began to take a new interest in old legends and ballads. As he listened to stories told by an old man of the village, he found himself making up tales of his own. Sometimes he wandered alone in the forest and sang songs as they came into his head.

From a distance he observed Eli Böen and her good friend, the pastor's daughter. He began to sing love songs. Arne did some carpentering and his work took him into the village more often. That winter Böen sent for Arne to do some carpentering. Arne's mother was disturbed because it had been Böen who had caused Nils to break his back years before. At first Böen's wife refused to speak to Arne. Eli Böen, who was attentive to him in the beginning, later ignored him. One day Arne brought word that the pastor's daughter was leaving the village. Eli fainted when she heard the news, for the two girls had been close friends.

Baard Böen tried to explain to Arne what had happened years before between Nils and himself. But he did not manage to make himself clear, and after many years he himself was not sure of the cause of their long-standing quarrel.

Eli's mother became friendly with Arne at last and she asked him to sing for Eli, who seemed to be recovering from her illness. While he sang, he and Eli felt a deep intimacy spring up between them. The next day, his work completed, Arne took his tools and left. From that time on he thought more and more about Baard Böen's daughter.

Arne had a friend, Kristian, who had gone to America. Now Kristian began to write urging Arne to join him, but Margit hid the letters as they came. Finally she went to the pastor for advice. He felt that Arne must be allowed to live his own life as he saw fit.

The farm was beautiful when spring came. On one of his rambles Arne came upon Eli and thought her more beautiful than he had ever seen her before. Margit took heart from his fondness for the girl. One midsummer evening she discovered Eli in the village and asked her to go for a walk. She took the girl to her homestead and showed her about, from the stables to the chest in which Arne kept the many gifts that were to belong to his bride, among them a hymn book with a silver clasp. On the clasp Eli saw her own name engraved.

Presently Arne appeared and later he walked with Eli back to her own home. They realized now that they were completely in love.

Shortly afterward they were married. Children stood by the church bearing bits of cake. Baard Böen, remembering his long-ago feud with Arne's father, marveled at this wedding of his daughter and the son of his old enemy.

ARROWSMITH

Type of work: Novel
Author: Sinclair Lewis (1885-1951)
Type of plot: Social criticism
Time of plot: Early twentieth century
Locale: United States and West Indies
First published: 1924

Principal characters:
MARTIN ARROWSMITH, a medical scientist
LEORA, his wife
DR. MAX GOTTLIEB, a scientist
GUSTAVE SONDELIUS, a scientist
TERRY WICKETT, Martin's friend
JOYCE LANYON, a young widow
DR. ALMUS PICKERBAUGH, a public health reformer

Critique:

Arrowsmith is one of the novels in which Sinclair Lewis has attempted to point out the insufficiencies and complacencies of American life. What *Babbitt* did for the American businessman, *Arrowsmith* was intended to do for the American doctor. The thesis of *Arrowsmith* would appear to be that the only decent way for a physician to serve mankind is by research. Using Martin Arrowsmith as his example, Lewis has tried to show that the progressive doctor is not appreciated in private practice; that the field of public health is politically corrupt; that the fashionable clinic is often a commercial enterprise; that even the best institutes of research are interested chiefly in publicity.

The Story:

Martin Arrowsmith was the descendant of pioneers in the Ohio wilderness. He grew up in the raw red-brick town of Elk Mills, in the state of Winnemac, a restless, lonely boy who spent his odd hours in old Doc Vickerson's office. The village practitioner was a widower, with no family of his own, and he encouraged Martin's interest in medicine.

At twenty-one Martin was a junior preparing for medical school at the University of Winnemac. Continuing on at the medical school, he was most interested in bacteriology and research and

the courses of Professor Max Gottlieb, a noted German scientist. After joining a medical fraternity, he made many life-long friends. He also fell in love with Madeline Fox, a shallow, pseudo-intellectual who was taking graduate work in English. To the young man from the prairie, Madeline represented culture. They became engaged.

Martin spent many nights in research at the laboratory, and he became the favorite of Professor Gottlieb. One day Gottlieb sent him to the Zenith City Hospital on an errand. There Martin met an attractive nurse named Leora Tozer. He soon became so interested in Leora that he became engaged to her as well. Thus young Martin Arrowsmith found himself engaged to two girls at the same time. Unable to choose between them, he asked both Leora and Madeline to lunch with him. When he explained his predicament, Madeline stalked angrily from the dining-room and out of his life. Leora, amused, remained. Martin felt that his life had really begun.

Through his friendship with Gottlieb, Martin became a student instructor in bacteriology. Leora was called home to North Dakota. Because of Leora's absence, trouble with the dean, and too much whiskey, Martin left school during the Christmas holidays. Traveling like a tramp, he arrived at Wheatsylvania, the town where Leora lived. In spite of the warnings of the dull Tozer family, Martin and Leora were married. Martin went back to Winnemac alone. A married man now, he gave up his work in bacteriology and turned his attention to general study. Later Leora joined him in Mohalis.

Upon completion of his internship, Martin set up an office in Wheatsylvania with money supplied by his wife's family. In the small prairie town Martin made friends of the wrong sort, according to the Tozers, but he was fairly successful as a physician. He also made a number of enemies. Meanwhile Martin and Leora moved from the Tozer house to their own home. When Leora's first child was born dead, they knew that they could never have another child.

Martin had again become interested in research. When he heard that the Swedish scientist, Gustave Sondelius, was to lecture in Minneapolis, Martin went to hear his lecture. In that way Martin became interested in public health as a means of controlling disease. Back in Wheatsylvania, still under the influence of Sondelius, he became acting head of the Department of Public Health. Because Martin, in his official capacity, found a highly respected seamstress to be a chronic carrier of typhoid and sent her to the county home for isolation, he became generally unpopular. He welcomed the opportunity to join Dr. Almus Pickerbaugh of Nautilus, Iowa, as the Assistant Director of Public Health, at a considerable increase in salary.

In Nautilus he found Dr. Pickerbaugh to be a public-spirited evangelist with little knowledge of medicine or interest in scientific control of disease. The director spent his time writing health slogans in doubtful poetic meter, lecturing to clubs, and campaigning for health by means of Better Babies Week, Banish the Booze Week, and Tougher Teeth Week. Martin was gradually drawn under the influence of the flashy, artificial methods used by his superior. Although he tried to devote some time to research, the young doctor found that his job took up all his time. While Dr. Pickerbaugh was campaigning for election to Congress, Martin investigated the most sanitary and efficient dairy of the town. He found that the dairy was spreading disease through a streptococcus infection in the udders of the cows. Against the advice of Dr. Pickerbaugh, Martin closed the dairy and made many enemies for himself. Despite his act, however, he was made Acting Director of Public Health when Dr. Pickerbaugh was elected to Congress.

In his new capacity, Martin hired a competent assistant in order to have more time for research in bacteriology. Largely because he fired a block of tenements infested with tuberculosis, Martin was asked to resign. For the next year he worked as staff pathologist of the fashionable Rouncefield Clinic in Chicago. Then publication of a scientific paper brought him again to the attention of his old friend and professor, Max Gottlieb, now located at the McGurk Institute in New York. Dr. Arrowsmith was glad to accept the position Gottlieb offered him.

At the McGurk Institute Martin devoted his whole time to research, with Gottlieb as his constant friend and adviser. He worked on staphylococcus germs, producing first a toxin, then an antitoxin. Under the influence of Gottlieb and Terry Wickett, his colleague at McGurk, Martin discovered the X Principle, a bacterial infection which might prove to be a cure for disease. Although Martin wanted to postpone publication of his discovery until he was absolutely certain of its value, the directors of the institute insisted that he make his results public at once. Before his paper was finished, however, it was learned that the same principle had already been discovered at the Pasteur Institute, where it was called a bacteriophage. After that disappointment, Martin began work on the possibility of preventing and curing bubonic plague with the phage, as the new antitoxin was called.

Meanwhile Gustave Sondelius had come to the McGurk Institute. He became so interested in Martin's work that he spent most of his time helping his young friend. When a plague broke out on St. Hubert, an island in the West Indies, Martin and Sondelius were asked to go there to help in the fight against the epidemic. Accompanied by Leora they sailed for the island of St. Hubert. Before leaving, Martin had promised Gottlieb that he would conduct his experiment deliberately by refusing to treat some of the plague cases with phage, so that the effects of the treatment could be tabulated.

The plague spread daily on the tropical island. Sondelius was stricken and he died. Martin was often away from his laboratory as he traveled between villages. During one of his trips Leora lighted a half-smoked cigarette she found on a table in his laboratory. The tobacco had been saturated with germs from an overturned test tube. Leora died of the plague before Martin's return.

Martin forgot to be the pure scientist. He gave the phage to all who asked for it. Although his assistant continued to take notes to carry on the research, Martin was no longer interested in the results. When the plague began to abate, he went back to New York. There, lonely and unhappy, he married Joyce Lanyon, a wealthy young widow whom he had met on St. Hubert. But the marriage was not a success. Joyce demanded more of his time than he was willing to take from research; he felt ill at ease among her rich and fashionable friends. When he was offered the assistant directorship of McGurk Institute, he refused the position. In spite of Joyce's protests, he went off to join his old friend, Terry Wickett, at a rural laboratory in Vermont, where they intended to experiment on a cure for pneumonia. At last, he believed, his work— his life—was really beginning.

ARS POETICA

Type of work: Poem on critical theory
Author: Horace (Quintus Horatius Flaccus, 65-8 B.C.)
First transcribed: 13-8 B.C.

To Horace, this poem was the last of his Epistles, but almost at once his contemporaries began referring to it as *Ars Poetica* (*The Art of Poetry*) and by "poetry" they meant any field of literary composition. Horace addressed it to his friend Lucius Calpurnius Piso, famous for his battles in Thrace, and to his two sons. Apparently the older son yearned for a career as dramatist or epic poet. Whether he was deterred, and kept his work unpublished for nine years, or whether his assassination while a praetor in Spain was the reason, no writing has survived bearing his name.

While not a formal treatise or abstract discussion, like the similarly named composition of Aristotle, the 476 lines of this unsystematic letter in verse influenced Joachim du Bellay (c. 1524—1560) in writing the manifesto of the Pleiad, and a century later inspired Boileau's *L'Art poétique* (1674) and Pope's *Essay on Criticism* (1711). Some of Horace's suggestions, like the classical five-act division of the drama, are no longer important, but today's writers still can learn much from the rest of the poem. The double purpose of literature, a mingling of "the useful with the sweet," has been quoted through the centuries in every literary movement.

One would be amused rather than impressed, begins Horace, by the painting of a creature with a horse's body and a man's head, with limbs from every sort of animal, adorned with feathers from a variety of birds. Yet poets combine just such outlandish elements, adding "purple patches" where they are entirely out of place in order to give color and brilliance to pompous openings in portions of their writing. Therefore he begins his *Art of Poetry* with a plea for simplicity and unity.

Addressing Piso and his sons directly, Horace confesses that most poets are misled by what looks like truth. When striving for brevity, the poet becomes unintelligible. Attempts to write smoothly result in loss of vigor and spirit. Aiming at grandeur, he becomes bombastic. Only when he is guided by art can a writer avoid some errors without committing worse ones. The remedy, therefore, is to select subjects equal to one's ability and to use appropriate language. Old words, properly used, seem new; new words, borrowed from the Greeks, may also have a place. Man is admired for making over nature when he builds harbors or drains marshes. Usage, then, should maintain or change the material and rules of speech.

Homer, according to Horace, showed the writer how to handle the deeds of kings and sad tales of war. No one is sure who invented the elegiac couplet, but Archilochus devised the iambus, used in tragic and comic drama; and since it was born of rage, it is designed to record man in action. The Muses gave the lyric for singing about victories, lovers, and gay banquets. All these meters have their specific uses and the poets would do well to employ them only in their appropriate places, though sometimes a writer of comedy may borrow from other forms of poetic art or an author of tragedies set aside his sesquipedalian words in favor of shorter ones to touch the hearts of his audience.

Feeling is the true test of literary worth, for beauty of writing is not enough. Unless a writer feels, he cannot make his audience feel. One style of writing goes with a gloomy face; another sort goes with an angry one, or a playful one. Nature first makes us reveal our feelings physically; then with the tongue for an interpreter she voices the emotions of the heart. There is also a difference in language between the gods and men, between old men and young, between merchants and farmers, among Colchians, Assyrians, and Thebans.

Either follow tradition or be consistent in your inventions, Horace advises. Achilles on the stage must be hot-tempered, appealing to the sword rather than to the law. Follow tradition and make Medea haughty, Ino tearful, and Ixion perjured. If the writer presents original characters, he must keep them consistent: do not let them be too bombastic or promise too much out of prudent fear that the mountain in labor will bring forth no more than a ridiculous mouse.

If the writer wishes the applause of his audience, he must paint accurately the characteristics of the four ages of man. The young boy is unsettled and changing; the beardless youth is fond of horses and dogs, boastful, scornful of advice; in middle age, man is ambitious but cautious; and the old man is surrounded by discomfort. Do not, therefore, attribute the wrong qualities to a stage of human life.

In touching lightly on the rules laid down by classical dramatists, Horace believed in the superiority of showing action rather than telling about it; but there are, he adds, things too horrible to be seen. He comments on the number of actors—only three—and the place of the chorus. He comments on the rules and restraints of satyric drama. Then, after an appeal that Greek, not Roman, tastes be followed in selecting verse forms, he embarks on a history of the theater.

Slightly confused, he gives Thespis credit for inventing the tragedy and traveling in a cart to put on plays in which the faces of actors were stained by dregs of wine. Then came Aeschylus, with the invention of the raised stage, the mask, and the buskins. Old comedy followed, soon to degenerate into license, and the chorus lost its role of abuse.

Roman playwrights, he continues, tried all forms of drama, but most were not successful because they were careless. Horace adjures his student reader to condemn any literary composition that has not been erased and amended. Even genius cannot discard rules. Characterizing himself, he says that he is too lazy to be a genius; he will perform his duty and criticize.

Answering the question of what to write, Horace declares that knowledge is the basis of good writing and that moral philosophy will supply matter. Life and manners should also occupy a writer's attention. The purpose of the poet should be to benefit and entertain. "He has received the votes who has mingled the useful and the sweet, by instructing and delighting the reader at the same time."

People do not always expect perfection from a poet. Some faults can be pardoned, for even Homer failed at times, though usually he excelled in his craft. But continued carelessness is unforgivable, and eternally second-rate material cannot be tolerated. A person who cannot play the game should keep off the field unless he craves the jeers of the spectators. If you write something, he told Piso's son, let the censor of plays see it; then show it to your father and me. Afterward, keep it in your desk for nine years. What you have not published, you can always destroy.

The final eighty lines of the poem deal with generalities. In the early days, says Horace, Orpheus represented the dignity of poets who, by their wisdom, distinguished between public and private property, divine and earthly things, lore and law. By their songs, they won honor. Homer and Tyrtaeus inspired men to battle; oracles guided men by their verses. It is a question for debate whether a poet is born or made, but at any rate, without art and study even a genius will fail.

The best of writers need criticism, but they should avoid mere flatterers. One good critic used to mark, for improvement and reworking, lines in poems submitted to him, and if the would-be poet defended his mistakes, the critic had no more to do with him. The honest critic puts black marks before poor verses as Aristarchus did to Homer. Self-willed poets will not like such treatment, comments Horace, but in that case they are not worth trying to save. They are probably mad, each one, like a bear, clawing at an innocent bystander. Such a poet will be your death, reading you his poetry.

ARTAMÈNE

Type of work: Novel
Author: Madeleine de Scudéry (1607-1701)
Type of plot: Sentimental romance
Time of plot: 500 B.C.
Locale: Asia Minor
First published: 1646-1653

Principal characters:
ARTAMÈNE, the Great Cyrus
CYAXARES, King of Cappadocia, then of Media
MANDANE, his daughter
PHILIDASPES, King of Assyria, in love with Mandane
THE KING OF PONTUS, in love with Mandane
ANAXORIS, in reality Aryante, Prince of the Massagetae, Thomyris' brother, in love with Mandane
PRINCE MAZARE OF SACIA, in love with Mandane
THOMYRIS, Queen of Scythia
SPARGAPISES, Thomyris' son
ARAMINTA, Princess of Pontus
SPITHRIDATES, in love with Araminta
PANTHEA, Queen of Susiana
MARTÉSIE, Mandane's maid of honor
METROBATE, a traitor

Critique:

Some books seem to have a universal value that transcends the time in which they were written. Others seem to be particularly representative of their epoch, and eventually stand as a milestone in the development of a genre. *Artamène, ou le grand Cyrus* belongs to the latter category. It consists of ten volumes, each in two books. In spite of its length, it has a remarkable unity of interest, if not of plot. The story is centered around the pursuit of Mandane by Cyrus, Mandane being constantly abducted by various other suitors. The author indulges in lengthy stories within the story. These successive stories are ingeniously knitted together, one character being introduced casually in one, and being caught up with later in another. The organization of the novel is such that it is actually quite difficult to read only parts of it and still understand it. This type of novel was expected to provide a pastime, in the literal sense of the word. Although this may seem ironic in view of its length, *Artamène* fulfilled this purpose. It provided noble sentiments together with a little learning. It is still possible to understand why it was such a great success.

The Story:

Cyrus, son of the King of Persia, had been given away as a child to a shepherd, who was ordered to kill the infant because his grandfather had been told by an omen that his grandson would eventually kill him. Instead, the shepherd had reared the boy to manhood and now, under the name of Artamène, he was the best general of Cyaxares, King of Cappadocia. He was also secretly in love with Mandane, Cyaxares' daughter.

The kings of Cappadocia and of Pontus had decided to settle a dispute between themselves by a combat, using two hundred men on each side. Artamène had been given the command of the Cappadocian warriors, to the great disappointment of his explosive rival, Philidaspes. Although all the odds were against him, Artamène was the only survivor and won the victory for the Cappadocians.

He discovered, however, that Philidaspes was also in love with Mandane. They had a violent fight and Cyaxares, unaware of the real cause of the quarrel, had them both put in prison.

There were other great battles fought, and Artamène, now out of prison, was again victorious. Then he disappeared and was believed dead. This was the occasion for Mandane to confess her love for him to her confidante, Martésie, a thing she had never dared do before. Eventually Artamène returned. He accidentally learned that Philidaspes was actually the prince of Assyria, heir to the throne of his mother Nitocris, and that he was plotting to take Mandane away. The King of Pontus had also become a new rival for the love of Mandane. To make matters worse, Thomyris, Queen of Scythia, who had never loved before, had fallen in love with Artamène the moment she saw him when he was sent on a mission to her court.

Philidaspes, now King of Assyria, had succeeded in taking Mandane to Babylon, where he pleaded with her to love him or at least to let him hope that she would, some day, accept his suit.

Meanwhile, Artamène, sent in pursuit of Mandane, had laid siege to mighty Babylon, but Philidaspes managed to escape to Sinope with Mandane and Mazare, the chivalrous prince of Sacia. Sinope was set afire and while the Assyrian king was locked up in a tower, Mazare took Mandane away to sea. A shipwreck brought her to the fortress of the King of Pontus.

When Cyaxares arrived at Sinope and failed to find his daughter, he also discovered that Artamène was in love with her. However, he still did not know the hero's real identity, and he was about to have him executed when the army assaulting the castle rescued Artamène and proclaimed him as Cyrus.

When Cyrus set out to get Mandane back, Philidaspes insisted on a paradoxical alliance in order to rescue their common love. They besieged Sardis and captured two hostages, Panthea, the wife of Abradantes, one of the enemy rulers, and Araminta, the sister of the Queen of Pontus. Unfortunately this action provoked Mandane's jealousy, and in a letter she accused Cyrus of using her as a mere pretext to further his ambition. She was particularly jealous of Araminta, whose lover Spithridates resembled Cyrus and could easily have been mistaken for him. Cyrus, with his best paladins, managed to enter Sardis, but Mandane was gone, carried away by the King of Pontus, and perhaps not unwillingly. The hunt for Mandane had to be resumed. Philidaspes stole away to search for Mandane by himself.

Cyrus then learned that the King of Pontus had taken Mandane to Cumae, a place protected by marshes and open to the sea on which she had so often been taken away from him. Meanwhile, the Queen of Corinth, who had conceived a romantic but platonic admiration for Cyrus, sent her fleet to help him. Martésie wrote that Mandane was at last no longer jealous, for Panthea had killed herself over the dead body of her husband, and Araminta had been taken away against her will by Prince Phraortes. Spithridates was desperate.

Cumae was captured and the lovers met at last. A certain Anaxoris had been instrumental in keeping Mandane from being carried away from Cumae. When Philidaspes turned up again to keep watch on Cyrus, he later entrusted Anaxoris with his secret, asking him to take care of Mandane should anything happen to him. Anaxoris, however, was actually Aryante, the prince of the Massagetae, and brother of Thomyris, the formidable Scythian queen. Aryante surrendered Mandane to his sister, and Cyrus went to fight Thomyris.

Spargapises, the son of Thomyris, considering himself disgraced because he had not been recognized when he was captured in battle, killed himself. Thomyris then threatened Cyrus by declaring that she would deliver Mandane's dead body to him unless he surrendered unconditionally. Aryante, not wishing to have Mandane murdered or to have Cyrus near her, sent him a message begging him not to surrender. A tremendous battle followed in which Cyrus set fire to some forests between the two armies. The unfortunate Spithridates, clad in a suit of armor given to him by Cyrus, was mistaken for Cyrus and was killed. His head was taken to Thomyris. Unfortunately, she was not the only one who was mistaken. Cyrus' troops gave up the fight and he was seized by an ally of Thomyris, but his captor later allowed him to escape because of his admiration for his noble prisoner. Cyrus escaped, but only after many difficulties. Thomyris then ordered Mandane killed, but a maid of honor was mistaken for her and killed in her place. Meanwhile, the queen's allies were preparing to desert her. When Cyrus' faithful friends arrived, she fled.

Now Cyrus and Mandane were free to wed, except that an ancient law stated that a prince or princess could not marry a foreigner. But an oracle declared that he who had conquered every kingdom in Asia could not be considered a foreigner in any of them. Thus, to the satisfaction of all concerned, the last obstacle to their union was cleared away.

THE ARTAMONOV BUSINESS

Type of work: Novel
Author: Maxim Gorky (Aleksei Maksimovich Peshkov, 1868-1936)
Type of plot: Family chronicle
Time of plot: c. 1862-1918
Locale: Russia
First published: 1925

Principal characters:
ILIA ARTAMONOV, the father
PETER ARTAMONOV, his oldest son
NIKITA ARTAMONOV, his hunchbacked son
ALEXEY ARTAMONOV, an adopted son
NATALIA BAIMAKOV, Peter's wife
ULIANA BAIMAKOV, widow of the late mayor and Ilia's mistress
ILIA, Peter's first son
YAKOV, Peter's second son
TIKHON VIALOV, a worker in the Artamonov factory

Critique:

Aleksei Maksimovich Peshkov, whose pseudonym was Maxim Gorky (the bitter one), was the son of poor parents and received no formal education. By the time he was nine years old he was earning his own living. During his long wanderings across Russia he educated himself and gained knowledge of all types of people. About 1900 he became a Marxist and was arrested for revolutionary activities. He was exiled in 1906 to Capri, but was permitted to return in 1913. In 1918 he joined the Bolshevik revolution and became one of the best-known writers of Communist Russia. His novels first excited Russian intellectuals but were popular with the masses after the revolution. In spite of his predominantly political influence he was not able to eliminate elements of romanticism in his novels, as is shown in his presentation of the pre-revolution characters of the *The Artamonov Business*. The author is here still far away from a purely socialistic novel, and he does not attempt to discard the strong influence which orthodox Christianity exercised on his heroes. As a description of the social climate in one particular Russian town before the revolution the novel is successful in its effects; however, if the writer intended also to make a plea for the revolutionary cause, it is not, on this thematic level, wholly convincing.

The Story:

A year or so after the liberation of the Russian serfs Ilia Artamonov arrived with his two sons, Peter and Nikita, and Alexey, his nephew and adopted son, in the little town of Dromov along the Vataraksha River. Ilia Artamonov had served as a bailiff to a prince, and the nobleman had recommended him highly to the authorities. Without giving the mayor of Dromov, Evgeny Baimakov, a chance for objections, Artamonov announced that he planned to build a linen factory and that he considered the mayor's daughter Natalia a good wife for his oldest son. Artamonov, disregarding the resentment his dictatorial behavior provoked in the town, went ahead with plans for the factory and preparations for Peter's marriage. The mayor, who died before the wedding, advised his wife Uliana to let Artamonov have his way. But Peter's marriage to the mayor's daughter and the prospect of employment for many citizens did not reduce the enmity felt toward the intruders.

When Uliana Baimakov became Ilia's mistress, she decided to live with the Artamonovs on the other side of the river where the factory was located. Ilia tried to be a strict but humane superior to his men. Among his workers, Tikhon Vialov was the most able, although he begged not to be promoted because he did not want to supervise others. Meanwhile, Nikita, the hunchback, had fallen in love

200

with Natalia, and when he overheard an unkind remark she made about him, he tried to hang himself. The attempt failing, Nikita entered a monastery.

The factory developed rapidly under Ilia's direction. Peter was the second in charge. Alexey, unhappy at the factory, wanted to join the army, but Ilia refused to give him permission to enlist.

When Natalia bore her first child, the baby died after five months. Another girl, Elena, followed. Then a much desired son, also named Ilia, was born. Alexey married a woman nobody in the family liked or understood.

During the transportation of a heavy steam boiler Ilia senior suffered a hemorrhage and died soon afterward. As time passed, Peter's only true happiness was his son. Against his wife's wishes he let Ilia attend a good secondary school away from Dromov. While Peter devoted his time almost exclusively to the factory, Alexey made the necessary business trips to trade fairs and to Moscow. Although Natalia gave birth to a second boy, Yakov, Ilia remained Peter's favorite.

In spite of all efforts to prepare Ilia as Peter's successor as the factory director, his son showed a completely different attitude. He liked to talk to Vialov, the philosopher among the workers, whom Peter despised; and he also formed a close friendship with an uneducated child of a worker. When Ilia, after completing his schooling, announced his desire to become a historian, his father objected because he still wanted Ilia to take over the factory. Ilia refused and left Dromov without receiving any financial assistance from his father. Thereafter Peter became an unhappy man; his wife could not please him, and he tried to find distraction with a local prostitute.

Often Peter had difficulty in controlling his temper, and one day he accidentally killed Ilia's former playmate. Vialov, too, irritated him with philosophizing whenever he had a question to ask. Hoping to find some spiritual guidance, Peter finally decided to visit his brother Nikita in the monastery. Nikita explained that he had failed in his efforts to become a good monk. Although he considered himself unworthy, the monastery valued him highly because he was able to give visiting pilgrims some comfort with patient ears and empty phrases.

When Peter failed to find peace of mind with Nikita, he attended a trade fair in a nearby city. Alexey had told him so many exciting stories about city life that he hoped to find distraction there. After a series of extended drinking sprees and orgiastic behavior with prostitutes, he was finally discovered by Alexey, who had heard from a friend of the family about Peter's disgraceful behavior. Back home, Peter heard rumors that his son had become a member of a revolutionary extremist party. He also detected unusual new ideas in Alexey's son Miron. Only his younger son, Yakov, seemed unconcerned about the new ideas that were spreading among workers. Yakov was not good-looking; however, Peter considered his interests, mainly girls, more normal than all the ideas expressed by the others, ideas which he believed a threat to the factory.

The rapid growth of the factory had brought a large settlement of workers to Dromov, along with many hardship cases. Peter tried to show his interest in his workers by building a new hospital or arranging a big party for them.

Alexey died suddenly. A telegram was sent to summon Nikita, but he had left the monastery. Only Vialov knew his address. After the funeral Nikita and Vialov were seen together frequently. Peter's feelings grew against all people who did not think primarily of the factory, and when Nikita died four days before the outbreak of World War I, he had no kind word for his dying brother.

When Peter grew too old for most of the factory work and Yakov took over in his place, Yakov also became concerned over the growing signs of unrest among the workers. One worker, who spied for him in the factory, became his oppressor. Early in the war many workers were drafted. Some returned, crippled, to the factory. Yakov's fear of being killed by his workers increased rapidly. With his mistress Pauline, a girl of easy virtue and expensive tastes, he planned to go away. Trying to avoid suspicion, he let Pauline leave Dromov first. His own plan was to meet her in Moscow with all the money he could raise. But he never arrived in Moscow. Reports reached Dromov that he had been robbed, killed, and thrown from the train.

Peter, who had tried to ignore all rumors about uprisings and a new way of life for the workers, lived in a state of semicoma and asked constantly the whereabouts of Ilia and Yakov. He failed to realize what was going on around him until one day, he felt a sharp sense of hunger and realized that he was in his garden house. Outside he saw a soldier. When Peter called for his wife, only Vialov came. He explained that Peter was a prisoner.

At first Peter thought Vialov was jeering at him. Later he believed that he had been taken prisoner because someone had learned the truth about the death of Ilia's former playmate. Vialov tried in vain to inform him about the revolution which had taken place and to explain that he was still alive only because of Ilia's influence. Peter thought Vialov had gone mad. When Natalia arrived with a cucumber and a piece of bread, Peter considered himself insulted that she dared offer him such meager food when he was so hungry. Angrily he threw the food away and with abusive words asked her to leave him alone.

AS I LAY DYING

Type of work: Novel
Author: William Faulkner (1897-1962)
Type of plot: Psychological realism
Time of plot: Early twentieth century
Locale: Mississippi
First published: 1930

Principal characters:
ADDIE BUNDREN, a dying old woman
ANSE BUNDREN, her husband
CASH,
DARL,
JEWEL, and
VARDAMAN, their sons
DEWEY DELL, their daughter

Critique:

Centered around the effect of Addie Bundren's death and burial on the members of her family, this novel has a powerful unity not always found in Faulkner's longer works. The author tells the simple story through the eyes and minds of each of his characters. This method of shifting the multiple points of view binds the Bundrens into a homogeneous group beset by the tragedy of Addie's death and the frustrations connected with her burial, yet each character emerges clearly with his own secrets, his own emotional abnormality.

The Story:

Addie Bundren was dying. She lay propped up in a bed in the Bundren farmhouse, looking out the window at her son Cash as he built the coffin in which she was to be buried. Obsessed with perfection in carpentry, Cash held up each board for her approval before he nailed it in place. Dewey Dell, Addie's daughter, stood beside the bed, fanning her mother as she lay there in the summer heat. In another room Anse Bundren, Addie's husband, and two sons, Darl and Jewel, discussed the possibility of the boys' making a trip with a wagonload of lumber to earn three dollars for the family. Because Addie's wish was that she be buried in Jefferson, the town where her relatives lay,

Anse was afraid the boys might not get back in time to carry her body to the Jefferson graveyard. He finally approved the trip and Jewel and Darl set out.

Addie died while the two brothers were gone and before Cash could finish the coffin. When it was obvious that she was dying, a Dr. Peabody was summoned, but he came too late to help the sick woman. While Dr. Peabody was at the house, Vardaman, the youngest boy, arrived home with a fish he had caught in the river; his mother's death somehow became entangled in his mind with the death of the fish and, because Dr. Peabody was there when she died, Vardaman thought the doctor had killed her.

Meanwhile a great rainstorm came up. Jewel and Darl, with their load of lumber, were delayed on the road by a broken wagon wheel. Cash kept working through the rain, trying to finish the coffin. At last it was complete and Addie was placed in it, but the crazed Vardaman, who once had almost smothered in his crib, tried to let his mother out by boring holes through the top of the coffin.

After Jewel and Darl finally got back with the wagon, neighbors gathered at the Bundren house for the funeral service, which was conducted by Whitfield, the minister. Whitfield had once been a lover of Addie's after her marriage, and Jewel, the son whom she seemed to favor, had been fathered by the minister.

Following the service, Anse, his family, and the dead Addie started out for Jefferson, normally one hard day's ride away. The rainstorm, however, had so swollen the river that the bridge had been broken up and could not be crossed by wagon. After trying another bridge, which had also been washed out, they drove back to an old ford near the first bridge. Three of the family—Anse, Dewey Dell, and Vardaman, with the assistance of Vernon Tull, a neighboring farmer—got across the river on the ruins of the bridge. Then Darl and Cash attempted to drive the wagon across at the obliterated ford, with Jewel leading the way on his spotted horse. This horse was Jewel's one great possession; he had earned the money to purchase it by working all day at the Bundren farm and then by working all night clearing ground for a neighbor. When the wagon was nearly across, a big log floating downstream upset the wagon. As a result, Cash broke his leg and nearly died; the mules were drowned; the coffin fell out, but was dragged to the bank by Jewel; and Cash's carpenter's tools were scattered in the water and had to be recovered one by one.

Anse refused the loan of anyone's mules, insisting that he must own the team that carried Addie to the grave. He went off to bargain for mules and made a trade in which he offered, without Jewel's consent, to give the spotted horse as part payment. When Jewel found out what his father had done, he rode off, apparently abandoning the group. Later it turned out that he had put the spotted horse in the barn of Snopes, who was dickering with Anse. And so they got their new mules and the trip continued.

By the time they arrived in Mottson, a town on the way to Jefferson, Addie had been dead so long that buzzards followed the wagon. In Mottson they stopped to buy cement to strengthen Cash's broken leg. The police and citizens, whose noses were offended, insisted that the wagon move on, but they bought the cement and treated the leg before they would budge. While they were in the town, Dewey Dell left the wagon, went to a drugstore, and tried to buy medicine which would abort the illegitimate child she carried, for she had become pregnant by a man named Lafe, with whom she had worked on the farm. The druggist refused to sell her the medicine.

Addie Bundren had been dead nine days and was still not buried. The family spent the last night before their arrival in Jefferson at the house of a Mr. Gillespie, who allowed them to put the odorous coffin in his barn. During the night Darl, whom the neighbors had always thought to be the least sane of the Bundrens, set fire to the barn. Jewel rescued the coffin by carrying it out on his back. Anse later turned Darl over to the authorities at Jefferson; they sent him to the asylum in Jackson.

Lacking a spade and shovel to dig Addie's grave, Anse stopped at a house in Jefferson and borrowed these tools. The burial finally took place. Afterward Dewey Dell again tried to buy her medicine at a drugstore. One of the clerks pretended to be a doctor, gave her some innocuous fluid, and told her to come back that night for further treatment. The further treatment took the form of a seduction in the basement of the drugstore.

Cash's broken leg, encased in cement, had by now become so infected that Anse took him to Dr. Peabody, who said that Cash might not walk for a year. Before starting on the trip home, Anse bought himself a set of false teeth that he had long needed. He then returned the borrowed tools. When he got back to the wagon he had acquired not only the new teeth but also a new Mrs. Bundren, the woman who lent him the tools.

204

AS YOU LIKE IT

Type of work: Drama
Author: William Shakespeare (1564-1616)
Type of plot: Pastoral romance
Time of plot: The Middle Ages
Locale: The Forest of Arden in medieval France
First presented: 1599-1600

Principal characters:
THE BANISHED DUKE
FREDERICK, his brother and usurper of his dominions
OLIVER, older son of Sir Rowland de Boys
ORLANDO, younger son of Sir Rowland de Boys
ADAM, a servant to Oliver
TOUCHSTONE, a clown
ROSALIND, daughter of the banished duke
CELIA, daughter of Frederick

Critique:

Shakespeare took most of the plot of this play from a popular novel of the period, *Rosalynde,* by Thomas Lodge. What he added was dramatic characterization and wit. *As You Like It* is a comedy compounded of many elements, but the whole is set to some of Shakespeare's loveliest poetry. Kindliness, good fellowship, good-will—these are the elements of *As You Like It,* and Shakespeare shows how much they are worth.

The Story:

A long time ago the elder and lawful ruler of a French province had been deposed by his younger brother, Frederick. The old duke, driven from his dominions, fled with several faithful followers to the Forest of Arden. There he lived a happy life, free from the cares of the court and able to devote himself at last to learning the lessons nature had to teach. His daughter Rosalind, however, remained at court as a companion to her cousin Celia, the usurping Duke Frederick's daughter. The two girls were inseparable, and nothing her father said or did could make Celia part from her dearest friend.

One day Duke Frederick commanded the two girls to attend a wrestling match between the duke's champion, Charles, and a young man named Orlando, the special object of Duke Frederick's hatred. Orlando was the son of Sir Rowland de Boys, who in his lifetime had been one of the banished duke's most loyal supporters. When Sir Rowland died, he had charged his oldest son, Oliver, with the task of looking after his younger brother's education, but Oliver had neglected his father's charge. The moment Rosalind laid eyes on Orlando she fell in love with him, and he with her. She tried to dissuade him from an unequal contest with a champion so much more powerful than he, but the more she pleaded the more determined Orlando was to distinguish himself in his lady's eyes. In the end he completely conquered his antagonist, and was rewarded for his prowess by a chain from Rosalind's own neck.

When Duke Frederick discovered his niece's interest in Sir Rowland's son, he banished Rosalind immediately from the court. His daughter Celia announced her intention of following her cousin. As a consequence, Rosalind disguised herself as a boy and set out for the Forest of Arden, and Celia and the faithful Touchstone, the false duke's jester, went with her. In the meantime, Orlando also found it necessary to flee because of his brother's harsh treatment. He was accompanied by his faithful servant, Adam, an old man who willingly turned over his life savings of five hundred crowns for the privilege of following his young master.

Orlando and Adam also set out for the

205

Forest of Arden, but before they had traveled very far they were both weary and hungry. While Adam rested in the shade of some trees, Orlando wandered into that part of the forest where the old duke was, and came upon the outlaws at their meal. Desperate from hunger, Orlando rushed upon the duke with a drawn sword and demanded food. The duke immediately offered to share the hospitality of his table, and Orlando blushed with shame over his rude manner. Moreover, he would not touch a mouthful until Adam had been fed. When the old duke found that Orlando was the son of his friend, Sir Rowland de Boys, he took Orlando and Adam under his protection and made them members of his band of foresters.

In the meantime, Rosalind and Celia also arrived in the Forest of Arden, where they bought a flock of sheep and proceeded to live the life of shepherds. Rosalind passed as Ganymede, Celia, as a sister, Aliena. In this adventure they encountered some real Arcadians—Silvius, a shepherd, and Phebe, a dainty shepherdess with whom Silvius was in love. But the moment Phebe laid eyes on the disguised Rosalind she fell in love with the supposed young shepherd and would have nothing further to do with Silvius. As Ganymede, Rosalind also met Orlando in the forest, and twitted him on his practice of writing verses in praise of Rosalind and hanging them on the trees. Touchstone, in the forest, displayed the same willfulness and whimsicality he showed at court, even to his love for Audrey, a country wench whose sole appeal was her unloveliness.

One morning, as Orlando was on his way to visit Ganymede, he saw a man lying asleep under an oak tree. A snake was coiled about the sleeper's neck, and a hungry lioness crouched nearby ready to spring. He recognized the man as his own brother, Oliver, and for a moment Orlando was tempted to leave him to his fate. But he drew his sword and killed the snake and the lioness. In the encounter he himself was wounded by the lioness. Because Orlando had saved his life, Oliver was duly repentant, and the two brothers were joyfully reunited.

His wound having bled profusely, Orlando was too weak to visit Ganymede, and he sent Oliver instead with a bloody handkerchief as proof of his wounded condition. When Ganymede saw the handkerchief the supposed shepherd promptly fainted. The disguised Celia was so impressed by Oliver's concern for his brother that she fell in love with him, and they made plans to be married on the following day. Orlando was so overwhelmed by this news that he was a little envious. But when Ganymede came to call upon Orlando, the young shepherd promised to produce the lady Rosalind the next day. Meanwhile Phebe came to renew her ardent declaration of love for Ganymede, who promised on the morrow to unravel the love tangle of everyone.

In the meantime, Duke Frederick, enraged at the flight of his daughter, Celia, had set out at the head of an expedition to capture his elder brother and put him and all his followers to death. But on the outskirts of the Forest of Arden he met an old hermit who turned Frederick's head from his evil design. On the day following, as Ganymede had promised, with the banished duke and his followers as guests, Rosalind appeared as herself and explained how she and Celia had posed as the shepherd Ganymede and his sister Aliena. Four marriages took place with great rejoicing that day—Orlando to Rosalind, Oliver to Celia, Silvius to Phebe, and Touchstone to Audrey. Moreover, Frederick was so completely converted by the hermit that he resolved to take religious orders, and he straightway dispatched a messenger to the Forest of Arden to restore his brother's lands and those of all his followers.

ASH WEDNESDAY

Type of work: Poem
Author: T. S. Eliot (1888-   )
First published: 1930

After the publication of *The Waste Land,* in 1922, had established his reputation as a major poet, T. S. Eliot wrote one important poem, "The Hollow Men" (1925), which seemed at that time to be a postlude to its predecessor but which now appears more as a prelude to *Ash Wednesday.* In any case, it should be read as a connecting link between the two longer poems. Its theme is the emptiness of modern intellectualism, which amounts only to

> Shape without form, shade without colour,
> Paralysed force, gesture without motion.

It is another aspect of the Waste Land, desiccated and meaningless, inhabited only by the empty and futile hollow men.

Ash Wednesday marks an important point in the author's poetic development, for it sprang directly from his acceptance of the Anglo-Catholic faith. This biographical aspect of the poem, even more than its theme, influenced its reception by Eliot's former admirers and caused a schism among them that gave an interesting insight into the modern mind.

The tone of the poem is the humility appropriate to Ash Wednesday, the first day of the penitential season of Lent; its theme is the dilemma of the modern man who wants to believe and who yet cannot bring himself to do so because of his dry, sterile intellectuality. This theme is stated in the first of the six parts: the poet, turning his irony upon himself, describes this characteristically modern predicament of a man caught in the web of his own intellectualizing but who can yet know that he must

> . . . pray that I may forget
> These matters that with myself I too much discuss
> Too much explain,

and that at this stage of religious experience the proper prayer is

> Teach us to sit still.

Throughout this opening section sound the echoes of the Penitential Office: "Turn thou us, O good Lord, and so shall we be turned" as well as of Guido Cavalcanti's poem, "In Exile at Sarzana."

The second part is based on a reminiscence of the Valley of Dry Bones described by Ezekiel, the language of which it echoes. Eliot once said in a lecture that the three white leopards could be taken as representing the World, the Flesh, and the Devil. They have fed on the body of the speaker, but Ezekiel was told to prophesy that these bones should live again, that "I [the Lord] shall put my spirit in you, and ye shall live, and I shall place you in your own land." There is also the figure of the Lady, who seems to play a role analogous to that of Beatrice as an intermediary; she is dressed in white, the color of Faith. The speaker, then, having been stripped of everything, has learned resignation; but through the intercession of the Lady and the prophecy of Ezekiel he has found hope.

The third section, with its description of the spiral stairway, obviously recalls Dante's winding ascent of the Purgatorial Mount. There seems to be no direct connection with any particular canto of the *Purgatorio,* only a linking of the journey of purgation with the penitential spirit of Lent. There is also the glimpse through the window of a scene suggestive of sensual pleasure that distracts the pilgrim from his journey. Dante is again

---

recalled in the fourth section, this time by the Earthly Paradise and the Divine Pageant at the end of the *Purgatorio.* Again there are echoes: of St. Paul's *Epistle to the Ephesians* and of the "Salve Regina."

For the fifth section Eliot made use of a sermon by Lancelot Andrews that he had already quoted in an essay on the Bishop: ". . . the Word of an Infant? The Word and not be able to speak a word?"—an elaborate play upon the word (speech), the Word (the Logos, the most abstruse of Christian doctrines), and the Word made Flesh.

The last section, doubling back upon the opening lines of the poem, suggests a scene in a confessional ("Bless me father") during which the beauty of the natural world intrudes into the mind of the speaker and distracts him from his proper meditation. Thus, the world seeks to draw us back to itself. Then, appropriately, the poem ends with words taken, with one slight change, from the Penitential Office for Ash Wednesday in the Book of Common Prayer:

And let my cry come unto Thee.

Thus, the poem deals with various aspects of a certain stage in religious experience: "Lord, I am not worthy"; it is a poem of spiritual, as Cavalcanti's was one of physical, exile. The dweller in the Waste Land who "cannot drink/there, where trees flower, and springs flow" must find his way back through peni-

tence, with the humble prayer: "Suffer me not to be separated."

This is a simpler poem than *The Waste Land,* though Eliot used much the same technical devices of ellipsis and echoes. It rises to heights of verbal beauty unequaled in any other contemporary verse. Its reception, however, was curious and not without irony. To many readers of the 1920's, Eliot had become the spokesman for the disillusionment of the now famous "lost generation"—a statement that he himself characterized as "nonsense." 1930, with its Marxian enthusiasm for proletarian literature, was probably the high point of the secular humanism of our time; Bertrand Russell's *A Free Man's Worship* was dominant. It was among the adherents to this secular humanism that Eliot's greatest admirers were to be found. For him to become a member of the Anglican Church and to write a poem with a deeply religious theme was to them a grievous shock. Some of them flatly refused to believe in his sincerity; his membership in the Church of England must be a pose, a kind of romantic, aesthetic Catholicism. To others, to whom religion was a retreat from reality, a "failure of nerve," he was a lost leader, a writer whose significant work had ended with "The Hollow Men." Yet it might not be an exaggeration to claim that the publication of *Ash Wednesday* marked the beginning of the swing from the intellectual Left to Right, with the consequent decline of the secular humanist attitude.

ASHES

Type of work: Novel
Author: Stefan Żeromski (1864-1925)
Type of plot: Historical romance
Time of plot: 1796-1812
Locale: Poland and Spain
First published: 1904

Principal characters:
RAPHAEL OLBROMSKI, a Pole
CHRISTOPHER CEDRO, his friend
HELEN, beloved of Raphael
PRINCE GINTULT, a nobleman
ELIZABETH, his sister
NARDZEVSKI, Raphael's uncle

Critique:

Much of this work is in the German romantic tradition. Żeromski describes nature in great detail and devotes long sections to philosophical speculations engendered by contemplation of nature. The tragic love affair of Helen and Raphael and the frequent unconnected sequences of action are reminiscent of Goethe. In contrast, the scenes descriptive of some of the Napoleonic campaigns are precise and realistic. As a historical novel, Ashes ranks high, and as an author Żeromski was acknowledged a master by Conrad.

The Story:

When he was very young, Raphael Olbromski paid a short visit to his uncle's secluded estate. Nardzevski, fond of his nephew, initiated him into the art of hunting. The fierce old man was a firm adherent to feudal times and treated his peasants as serfs. Casper, his huntsman, was his only intimate. Raphael's visit came to a sudden end with the arrival of an Austrian official.

The Austrian lectured Nardzevski severely on the necessity of paying the new taxes and modifying his treatment of his peasants, but the old man had no intention of truckling to the Austrians. To emphasize his attitude, he practiced his pistol marksmanship in the dining hall.

Defiantly Nardzevski ordered his steward to summon all the peasants in the morning and to arrange for a public flogging of a miscreant. Raphael never learned what happened afterward because early in the morning he was bundled into a sleigh and sent home.

A great sleighing party one winter attracted all the gentry. Raphael, mounted on a spirited horse, followed Helen's sleigh closely. The party stopped to dance at Raphael's poor house, and his aristocratic father staged a big celebration. During the affair Raphael managed to tell Helen that he would come to her window some midnight. The party lasted for two days, but Raphael missed much of it because he slept in a drunken stupor.

At school Raphael was no student, but he was a leader. One evening he and Christopher stole a rowboat and went out into the ice-packed Vistula. When they tried to land, the thin shore ice broke and the boys were soaked. As they went on toward school, they sank into a bog. They were nearly frozen before Raphael took vigorous measures. He tore off his clothes and those of the weakened Christopher, and the boys pummeled each other to get warm. Then, quite naked, they ran back to school, to be caught as they tried to slip inside. Christopher fell ill with fever, and Raphael

ASHES by Stefan Żeromski. Translated by Helen Stankiewicz Zand. By permission of the publishers, Alfred A. Knopf, Inc. Copyright, 1925, as POPIOLY by Stefan Żeromski. Copyright, 1928, by Alfred A. Knopf, Inc.

as the leader was sentenced to be chastised. When the beadle tried to carry out the punishment, Raphael drew a knife, wounded the beadle, and escaped.

His father, when he arrived home in disgrace, imprisoned him in a small room and forbade the family to speak to him. Later he had to spend months working with the peasants. One night Raphael took a fine mare from the barn and rode through a storm to Helen's house. When a watchman came upon them in an outbuilding, Helen got back to her bedroom safely, but Raphael barely escaped ahead of the fierce watchdogs.

A storm came up. Raphael was followed by four wolves. When his horse stumbled, the wolves were on him. Three brought down the horse; Raphael killed the fourth with his hands. Gravely wounded, he was found by an old peasant and taken home. When he recovered, he was cast out of the family and sent to live with his older brother Peter, who had been cast out years before.

Peter, in poor health from war wounds, lived quietly. Raphael spent delightful months in idleness until the arrival of Prince Gintult, an old comrade of Peter's. Peter and the prince had angry words on the treatment of peasants, and as the result of the quarrel Peter had a hemorrhage and died. With no home and melancholy with memories of Helen, who had been taken out of the country, Raphael went to stay with the prince.

In the noble household Raphael was half family, half guest. The prince gave him money for clothes and others gave him errands to run. Raphael was particularly attracted to the prince's sister Elizabeth, a haughty young girl. One day, while they were riding in a group, Elizabeth's horse ran away. Raphael rescued her and made the mistake of kissing her as he held her in his arms. She slashed his face with her whip.

The prince suddenly departed on a voyage to Venice and Paris, after paying Raphael's lodging in a school for a year. Raphael studied fairly well and spent his time profitably. When he was forced to return home, his stern father outfitted him in work clothes and for four years he worked on the farm. His release came with an offer of a position from Prince Gintult.

In Warsaw, Raphael served as secretary to the prince, who was writing a vague philosophical treatise on Freemasonry. In order to continue the work on the secret lodge, Raphael was taken into the Masons; soon afterward he was accepted in society. Through the lodge, he met Helen again.

Abruptly Raphael and Helen fled to the country to enjoy their love. One night they slept in a cave in the mountains. Although Raphael was armed, brigands overpowered him as he slept and bound him while they had their sport with Helen. She escaped their clutches at last and jumped over a cliff.

While he was searching for Helen's body and tracking the brigands, Raphael was arrested by a patrol. He did not dare give his right name or mention Helen for fear of defiling her memory, and while in prison he had a long siege of fever. More than a year passed before he was released.

Penniless and tramping aimlessly about the country, Raphael fell in with his old friend Christopher. The reunited friends spent happy months on Christopher's estate. Then a soldier who had been with Napoleon for twelve years fired their imagination, and they decided to leave that Austrian-dominated part of Poland and join the emperor. Aided by Elizabeth, who was now married and living near the border, they made a daring escape across the frontier.

Christopher, as an enlisted man, crossed Europe with Napoleon and took part in the Spanish campaign. His most vivid impressions were those of the siege of Saragossa, where he distinguished himself for valor and saved a young girl from soldiers who sacked a convent and raped the nuns. He was thrilled when Napoleon abolished the Inquisition. After he had been wounded, he saw the emperor at close hand.

Raphael saw action in Poland, where the Austrian legions were too strong for Napoleon's forces. Once the Poles were preparing to demolish a church, held by the enemy. Prince Gintult, fighting as a civilian, attempted to save the church by interfering with the cannoneers, and Raphael helped him. For his deed the prince was cut down by an officer's sword. In the confusion Raphael carried the wounded nobleman away to his father's house.

When the fighting died down, Raphael was discharged. He went to live at his uncle's old estate, and for a time he was happy there. He rebuilt the barns demolished by the soldiers and cleared land. Then he began building a house. Just as he was finishing, Christopher arrived. Invalided out of the army, but well again, he was impatient for action. Reluctant to leave his home, Raphael objected at first; but finally he agreed to accompany his friend. In the middle of August, 1812, the Polish Corps was united with the Grand Army, and Raphael returned to serve the emperor. At Orsha, Napoleon reviewed his hordes of Polish, Dutch, Italian, and German soldiers.

AT THE SIGN OF THE REINE PÉDAUQUE

Type of work: Novel
Author: Anatole France (Jacques Anatole Thibault, 1844-1924)
Type of plot: Humorous satire
Time of plot: Eighteenth century
Locale: France
First published: 1893

> *Principal characters:*
> JACQUES MÉNÉTRIER, a young scholar
> MAÎTRE JÉRÔME COIGNARD, an abbot
> CATHERINE, a temptress
> JAEL, a Jewess
> MONSIEUR D'ASTARAC, a philosopher

Critique:

At the Sign of the Reine Pédauque (*La Rôtisserie de la Reine Pédauque*) was the first of France's many works to exhibit in full his peculiar talents. This tale is gusty in outline and overlaid with vast erudition in philosophy and in ancient history. In plot the novel is reminiscent of *Tom Jones* but the treatment is pure Gallic. France's humor is always subtle and at times wicked. In the Abbé Jérôme he has created a memorable character, the fluent, scoundrelly cleric who becomes a sympathetic creation.

The Story:

Jacques Ménétrier's father was a merry cook and his mother a long-suffering, plain woman. The father spent several hours each night at a nearby tavern in the company of Jeannette, the hurdy-gurdy woman, and Catherine, the lace maker. Both ladies helped him relive his lusty youth.

When Jacques was six, he was stationed all day long in the chimney corner to turn the spitted roasts. His time was not altogether wasted, however, for he learned his letters at the same time from a beggar Capuchin, Brother Ange. The good Brother Ange ate well at the common table in return for his services, and in secret he sighed for Catherine.

After a drunken brawl, Brother Ange was imprisoned, and Maître Jérôme Coignard, a Greek and Latin scholar, became Jacques' tutor. As he grew to young manhood he progressed rapidly under the scholar's teachings.

Jeannette, complaisant with all, initiated Jacques into the mysteries of love, but, perversely, Jacques was attracted to Catherine, who made fun of Jacques' beardless chin and refused to take him seriously. Jacques and his father were greatly discomfited when she ran away with Brother Ange.

One evening a tall, gaunt philosopher entered abruptly, crying that he saw a salamander in the fireplace. Vigorously stirring the ashes, he asked the company if they saw anything. Only Jacques thought he saw the outlines of a beautiful woman in the smoke. The philosopher was much pleased with Jacques' discernment.

When Monsieur d'Astarac, their strange visitor, learned that the Maître Jérôme could read Greek easily, he arranged to have the abbot and Jacques come live with him.

At the ruined estate of the philosopher, the two friends were astonished by the rich library. In spite of crumbling walls and overgrown grounds, d'Astarac was evidently wealthy as well as learned. Maître Jérôme was set to work translating the ancient works of Zosimus the Panopolitan, with Jacques as his helper. According to d'Astarac, the only other inhabitant of the estate was Mosaïde, a learned Jew over a hundred years old. The Jew lived mysteriously withdrawn in a separate cottage, where he worked on old Hebrew manuscripts.

After several tranquil months Jacques went for an evening walk into Paris. Brother Ange came up and whispered that a lady was eagerly awaiting him in her carriage. At the rendezvous Jacques found Catherine seated in an elegant coach. Astonished at her magnificence, Jacques learned that she was now the mistress of de la Guéritaude, a tax collector. Then they kissed fervently and made an appointment for later that night.

On Jacques' arrival, the house where Catherine lived was in disturbance. She, half-dressed, was shrieking at the door and lackeys were pursuing Brother Ange with spears. De la Guéritaude had surprised her with her monk. Jacques comforted Catherine ardently, but when de la Guéritaude returned he rudely shoved Jacques into the street and slammed the door.

Soon afterward d'Astarac summoned Jacques to a private conference in a secret laboratory, where he told the young man that he would reveal some of the mysteries of philosophy. The spirit world consisted of sylphs, males who helped philosophers, and salamanders, beautiful females in search of human lovers. Since Jacques was well on his way to being a philosopher and since he had little to do with carnal women, d'Astarac would show him how to summon a salamander. Guiltily thinking of Catherine, Jacques agreed to try.

D'Astarac helped him open a crystal ball filled with stardust. Feeling overwhelmed, Jacques sank down and d'Astarac left him. After a few minutes Jacques looked up to see in front of him a voluptuous, dark-haired woman. Although she resisted his advances for a time, she accepted him as her lover, and they spent the night together.

Jacques soon learned that she was no salamander; she was Jael, niece of Mosaïde. The fierce old Jew kept her secluded, hiding her from Christian eyes, but Jael came frequently to his room despite the uncle's vigilance. One early morning Maître Jérôme saw her leaving and traced her to Mosaïde's cottage. Although Jael slipped inside unseen, Mosaïde saw the abbot from his window and cursed him in Hebrew and Spanish. Not to be outdone, Maître Jérôme cursed the Jew in French and Latin.

That evening, as Maître Jérôme and Jacques passed Catherine's house, she greeted Jacques with great affection from her doorway. Someone inside slapped her sharply and pulled her inside. It was the noble d'Anquetil, Catherine's new lover. He invited them in, pleased that he had Jacques for a rival instead of the begging Capuchin.

The four spent an agreeable evening at the card table. Maître Jérôme always won. Catherine sat snuggled close to d'Anquetil, and while vowing eternal fidelity to him pressed Jacques' foot under the table. Suddenly there was a thunderous rapping outside. De la Guéritaude had returned, furious at being locked out of the house he rented for Catherine.

The four revelers brawled with the tax collector, injuring him gravely and killing one of his lackeys. Jacques, Maître Jérôme, and d'Anquetil fled to d'Astarac's estate for safety. Jacques put the nobleman in his own room and went to talk with the philosopher, although it was almost morning. Unfortunately, Jael came visiting, and before she could flee d'Anquetil was smitten with her charms.

D'Anquetil, who had hired carriages so that they could flee the police, wanted to take Jael with him. To Jacques' horror, Jael agreed after being promised a set of silver plate and a monthly income. In the morning d'Anquetil and Jael set off in a closed coupé, followed by Maître Jérôme and a morose Jacques.

During the journey Jacques reproached Jael for her easy switch of lovers, but she took a practical view of the matter. A set of silver plate could not be ignored. One night at an inn Jael left d'Anquetil's room to visit Jacques, who was thereafter somewhat more content.

From Jael, Jacques learned that Mosaïde was not a hundred years old, but barely sixty; and instead of being a famous scholar, he was a banker who had fled Spain after killing a Christian. Furthermore, Mosaïde was Jael's lover.

Shocked by these disclosures, Jacques was uneasy at the sight of a mysterious carriage which followed them closely. His apprehensions were justified one night when they ran into a bridge and broke a wheel. Jacques, d'Anquetil, and Jael waited for repairs in a nearby dell, while Maître Jérôme searched the wreckage for bottles of wine.

In the darkness Mosaïde, who had been following the runaways, fell upon the abbot and wounded him mortally, for the jealous Jew thought that Maître Jérôme had stolen Jael. The monk died in a neighboring village, where he had been carried for medical aid. Jacques, mourning his tutor and friend, returned to his parents in Paris.

Later Jacques went to pay a visit to d'Astarac. When he arrived at the estate, he saw the big house blazing fiercely. The philosopher was burned to death in the fire, and Mosaïde drowned in a swamp as he tried to run away. Gradually, the memory of Jael becoming less poignant, Jacques found his true vocation. He became a bookseller and supported his father and mother in dignity in their old age.

ATALA

Type of work: Novel
Author: François René de Chateaubriand (1768-1848)
Type of plot: Philosophical romance
Time of plot: Early eighteenth century
Locale: Louisiana
First published: 1801

Principal characters:
ATALA, an Indian maiden
CHACTAS, beloved of Atala
FATHER AUBRY, a missionary

Critique:

A tale of passionate but pure love, *Atala* is another of the stories of the Noble Savage which began to find such favor in the early nineteenth century. Against a background of the primitive American wilderness, the two lovers and the gentle priest wage a winning battle against sin and paganism. Simplicity and complexity of character are vividly contrasted, the two meeting in Christian faith in the goodness of God. *Atala* was the first of Chateaubriand's romances to be published, and the book had a tremendous vogue in its own day. The novel was originally planned as part of a much longer work, *The Natchez,* based on Chateaubriand's travels on the American frontier and influenced by his romantic philosophy.

The Story:

Chactas was an old, blind, and wise Indian of the tribe of Natchez, whose hunting ground was in the territory of Louisiana. Because of his great age and deep wisdom gained through countless years of tragic misfortune, Chactas was the patriarch of the tribe. Thus it was that when a young Frenchman named René presented himself for membership in the tribe in the year 1725, it was Chactas who questioned him to determine his fitness to join the Natchez nation. Finding René fixed in his determination to become a savage, Chactas accepted him. As the Indians prepared for a beaver hunt, Chactas—even though he was blind—was made the leader of the party. One night as they lay in their ca-

noes Chactas recited to René the story of his adventures.

When Chactas had lived but seventeen summers, his father was killed in battle and he himself was taken prisoner by the enemy and led away by the Spaniards to St. Augustine. There he was befriended by an old Castilian named Lopez and his sister. The two white people cared for the young savage and tried to educate him as their son. But after thirty moons had passed, Chactas tired of this civilized life and begged Lopez to allow him to return to his people. Lopez, knowing the dangers awaiting a lonely youth in the forests, tried to dissuade Chactas at first. At last, seeing that the youth was firm in his resolve, the old man sent him away with his blessing.

The warning given by the good Lopez soon proved right. Chactas, having lost his way in the woods, was captured by an enemy tribe and taken to their village to await death by burning. Because of his youth and bravery, the women of the tribe took pity on him. One night, as he sat by the campfire, he heard a rustling and then felt the presence of a woman beside him. In low tones she told him that she was Atala, daughter of the chief and his dead wife. She asked Chactas if he were a Christian, and when he told her that he had not forsaken the gods of his father, she departed.

For many days the tribe marched, taking Chactas with them, and each night Atala visited him by the fire. One night, after Chactas had been tied to a tree, Atala appeared and told his guard that

215

she would watch the prisoner for a time. Since she was the daughter of the chief, the guard gladly gave her his place. Quickly she untied the cords and gave Chactas his freedom. But he as quickly placed the cords in her hand, telling her that he wanted to be chained to her forever. She cried out in anguish that their religions separated them. She also seemed to have some other terrible secret that she feared he would learn. Atala begged him to flee without her, but Chactas said that he would rather die by fire than leave her. Neither would change, and so Atala tied Chactas again, hoping that soon he would change his mind. Each night they slipped off into the woods together, but Chactas did not possess her, for her God helped her to deny her passion for her beloved. She prayed that the savage boy might give himself to her God so that one barrier to their love would be broken.

One night her father's warriors discovered them together. Chactas was returned to the camp and placed under heavy guard. The tribe marched on and came at last to the place where Chactas was to be burned at the stake. From far and near Indians gathered to witness his torture and death at a Feast of the Dead. Chactas was prepared for his ordeal in the manner of savages, his body being painted and then laid on the ground, with guards lying across the ropes so that they might feel the slightest movement of the prisoner's body. But in spite of the great precautions, Atala again freed him by a ruse, and they made their escape into the forest. Although they were pursued, the Indians were so drunk from celebrating the Feast of the Dead that the pursuit was only half-hearted, and the lovers had little trouble in eluding them.

But the wilderness almost conquered the fugitives, who were ill-prepared for the hardships they now had to endure. Their fates joined, Atala proclaimed her love for Chactas but said that they could never marry. Although she gave their differences in religion as the only reason, Chactas felt that there was more she feared to tell him. At last, upon his urging, she told him her secret. She was not the daughter of the chief, but the illegitimate child of a white man and the chief's wife. When Chactas learned that the white man was his old friend Lopez, he loved her as a sister as well as a lover. It was through Lopez that she had gained her Christian faith, transmitted to her by her mother.

A terrible storm drove them to the shelter of a tree, and while in that refuge they saw approaching a dog and an old hermit. The hermit was a missionary, Father Aubry, who took them to his grotto and gave them food and shelter. Chactas feared to go, for he was not a Christian, but Father Aubry said that he was one of God's children and made him welcome. When he promised to instruct Chactas in Christianity so that he and Atala could be married, the girl paled at his words.

They learned that Father Aubry had spent almost his entire life among the savages, even though he could have had a more comfortable life in Europe. A good man, he considered it a privilege and not a sacrifice to endure the hardships and dangers of the wilderness. Atala and Chactas became a part of the little community of Christian savages over whom the good priest presided. After a time Chactas began to feel the spirit of God in his heart.

One day, returning from a pilgrimage with Father Aubry, Chactas found Atala apparently dying from a mysterious fever. Then they learned what her true secret had been. On her deathbed Atala's mother had taken the girl's vow that she would always remain a virgin. Her own sin had made her want to protect her daughter, and Atala, knowing nothing of real love, had given her vow which could never be broken. When Father Aubry told the lovers that the bishop in Quebec could release her from her vow, Chactas' heart grew light. In real anguish Atala then told them that she had taken poison because she had believed Chactas forever denied to her. There were no remedies for the poison, and so, after receiving the blessing of the priest and the promise of Chactas that he would embrace the Christian religion so that they could be joined in heaven, the poor virgin expired.

With the priest's aid Chactas buried his beloved. Then he said goodbye to Father Aubry and once more began his wanderings. Many years passed before

he received baptism in the faith of his beloved Atala.

And many years more were to pass before the daughter of René, whom Chactas had adopted, took the bones of Atala and Father Aubry and Chactas to the land of the Natchez for burial. Chactas and Father Aubry had been killed by savage enemies. The daughter of René told a curious traveler that he should not grieve. The three friends were together with God.

217

ATALANTA IN CALYDON

Type of work: Poem
Author: Algernon Charles Swinburne (1837-1909)
Type of plot: Classical tragedy
Time of plot: Remote antiquity
Locale: Ancient Greece
First published: 1865

Principal characters:
ŒNEUS, King of Calydon
ALTHÆA, his wife
MELEAGER, their son
ATALANTA, a virgin huntress
CHORUS

Critique:

Atalanta in Calydon, typical of the Victorian treatment of Greek tragedy, was the first of Swinburne's longer works to attract marked critical notice. As in the case of Swinburne's other poetic dramas, it was not written for stage presentation, but for reading. One of the Pre-Raphaelites, Swinburne was criticized for using too much intensity and too violent colors in his poetry. In this poem his intensity and violence are very much the essence of the passionate and soul-stirring description of the characters' fateful existence.

The Story:

Œneus, father of Meleager, had offended Artemis, goddess of the hunt, by offering sacrifices to all the gods except her. As a punishment for his negligence Artemis had sent into Calydon a wild boar that ravaged the land and the crops.

Althæa, embittered by the curse, refused to pay homage to Artemis and raged against the gods. Althæa was a woman of strong will and determination. Years before, when her son Meleager was born, she had had a strange dream concerning his birth. In the dream three spinning women, the Fates, had visited Althæa and had promised for Meleager strength, good fortune, and a bounteous life until the brand on the hearth burned out. On hearing the last part of the prophecy, Althæa had sprung from her bed, grasped the burning brand, and beaten and trampled the heat from it with her bare hands and feet. Then, to guard Meleager's life, she had hidden the brand.

Again she had dreamed that the heatless brand burst into flame as a bud bursts into flower; and with this strange phenomenon Death had come to blow charred ash from the brand into her breast, but there Love had quenched the flame. The omen presaged for Althæa the security of her family; but in spite of her great pride she was not unmindful of the lots which the gods might cast for mortals. These thoughts were in her mind as she went to arm Meleager for the boar hunt. Never had there been born so strong a man of royal birth as Meleager.

The Chorus, reviewing the life span of man, summed up this existence as a passing between a sleep and a sleep.

The warriors of Arcadia were to join the Calydonians in the hunt, and Meleager and Althæa discussed the qualities and characteristics of these men, among them the valiant sons of Leda, Althæa's sister. Meleager described Toxeus and Plexippus, Althæa's brothers, as undoing their deeds with too much talk. Althæa counseled her son against too great pride in earthly accomplishments and advised him to submit his soul to fate. The Chorus admonished Meleager to follow his mother's counsel.

Meleager, recounting the many tumultuous battles he had experienced, pointed out to his mother that in all these frays he had never seen evidence of the infallible gods to whom she and the Chorus would have him submit.

Œneus reported the coming of the Arcadians and said that among them was a woman armed for the hunt. Although Œneus wished to have this woman shown great respect because of her favor from the gods, he warned Meleager against becoming infatuated with her beauty. Althæa, recalling the prophecies of the Fates regarding Meleager's career, added to her husband's warning against earthly love. Again imploring her son to give himself to fate, she told him that he would not die as ordinary men die and that his death would be her death as well. Meleager declared his boundless love for his mother and expressed respect for her teaching. Ever faithful to Zeus, the sole determiner of things, he prepared for the hunt.

The Chorus, philosophizing on Love, saw her blind as a flame, covered by earth for hiding, and fronted by laughter to conceal the tears of desire. According to the portent of the Chorus, man and maid would go forth; the maid's name, Fate; the man's, Death. The Chorus lamented also the meagerness of life's span. This futility, an evil blossom born of sea foam and blood froth, had come into existence with Aphrodite, goddess of love. Before, there had been joy upon the earth, but Aphrodite's influence had resulted in suffering, evil, and devastation.

In the hunt, as predicted, Meleager met the Arcadian maiden. She was Atalanta, the virgin priestess of Artemis, whom Œneus had neglected in his sacrifices and who had sent the wild boar to ravage Calydon. Atalanta invoked Artemis to favor Meleager that he might be victorious in the hunt. Meleager, confessing his love for Atalanta, was taunted by his uncles, Toxeus and Plexippus, for his woman-tonguedness. Althæa pleaded for peace among her kinsmen lest words become snakes and poison them against each other.

The hunt proceeded. According to a message sent by Œneus to Althæa, the expedition demanded energy, courage, and hunting strategy. The boar, crazed by the chase and by the numerous wounds inflicted, charged Meleager, who with all daring and skill slew the animal, thereby ridding Calydon of its curse. Althæa offered praise to the gods. A messenger who had brought the message to Althæa added that pride in earthly accomplishments would bring about destruction.

The Chorus, chanting a song of thanksgiving to the gods, was hushed by the messenger, who ordered them to change their songs to wails of pity because Toxeus and Plexippus had been slain.

Althæa, lamenting the death of her brothers, found comfort in the thought that Meleager would avenge them. The messenger questioned whether her son should slay himself. When Althæa threatened him for his ambiguity, the messenger bluntly informed her that Meleager had slain his uncles.

After the boar had been killed, Toxeus and Plexippus requested that the head and the hide be kept as a monument in Calydon; but Meleager, enamoured of Atalanta, gave her the spoils of the hunt. Pleased with this token of his devotion, Atalanta laughed. The Calydonians construed her reaction as a taunt and sought to destroy her. In furious fighting to protect the maiden, Meleager killed his uncles. Althæa recalled her brothers' kindnesses in their childhood, anticipated her sister's scorn for Meleager's crime, and accepted her fate as a victim of many curses.

The Chorus, endeavoring to comfort Althæa in the loss of her brothers, was rebuked. Had Toxeus and Plexippus died in sacrifice or battle, Althæa maintained, their lives would not have been in vain; but knowing that they had been slain by her son, she could never become reconciled to their deaths or to his crime.

In Meleager's deed, caused by excessive earthly pride and undue desire for attainment, Althæa sensed her error in taking the burning brand from the fire at the time of his birth. Stoically she thrust the brand into the fire that it might be consumed at last. Althæa suffered with torment and anguish as the Chorus described the burning, which resulted in Meleager's death after his return from the hunt.

Meleager reviewed his existence without remorse and besought Œneus and Althæa not to let his name die among men. He described his passing as an empty night harvest in which no man gathers fruit. Althæa died of sorrow. Atalanta, hailing Meleager's greatness, returned to Arcadia. Œneus ruled alone in Calydon.

AUCASSIN AND NICOLETTE

Type of work: Tale
Author: Unknown
Type of plot: Chivalric romance
Time of plot: Twelfth century
Locale: Provence, in France
First transcribed: Fourteenth-century manuscript

Principal characters:
COUNT GARIN DE BEAUCAIRE
AUCASSIN, his son
NICOLETTE, a slave girl

Critique:

Aucassin and Nicolette is considered by many scholars to be the masterpiece of the romances of chivalry. It is written in what is called the *chante-fable*, or song-story style—a prose tale containing verse passages which are sung by a minstrel. In it are found certain Oriental elements and much folklore.

The Story:

Count Bougars de Valence and Count Garin de Beaucaire were at war. Count Garin had one son, Aucassin, who was so smitten by love that he would neither accept the duties of knighthood nor participate in his father's quarrel, unless his father consented to his love for Nicolette. She was a slave girl, bought by a captain of the town from the Saracens and reared as his own daughter. Count Garin agreed to the marriage of Aucassin to any daughter of a king or count, but not to Nicolette. He went to see the captain and told him to send Nicolette away. The captain said that he would keep Nicolette out of sight, and so she was imprisoned in the high chamber of a palace with an old woman to keep her company.

Rumors sped through the countryside: Nicolette was lost; Nicolette had fled the country; Nicolette was slain by order of Count Garin.

Meanwhile the war between the two counts grew more fierce, but Aucassin still refused to fight. Father and son then made a covenant; Aucassin would go into the battle, and if God willed that he should survive, the count must agree to allow him two or three words and one kiss from Nicolette. Aucassin rode into the fray, but thoughts of Nicolette so distracted him that he was captured. Then Aucassin reflected that if he were slain, he would have no chance at all to see Nicolette. Therefore he laid his hand on his sword and began fighting with all his strength. He killed ten knights and wounded seven and took Count Bougars prisoner. But when Count Garin refused to keep the covenant, Aucassin released Count Bougars. Aucassin was cast into a dungeon.

Nicolette, knowing her companion to be asleep, escaped from her prison by a rope made of bed linen and went to the castle where Aucassin lay. While they exchanged lovers' vows, the guards came searching for Nicolette, as her escape had been discovered. But a friendly sentinel warned Nicolette of their coming. She leaped into the moat and, bruised and bleeding, climbed the outer wall.

Nicolette fell asleep in a thicket near the castle. Next day she saw some shepherds eating their lunch at a fountain nearby. She asked them to take a message to Aucassin, saying there was a beast in the forest and that he should have this beast and not part with one of its limbs for any price. Nicolette built herself a lodge within the forest and waited to prove her lover's faith.

Aucassin was taken from his prison and allowed to attend a great feast, but he had no joy in it. A friendly knight offered his horse to Aucassin and suggested that he ride into the forest. Aucassin was only too happy for a chance to get away. He met the shepherds by the fountain and heard what Nicolette

221

had told them. Aucassin prayed God that he would find his quarry.

He rode in all haste through the thorny forest. Toward evening he began to weep because his search had been fruitless. He met a huge, ugly fellow, leaning on a terrible cudgel. Aucassin told him that he mourned for a white hound he had lost. The burly fellow scornfully replied that he had lost his best ox and had searched fruitlessly for three days without meat or drink. Aucassin gave the man twenty sols to pay for the beast. They parted and went their separate ways.

Aucassin found the lodge built by Nicolette and rested there that night. Nicolette heard Aucassin singing and came to him. The next day they mounted Aucassin's horse and journeyed until they came to the seas. Aucassin and Nicolette embarked upon a ship. A terrible storm carried them to Torelore. First Aucassin fought with the king of that strange land and then freed the king of his enemies. He and Nicolette lived happily in Torelore until Saracens besieged the castle and captured all within it. Aucassin was put in one ship and Nicolette in another. A storm scattered the ships, and that in which Aucassin was a prisoner drifted ashore at Beaucaire. He was now the Count of Beaucaire, his parents having died.

Nicolette was in the ship bearing the King of Carthage, who was her true father. They did not recognize each other because Nicolette had been but a child when she was stolen. But when she saw the walls of Carthage memory came back to her, and she revealed her identity in a song. The king gave her great honor and desired to marry her to a king of the Saracens, but Nicolette remained steadfast in her love for Aucassin. She disguised herself as a minstrel and took ship for Provence, where she traveled from castle to castle until she came to Beaucaire.

In the great hall Nicolette sang of her adventures. When Aucassin heard her song, he took her aside and inquired concerning Nicolette. He asked her to return to the land where Nicolette lived and bring her to him. Nicolette returned to the captain's house and there she clothed herself in rich robes and sent for Aucassin. And so at last they were wedded and lived long years with great joy.

THE AUTOBIOGRAPHY OF BENJAMIN FRANKLIN

Type of work: Autobiography
Author: Benjamin Franklin (1706-1790)
Time: 1706-1757
Locale: Boston, London, Philadelphia
First published: 1791; first printed in Paris, as *Mémoires*

> *Principal personages:*
> BENJAMIN FRANKLIN
> JOSIAH FRANKLIN, his father
> JAMES FRANKLIN, his brother and first employer
> SIR WILLIAM KEITH, Governor of Pennsylvania
> MR. DENHAM, a merchant
> MR. MEREDITH, Franklin's partner in the print shop
> ALEXANDER HAMILTON
> GOVERNOR MORRIS

Addressing himself to his "Dear Son," Benjamin Franklin first began in Twyford, England, at the age of sixty-five, to set down reminiscences of his early days. For years he had been collecting data about his ancestors, who had lived in Ecton, Northamptonshire, as far back as 1555, the oldest date of the town records; and he thought that his son William Franklin (1731-1813) would someday be interested in the "circumstances" of his father's life, just as Franklin had delighted in anecdotes relating to his family.

The work was composed in installments, the first section, dealing with Franklin's first twenty-four years, the product of a week of leisure in England in 1771. Then, because of his political activities abroad and at home, he had no further opportunity to continue his task until the urgings of friends persuaded him to resume his writing in 1783. The final section was probably written between November, 1789, and April, 1790. Titled *Mémoires,* it was first printed in France in 1791. No complete text appeared until 1868.

In spite of the lengthy period of composition, only Franklin's life before July, 1757, is covered, with a few comments on his activities in the following year. But the failure to complete the *Autobiography* beyond his fifty-first year does not mean that Franklin failed to write of his activities over the next thirty years. Some of his most important diplomatic missions are reported in individual compositions, such as the sample he showed to Jefferson of the "history of my life" that he said he was preparing. They cover "Negotiations in London for Effecting a Reconciliation between Great Britain and the American Colonies" and the "Journal of the Negotiations for Peace with Great Britain from March 21st to July 1st, 1782."

In addition, this indefatigable letter writer filled his correspondence (in many ways the most interesting part of his writing) with details and sketches. Some of the most complete are the letters to his wife, whom he addressed as "My dear Child." By combining the correspondence chronologically, a biographer can obtain Franklin's personal reactions to practically everything that happened to him. These letters show Franklin as the first real American who stood apart from European influences.

The Franklin family, whose ancestors had lived in the Northamptonshire village of Ecton from the time they assumed a surname originally signifying a middle-class landowner, was transplanted to Boston about 1682, when Benjamin's father Josiah brought his wife and several children to Massachusetts. After his wife's death, the older Franklin remarried. Benjamin, born of the second marriage, was the youngest son of seventeen children. Fond of study and quickly learning to read, Benjamin was destined for the ministry until his father, a tallow-candler and soap-boiler by trade, began calculating the cost of education and the pitiable salary received by most ministers. So the boy was taken out of school to learn a trade. After a brief period as his father's assistant he was, at the age of twelve, apprenticed to his half brother James, a printer. In his brother's shop he saw his first writing in print, topical ballads written to be sold in the streets.

He continued to read: *The Pilgrim's Progress*, Plutarch's *Parallel Lives*, essays by Defoe, Burton, and Mather. A volume of the *Spectator*, acquired by chance, revealed to him the importance of style and, like Robert Louis Stevenson at a later date, he taught himself by rewriting and comparing sentences. From this printshop came the fifth—Franklin mistakenly says the second—newspaper in America, the *New England Courant*, to which Franklin became an anonymous contributor.

Quarrels with his brother eventually sent the seventeen-year-old apprentice to Philadelphia looking for employment. His arrival early in the morning, with three-penny-worth of rolls in his mouth and under his arms as he walked up Market Street past the home of Miss Read, whom he was to marry later, was Philadelphia's first sight of one of its most distinguished citizens.

Neither Bradford nor Keimer, the only printers in Philadelphia, was very advanced. After the boy found a place in Keimer's shop, his wide reading and his ability to talk and to listen brought him many friends. Finally Governor Keith offered to send him to England to buy type and equipment for a shop of his own. Arriving in London, he learned that Keith, whose credit was not good, had provided nothing but promises. To support himself, Franklin found work in a printing house. After eighteen months he was happy to accept the offer of a merchant who wanted him to take back to America a consignment of merchandise. Back in Philadelphia, he worked for a time in Keimer's shop; then, finding a

partner in Hugh Meredith, he and the Welsh Pennsylvanian set up their own establishment. They prospered and in 1729 Franklin became the sole proprietor, having bought out Meredith, whose drinking habits were distasteful to the temperate, frugal Franklin. He branched out as a stationer. In 1730 he founded the *Pennsylvania Gazette* and also married Miss Read. At this point the first section of the *Autobiography* ends.

In 1784, in Passy, France, Franklin again began to write his story, this time addressed more generally to the reading public than to his son. With friends interested in scientific and intellectual matters he had in 1743 founded a Junto for their mutual exchange of ideas and intellectual improvement; this was later to become the American Philosophical Society. The members sponsored a library for the use of the public.

Now that he had educated himself, Franklin sought moral perfection. He set down twelve virtues, then added a thirteenth, Pride, at the suggestion of critical friends. But he had reason to be proud. He had learned to speak fluent French, Spanish, and Italian. His civic spirit, born when he was appointed postmaster of Philadelphia, induced him to reorganize the fire department, start a movement to pave and light the streets, and to establish an academy which later became the University of Pennsylvania. The death of a son from smallpox caused him to argue for inoculation against the disease. He invented an improved form of heating stove and offered it free for general use, only to learn that he had brought wealth to one stove manufacturer. Meanwhile, beginning in 1732, he published *Poor Richard's Almanack*, the usual collection of agricultural and astronomical data to which he added a compendium of practical wisdom and moral maxims. This venture also brought him wealth and enabled him to retire from active business in 1748.

His thoughts about defense caused him to campaign for the establishment of a militia, but this man who so candidly confessed his "errata," his mistakes, was too well acquainted with himself to accept the appointment as their colonel. Other civic improvements, when initiated by others, needed his approval before his fellow citizens would adopt them. He extended his influence beyond his own city to the whole colony, and to other colonies. Yale and Harvard awarded honorary degrees to this self-taught scholar, and he was elected to membership in cultural and scientific societies at home and abroad.

Braddock sought Franklin's advice in campaigning against the Indians, only to disregard it with disastrous results. After selling out his shop to his foreman, he occupied his time with philosophical concerns and scientific experiments, particularly those relating to electricity. His theories, when ignored or contradicted abroad, led to his experiments with lightning in 1752.

Having represented Pennsylvania at the Albany Congress of 1754, he was chosen to represent it in protests to the English crown. His arrival in England, July 27, 1757, is the last date in his story of himself.

THE AUTOBIOGRAPHY OF BENVENUTO CELLINI

Type of work: Autobiography
Author: Benvenuto Cellini (1500-1571)
Type of plot: Chronicle of adventure and art
Time of plot: 1500-1562
Locale: Italy and France
First published: Sixteenth-century manuscript

Principal characters:
BENVENUTO CELLINI, goldsmith, artist, sculptor
POPE CLEMENT VII
POPE PAUL III
FRANCIS I, King of France
COSIMO DE' MEDICI, Duke of Florence
BANDINELLO, a rival sculptor

Critique:

The *Autobiography of Benvenuto Cellini*, written 1558-1562 and circulated in manuscript form until printed in 1730, is perhaps the finest document left to moderns from the period of the Italian Renaissance. In its pages we view intimately, through the eyes of an artistic and adventurous contemporary, the men, women, princes, dukes, and popes of the sixteenth century. In addition, we see the artists who produced some of the great pictures and sculpture which we take more or less for granted. In Cellini's backward glances we can feel some measure of the pangs and troubles and joys that went into those art works and the climate of culture which produced them. To judge Cellini and his contemporaries by twentieth-century standards is common enough to bear comment. It suffices to say that no one can appreciate Cellini as a man and as an artist who does judge by current standards. He was a product of his time, and on that basis he must be judged as an author, a man, and an artist.

The Story:

At the age of fifty-eight Benvenuto Cellini began to set down his memoirs. He related first a fictional version of the founding of Florence by his ancestors and then began the story of his life.

Benvenuto, destined by his father to be a musician, was as a lad taught to play the flute and sing by note. But lessons in music from his father failed to interest him, and at the age of fifteen Cellini apprenticed himself to a goldsmith. Cellini said of himself that he had a natural bent for the work and in a few months he had surpassed men long in the trade.

As an apprentice and, later, as a journeyman goldsmith, Cellini on his travels through Italy did fine work and acted the part of a bravo. He became an excellent swordsman and handler of the poniard, as he proved when he killed an enemy in a street brawl.

In 1527 the Constable of Bourbon marched on Rome and besieged Pope Clement VII in his fortress. Cellini, then in Rome and in sympathy with the pope, served the pontiff valiantly as an artillerist and as a goldsmith, having been commissioned by the besieged prelate to melt down much jewelry and turn it into a more transportable form. Later he boasted that during the siege he had killed the Constable of Bourbon and wounded the Prince of Orange.

After the siege was lifted and a truce declared, Cellini returned to Florence and killed his brother's murderer. He later went to Mantua. Ill with fever in that city, he returned to Florence. When Pope Clement declared war on that city, however, Cellini left his shop and trade to enter the papal service. While in Rome he made a medallion of tremendous size for the papal cope, a work which was the beginning of his fortunes. It was a splendid button, pleasing greatly the pontiff for whom it was made. From then on, during Clement's life, Cellini did much work for the papacy.

Cellini's career under Pope Clement was a stormy one. His fiery temper often caused him no end of trouble; for example, he received the commission of the papal mint and then lost it because of his foolhardy and unmannerly actions.. He killed another enemy in a quarrel but was lucky enough to be pardoned by his patron.

Cellini's great commission from Pope Clement was for a gold chalice. The chalice was never finished, for Clement died too soon. During the last years of his life, however, the chalice was a matter of contention between the pope and his goldsmith. Cellini, an independent and temperamental workman, often got into trouble because of the slowness with which he worked. And the pope, according to Cellini's account, often forgot that gold was needed to make the vessel.

Upon the accession of Cardinal Farnese as Pope Paul III, Cellini went into his service for a time. But Cellini was away from Rome a great deal, at one time taking service with Cosimo de' Medici, Duke of Florence. Upon his return Cellini was imprisoned on a charge of homicide. The pope granted him a safe-conduct for a time, but eventually he was imprisoned. Only after many difficulties did he receive a pardon for the slaying.

Cellini came to the notice of Emperor Charles V when that monarch visited Rome and was presented by the pope with a Book of Hours bound into a gold cover encrusted with jewels, the work of Cellini. A short time later Cellini was sent for by Francis I, King of France, but before he could leave Rome he was accused of theft and thrown into prison by the pope's *bargello*, or police force. Cellini cleared himself of the charge, but he had made so many enemies that he was kept in prison for many months and suffered, at times, cruel punishment.

Action on Cellini's behalf by King Francis only served to make his lot harder. At last Cellini managed to escape by using bed sheets to lower himself from the prison tower and to get himself over the prison walls. Having broken his leg in his flight, he was recaptured. Released after a long period of confinement, he found asylum with a French cardinal and finally with the aid of Cardinal d'Este of Ferrara made his way to France.

In France, with King Francis as his patron, the goldsmith and artist turned to sculpture. He executed an amazing statue of Jupiter for the king and also constructed the large statue of the nymph of Fontainebleau. But Cellini made an enemy of Madame d'Etampes, the king's mistress, who made his career difficult and his life dangerous, and the Cardinal of Ferrara did not fulfill the promises he had made. Cellini's amorous adventures also got him into many difficulties.

In desperation, and with some hopes of a better future, Cellini left France and returned to his native Florence in 1545, there to find protection under the patronage of Cosimo de' Medici.

In Florence he made an enemy of the Duchess of Florence and a famous sculptor, Bandinello, whose work Cellini reviled in public and to the sculptor's face. As in France, a woman's enmity, the dislike of fellow artists, the pettifogging of minor officials, and small commissions used up Cellini's valuable time in Florence. Nevertheless, while there, in the years after 1545, Cellini did his greatest work, a bronze Perseus of which he was extremely proud.

Following the completion of that statue, Cellini went to work on other pieces, including a tremendous crucifix with a mausoleum at its base, to hold his body when he had died.

While working in Florence for the duke, Cellini bought some farm land which, failing to bring him the revenues he had been promised, embroiled him in a long and upsetting litigation. That trouble, plus the enmity of the duchess, finally drove him from Florence. In 1562, while the duke and his family were away on a journey, Cellini left Florence and headed for Pisa. With that final entry, the departure for Pisa, Cellini ended his memoirs, though he lived for eight more years.

THE AUTOCRAT OF THE BREAKFAST-TABLE

Type of work: Informal essays
Author: Oliver Wendell Holmes (1809-1894)
Time: 1857-1858
Locale: Boston
First published: 1858

Principal characters:
THE AUTOCRAT
THE SCHOOLMISTRESS,
THE DIVINITY-STUDENT,
THE OLD GENTLEMAN, and
THE YOUNG FELLOW CALLED JOHN, the Autocrat's fellow boarders
THE LANDLADY
THE LANDLADY'S DAUGHTER
BENJAMIN FRANKLIN, the Landlady's son
THE PROFESSOR, and
THE POET, friends of the Autocrat who, though never present, contribute to the discussion

At one point in the recounting of his breakfast-table experiences, the Autocrat observed that, since medieval times, the reputation of Aristotle had passed through two stages and was then (one hundred years ago) entering its third. First came the period of idolization when everything attributed to the Greek sage was accepted not only as scientifically sound but as absolute and ultimate truth. Then came the period of critical examination, the stage at which his scientific inaccuracies were discovered and, as a result, all of his ideas belittled and discredited. Finally, in Dr. Holmes' time, there was the third stage, the enlightened period when the scientific inaccuracies were excused, being viewed in historical perspective as unavoidable, and the value of his philosophical insights reasserted.

On a smaller time scale, the reputation of Oliver Wendell Holmes, along with that of the Cambridge-Boston group as a whole (as opposed to that of the Concord group), has gone through the first two of these stages but shows no signs, as yet, of entering the third. Although few, and certainly never Dr. Holmes himself, actually believed that Boston was "The Hub of the Universe," Harvard Yard and the eastern end of Beacon Street (including the first eight doors on Arlington Street

so as to take in the offices of the *Atlantic Monthly*) were for better than half a century regarded as the dual nerve center, as it were, the cerebrum and cerebellum, of American culture. A Cambridge-born Harvard Professor of Anatomy, a member of the Saturday Club, a resident of Beacon Street, Dr. Holmes did not merely share in such regard; he helped to create it. It was he, in fact, who coined the term, "The Hub." (But the original statement, as it appeared in Chapter VI of *The Autocrat of the Breakfast-Table*, was made, not by a Bostonian, but an outlander whose remark was, "Boston State-House is the hub of the solar system.") As lecturer, poet, novelist, biographer, and, most of all, perhaps, as the author of *The Autocrat of the Breakfast-Table* and later *The Professor at the Breakfast-Table* (1860) and *The Poet at the Breakfast-Table* (1872), Dr. Holmes helped to establish in the public mind a concept of Bostonian wit, sensibility, and culture.

Gradually—not suddenly as did the Wonderful One-Hoss Shay (Chapter XI of *The Autocrat*)—the reputations of many of the New England writers seemed autumnal and dry, and a season of critical neglect set in. Today, however, the situation has somewhat changed. Hawthorne has been resurrected by the

New Critics; the cautiously radical Emerson has been turned into a spokesman for the Neo-conservatives; and Thoreau is a pet nonconformist in these conformist times. The Concordians have entered their third stage, but not the Cambridge-Bostonians. Yet, while it is no doubt true that the poetry of the Cambridge-Boston group is a mixture of neoclassic moralizing combined with a nostalgic and academic romanticism, it should be remembered that Longfellow had a gift for storytelling, that Lowell was a sprightly satirist, and that Holmes possessed wit, urbanity, a background of knowledge, and a tolerant, all-encompassing view of life, the like of which has not appeared in English letters on either side of the Atlantic since his death.

It can be argued that in regard to Holmes such qualities did not produce the reputation, but are deduced from it, that the alleged wit and urbanity are really provincial smugness, and that what passes for a tolerant and total life-view is in reality a carefully cultivated dilettantism. Such arguments have been made, but they neglect both the facts provided by history and the literary evidence provided by *The Autocrat of the Breakfast-Table*. The facts show that Holmes was learned in both science and humane letters and that he was one of the foremost advocates of technological progress in the nineteenth-century United States. One English critic has said that he, rather than Emerson, deserves the title, the "American Montaigne."

It is on an objective reading of *The Autocrat of the Breakfast-Table* that the case for Holmes must finally rest. *The Autocrat* appeared originally in the first twelve issues of the *Atlantic Monthly* (1857-1858) and was published in book form directly after this appearance. Its plan is simple enough: the Autocrat lives in a Beacon Hill boarding house; the essays are, we are told, reports, somewhat condensed, and interlarded with the Autocrat's comments, of the conversations that take place each morning at the breakfast table of this remarkable establishment, a table at which is found a most heterogeneous collection of boarders. Each has his say occasionally, but his main purpose is to provide a sounding board for the wit and philosophizing of the Autocrat. There is conversation, but mostly (as it is finally reported, in any case) there is monologue. The varied responses of the boarders allow Holmes' wit to play over a wide range of subjects, to jump easily from point to point, and to juxtapose ideas that have no apparent relevance.

The result may seem chaotic at first. One is carried along by the bubbling cleverness easily enough, but apparently to no particular place. For example, the topics of the first chapter are, in order of appearance: (1) the algebraic classification of minds; (2) the value of mutual admiration societies; (3) the meaninglessness of brute fact; (4) the typing of various kinds of speakers; (5) the dangers of specialized learning; (6) an attack on the use of puns (Holmes deplores the use of them here but cannot always resist them; later, for example, he speaks of the landlady's economically-minded poor relation as standing by her guns, "ready to repel boarders"); (7) the poverty of pure logic as opposed to common sense; (8) the foibles of young poets; (9) the superiority of men of family over self-made men, *"other things being equal"* (Holmes' italics); (10) the rendering of a pair of poems. Holmes makes these points interesting in themselves, but there seems to be little connection between one and another. As the reader continues, however, he becomes aware that certain ideas are recurrent; that certain themes are announced, dropped, but repeated later with variations; that there are psychological connections in the apparently chance juxtapositions of ideas—that the whole thing develops in a geometric, not in an arithmetic, progression.

The effect is produced by a means that

is at the same time modern and meta-physical. Holmes was a Proper Bostonian, a Victorian American, and it has been said that his sympathies lay with the eighteenth century, that he was at heart a Neo-Johnsonian. This assertion is in some respects valid. But if his conscious affinities turned back one hundred years, his unconscious ones turned back two. Andrew Lang notes "a fleeting resemblance to Sir Thomas Browne," a resemblance based on "a community of professional studies," but this similarity between Holmes and the author of *Religio Medici* and *Urn Burial* is not explained simply by the fact that both were medical men. Holmes possessed the "divided sensibility" found also in the metaphysical school; and Browne, it is now acknowledged, was a metaphysical poet writing in prose. This division in Holmes, obscured as it is by his neoclassical pose, has been too often neglected.

He was divided along a different axis from Browne's, for he lived under different conditions; but the division is still there. First was the religious division: Holmes had disavowed the Puritanism of his fathers, but the scars of his youthful indoctrination were never completely gone. More important, perhaps, at least as far as its reflection in *The Autocrat of the Breakfast-Table* is concerned, is his divided allegiance between Brahminism, which stood for all the deeply rooted things that meant the good life to him, on the one hand, and science, which meant technology and, with it, the unleashing of those forces, human and mechanical, that would destroy Brahminism, on the other. The division could not exercise itself in Holmes' poetry because the moralizing-romantic tradition was too binding. But when Holmes found in his hands a form free from restrictions and with which he could experiment as he wished, his divided sensibility found expression in the essay through the use of what are very close to metaphysical techniques.

First, there is the juxtaposition of topics. The most extreme, and the one that most strongly anticipates the modern reflection of the metaphysical, is Chapter IX, in which Holmes presents a series of childhood reminiscences—the stuff of poems:

Many times I have come bearing flowers such as my garden grew; but now I offer you this poor, brown, homely growth, you may cast it away as worthless. And yet—and yet—it is something better than flowers; it is a *seed-capsule*.

There is also the shift in prose styles—from the colloquial or the scientific to the lofty and poetic—a device that harks back to the style of Browne. But most important are the similitudes—the similes, the metaphors, the extended analogies. *The Autocrat of the Breakfast-Table* is full of them. But the important thing is that they are functional, not decorative; they are the very fabric of the work. Holmes uses them to bring into focus the two parts of his divided world. Science and beauty stand for the two parts of the key dichotomy, represented in character by Holmes' own two alter egos, the Professor and the Poet, and playing their dual parts in all of the analogies:

We get beautiful effects from wit—all the prismatic colors—but never the object as it is in fair daylight. A pun, which is a kind of wit, is a different and much shallower trick in mental optics; throwing the *shadows* of two objects so that one overlies the other. Poetry uses the rainbow tints for special effects, but always keeps its essential object in the purest white light of truth.

Through the interplay of these two conflicting worlds, by means of analogy and opposition of character, the themes of the work are brought out. They appear as questions, not as answers, for awareness of the divided world permits no dogmatic assertions. What is love and what is beauty? How are human communication and expression achieved? What, after all, is really important? And how can it be found—by sculling beneath the bridges of the Charles, by searching for seed capsules of poetry in one's memory, or by counting the rings of an elm that stood when Shakespeare was a boy?

To bring out these questions in a meaningful way is a decided literary achievement. Not that *The Autocrat of the Breakfast-Table* is entirely a great literary work. Holmes cannot maintain his metaphysical detachment. He becomes too concerned with his characters and they begin to lose their reflecting qualities. He becomes too concerned with love: in the end the Autocrat and the Schoolmistress degenerate into the principal figures of a rather sentimental romance. So there are weaknesses, true; but they are not the weaknesses for which the "Genteel Tradition" is usually condemned. Only half of Holmes was in that tradition anyway. In respect to that other half, he deserves to have his reputation advanced to its third stage.

THE AWAKENING OF SPRING

Type of work: Drama
Author: Frank Wedekind (1864-1918)
Type of plot: Psychological realism
Time of plot: Nineteenth century
Locale: Germany
First presented: 1891

Principal characters:

MELCHIOR GABOR, an intelligent high school boy
MORITZ STIEFEL, his friend
WENDLA BERGMANN, a schoolgirl, aged fourteen
MRS. BERGMANN, her mother
MRS. GABOR, and
MR. GABOR, Melchior's parents
MARTHA, and
THEA, schoolgirls
ILSE, a young prostitute and model
RENTIER STIEFEL, Moritz' father
A MUFFLED GENTLEMAN

Critique:

In *The Awakening of Spring,* Wedekind presents a plot stripped to its naturalistic essentials: the suffering inflicted on the very young when their burgeoning native, erotic consciousness confronts the deadly, adult, hypocritical unconsciousness of the society to which they are answerable. The plot is, however, only the crude skeleton for a powerful anti-naturalistic dramaturgy which relies on its own intractable poetic logic. Within a loose episodic structure, scenes are articulated by means of ironic parallel actions, and an unsubtle but dramatically effective use of symbolic references. Dramatic tension depends not upon the formal plot revelations, but on swift modulations of response elicited in the spectator by the mixture of satire and tragedy; caricature yields to lyrical statement, the horrific yields to the commonplace, the commonplace to that realm of parable inhabited by the existential absurd—or rather haunted, in this case, by the figure of the muffled gentleman, to whom the play is dedicated.

The Story:

Wendla hung up again in the closet the long, grown-up dress which her mother had just completed, protesting that she did not see why next year would not be soon enough to put on such a penitential garment. Mrs. Bergmann acquiesced with motherly affection to her daughter's wish to continue wearing, for the present, the freer, familiar clothes of childhood, remarking at the same time on the fact that Wendla had retained her childhood grace without a trace of the gawkiness usual to her age. Mrs. Bergmann was not without misgivings, even while she cherished that appearance of innocence and grace, and she expressed her uneasiness in various equivocating substitutes for her real fears, all of which Wendla gaily laughed away.

Melchior Gabor, Moritz Stiefel, and their classmates broke up their games to go prepare their homework. Moritz and Melchior, walking home in the spring night, became involved in a discussion of the meaninglessness of the exam system and the sexual phenomena of adolescence which they were beginning to experience. For Moritz, the mysterious sexual pressures were a great burden, partly because they hindered his already desperate attempts to meet the rigid demands made upon him by school and parents. Though a poor student, and excessively timid, he possessed an acute sensitivity in certain areas which went unrecognized by all but Melchior, who was his closest friend and,

233

unlike Moritz, an extremely promising student. The ease with which Melchior dealt with his schoolwork left him time not only for metaphysical speculation, but for a scholarly acquisition of the facts of reproduction, which he now offered to impart. Moritz accepted Melchior's offer on the condition that the facts be in written form and slipped into his books where he could come upon them as if by chance.

On a blustery spring day not long afterward, Wendla, Thea, and Martha also exchanged confidences on the subjects of parental tyranny, love, marriage, and children, embellishing their remarks with the gaudy and arbitrary imagination of childish ignorance. The talk turned to boys of their own age, and to the peculiar behavior which they sometimes exhibited. Wendla disclosed that Melchior had once told her he believed in nothing. Mention of the spring floods revealed the fact that Melchior had come near drowning in one of the swollen streams, but was saved by his ability as a swimmer.

In another gathering of the schoolboys, it was revealed that Moritz had illicitly entered the staff common room (repository of all records), driven by the desire to learn whether he was to be promoted. When Moritz appeared, dazed by his own boldness but relieved by the knowledge of a provisional remove, he was taunted by the boys for his statement that he would have shot himself had he not received it.

Melchior and Wendla met by chance in the woods, where Wendla had gone to gather woodruff for her mother and had stopped to daydream by a brook. Melchior persuaded her to sit down and asked if she enjoyed going among the poor to take them food and money, errands on which she was often sent by her mother. Wendla's answer, that it gave her pleasure, began an argument on the reality of virtue and selflessness.

Wendla also confessed that she daydreamed of being a poor beggar child, beaten by a cruel father, although she herself had never been beaten. She picked a switch and begged Melchior to strike her, to show her how such punishment felt. The boy at first refused; then, as she persisted in her request, he threw the stick aside and pummeled her with his fists before he ran away into the wood, crying out in anguish.

Moritz found himself again on the verge of school failure. While reading *Faust* with Melchior, he related his grandmother's story of the headless queen, a tale which had been haunting him during his studying. It told of a fabulously beautiful queen unfortunately born without a head who was one day conquered by a king who happened to be provided with two heads that argued constantly. The court wizard gave one to the queen, on whom it proved surpassingly becoming, and the two were married with great joy, the heads now being on the best of terms. Melchior's mother entered with tea and words of encouragement for Moritz. Noticing the *Faust,* she wondered if they ought to be reading it, saying elliptically, however, that she preferred to place her trust in Melchior rather than in pedagogical principles. Realizing that she was thinking of the Gretchen episode, they became annoyed, Melchior because everyone insisted on acting as if the world turned on nothing but obscenities, Moritz because he had begun to fear that it actually did. He had received Melchior's sex essay which affected him like a series of dim recollections. He was disposed to exalt the satisfaction experienced by the woman, and regarded that of the man as insipid.

Meanwhile, Wendla persistently interrogated her mother on the subject of her sister's latest baby. She mocked her mother's giggling fairy tales by pretending to see a ridiculous vision outside the window. At Wendla's insistence, Mrs. Bergmann was forced to begin telling her daughter how babies come about, but finally she managed to evade the issue by saying that the things required were marriage and an enormity of love which Wendla was too young to comprehend.

A short time later Wendla went looking for Melchior and, disarmed by his intensity and his tortured insistence that there is no such thing as love, she remained with him in the hayloft, where she conceived a child.

Moritz finally reached the end of his resources and, at the brink of suicide over the realization that he was about to fail, wrote to Mrs. Gabor for a loan which would enable him to leave home. She, considering it her duty to refuse, appealed to his common sense and better nature. At dusk, in a parting soliloquy pervaded by his unfailing wry humor but mixed with self-pity, he concluded that life was not his responsibility. The Headless Queen beckoned. Life was a matter of taste. His only regret was in not having known sexual fulfillment, the most human experience of all. When Ilse, a young model with an insatiable appetite for life, appeared to tempt him with tales of her warm, carefree, animal existence, he wavered but then rejected the opportunity she offered.

Moritz' suicide precipitated an investigation on the part of the school officials. Melchior, charged with indecency on the basis of the notes on sex discovered among Moritz' books, became the scapegoat.

At the funeral service Moritz was condemned for his crime against man and God by the adults in attendance. Rentier Stiefel comforted himself by repeating he had never cared for the boy from a child; he was no son of his. The pastor urged with consummate coarseness that he seek comfort in the arms of his wife. While the reaction of the schoolboys at the funeral was largely one of curiosity as to the exact manner of the suicide, Martha and Ilse brought to the grave a profusion of flowers. Ilse had discovered the suicide pistol and concealed it.

Mrs. Gabor, meeting with indignation her husband's determination to send Melchior to the reformatory, defied anyone to perceive moral corruption in what the boy had written; but she was unable to stand up to the discovery that Wendla was pregnant, and Melchior responsible.

Shortly after her discovery of the cause of her illness, Wendla succumbed to the combined concoctions of Dr. Von Brausepulver and Mother Schmidt for inducing abortion. After her death, Melchior, hounded by society and by his own self-contempt, managed to return to look at her grave. As he wandered enviously among the graves, he encountered Moritz Stiefel, with his head under his arm, who attempted to persuade Melchior to join him in his life among the dead, which he pictured as a fabulous if grotesque freedom. While Melchior hesitated, a muffled gentleman appeared to take Moritz to task for his attempt, his lack of a head, and his general crumbling condition. He accused Moritz of charlatanism and asked Melchior to submit himself to his care. Melchior, contending that he could not entrust himself to a masked unknown, subjected the muffled gentleman to questions regarding his moral position. Moritz admitted that he had been boasting and urged Melchior to accompany the muffled gentleman, who was, in any event, alive. The two alive withdrew together while Moritz returned to warm himself with putrefaction.

235

THE AXE

Type of work: Novel
Author: Sigrid Undset (1882-1949)
Type of plot: Historical chronicle
Time of plot: Late thirteenth century
Locale: Norway
First published: 1925

Principal characters:
OLAV AUDUNSSON, master of Hestviken
STEINFINN TORESSON, his foster father
INGEBJÖRG JONSDATTER, Steinfinn's wife
INGUNN, Steinfinn's daughter, betrothed to Olav
TORA, another daughter
ARNVID FINNSSON, Steinfinn's kinsman
KOLBEIN TORESSON, Steinfinn's half-brother
TEIT, an Icelander, a clerk

Critique:

The Axe is the first volume of a tetralogy—the others are *The Snake Pit, In the Wilderness,* and *The Son Avenger* —published under one title, *The Master of Hestviken.* These four books together make up a great historical chronicle, a great religious novel, and a novel of character. In this story of thirteenth-century Norway, Sigrid Undset presents a massive picture of human conflicts which are universal and timeless. As a study of man's faith, the novel shows a world poised between the old pagan spirit and Christian belief and practice. Olav Audunsson, her chief character, is the medieval man, virile yet innocent and meek in his simple goodness. *The Axe* tells the story of a murder which he never dared confess without the certainty of harming others, a crime which was to burden his conscience and influence his actions for the rest of his days.

The Story:

The troubles of the Steinfinnssons began when Tore Toresson sent his youngest son to the royal bodyguard at Bergen. There Steinfinn Toresson saw Ingebjörg Jonsdatter, who had come from Denmark with young Queen Ingebjörg, and he fell in love with her. But King Magnus had already promised the girl to his friend, Mattias Haraldsson. Steinfinn was in the Orkneys that winter. The next summer he went to Bergen and stole Ingebjörg out of the king's court.

Although Tore was displeased with his son, he gave the couple the manor at Frettastein, where they lived as if in lawful wedlock. After a time the queen reconciled all concerned, and Steinfinn and Ingebjörg held their wedding at the royal court in Oslo. Ingunn, their first child, was three when her parents were wed.

Meanwhile Mattias Haraldsson had gone into foreign lands, so that Steinfinn had little thought of his ill will. When Steinfinn and Ingebjörg had been married about seven years, however, Mattias came one night with his men, bound Steinfinn, and shamed him before his household. After Mattias rode home to his own manor, young Olav Audunsson cut his foster father's bonds. Steinfinn swore that he would not sleep with his wife until he could show the world that she was his without Mattias' leave.

But Steinfinn had no revenge at that time, for Mattias sailed again to foreign lands. Meanwhile life grew slack and somber at Frettastein. Steinfinn was much in the company of Kolbein, his grim half-brother, and Ingebjörg lived in a house apart with her women and her two small sons, Hallvard and Jon. Ingunn and Tora, the older daughters, would have been left to themselves if it had not been for Olav Audunsson, Steinfinn's foster son.

Olav's father had been Audun Ingolfsson of Hestviken; his mother had died at his birth. One summer, when Steinfinn met Auden at the Thing, the man from Vik said that he was soon to die. There was much drinking that night, and it seemed good sport to betroth little Ingunn to Olav. Next morning Steinfinn would have cried quits on the agreement, but Audun held him to his word. So Olav grew up at Frettastein. An aged kinsman managed his estate at Hestviken.

All his life Olav remembered a day just past his sixteenth year. The edge of his ancient Viking ax, Kin-fetch, being blunted, he took it to an armorer in Hamar. Ingunn stole away from the house to go with him, and the two rowed up the fjord under sunny skies. Later he never knew whether his deep feeling of pleasure came from a sudden, disturbing sense of Ingunn's loveliness, the summer light over the town, or the vesper service he and Ingunn went to before they started home through the dark; but he always thought that day the happiest of his life.

Arnvid Finnsson, Ingunn's cousin, brought word that Mattias was at Birid, and two days later Steinfinn and his kinsmen, Olav among them, rode away. There was great merriment at Frettastein when they returned. Mattias and his housecarls had been taken by surprise, and Steinfinn had killed his enemy in fair fight. Steinfinn, badly wounded, laughed at his own hurts. After he and Ingebjörg went to their loft-room, the dancing and drinking continued, and some became wanton. Half-tipsy, Olav went with Ingunn to her loft.

That night Ingebjörg died suddenly in her sleep and Steinfinn's wounds reopened. From that time on he grew steadily weaker. While he lay dying, Arnvid asked him to declare the marriage of Ingunn and Olav but he refused, saying the settlement had never been clearly drawn. After Steinfinn's death Olav found

among his own gear the betrothal ring he had given Ingunn many years before. He suspected Kolbein of that sly attempt to repudiate the betrothal.

Arnvid stayed on at Frettastein for a time. That fall Olav spent many nights with Ingunn in her loft. When Arnvid finally learned how matters stood, he advised Olav to lay the case before Bishop Thorfinn in Hamar and to claim that he had only fulfilled a marriage contract which Ingunn's kinsmen had broken. Bishop Thorfinn was a stern man but just, and he saw that Olav had some right in the wrong he had done. All might have gone well for the lovers if the Kolbeinssons had not quarreled with Arnvid and Olav in the convent guest house at Hamar. At last, unable to endure their taunts, Olav raised Kin-fetch and struck down Einar Kolbeinsson.

Proclaimed an outlaw, Olav fled to Sweden, and Ingunn went to stay with Arnvid at Mickleböard. There she was taken with an illness so strange that Arnvid's mother accused the Kolbeinssons of witchcraft. After her recovery the girl went to live with her aunt, the Lady Magnhild of Berg. Olav, meanwhile, had gone to his mother's kinsmen in Denmark. Tora married Haakon Gautsson and came to visit at Berg, where her first child was born. Ingunn wished for a husband and child of her own, but she grew stubborn when her relatives talked of marrying her to any of the young men who came wooing.

Four years later Olav returned in the train of Earl Alf Erlingsson, Queen Ingebjörg's liegeman. On promise of penance and payment of blood-atonement to Kolbein for Einar's slaying, the Steinfinnssons acknowledged him as Ingunn's betrothed. Then the queen died and her son proclaimed Alf and all his men outlaws. Word came that Olav had followed Alf to Sweden. Once more Ingunn was left to wait at Berg.

One summer Teit, an Icelander, came on business to the manor. Mistaking Ingunn for a servant, he was not abashed when he learned that she was a daughter of the house. Ingunn liked the clerk's pert speech and merry ways. At last, out of weakness and pity, she let him stay with her in the house she shared with her aged grandmother. When Olav, no longer an outlaw, came home in the spring, she was carrying Teit's child.

Olav was dismayed when he learned how things were with Ingunn, but he felt bound to her by every tie between them in the past. Bitter because he could not part from her, he offered to claim that he had gone secretly to Berg during his outlawry and that the child was his. Shamed, Ingunn refused so unseemly an offer.

Olav was staying with the Preaching Friars in Hamar. Teit, believing that Olav no longer wanted Ingunn, proposed to Olav that he accompany the Icelander when he went to Arnvid to plead for Ingunn's hand. As Olav prepared for the journey, Kin-fetch, hanging on the wall, rang—old superstition said that when the ax sang, death would follow. That night, at the *sæter* where they stopped to rest, Olav killed Teit and burned the hut. Although he knew he could never confess his deed without shaming Ingunn, he felt that her secret was safe.

When Ingunn's child, a boy, was born, Lady Magnhild gave it to a foster mother, a forester's wife. A short time later Olav went to claim his bride. After years of waiting it was a sorry bridal ale they drank at their wedding feast.

BABBITT

Type of work: Novel
Author: Sinclair Lewis (1885-1951)
Type of plot: Social satire
Time of plot: The 1920's
Locale: Zenith, fictional Midwestern town
First published: 1922

Principal characters:
GEORGE F. BABBITT, a middle-aged real estate broker
MYRA, his wife
TED, their son
VERONA, their daughter
PAUL RIESLING, Babbitt's friend
ZILLA, Paul's shrewish wife

Critique:

Babbitt is a pungent satire about a man who typifies complacent mediocrity. George F. Babbitt, as standardized as his electric cigar lighter, revels in his own popularity, his ability to make money, his fine automobile, and his penny-pinching generosity. Babbitt worships gadgets. He praises prohibition and drinks bootleg whiskey, bullies his wife, ogles his manicurist. Though he is constantly discontented with the life he leads, he is thoroughly satisfied with George F. Babbitt. Because his character is grounded in realism, Babbitt is one of the most convincing characters in American literature.

The Story:

George F. Babbitt was proud of his house in Floral Heights, one of the most respectable residential districts in Zenith. Its architecture was standardized; its interior decorations were standardized; its atmosphere was standardized. Therein lay its appeal for Babbitt.

He bustled about in a tile and chromium bathroom in his morning ritual of getting ready for another day. When he went down to breakfast, he was as grumpy as usual. It was expected of him. He read the dull real estate page of the newspaper to his patient wife, Myra. Then he commented on the weather, grumbled at his son and daughter, gulped his breakfast and started for his office.

Babbitt was a real estate broker who knew how to handle business with zip and zowie. Having closed a deal whereby he forced a poor businessman to buy a piece of property at twice its value, he pocketed part of the money and paid the rest to the man who had suggested the enterprise. Proud of his acumen, he picked up the telephone and called his best friend, Paul Riesling, to ask him to lunch.

Paul Riesling should have been a violinist, but he had gone into the tar-roofing business in order to support his shrewish wife, Zilla. Lately she had made it her practice to infuriate doormen, theater ushers, or taxicab drivers, and then ask Paul to come to her rescue and fight them like a man. Cringing with embarrassment, Paul would pretend he had not noticed the incident. Later, at home, Zilla would accuse him of being a coward and a weakling.

So sad did Paul's affairs seem to Babbitt that he suggested a vacation to Maine together—away from their wives. Paul was skeptical, but with magnificent assurance Babbitt promised to arrange the trip. Paul was humbly grateful.

Back in his office Babbitt fired a salesman who was too honest. When he got home, he and his wife decided to give a dinner party, with the arrangements taken bodily from the contents of a woman's magazine, and everything edible disguised to look like something else.

The party was a great success. Babbitt's friends were exactly like Babbitt. They all became drunk on prohibition-period gin, were disappointed when the cocktails ran out, stuffed themselves with food, and went home to nurse headaches.

The next day Babbitt and Myra paid a call on the Reislings. Zilla, trying to enlist their sympathy, berated her husband until he was goaded to fury. Babbitt finally told Zilla that she was a nagging, jealous, sour, and unwholesome wife, and he demanded that she allow Paul to go with him to Maine. Weeping in self-pity, Zilla consented. Myra sat calmly during the scene, but later she criticized Babbitt for bullying Paul's wife. Babbitt told her sharply to mind her own business.

On the train, Babbitt and Paul met numerous businessmen who loudly agreed with each other that what this country needed was a sound business administration. They deplored the price of motor cars, textiles, wheat, and oil; they swore that they had not an ounce of race-prejudice; they blamed Communism and socialism for labor unions which got out of hand. Paul soon tired of the discussion and went to bed. Babbitt stayed up late, smoking countless cigars, and telling countless stories.

Maine had a soothing effect upon Babbitt. He and Paul fished and hiked in the quiet of the north woods, and Babbitt began to realize that his life in Zenith was not all it should be. He promised himself a new outlook on life, a more simple, less hurried way of living.

Back in Zenith, Babbitt was asked to make a speech at a convention of real estate men which was to be held in Monarch, a nearby city. For days he tried to write a speech about the good life, as he now thought of it. But at the convention he scrapped his speech, declaimed loudly that real estate was a great profession, that Zenith was God's own country—the best little spot on earth

—and to prove his statements quoted countless statistics on waterways, textile production, and lumber manufacture. The speech was such a success that Babbitt instantly won recognition as an orator.

Babbitt was made a precinct leader in the coming election. His duty was to speak to small labor groups about the inadvisability of voting for Seneca Doane, a liberal, in favor of a man named Prout, a solid businessman who represented the conservative element. Babbitt's speeches helped to defeat Doane. He was very proud of himself for having Vision and Ideals.

On a business trip to Chicago, Babbitt spied Paul Reisling sitting at dinner with a middle-aged but pretty woman. Later, in his hotel room, Babbitt indignantly demanded an explanation for Paul's lack of morality. Paul told Babbitt that he could no longer stand living with Zilla. Babbitt, feeling sorry for his friend, swore that he would keep her husband's secret from Zilla. Privately, Babbitt envied Paul's independence.

Babbitt was made vice-president of the Booster's Club. He was so proud of himself that he bragged loudly when his wife called him at the office. It was a long time before he understood what she was trying to tell him; Paul had shot his wife.

Babbitt's world collapsed about him. Though Zilla was still alive, Paul was in prison. Babbitt began to question his ideas about the power of the dollar. Paul was perhaps the only person Babbitt had ever loved. Myra had long since become a habit. The children were too full of new ideas to be close to their father. Babbitt felt suddenly alone. He began to criticize the minister's sermons. He no longer visited the Athletic Club, rarely ate lunch with any of his business acquaintances.

One day a pretty widow Mrs. Judique, came to his office. She became his mistress, and Babbitt joined her circle of Bohemian friends. He drank more than he had ever drunk in his life. He spent money wildly. Two of the most powerful men in town requested that he join the Good Citizen's League—or else. Babbitt refused to be bullied. For the first time in his life he was a human being. He actually made friends with his arch-enemy, Seneca Doane, and discovered that he liked his liberal ideas. He praised Doane publicly. Babbitt's new outlook on life appealed to his children, who at once began to respect him as they never had before. But Babbitt became unpopular among his business-boosting friends. When he again refused to join the Good Citizen's League, he was snubbed in the streets. Gradually Babbitt found that he had no real resources within himself. He was miserable.

When Myra became ill, Babbitt suddenly realized that he loved his colorless wife. He broke with Mrs. Judique. He joined the Good Citizen's League. By the time Myra was well again, there was no more active leader in the town of Zenith than George F. Babbitt. Once more he announced his distrust of Seneca Doane. He became the best Booster the club ever had. His last gesture of revolt was private approval of his son's elopement. Outwardly he conformed!

THE BACCHAE

Type of work: Drama
Author: Euripides (480-406 B.C.)
Type of plot: Classical tragedy
Time of plot: Remote antiquity
Locale: Thebes, in Boeotia
First presented: c. 405 B.C.

Principal characters:
DIONYSUS, god of the vine
PENTHEUS, King of Thebes
CADMUS, grandfather of Pentheus and former king
TIRESIAS, a Theban seer
AGAVE, Pentheus' mother

Critique:

In this sinister drama, Euripides would seem to have attempted the impossible; that is, to condemn religious excess and at the same time to accept the myth of a man who died for disapproving of religious excess. It has been said that *The Bacchae,* posthumously staged, was a recantation, marking Euripides' acceptance of the nature-worship aspects of the Dionysiac cult. If so, the play can still be interpreted as a warning against excess. In this drama Euripides was also an accurate observer of Nature. As half-man, half-god, Dionysus is exasperating in his divine self-sufficiency; as a symbol of certain aspects of brute Nature, he is terrifying.

The Story:

Visited by Zeus, Semele, daughter of Cadmus, the King of Thebes, conceived a child. While she was still carrying her unborn child, she prayed to see Zeus in all his regal splendor. Zeus accordingly appeared to her in the form of a bolt of lightning; Semele was killed instantly. Zeus took the prematurely born child he had fathered and placed him within himself.

In its proper time the child was born again and was named Dionysus. When he grew up and became the god of revelry and wine, men established a cult for his worship. The cult of Dionysus spread throughout western Asia, but it had not yet gained a real foothold in Europe.

Dionysus, the god-man whom his devotees associated with the vine and with the ecstasies derived from the juice of the grape, decided that Thebes, home of his ancestors, would be the logical place for the beginning of his cult in the West. At first Theban resistance to Dionysiac behavior balked his efforts, and many Thebans refused to believe that he was a son of Zeus. Pentheus, grandson of Cadmus and cousin of Dionysus, ruled as King of Thebes. Dreading the disorders and madness induced by the new cult, he stubbornly opposed its mysteries, which hinged largely upon orgiastic and frenzied Nature-rites.

A group of Eastern women, devotees of Dionysus, called upon the Theban women to join them in the worship of their beloved god. During the ceremonies blind Tiresias, an ancient Theban prophet, summoned old Cadmus, now withdrawn from public life, to the worship of Dionysus. Performing the frenzied rites, the two old men miraculously regained youthful vigor.

Pentheus, enraged because some of his people had turned to the new religion, imprisoned all women who were caught carrying any of the Bacchic symbols, wine, an ivy crown, or a staff. He rebuked his aged grandfather and accused Tiresias of responsibility for the spread of the cult in Thebes. Tiresias championed Dionysus, declaring that wine provided men with a temporary release from the harshness and miseries of life. The Theban maidens, he said, were exalted and purified by the Bacchic ecstasies. Old Cadmus seconded the words of Tiresias and offered to place an ivy wreath on Pentheus' brow. Pentheus brushed it aside and ordered some of his soldiers to destroy Tiresias' house; others he directed to seize a mysterious stranger, a priest of Dionysus, who had a remarkable influence over Theban women.

When the stranger, Dionysus in disguise, was brought before the king, all the Theban women who had been jailed suddenly and mysteriously found themselves free in a forest where they were engaged in worship of Dionysus. Meanwhile, in the city, Pentheus asked the prisoner his name and his country. Dionysus answered that he was from Lydia, in Asia Minor, and that he and his followers had received their religion from Dionysus. He refused, however, to tell his name. When Pentheus asked to know more about the strange religion, Dionysus said that this knowledge was reserved for the virtuous only. Pentheus impatiently ordered a soldier to cut off Dionysus' curls, which the prisoner had said were dedicated to his god. Then Pentheus seized Dionysus' staff and ordered him to be imprisoned. Dionysus, calm in spite of these humiliations, expressed confidence in his own welfare and pity at the blindness of Pentheus. Before the guards took Dionysus to be imprisoned in the royal stables, he predicted catastrophe for Pentheus. The king, unmindful of this prophecy, directed that the female followers of Dionysus be put to practical womanly labors.

From his place of imprisonment Dionysus called out encouragement to his devotees. Then he invoked an earthquake which shook the foundations of Pentheus' fortress. Flames danced on Semele's tomb. Dionysus appeared, mysteriously freed from his prison, and rebuked his followers for any doubts and fears they had ex-

pressed. He had cast a spell on Pentheus, who in his mad frenzy mistook a bull for Dionysus and chained the animal in its stall while the god-man looked on. Another earth tremor tumbled the royal fortress in ruins.

Pentheus, enraged at seeing Dionysus free, ordered his guards to shut the gates of the city. At the same time a messenger reported that many Theban women, among them Agave, mother of Pentheus, were on nearby Mount Cithaeron observing Dionysiac rites that were partly a dignified and beautiful Nature-worship, partly the cruel slaughter of cattle. A battle had taken place between the women and Boeotian peasants, but the frenzied women, although victorious over the peasants, did not harm them. Pentheus ordered the immediate suppression of the cult. Dionysus offered to lead the women back to the city, but he declared that if he did so the women would only grow more devoted to the man-god.

When Pentheus imperiously demanded that his orders be obeyed, Dionysus cast over him a spell which made the king express a desire to see the women at their worship. In a trance, he resisted only feebly when Dionysus dressed him in woman's clothes in order that he might not be detected by the women, who were jealous of the secrecy of their cult. Pentheus, in fact, was almost overcome by Dionysus' charms as the god led him to Mount Cithaeron.

On the mountain Pentheus complained that he could not see the rites because of the thick pine forest. Dionysus immediately bent a large pine tree to the ground, set Pentheus in its topmost branches, and gently let the tree return to its upright position. At that moment the man-god disappeared, but his voice boomed out to his ecstatic devotees that a great enemy of the cult was hidden in the tall tree. The women, wild with fury, felled the tree, Pentheus with it. Agave, in a Dionysiac frenzy, stood over her son. He frantically threw off his feminine dress and pleaded with her to recognize him, but in her Bacchic trance she imagined him to be a lion. With prodigious strength she tore off his left arm at the shoulder. Her sisters, Ino and Autonoë, joined her and together the three women broke Pentheus' body to pieces. Agave placed his severed head on her wand and called upon the revelers to behold the desert-whelped lion's head that she had taken.

Cadmus and his attendants carried the maimed body of his grandson back to the city. When Agave displayed her bloody trophy, the old man could only feel the deepest pity for his daughter in her blind excess. When Agave awoke from her trance and recognized the head of her beloved son on her wand, she was bewildered and grief-stricken. Cadmus, mourning the violence that had occurred, urged all men to comply with the wishes of the Olympian deities.

Dionysus returned in his divine form and prophesied that Cadmus and his wife, Harmonia, transformed into dragons, would overcome many Grecian lands before they died. He showed no sympathy for Agave, who cried out that she had been guilty of sinning against him. He doomed her and her sisters to wander without respite until death overtook them.

BACK TO METHUSELAH

Type of work: Drama
Author: Bernard Shaw (1856-1950)
Time: The past and the future
Locale: The Garden of Eden, Mesopotamia, the British Isles
First presented: 1922

Principal characters:
ADAM
EVE
CAIN
THE SERPENT
CONRAD BARNABAS, a biologist
FRANKLYN BARNABAS, his brother, a theologian
WILLIAM HASLAM, a rector, later Archbishop of York
A PARLOR MAID, later Mrs. Lutestring, Domestic Minister
JOSEPH P. B. B. BARLOW, an elderly gentleman
BADGER BLUEBIN, Commonwealth Prime Minister
A HE-ANCIENT
A SHE-ANCIENT
LILITH, mother of mankind

Back to Methuselah is Shaw's only major drama of ideas which falls flat as a play. It is true that both *Man and Superman* and *Major Barbara* contain lengthy speeches which contribute little to the action, but Shaw's mastery of idiosyncrasy and dialogue compensates for those stretches of verbosity and often justifies them. *Back to Methuselah,* however, has no such redeeming stylistic touches. For the most part, the dialogue is declamation and the characters are orators. Worst of all, talk takes the place of action—ninety thousand words of talk in the play itself and thirty thousand in the preface which Shaw the essayist wrote to explain the dramatist's ninety thousand.

The play does have moments in which theatricalism relieves the tedium of the talk. In one scene, for example, a make-believe sibyl appears to the accompaniment of lightning and thunder. In another, a full-grown girl is hatched from an egg. In still another, characters appear on a simulated television screen. But all these devices are so obviously contrived that they fail to delight.

Properly speaking, *Back to Methuselah* is not a play at all. A far more appropriate designation is the subtitle Shaw gave it: *A Metabiological Pentateuch.* It

is a pentateuch because it consists of five separate plays which add new information to the Bible. It is *biological* because the information concerns evolution. It is *metabiological* because the concept of evolution expounded in the play transcends the conventional theory of Darwin. *Back to Methuselah* is Shaw's attempt to explain the theory of Creative Evolution to a public unwilling or unable to read biological treatises. That the public might be unwilling or unable to sit through a play which takes two or three evenings to perform apparently did not worry him.

Yet *Back to Methuselah* is an important play: a work important in the development of modern drama because it stretched the drama of ideas as far as it could go and important in the body of Shavian drama because it contains the core of Shaw's philosophy.

The theme of the play and the central tenet of Shaw's belief and teaching is that man does not live long enough but that he could if he would. As soon as man has lived long enough to acquire the knowledge and experience to solve some of the problems of life, life ends. The knowledge and experience are wasted. Life itself is wasted. Such waste, in Shaw's belief, is shameful, for all that man must do to avoid it is resolve to live longer. What man wants, he can have, whether it be an extra head, arm, leg, or additional years of life. This is the secret of Creative Evolution: species acquire new characteristics not through random mutations which are confirmed or rejected in the struggle for existence but through the recognition that new characteristics are needed and then the desire, conscious or unconscious, for their development. A disciple of Lamarck and Samuel Butler, Shaw believed that man could create his own evolution. In *Back to Methuselah* he attempts to show how and why.

Creative Evolution, according to Shaw, was one of the mysteries which the Serpent explained to Eve in the Garden of Eden—the setting of "In the Beginning," the first part of the pentateuch. Paradoxically, the great problem of life in the Garden was not how to extend life but how to end it. Faced with the horrible prospect of living forever, Adam longs to die and yet is unwilling to end life on earth. The Serpent solves the dilemma for him by explaining to Eve the doctrine of creative imagination. All they need to do to die is to will to die; to ensure the perpetuation of life, to create new life. The secret of creation is one the Serpent is only too willing to whisper in Eve's ear.

The second act, which takes place a few centuries later, is a variation on this theme of life and death. It is actually a debate on the purpose of life, with Adam, Eve, and Cain taking three different views. Adam contends that the purpose of life is to live, quietly working to pass away the years. Cain, the inventor of murder, believes that to live bravely, daring death and dying gloriously is the goal of man. Eve, believing that there is something nobler than either working or fighting, scoffs at both. Though she has not yet discovered just what it is, she has hope that man will find and cherish it.

By 1919—the date of "The Gospel of the Brothers Barnabas," the second part of the pentateuch—the triumph of Cain's apostles of death and destruction has shortened man's life span to its current length. But Franklyn and Conrad Barnabas have rediscovered the Serpent's secret of Creative Evolution and have settled on three hundred years as the ideal life span. Their task is to convince enough people that extending life is possible, then let nature do the rest. Although they are notably unsuccessful in persuading two politicians, Burge and Lubin, to adopt "Back to Methuselah" as the Liberal Party slogan, they remain confident that someone will soon live for three hundred years.

By 2170, the date of "The Thing Happens," the miracle has been accomplished. The Archbishop of York and Mrs. Lutestring, both of whom had been exposed to the Barnabas gospel, have lived 283 and 274 years respectively. Except for their ages, both are typical Shavian heroes in that they are so superior to a conventional society that society rejects and despises them. Their plight is more ironic than that of most Shavian heroes because by 2170 England is a Utopia, albeit a bureaucratic Utopia, administered by Chinese men and African women. When confronted with the prospect of a race of supermen, the rulers of the Utopia can only contemplate their own impotence.

By 3000, the date of "Tragedy of an Elderly Gentleman," the rulers' worst fears have materialized: the new race has expropriated the British Isles for its own use and banished ordinary mortals. The thematic significance of this section of the play is drawn from the contrast between the new race and the old. From Baghdad, the new capital of the British Commonwealth, comes a politician posing as a statesman to seek counsel from the supermen. The supermen are so contemptuous of the politician's intellect that they present the advice, which itself is humiliating, through a humbug oracle. True to form, the politician ignores it, fabricates his own counsel, and departs. An elderly gentleman, a member of the delegation, decides to remain behind, but he is so feeble in contrast to one of the super beings that he dies upon meeting her gaze.

By 31,920, the ordinary human race is extinct. Children are hatched from eggs at the age of seventeen and live indefinitely. "As Far As Thought Can Reach," the fifth and last section of the play, sketches the development of the new human being, who, after a four-year accelerated intellectual and physical growth devoted to playing, dancing, and mating, becomes an "Ancient," one who devotes himself to pure thought and whose goal is existence as pure, disembodied thought.

That this goal will be reached is affirmed by Lilith, the mother of Adam and Eve, in the closing speech of the play.

In fact, the only reason Lilith has permitted the human race to evolve is that it has been striving toward such a goal. But, Lilith concludes, the attainment of the goal is merely a step in a greater plan, the nature of which even she knows nothing.

In such a fashion Shaw finally reaches the conclusion that life, some form of life, will endure. Admittedly, the conclusion is not a profound one, but the insistence that man can forge his own destiny and create his own form of life is well worth considering if only because it is the underlying assumption of every one of Shaw's major plays.

BAMBI

Type of work: Novel
Author: Felix Salten (1869-1945)
Type of plot: Pastoral allegory
Time of plot: Indefinite
Locale: The woods
First published: 1929

Principal characters:
BAMBI, a deer
THE OLD PRINCE, a stag who befriends Bambi
BAMBI'S MOTHER
FALINE, Bambi's cousin
GOBO, her brother

Critique:

Bambi is one of the few · successful attempts to humanize animals in fiction. A fairy tale for children, but an allegory for adults, the book tells the story of a deer who learns that he must travel alone if he is to be strong and wise.

The Story:

Bambi was born in a thicket in the woods. While he was still an awkward young fawn, his mother taught him that he was a deer. He learned that deer did not kill other animals, nor did they fight over food as jaybirds did. He learned, too, that deer should venture from their hiding places to go to the meadow only in the early morning and late in the evening and that they must rely on the rustle of last year's dead leaves to give them warning of approaching danger. On his first visit to the meadow Bambi had a conversation with a grasshopper and a close look at a butterfly.

One evening Bambi and his mother went to the meadow again. On his second visit he was introduced to the hare, an animal with big, soft eyes and flopping ears. Bambi was not impressed. The little deer was considerably happier to meet his cousins, Gobo and Faline, and their mother, Ena. The two families were about to separate when two stags with spreading antlers on their heads came crashing out of the forest. Bambi's mother explained that the larger, statelier stag was Bambi's father.

As he grew older, Bambi learned the sounds and smells of the forest. Sometimes his mother went off by herself. Missing her one day, Bambi started out to look for her and came upon his cousins in the meadow. Faline suggested that both their mothers might have gone to visit their fathers. Bambi decided to continue his search by himself. As he stood at the edge of a clearing, he saw a creature he had never seen before. The creature raised what looked like a stick to its face. Terrified, Bambi ran back into the woods as fast as he could go. His mother appeared suddenly, and they both ran home to their glade. When they were safe again, Bambi learned that he had seen a Man.

On another day he began to call for his mother. Suddenly a great stag stood before him. Coldly he asked Bambi why he was crying, and told him that he ought to be ashamed of himself. Then he was gone. The little deer did not tell his mother of his experience, nor did he call her any more. Later he learned that he had met the Old Prince, the biggest and wisest stag in the forest. One morning Bambi was nibbling in the meadow with his mother when one of the stags came out of the forest. Suddenly there was a crash. The stag leaped into the air and then fell dead. Bambi raced away after his mother. All he wanted was to go deeper and deeper into the forest until he could feel free of that new danger. He met the Old Prince again. When Bambi asked him who Man was, the stag only replied that he would find out for himself. Then he disappeared.

The forest gradually changed as summer passed into fall and then into winter. Snow fell, and grass was not easy to find. All of the deer became more friendly during the cold months. They would gather to talk and sometimes even one of the stags would join them. Bambi grew to admire the stags. He was especially interested in Ronno, the stag who had escaped after a hunter had wounded him in the foot. The constant topic of conversation was Man, for none of the deer could understand the black stick he carried. They were all afraid of it.

As the winter dragged on, the slaughter of the weaker animals in the forest began. A crow killed one of the hare's children. A squirrel raced around with a neck wound a ferret had given him. A fox murdered a pheasant. A party of hunters came into the woods with their noise-making sticks and killed many of the animals. Bambi's mother and his cousin Gobo were not seen again.

That spring Bambi grew his first pair of antlers. With his mother gone, he had to spend most of his time alone. The other stags drove him away when he tried to approach them, and Faline was shy with him. Deciding one day that he was not afraid of any of the stags, Bambi charged at what he thought was one of his tormentors in a thicket. The stag stepped aside, and Bambi charged past him. It was the Old Prince. Embarrassed, the young deer began to tremble when his friend came close to him. With an admonishment to act bravely, the older deer disappeared into the woods.

A year later Bambi met Faline again, and once more they played as they had when they were very young. Then an older stag named Karus appeared and tried to block Bambi's way. When Bambi attacked him, Karus fled, as did the stag named Ronno, who had been pursuing Faline.

Faline and Bambi ventured into the meadow one day and there saw a stranger nibbling the grass. They were surprised when he came skipping up to them and asked if they did not know him. It was Gobo. Hunters had caught him and kept him until he was full-grown. Then he had been sent back to join his family in the forest. His mother was delighted to see him once more.

Gobo explained his absence to an admiring audience, and praised Man for his kindness. While he was talking, the Old Prince appeared and asked Gobo about the strip of horsehair around his neck. Gobo answered that it was a halter. The Old Prince remarked pitingly that he was a poor thing, and vanished.

Gobo would not live as the other deer in the forest did. He insisted on going about during the day and sleeping at night. He had no fear about eating in the meadow, completely exposed. One day, when a hunter was in the woods, Gobo declared that he would go talk to him. He walked out into the meadow. Suddenly there was a loud report, Gobo leaped into the air and then dashed into the thicket, where he fell mortally wounded.

Bambi was alone when he met the Old Prince for the first time since Gobo's death. They were walking together when they found a hare caught in a noose. Carefully the Old Prince managed to loosen the snare with his antlers. Then he showed Bambi how to test tree branches for a trap. Bambi realized for the first time that there was no time when Man was not in the woods.

One misty morning, as Bambi stood at the edge of the clearing, a hunter wounded him. He raced madly for the forest, and in its protection lay down to rest. Soon he heard a voice beside him, urging him to get up. It was the Old Prince. For an hour the veteran led Bambi through the woods, crossing and recrossing the place where he had lain down, showing him the herbs which would stop his bleeding and clear his head. He stayed with Bambi until the wound had healed.

Before he went off to die, the old stag showed Bambi a poacher who had been killed. He explained that man, like animals, must die. Bambi understood then that there is someone even more powerful than Man.

Walking through the forest one day, Bambi spied a brother and sister fawn crying for their mother. As the Old Prince had spoken to him so many years before, he asked them if they could not stay by themselves. Then, as his friend had done, he vanished into the forest.

BARABBAS

Type of work: Novel
Author: Pär Lagerkvist (1891-   )
Type of plot: Realistic symbolism
Time of plot: First century
Locale: Palestine, the Near East, Rome
First published: 1949

Principal characters:
BARABBAS, the robber freed in Christ's stead
A GIRL, unnamed, formerly intimate of Barabbas
SAHAK, a fellow slave of Barabbas, an Armenian Christian
THE ROMAN GOVERNOR
MARY
PETER
LAZARUS

Critique:

Barabbas in surface and in details of action and characterization seems a very realistic historical novel. In this fable, however, Lagerkvist has created a symbolic story which treats a primitive man's unwitting search for God. His portrait of the criminal Barabbas' emerging conscience patterns the emergence of Christian doctrine from the superstition and bewilderment which, the author implies, were the first reactions of the populace to the Crucifixion. The symbolic meaning of Barabbas' story is probably to be extended to include the blind search of all men of all times for belief. In 1951, two years after the appearance of this novel, Lagerkvist was awarded the Nobel Prize for literature.

The Story:

At Golgotha, Barabbas, watching the Crucifixion from which he had suddenly been saved, was startled by the words uttered by the figure on the cross: "My God, my God, why hast thou forsaken me?" Even stranger to him was the darkness which seemed to come over the world. As he was leaving the scene he was also disturbed by the look of silent reproach directed at him by the dead man's mother.

Back in Jerusalem, he met and walked with a young girl, whom he had known before. The girl, who had a harelip, went with him to a dive where some of his low companions were gathered. Barabbas and the people there discussed Barabbas' rescue and the strange rabbi who had made such extreme claims and yet permitted himself to be crucified like any criminal. Barabbas was considerably relieved that the people in the café did not believe in the rabbi's divinity, though he was rather troubled that they had not even noticed the darkness which had for a while hung over the land. The young girl having left the dive, Barabbas indulged, as a kind of escape from his worries, in a drunken debauch with one of the patrons of the café—a fat, crude woman.

Later Barabbas met a red-bearded follower of Christ who expected Christ to rise from the dead the next day. He explained some of Christ's teachings to Barabbas, but shamefacedly admitted that before the end he had denied Christ. The girl with the harelip, to whom Barabbas also talked about Christ, said that she had met Him. She was wilder in her predictions than was the red-bearded man; she expected the millennium and divine miracles any day. Superstition did not blur everything, however, for she told Barabbas that Christ's message was one of love. Barabbas thereupon went to the grave, and watched all night, but saw nothing. The next day, however, the stone was gone from the entrance. He believed that the followers of Christ had taken the body; the girl thought He had risen.

Barabbas asked the followers of Christ about these events, but found little satisfaction in their answers. He could not understand One who used His power by refraining from using it. Barabbas was later taken to a man who had been dead four days and had been raised again by this rabbi. This man told Barabbas that death was nothing; it was there, but it signified nothing. He added that after one had experienced death, life also was as nothing. As Barabbas further questioned the followers of Christ, it became clear that though they were believers they were quite confused as to the meaning of all these happenings. When the followers learned Barabbas' identity, as sooner or later they did, they naturally hated him.

About this time Barabbas became estranged from his fellows in the low life of Jerusalem—so much so that he left off his sensual life. The fat woman, his sometime lover, thought that Christ's soul had possessed Barabbas. One day, by accident, Barabbas was present at a church meeting and heard a rather disappointing sermon by the red-bearded man who had denied Christ. The snuffling testimony of witness given by the harelipped girl he found even more distasteful; yet later, when a blind man denounced the girl as a Christian, Barabbas knifed the first person who stoned her. She died a humble martyr, but one who saw Christ as she died. Barabbas carried her body to the grave of a baby she had had; Barabbas had been the father of that child.

A short time later Barabbas left Jerusalem and returned to the robber band which he had at one time led. The robbers were distressed by his seeming character change: formerly the boldest of all, he had become apathetic. So bold had he been that years ago he had fought and

killed and supplanted the bandit leader; thus he had come by the scar on his face. What none of the characters knew was that Eliahu, whom Barabbas had killed, was his own father. Sensing that he no longer fitted in with the robber band, Barabbas silently stole away from the camp.

For an indeterminate period Barabbas wandered the face of the earth. Later he was enslaved and put to mining for the Romans. There he met Sahak, a slave who was thrilled by the knowledge that Barabbas had seen Christ. Without revealing to Sahak the true nature of that relation, Barabbas increased the details of Sahak's belief by telling him things about Christ. Some of these were lies, such as that he had seen an angel come down from the sky on the night that he had watched outside Christ's tomb. After a time Barabbas apathetically suffered Sahak to enter into Christian observances with him. He even permitted Sahak to draw Christ's symbol on his slave's disk, and for a time he prayed with him. Years later a new mine overseer, attracted to Christianity but mystified by its doctrine of love, noticed the two slaves, bound to each other by a chain. The overseer, having talked to them about Christianity, was moved to secure positions above ground for the two men. Though still slaves, Sahak and Barabbas were at any rate free of the deadly conditions of primitive mining.

Matters soon changed when the Roman governor of the territory learned through another slave that both men were Christians. Sahak refused to renounce his faith. Barabbas, who by this point would have liked to believe in Christ but could not, readily renounced his. He let the governor scratch through the sign that Sahak had put on his disk. He then had to witness Sahak's crucifixion, but he himself was rewarded. He was relieved when no miraculous occurrences accompanied the death of Sahak.

When the pagan but kindly Roman governor retired to Rome, he took Barabbas with him. Once Barabbas went to the catacombs to see a Christian religious service, but no worshipper was there. In the darkness of the catacombs he felt terribly alone. He also felt that, as he had dreamed one night, he was still chained to Sahak, just as he had been during the days when he had pretended to believe.

After he had left the place of the dead, he smelled fire; flames were everywhere. He thought that Christ had returned to save the world, the first step of which would be to destroy Rome—for Rome felt that Christ was the enemy. Barabbas seized a burning brand and began to set everything afire that he could; he thought, wildly, that he was helping the Christians and his Saviour.

Thrown into prison with the Christians, Barabbas learned that there had been no service in the catacombs because the followers had been forewarned that an attack was to be made on them. The fires were probably set by agents or spies to discredit further the Christians.

The Christians in the prison naturally denied that Barabbas, who had been caught red-handed, was one of them.

When they protested to the jailer, the man showed as evidence Barabbas' disk, which still had the Christian symbol dimly scratched on it. A venerable old man among the Christians turned out to be one whom Barabbas had met before, the man who had denied Christ. Now he explained to Barabbas that it was Caesar who had set the fires, not Christ; it had been Caesar, therefore, whom Barabbas had helped by trying to burn Rome. Christ's message was still that of love.

To the others the old man added that they must not condemn Barabbas, though he was the Acquitted One. He continued that Barabbas was unhappy, and he had to wear his crossed-out disk. The others were also weak and full of faults; their belief had come from God. They must not condemn a man who had no god in whom to believe.

Soon the Christians were led out in pairs to be crucified, but Barabbas was taken alone. When death was coming, he spoke rather ambiguously into the darkness, saying that he delivered up his soul "to thee."

THE BARBER OF SEVILLE

Type of work: Drama
Author: Pierre Augustin Caron de Beaumarchais (1732-1799)
Type of plot: Romantic comedy
Time of plot: Eighteenth century
Locale: Seville, Spain
First presented: 1775

Principal characters:
FIGARO, the barber of Seville
COUNT ALMAVIVA, a Grandee of Spain
BARTHOLO, a doctor
ROSINE, his ward
DON BAZILE, Rosine's singing-master

Critique:

Although the plot of *The Barber of Seville* has been used many times by dramatists and composers, Beaumarchais seems to have a fresh approach to the story. It is on this gentle comedy that Rossini's famous opera is based. The play is fast-moving and brisk. It has all the necessary ingredients for a romantic comedy: intrigue, wit, clear-cut characterizations, satire, and a well-defined plot. Indeed, the plot is more important than the actors themselves, even though Figaro, the barber, has become famous in the literature of all countries. Beaumarchais' style served as a model for many dramatists who followed him.

The Story:

Count Almaviva was so much in love with Rosine, the ward of Dr. Bartholo, that even though he had never spoken to her he had left Madrid and the pleasure of the court in order to be near her in Seville. Because her guardian desired to marry her, he kept the young girl locked in her room. To help him in his suit the count enlisted the aid of Figaro, the barber and apothecary of Bartholo.

A note Rosine threw from her window convinced the count that she returned his love. At Figaro's suggestion, the count then disguised himself as a soldier seeking quarters for the night. He called himself Lindor, the name Figaro had used in telling Rosine of her unknown lover. When Bartholo, suspicious of everyone who might come near Rosine, refused to give the disguised count lodging, the count managed to slip a note to Rosine before Bartholo ordered him from the house. Bartholo forced Rosine to show him the note, but she cleverly tricked him into reading another letter which she had received from her cousin. Still his suspicions were not allayed.

His first plan having failed, the count, with the help of Figaro, disguised himself as a student. Calling himself Alonzo, he told Bartholo that he had been sent by Don Bazile, Rosine's music teacher. His story was that Don Bazile was ill and had asked Alonzo to take his place. Bazile was a party to Bartholo's plot to force Rosine to marry him the next day. Figaro, having learned of this plot, had given the count the information so that he could pretend to help Bartholo. The count gave Bartholo a letter which he claimed would help Bartholo in his suit. They would tell her that another woman had given it to Bartholo, a woman with whom the count was supposed to be in love.

The count thought that by pretending to help Bartholo he could be alone with

Rosine and tell her his plans to rescue her from the old man. But again Bartholo would not leave them alone together until Figaro managed to trick him into leaving the room. Then Figaro stole the key to Rosine's room from the old man's key ring. When Bartholo returned to the room, the music lesson seemed to be in progress. Then Don Bazile himself was announced. It took all of Figaro's ingenuity to keep him from revealing Alonzo as an impostor. Figaro and the count at last managed to get Don Bazile out of the house before Bartholo began to suspect the truth. But Bartholo, suspicious of everyone, sneaked behind the count and Rosine and overheard enough to make him decide to investigate Don Bazile's strange behavior and apparent bewilderment.

Don Bazile confessed that he knew nothing of his supposed illness and had never before seen the so-called Alonzo. This confirmation of his suspicions made Bartholo uneasy. Although he feared that Alonzo was the count's friend, he did not suspect that Alonzo was the count himself. He told Don Bazile to arrange to have the notary come at once to perform his marriage with Rosine.

Immediately afterward he went to the young girl's room and showed her the letter the count had given him. Instead of the help the count expected from the letter, however, it worked against him. Bartholo told Rosine also that her young lover would pretend to rescue her, but in reality he planned to sell her to the count. Since Rosine too did not know the real identity of the man she called Lindor, she believed Bartholo and promised to marry him at once. She also told him of Alonzo's plan to steal into her room that night and carry her off. Bartholo left her to arrange for the police to come and apprehend the kidnaper.

While Bartholo was gone, the count and Figaro climbed up a ladder and entered Rosine's room. Thinking him to be Lindor, she scorned the count and

accused him of a plot to sell her to the count. The count then threw aside his disguise. He told her he was the Count Almaviva, that in his love for her he had followed her hopelessly for the past six months. Rosine was so overcome that she fainted. When she was revived, she told them of her loss of faith and of her promise to marry Bartholo. She told them also of Bartholo's knowledge of the plan to carry her away. Already the ladder had been removed from her window and the police were on the way.

When all looked blackest, Don Bazile appeared with a notary, as Bartholo had instructed him to do. The notary knew only that he was to perform a marriage here and another marriage at the home of Figaro. Here he was to marry Bartholo and a young lady named Rosine. At Figaro's he was to marry Count Almaviva and a young lady named Rosine. By some clever and rapid talking, the count and Figaro were able to convince the notary that he was merely confused. Don Bazile was more difficult, but he finally decided the money the count slipped into his hand was more important than his loyalty to Bartholo. He signed the marriage contract as a witness just before Bartholo burst into the room with many policemen and a justice of the peace.

Bartholo ordered the justice of the peace to arrest the count, but that civil servant was too much impressed with Count Almaviva's high position to risk offending him. Bartholo, anxious to marry his ward, then ordered the count out of the house. When he learned that the count and Rosine had just been married, and that the contract was legally signed, he was infuriated and tried in vain to keep Rosine from leaving with her husband. By threatening Bartholo with a demand for an exact accounting of his ward's property, an exposé which Bartholo dared not allow, the justice of the peace was able to persuade the old man to sign the marriage certificate, thus giving his consent to the marriage of Rosine. Bartholo could not understand how his plans had failed. Figaro told him that youth and love could always defeat an old man's schemes.